P9-DGB-416

This Book Comes With a Website

Nolo's award-winning website has a page dedicated just to this book, where you can:

KEEP UP TO DATE – When there are important changes to the information in this book, we'll post updates

READ BLOGS – Get the latest info from Nolo authors' blogs

LISTEN TO PODCASTS – Listen to authors discuss timely issues on topics that interest you

WATCH VIDEOS – Get a quick introduction to a legal topic with our short videos

You'll find the link in the appendix.

And that's not all. Nolo.com contains thousands of articles on everyday legal and business issues, plus a plain-English law dictionary, all written by Nolo experts and available for free. You'll also find more useful **books, software, online services,** and **downloadable forms.**

 NOLO
LAW for ALL

Get updates and more at

4th Edition

Effective Fundraising for Nonprofits

Real-World Strategies That Work

Ilona Bray, J.D.

FOURTH EDITION	AUGUST 2013
Cover Design	SUSAN PUTNEY
Book Design	TERRI HEARSH
Proofreading	SUSAN CARLSON GREENE
Index	UNGER INDEXING
Printing	BANG PRINTING

Bray, Ilona M., 1962-
  Effective fundraising for nonprofits : real-world strategies that work / by Ilona Bray, J.D.
-- 4th edition.
      pages cm
  Includes bibliographical references and index.
  ISBN 978-1-4133-1923-1 (pbk.) -- ISBN 978-1-4133-1924-8 (epub ebook)
  1. Fund raising--United States. 2. Nonprofit organizations--United States--Finance. I.
Title.
  HG177.5.U6B73 2013
  658.15'224--dc23

                              2013011390

This book covers only United States law, unless it specifically states otherwise.

Please note

We believe accurate, plain-English legal information should help you solve
many of your own legal problems. But this text is not a substitute for
personalized advice from a knowledgeable lawyer. If you want the help of a
trained professional—and we'll always point out situations in which we think
that's a good idea—consult an attorney licensed to practice in your state.

Dedication

To my mother, who showed me how commitment to a cause can help you accomplish things you never thought possible; and my father, who knows how to greet each new day with entrepreneurial optimism.

Acknowledgments

This book was envisioned as a collaborative effort, in which the voices of many nonprofit staff and experienced fundraising experts would be heard. Still, I was overwhelmed by the generosity with which the people named below offered their time, knowledge, and stories of successes as well as frustrations. You'll see many of their names and stories within the book—others preferred to play a more behind-the-scenes role. My deepest thanks to all of them for their contributions, and for keeping me inspired during the many months of pulling this book together. In addition, I'd like to thank the various organizations whose sample letters and printed materials you'll see throughout the book (not listed below).

Lauren Brown Adams, nonprofit fundraising consultant

Sophie Lei Aldrich, Fu Jen University Foundation

Bob Baldock, KPFA Radio

Randolph Belle, formerly of the East Bay Nonprofit Center

Robert Brenneman, Project Open Hand

Jennifer Castner, the Altai Project

Sarah Clark

M. Eliza Dexter, formerly of Save The Bay (Oakland)

Grant Din, Angel Island Immigration Station Foundation

Laurie J. Earp, Earp Events and Fundraising

Lisa Ruth Elliott, formerly of Zen Hospice Project

Jan Etre, KPFA Radio

Judy Frankel, formerly of Project Open Hand

Susan Freundlich, National Writing Project

Lupe Gallegos-Diaz, Chicana Latino Student Development Office at UC Berkeley

Karen Garrison, formerly of Bernal Heights Neighborhood Center

Jennifer Gennari, consultant, formerly with Greenbelt Alliance

Leanne Grossman, writer, formerly of Global Fund for Women

Christine Grumm, consultant, formerly of the Women's Funding Network

Keven Guillory, KQED Radio

Linda Solow Jaffe, J.D., CFRE, Special Olympics Northern California and Nevada

Pat Joseph, formerly of Sierra Club

Don Kiser, formerly of the Human Rights Campaign

Lynn Eve Komaromi, Berkeley Repertory Theatre

Greg Lassonde, Legacy Giving Specialist

Marisa Lianggamphai, formerly of the World Institute on Disability

Harry Lin, formerly of KQED Radio

Jim Lynch, TechSoup Global

Sonja Mackenzie, former board co-president of WORLD

Mike Maxwell, nonprofit professional

Kate McNulty, Golden Gate University

Susan Messina, National Hospice Foundation

Nick Parker, formerly of the California School Age Consortium

Peter Pearson, The Friends of the Saint Paul Public Library

Sharon Rabichow, Save the Redwoods League

Angelina Ramsay, marketing professional

Peggy Rose, formerly of the San Francisco Mime Troupe

Ron Rowell, Common Counsel Foundation

Jim Schorr, formerly of Juma Ventures

Duane Silverstein, Seacology

Joseph Smooke, formerly of Bernal Heights Neighborhood Center

Elizabeth Stampe, Walk SF

JoLynn Taylor, WildCare

David Thorpe, Housing Works

Anthony Tusler, Disability Resource Center, Sonoma State University

Amanda Vender, DAMAYAN

Mona Lisa Wallace, formerly of the East Bay Nonprofit Center

Anita Wetzel, Women's Studio Workshop

Debra and Rich Whitall

Lauren Williams

Jason Wilson, Share Our Strength

J.R. Yeager, CompassPoint Nonprofit Services

Audrey Yee, Golden Gate National Parks Conservancy

Many of my colleagues at Nolo also helped with the current and earlier editions of this book in important ways: **Marcia Stewart**, with early conceptualization and advice; **Stan Jacobsen,** with research; **Jake Warner,** whose first-draft edits incorporated his own extensive nonprofit as well as business experience; final editor **Lisa Guerin,** who took the manuscript up a notch with her wit and practical instincts; **Tomek Pilch**, for SEO tips; **Wendy Copley,** with technical advice on blogging; and the production folks, with all-important design and graphics help, including **Jaleh Doane, Emily Dunn, Susan Putney,** and **Toni Ihara**.

A final special "thank you" to **C.S.** and other friends, for ongoing support, and for apparently remembering my name even after many months of self-imposed hermitage.

About the Author

Ilona Bray has worked and volunteered with various nonprofit agencies in numerous capacities, including development director, staff attorney, department manager, and advisory council member. Bray is now a legal editor at Nolo and the author of other Nolo books, including *Becoming a U.S. Citizen*.

Table of Contents

Your Fundraising Companion

If you think you don't have time to read a book on fundraising, you're not alone. I've worked in some of the hardest-to-fund nonprofits around and fully appreciate that you may be reading this while simultaneously gulping down lunch and photocopying a grant proposal. But you probably know in your heart that when a person is too harried to learn to do fundraising right, mistakes and inefficiency are the inevitable result.

With all this in mind, I'm going to skip the traditional lectures on personal philosophy and fundraising history and get right to the heart of the matter: how this book will help you succeed as a fundraiser. It's an attempt to distill and assemble, in plain English, the most important things you need to know in order to do your fundraising job well (most likely as a development director or staff person, executive director, or board member). I won't be expounding new theories of nonprofit philosophy, or giving you touchy-feely ways of using Jungian symbols to contemplate your mission. (I've sat through too many meetings and retreats that did just that, without giving me any new information on how to actually raise money.)

Instead, I'll discuss how fundraising is being done, at its best, today. Gone are the days when a nonprofit could charm people with its desperation and grassroots inefficiencies. You'll learn how current technology, business savvy, and public attitudes toward nonprofits are shaping the fundraising environment. You'll get right into the nuts and bolts of how to plan your fundraising strategy, assemble the right people, technology, and other tools you'll need in order to maximize your returns, attract supporters, ask for gifts from individuals, businesses, and foundations, and much more.

Though this book will teach you the basics, it will also help you to think creatively. By understanding how other nonprofits are raising funds, you'll be better able to think up ways to outdo them or to see where you might bend the rules a bit. Throughout the chapters, you'll find stories from experienced development professionals—many of them at small, struggling nonprofits whose constraints may be similar to yours—who've employed interesting strategies to gain fundraising success.

The question is, how much of this book do you really need to read? Everyone should start with Chapter 2, which lays out all the tools you'll need for effective fundraising, including staffing, personal skills, and technology. Also take a look at Chapters 11, 12, and 13, which explain how to bring visibility to your organization—and therefore potentially higher donations from all possible sources—through printed materials, the media, and your website.

After these, you can decide which additional chapters to refer to based on the types of fundraising your organization plans to engage in—choices you can make after reading Chapter 3, where you'll find instructions and worksheets that will help you create a fundraising plan that strategically uses your organization's existing strengths and assets.

Other chapters cover fundraising methods. I'll preview those chapters here, especially for those readers who may be new to the fundraising field or whose organizations are considering branching into new types of fund-raising. Even if you don't use these methods now, many of the first-edition readers of this book report keeping it on their shelves for ongoing reference.

Chapter 4, Attracting Individual Supporters. The real, everyday people who believe in your organization should probably be its bread and butter. Their donations are a sign of community relevance and support and (conveniently for your organization) come with very few strings attached. Yet many new fundraisers, as well as established organizations, come to rely too much on foundation grants, at the expense of paying attention to individual supporters. Read this chapter to learn how to reverse that trend and gain or expand your community support.

Chapter 5, How to Keep the Givers Giving. Your new supporters probably won't give very large gifts, and they're statistically likely to leave in a couple of years unless you take active steps to increase their interest in, and connection to, your organization. Read this chapter to learn how to analyze your donor base and further engage donors through personal contacts, appeal/renewal letters or emails and other communications, and invitations to volunteer at or attend other activities sponsored by your organization. Sample letters are included.

Chapter 6, Midscale and Major Donors. This chapter explains how to identify your most committed supporters and encourage them to give more. New fundraisers who have some anxiety about asking for major gifts will especially appreciate this chapter's gradual approach to building relationships between their organization and their potential major donors before popping the money question. It includes an extensive list of websites to help you do background research on prospective major donors.

Chapter 7, Funds From the Great Beyond: Bequests and Legacy Gifts. This final chapter on working with individual donors focuses on offering them alternative ways to give, namely through wills and living trusts. This chapter isn't appropriate for an organization whose existence is temporary or tenuous, because it involves planning around events that may take place far in the future (usually, a donor's death). However, the chapter will show how smaller, grassroots organizations can start programs to attract inheritance gifts without worrying about the more financially complex arrangements that some larger organizations are able to offer (such as charitable annuities). The chapter also provides plain-English explanations of these more complex arrangements, so you can plan your transition toward offering them.

Chapter 8, Special Events. There's almost no organization that won't put on a special event at some point in its existence, both because it's fun and because the simpler events, such as bake sales and garage sales, offer a quick way to raise money without much advance planning or experience. However, the bigger the party, the greater the chance that it will be a flop, financially and otherwise. This chapter explains how to choose an event that's most likely to be a success for your organization and how to maximize the fundraising potential of virtually every kind of special event, from auctions to walkathons. It includes budget worksheets that will help you make sure your event will bring in money.

Chapter 9, Raising Money Through Business or Sales Activities. If your bake sale went well, why not open a bakery? Thinking along these lines, many nonprofits have been exploring ways to make money through business activities, thereby reducing their reliance on foundations and the more limited donor—as opposed to consumer—pool. Unfortunately, enthusiasm has exceeded planning in many cases, and all too many nonprofit-run businesses have failed. Read this chapter to learn where others went wrong, how IRS requirements affect your business possibilities, and how to develop your own viable business idea, assess the competition and set appropriate prices, and launch your business in a gradual, low-risk way. Or, learn how to enter business at a less ambitious scale, such as through partnerships with existing businesses. This chapter includes a checklist that will help you identify a winning business idea.

Chapter 10, Seeking Grants From Foundations, Corporations, and Government. Nonprofits cannot live on grants alone, though many try. Nevertheless, grant funding, from foundations, corporations, and local or federal government sources, continues to have an important place in almost every nonprofit organization's budget. Such funding is especially good for jump-starting a new project or initiative. Even if you've written grant proposals before, you'll want to read this chapter for tips on how to excite a foundation's interest in your organization before you start writing; how to fully address every important component of a grant proposal; and how to write in a voice whose clarity and passion wake up the overburdened reader at the other end. It includes worksheets for breaking down and comparing different grant possibilities and a sample query letter.

So, enough preliminaries. It's time to learn how you can raise more money for your group—and create the long-term relationships with your community, supporters, and foundations that lead to sustained fundraising success.

TIP

Look in Appendix A and the Nolo website for handy worksheets. Various worksheets and checklists are presented throughout this book. You'll find the blank versions at the back of the book and online versions at www.nolo.com; see Appendix B for the exact link.

Fundraising Tools

Since the days when fairy tales were first told, people have been looking for a way to spin straw into gold. Unfortunately, this impulse remains alive in too many of today's nonprofits. With sources of new money hard to come by and old revenue streams threatening to dry up—not to mention staff members and volunteers overextending themselves to do the basic work of the organization—the fundraising office is often expected to perform feats of magic, sometimes with few more resources than the legendary pile of straw.

Don't allow your organization to be trapped into this kind of fairy-tale thinking. Until your group understands that its success will depend, in large part, on your fundraising efforts—and is willing to invest in the people, resources, and technology necessary to do the job right—you'll be spinning your wheels rather than spinning gold. And investing in fundraising should never mean investing only in activities that will produce immediate results: A successful fundraising program must also budget for the long term, with plans for such things as donor recruitment, cultivation, stewardship, and acknowledgment. These activities may not yield the immediate payback that writing a grant proposal would, but they will provide a solid foundation for the rest of your fundraising structure.

This chapter introduces the tools you'll need to create and execute a successful fundraising effort. The way you use these resources will depend on your group's size and experience, but most groups, no matter how large or small, use some combination of these basic tools to raise money.

This chapter covers:
- how the position of each person in your organization—including volunteers and paid staff—can play a role in fundraising
- personal skills that any development professional will need to have or develop, and
- equipment and technology for fundraising, including computer and Web tools.

RESOURCE

Need help with legal tasks like incorporating your nonprofit? This book assumes that your organization has already taken care of some legal and tax basics—namely, forming a nonprofit corporation and successfully applying for

501(c)(3) tax-exempt status and any required state tax permits. In addition, most states require you to register with their attorney generals before soliciting funds within those states (even via the Internet!), and many states also require you to report on your fundraising expenditures and revenues. For step-by-step instructions on incorporating your nonprofit and applying for tax-exempt status, see *How to Form a Nonprofit Corporation* (national and California versions), by Anthony Mancuso (Nolo). Then check out *Nonprofit Fundraising Registration: The 50-State Guide*, by Ronald J. Barrett and Stephen Fishman, J.D. (Nolo).

Fundraising People

In an ideal situation, your well-recognized and highly successful nonprofit would have a bustling staff of paid fundraising professionals, each with separate responsibilities and areas of expertise. Unfortunately, this level of organization and professionalism is far beyond the financial reach of most nonprofits. More often, you'll need to cobble together a mix of as many board members and other committed volunteers as you can recruit to the fundraising cause, hopefully with the assistance of one or more paid fundraising staffers.

The roles and functions of various fundraising positions are covered below, including how to involve and motivate your fundraising team. Don't worry if your organization doesn't have all of these people in place. Especially during a nonprofit's early years, it's common for several people to wear two or more hats—your best fundraiser may also serve as your volunteer coordinator, your executive director, or even the president of your board of directors.

Those who might participate in your fundraising efforts include:
- the executive director
- the development director
- the board of directors
- an advisory council
- other paid development staff
- paid staff in nondevelopment roles
- other volunteers, and
- outside consultants.

> ### TIP
> **Track your own hours to find out your staffing needs.** If you have the chance to expand your development staff, you'll need to figure out what type of help will give you the most bang for your buck. The answer may be no farther away than your own workday. Try keeping track of where each hour goes. Even quickly scribbling entries such as "9:30 to 11:00 planning meeting, 11:00 to 12:30 research" can reveal that you spend hours in ways you wouldn't have guessed. If, for example, you find that most of your time is spent on events planning, it might be worth contracting with an outside events planner rather than putting a new person on salary. Or, if most of your hours go toward clerical tasks, you might save some money by hiring a support staffer.

The Executive Director

Fundraising is, or should be, part of every executive director's (ED's) job description. This includes getting to know the organization's supporters, meeting individuals to solicit major gifts, interacting with staff at foundations, reviewing grant proposals, helping oversee special events, speaking at events, and more. Sounds like a lot of hours, doesn't it? And most EDs already have plenty on their plates concerning their organizations' missions, programs, and personnel. But any ED who doesn't somehow make the time for fundraising activities isn't fulfilling the job requirements, period.

> ### TIP
> **Former development directors can become great EDs.** According to J.R. Yeager, a project director with CompassPoint (www.compasspoint.org) who specializes in executive transitions, "Many skilled, well-organized development directors are ready and well positioned to step into the role of ED, particularly with smaller nonprofits. Most smaller organizations truly need their ED to do much of the fundraising. As for the other parts of the ED's job, these can be supported (for example, the board treasurer and outside auditor can help with budgeting and financial matters) and ultimately learned as the new ED grows into the job."

The smaller your organization's staff, the more time your ED will have to spend on fundraising. But if your organization can afford to hire a development director, the ED might be tempted to delegate as many activities as possible to that person. This can be a mistake. To the outside world, the ED is the face of your organization, the person who (rightly or wrongly) is seen as having the fullest sense of how your organization's need for money intersects with its mission, goals, and day-to-day work. Whether you are pursuing a large grant or trying to coax a major donor to increase support, the ED is usually the best staff person to close the deal.

Fortunately, the ED won't be solely responsible for all or even most parts of the fundraising process. The ED should help solicit major gifts, for example, but need not be present for every gift request. Nor will the ED have to be involved in the day-to-day work of staying in close contact with major donors. Your board and staff members may also participate, depending on who is being approached. And when it comes to grant applications, the ED's role should be limited to reviewing proposals, not writing them. If you can afford a development director, grant writing and other behind-the-scenes tasks will be done by that person. If not, your organization may use board members and other volunteers, as well as paid consultants and freelance contractors, to do this day-to-day work.

On the other side of the coin, an ED must be willing and able to share fundraising tasks with other board and staff members, especially the development director. An ED who can't bear to part with these tasks, or won't trust others with them, can spell trouble for an organization's long-term survival. Over and over, one hears stories of a charismatic, successful ED who successfully grows a small nonprofit—but then continues to attempt to single-handedly raise all the money and lead the organization. Over the long haul, such EDs tend to either burn out from overwork, neglect important tasks while trying to cope with too many others, or, in the worst possible scenario, move on to another job, leaving the nonprofit with a huge leadership and fundraising void. J.R. Yeager of CompassPoint notes that, "The wise organization (no matter its size) engages in 'succession planning.' This means having an internal structure in place where a formal and clear line of succession, cross-training, and information sharing is planned in advance, so that a 'void' will not happen—or will at least be minimized if an organization's ED departs."

The Development Director

Perhaps you are the development director at your nonprofit, or perhaps you are a board member or an ED of a smaller organization that hasn't yet mustered up the funds to hire for this position. Although some small nonprofits that plan to stay small—let's say, Friends of the Rose Garden—find it practical to delegate fundraising to volunteers, most growing organizations will find it highly cost-effective to hire a part- or full-time development director. (The median salary that development directors command is $96,645, (according to the *Wall Street Journal*'s "Salary Wizard.")

Ideally, a full-time development director's role is to oversee all aspects of the fundraising process, including planning the fundraising strategy, gathering input from the board and ED, identifying potential funding sources, and ensuring smooth operation of fundraising activities. Typically, however, the development director's role also includes carrying out practically every other aspect of the fundraising program: writing appeals, newsletters, acknowledgment and stewardship correspondence, and grant proposals; meeting with donors to solicit gifts; coordinating events; and more.

When this turns into busywork, it can prevent the development director from concentrating on important fundraising tasks. It will, therefore, be key to your group's long-term success to identify other people who can help take care of discrete or routine tasks.

A successful development director brings certain skills and abilities to your organization. Among the most important is good communication—in writing as well in person. You need a "people person"—someone who not only can express him- or herself, but also genuinely enjoys interacting with others. Remember, asking for money is just a small part of the greater—and often more fulfilling—process of building the nonprofit's relationship with donors.

Unfortunately, experienced and personable development directors are hard to find. There are more organizations seeking development directors than there are people up to the challenge, which means that the best can pick and choose where they work. Those with an ounce of savvy won't hitch their wagons to organizations that are teetering on the edge of financial collapse, dealing with internal dissension, or experiencing other serious problems. Less-established organizations often have to compromise by, for example, sharing a development director with another (noncompetitive) organization, hiring someone who isn't fully qualified for the job, or hiring a part-time or assistant development director. Such a group usually gives the ED primary responsibility for fundraising.

> **TIP**
>
> **A little recognition goes a long way.** Smart EDs and board leaders know that a dedicated and effective development director may easily burn out. One way to prevent this is to make fundraising a high priority and encourage all key people to participate without whining. Another is to recognize the development director's hard work by thanking him or her, sincerely and in front of others, for jobs well done. Too often, recognition goes primarily to board members and volunteers, as if receiving a salary diminishes the value of the passion and energy the development director throws into a project. Don't make this mistake!

Board of Directors

By law, every nonprofit must have a board of directors (sometimes called a board of trustees, a board of governors, or another similar term). This is usually a volunteer group of about 12 to 15 people, whose responsibilities include overseeing the organization and being accountable for its compliance with legal and other requirements. Board members are not mere figureheads: If they neglect their duties and your organization is sued or collapses as a result, they can be held financially accountable. (Many boards buy insurance to guard against this type of liability.)

As a practical matter, a good board not only sets the direction of your programs, but will also be critical to the success of your fundraising efforts, both by making fundraising an organizational priority and by participating personally. To this end, it's a big help to have someone on the board with a thorough understanding of nonprofit budgeting and finance. There's little point in working hard to raise money if the board can't make sure that the organization is meeting its financial obligations and spending wisely.

Find Board Members Who Are Willing—
And Able—To Raise Money

Unfortunately, there's often a wide gap between what nonprofits hope board members will do for them and how prospective board members envision their roles. In my earlier life as a corporate law associate, for example, my law firm employer encouraged me and my fellow associates to join nonprofit boards. The firm wanted us to get involved with the "community"—that is, with people whose incomes were high enough to hire lawyers—by any means necessary, and offered to help us get onto the board of just about any organization we wanted—the opera, the symphony, whatever. That sounded good to me: I envisioned myself sitting around a meeting table, mulling over a group's mission and giving sage advice. In short, like most novice board members, I was clueless. I not only had no idea about the depths of a board's responsibilities, I hadn't even considered that it might include plenty of time fundraising. Worse yet, I was only a few years out of law school, with little life experience beyond minimum wage summer jobs, so I was spectacularly ill-equipped for this role. (Luckily, I quit corporate law before inflicting myself on any boards.)

What lessons can be gleaned from my experience? Willing board members may be easier to find than you think, but:

- You must be selective to find the ones with the knowledge and experience you need.
- You need to be up-front about your fundraising expectations.

Most board members serve terms of only three years, with one or more renewals allowed. Check your bylaws to be sure—and think about amending the bylaws if your board members can serve "life terms," and you've got a few who are running low on energy and ideas. (Or think about enforcing your bylaws if people are overstaying their prescribed welcome!) If your board members serve limited terms, you must build a process to incorporate new board members into the ongoing work of your organization.

If you are new to the nonprofit world, you may wonder why anyone would voluntarily commit many hours per month to a demanding position, usually on top of work, family, and other responsibilities. A few board members are truly selfless—they live to help others. Some are newly retired, with an adequate income and time on their hands. Most are hard-working people genuinely interested in the cause, who hope that they'll be able to fit board responsibilities into their already-stretched schedules. Unfortunately, too many busy people turn out to be unrealistic in their hopes and end up unable to do much more than attend meetings (if that). Finally, there are the staff of corporate law and accounting firms and other companies that have a material interest in encouraging their employees to join boards. Even this category isn't all bad, especially if you can make use of their professional skills (but realize that nonprofit finance and law are specialty areas that your average accountant or lawyer will know nothing about).

No matter people's motivations, many of them will have trouble making the kind of long-term commitment that active board membership entails. At the same time, organizations have a larger pool of potential volunteers who might be interested in more substantial work than the odd photocopying job. Recognizing this, some nonprofits are rethinking how their boards are structured, perhaps paring them down to ten or fewer members, but asking these members to farm out work—including some fundraising—to committees. The committees may be composed of nonboard volunteers who can commit to the occasional sprint of activity—say, a donor campaign or a special event—but not the marathon of full board membership.

Recruiting board members is a topic well covered in other places (see the resource list at the end of this section), so this book won't go into detail.

No matter what else they bring to the table, however, you must make sure that potential new board members have an interest in fundraising—and understand that this will be a substantial part of their role. Because there are so many ways to raise money, there's a role for any willing board member to play. You can help by preparing materials that excite potential board members' interest, such as a packet of items highlighting your organization's mission, fundraising activities, and accomplishments. You should assemble a more extensive selection of such materials for purposes of training new board members.

Board Donations

Some organizations give prospective board members a very clear up-front understanding of their fundraising responsibilities, by asking them to commit to making a major financial contribution every year. You might require board members to contribute a set amount or base contributions on a sliding scale.

Asking board members for donations may seem odd—after all, they are already asked to give generously of their time, and now they're being told they have to pay dearly for the privilege. One reason for this practice is that board members will be much better at soliciting large gifts from others if they can say that they've given themselves. It demonstrates their commitment to the cause and their confidence that the donation will be well spent. Perhaps more importantly by now, potential donors—individuals as well as foundations—have learned to ask, "How much have board members given?" You might literally lose out on a grant opportunity because the foundation was unimpressed by your level of board giving.

For example, one environmental organization I know of not only specifically requires each board member to make a $10,000 donation as a condition of service, but also makes clear that each member's primary role will be fundraising. When the organization needs advice concerning the technical parts of its mission or activities, it turns to a separate advisory board, made up of scientists and other experts. This organization believes that policymaking and fundraising are the major roles of the board. Their experienced staff and advisers, they feel, are in the best position to know how the organization should be run. While there's merit to this approach, it also has a downside: If key staff members leave, or the organization faces another crisis or turning point, the board will not be well equipped to step in and provide continuity or plot a new course.

Of course, your organization will need to decide for itself—based in part on what kind of work you're doing and what community you serve—whether to solicit mostly affluent board members, or to ask for a particular monetary commitment. (For less-well-off board members, an alternative to the up-front donation might be to ask them to bring in an equivalent amount of money from a new donor or business.) For many community-based organizations or small advocacy groups, creating a financial requirement for entry could be just plain misguided. You might be lucky to have even a few affluent members. And the last thing you want is for representatives of a low-income community or dedicated former clients to be shut out. However, that doesn't mean you can't still ask a financially able board member to make a major gift.

Board Involvement in Fundraising Activities

There is virtually no limit to what your board members can do to help raise funds for your organization—other than each member's own interests and time constraints. Board members can help plan your fundraising program, spearhead or help carry out a special event, represent your organization in public, provide names of likely supporters, approach supporters for gifts, host house parties or other events, institute giving programs within their own workplaces, coordinate a new member drive, write personal letters, make phone calls thanking people for gifts, and much more. All of this will help take some weight off the shoulders of your in-house development staff. The wide variety of possible fundraising roles also allows board members who are reluctant to ask for major gifts to find a role behind the scenes.

A well-run nonprofit will ask a great deal of board members, at the same time being sensitive to cries of "Enough!" Once board members become genuinely committed to your organization, they are more likely to stay interested and involved if you call on them for help on a regular basis. Performing minimal board activities—attending meetings and the occasional workshop, for example—can be less than soul satisfying. Ideally, you want board members to see that raising the money your group absolutely needs to do its good work can be the most rewarding part of board membership. Properly orchestrated, fundraising gets people out from behind the meeting table and into the community, where they can share what excites them about your organization. It also gives them a chance to enjoy the company of their fellow board members on a less formal basis, thus helping them form enduring friendships.

RESOURCE

Need more information? For more on recruiting, structuring, and developing a strong, dynamic board, see:

- *Boards on Fire! Inspiring Leaders to Raise Money Joyfully,* by Susan Howlett (Perfect Paperback)
- *BoardSource,* a membership-based group that offers consulting, training, and various publications, at www.BoardSource.org, and
- *The Truth About What Nonprofit Boards Want,* by June J. Bradham (Wiley).

What If the Board Just Won't Fundraise?

Coping with board members who won't take the fundraising ball and run with it is a common problem in the nonprofit world. If you're a development staffer, it shouldn't be your responsibility to talk balky board members into helping raise money—this is the job of the board president or the chair of the development committee. However, because you're being judged by how much money you raise, you may find yourself with a vested interest in getting board participation. Here are some potential ways to approach this problem:

- **Identify the board's strongest leaders.** Often, all it takes is one committed person on the board to inspire the others to put their shoulders to the wheel. For example, Grant Din, former executive director of San Francisco–based Asian Neighborhood Design (www.andnet.org), recalls, "We had one board member who was a development director at another nonprofit, which was perfect, because he could emphasize the importance of fundraising—and not have others tune him out the way they might if a staff member said the same thing. We also had another board member who really pushed for full participation by the board, and the two of them tried to create more of a giving and getting environment. As a board member for other nonprofits, I try to support the development staff by talking up the importance of board involvement in fundraising."

- **Make sure your board members understand and care about your organization's mission.** Some board members feel distant from the organization they serve. They may have joined the board for personal or career reasons rather than commitment to your cause. Will attending board meetings cure this? Not likely, if they consist of a superficial report by the ED and hours spent worrying about financial issues. But you can jazz up board meetings—for example, by bringing staff members to talk about what they're currently doing. Do some "show and tell"—sample projects, art works by clients, videos, testimonials by local activists, or anything else that might rev up the board and get them to do something more than just sitting back and voting. And serve food!

- **Enlist an outside voice.** Consultants are available to address a board meeting, lead a board retreat, and more. (Ask colleagues at other nonprofits to recommend a good one.) Or, you might arrange a webinar through Grassroots Fundraising Institute; see www.grassrootsfundraising.org.

Advisory Council

A nonprofit isn't required to have an advisory council (or board or committee), but there are many good reasons to establish one. An advisory council is a group of people whose responsibilities include little more than—as the name suggests—offering advice and input on what the nonprofit is or should be doing. Members might be experts in a certain field, represent a community you'd like information from, be well known, or be past staff or board members whose experience you don't want to lose—but who aren't able to commit to board membership.

For fundraising purposes, your advisory council can be a source of additional friends. At a minimum, members' names should be added to your mailing lists. Their quasiceremonial role makes them particularly well suited to special events—you might call on them to buy seats, sell tickets to their friends, greet arriving guests, make speeches or presentations, and more. As the advisory council members develop an increased sense of connection to your organization, you may be able to solicit them for major gifts. And you should, of course, find out about their other experience and interests; they may be willing to put in some short-term volunteer time on fundraising activities.

When it comes to the famous folk, your expectations of their actual participation should be minimal. You might be content for them to lend nothing more than their name, so that it appears anyplace that you list people associated with the organization—perhaps on your letterhead, website, newsletter, and in other publications. Your cause gains credibility, and the person named enhances his or her reputation by appearing to be caring and compassionate. If such people actually show up for your meetings, it's a bonus.

Other Paid Development Staff

Although there's always pressure to run a lean development office (so as to minimize the percentage of the organization's money spent on fundraising), penny-pinching isn't always a good thing. If your potential donor pool is large enough, you may actually become more efficient at raising money by hiring more people.

If you are able to bring on help, you'll need to confront the pleasant problem of figuring how to divide development responsibilities among a small staff. Although how you do this will depend in part on your organization's structure and fundraising strategies, a first priority is usually to hire a "development assistant," someone to handle the mail, enter names and other information on supporters into your database, check for any email correspondence, prepare and mail thank you letters, and handle other day-to-day tasks. Obviously, these chores could also be handled by a dedicated volunteer or another clerical person in your office (such as a receptionist), but the person will need sufficient oversight to make sure that the tasks get done on time and that the paperwork doesn't get jumbled with other matters unrelated to fundraising.

If you don't have someone who will handle these tasks promptly and well, then you'll inevitably discover, while you're busy racing toward a grant deadline or staging an event, that important details have fallen through the cracks. The hazards of letting these matters slide are dealt with in other chapters—for example, Chapter 5 discusses how quickly you can lose a supporter's loyalty if the thank-you letter is sent out late.

A midsize organization may be able to afford a three-person department, adding a "development associate" to the mix. This is typically someone at a junior professional level, who works side by side with the development director, handling similar but less critical tasks. The associate would also have less responsibility for fundraising planning and dealing with key donors, and would be presumed to be "in training" for a director role.

Larger organizations often split fundraising tasks into subject areas, assigning a development officer to each. For example, care and feeding of major donors might be assigned to one person, while another is responsible for writing grant proposals. A few nonprofits, such as universities, have development officers who spend much of their time just researching future funding prospects.

Paid Staff in Nondevelopment Roles

A truly successful fundraising office will always be in close communication with the rest of the organization and able to call on program staff as needed. For starters, you want program people to keep your office informed about what they're doing, supplying you with interesting stories (with photos, if possible) to illustrate the important work donors are funding.

As a development staffer, much of your job is to explain the importance and success of your organization's work to the outside world. But simply repeating your mission ad nauseam is not going to bring in the donations you need. To be truly effective, you need details—colorful, lively stories of difficult situations that your organization confronted and hopefully helped to overcome, for presentation in your appeal letters, newsletter, Facebook page, and more. Here are some examples of compelling stories from my own days as an immigration attorney at a nonprofit:

- a father who literally got off his deathbed to take the citizenship exam and thereby ensure faster immigration for his children
- a Somali youth who was beaten in intertribal violence and who was desperate to get through the immigration process fast enough to go search for his missing mother, and
- a Guatemalan who'd watched his entire village massacred by the army only to have an unsympathetic immigration judge deny his case because conditions had supposedly "improved" in Guatemala.

Because all of these stories so graphically illustrated the important work our group was doing, they were good material to communicate to potential donors—but not all of them saw the light of day. Unfortunately, because few nonprofits foster communication between program and fundraising staff, program staff members don't even recognize their crucial role in the fundraising process. They may resent being asked to weigh down their schedules or dirty their hands with the business of fundraising. If this is your situation, try gentle persuasion rather than a frustrated lecture. Take a few key staff members to lunch, ask them about what they're doing, and find out what fascinates—or frustrates—them about their work. This information will give you a fuller sense of what your organization does beyond its mission statement, and what challenges it faces day to day. But don't finish dessert without explaining how you communicate with key donors and funders who are likely to give more if they understand why your group's current work is so important.

How Share Our Strength Gathers Its Stories

Between needing content for its fundraising appeals, website, email updates, and several bloggers, Share Our Strength and its No Kid Hungry Campaign are, well, hungry for regular information from program staff. How else will its communicators find out about things like the volunteer who drives around in a non-air-conditioned truck to deliver summer meals to hungry children, or the mother who declared that, thanks to the Cooking Matters class, she could triple the value of her WIC check?

Opening the channels of communication wasn't something that happened by accident, however. As Jason Wilson, Associate Director of Digital Communications explains, "We've deliberately created a culture of storytelling within our organization. This involved identifying members of each department or team and making story transmission part of their responsibilities. They are literally asked to set aside time to tell the story of the work that's happening, and then to connect with the people who are putting this information together for the Web or other materials.

"Once we got this culture built, and staff people began to see their stories presented—perhaps in an email campaign or as online content—they realized the double satisfaction in not only accomplishing something through their day-to-day work, but also through the telling of that story.

"There's no set schedule for sharing—either the staff will pass news along, or the people in charge of content may approach them with questions like, "We're looking for stories about X, what do you have to share?"

"An effort like this really needs to be organization-wide, and involve accountability. For our team members, storytelling is a formal part of their performance goals."

When you later use information a staffer gave you, be sure to show the staffer the appeal letter, or tell him or her about your successful meeting with a supporter or foundation officer. Some development professionals distribute brief emails or memos to staff describing recent fundraising efforts and successes, or post the classic thermometer to show progress toward a fundraising goal. Though you can do most of this casually and quickly, it's got a name—internal marketing. And it's a valuable tool for getting people within your organization to see how, by working closely with you, they can benefit through increased funding and recognition for their work.

Your next step may be to request something more systematic from staff members. For example, you could ask program staff to write up regular reports on their activities or to simply stop by and let you know whenever something interesting happens. Asking program staff members to take photographs or videos of their work is also a great way to get them involved. A nonprofit can always use photos to illustrate its social networking pages, website, newsletters, brochures, and annual reports. A program staffer who is doing fieldwork—for example, visiting a project in the Maldives or taking children on a hike to see native wildflowers—should always bring a camera. Even in-house program staff consulting with clients over a desk should be encouraged to snap a few shots (with the client's permission of course), in order to put a face to your work.

> ## CAUTION
> **Go light on the disaster shots.** Although evocative photos of grieving family members and emaciated victims are undoubtedly moving and can be of some use in fundraising, more upbeat pictures showing your successes are usually even more effective. For example, a photo of the new buds of a nearly extinct flower that your group helped preserve will be far more powerful than a photo of the cracked cement that previously covered its habitat.

If your organization holds staff meetings, make sure all development staff attend. If you're a development staffperson, this will give you a chance not only to keep abreast of what's happening, but also to give a regular report on the fundraising office's activities. Such reports should include more than dry numbers, but also convey your hopes, challenges, and disappointments. Staff meetings can also provide a convenient forum for holding a general fundraising training. Such trainings can cover basic issues like the importance of developing an extensive list of supporters, how staff can help contribute names, how they and their clients can help represent the organization on their Facebook pages or at special events or meetings with funders, and what your organization's strategic plans are for the future, fundraising plans included. Also encourage brainstorming about fundraising. A staffer may have the next great idea for bringing in support.

As program staff hopefully get more attuned to the symbiotic relationship between themselves and your fundraising staff, you'll want to encourage the more charismatic ones to help you with occasional, specific fundraising activities—for example, participating in an important presentation to a potential major supporter or a foundation or writing or editing a portion of a grant proposal. While you must make sure that this doesn't prevent staffers from fulfilling their primary responsibilities, such involvement can be highly effective. A staff member who works directly with clients or issues is often the most eloquent and credible person to explain your nonprofit's work to the outside world.

Other Volunteers

Many nonprofits begin their lives with an all-volunteer fundraising effort, often led—initially, at least—by a few dedicated board members. Even some established organizations rely heavily on volunteer participation or have more volunteers than paid staff. (Americans volunteer around eight billion hours every year.)

The development office is certainly one place where volunteers can be useful, whether for ongoing office support or for labor-intensive, one-time projects, such as mailings or telethons. Not only do volunteers allow you to shift a lot more sand than would otherwise be possible, but they can also substitute for paid staff, especially if you can find competent people willing to work for several months at a time.

In many programs, volunteers aren't terribly difficult to recruit. You can advertise volunteer opportunities in your written materials, work with local volunteer placement organizations, and check with local colleges and schools, some of which require students to perform community service as part of their curriculum. There are also numerous Web matching services, as detailed in "Get Help From Volunteer Matching Organizations," below.

What's far more difficult is keeping volunteers around for more than a day or two and managing them effectively. If you're going to inspire volunteers to provide you with meaningful free service over the long term, you must keep certain cardinal rules in mind:

- Understand and respect people's motives for volunteering.
- Train volunteers well and ask for a specific commitment.
- Make volunteering as convenient as possible.
- Find ways to allow volunteers to have fun.
- Show your appreciation early and often

TIP

Big businesses may offer their paid staff as volunteers. While they don't get a tax deduction for these contributions, businesses do get goodwill, an opportunity for employee bonding, and an investment in a more economically stable community. Your best bet is to approach businesses that are geographically near to your organization, especially ones whose goods or services your staff or clients might later purchase. Be ready to point out how, through your newsletter or other means, you'll publicly recognize their businesses' contributions.

Cater to Volunteers' Motives

Most people who agree to volunteer for your organization will be drawn to your cause, intellectually or emotionally. They really care about fair housing, avoiding conflict through mediation, or giving inner city kids a chance to develop their intellects by playing chess. But sincere interest in your mission is not the only reason that volunteers show up on your doorstep. Of equal importance to many volunteers is the chance to meet new people, develop skills, and feel needed. If a volunteer shows up full of energy and enthusiasm, and you ask that volunteer to photocopy stacks of reply cards for hours, you may never see him or her again.

This can be a hard lesson to learn. After all, the photocopying is crying out to be done, and you don't have the time to create work that will keep every new, inexperienced volunteer happy. But many organizations rely too heavily on their volunteers for thankless tasks, only to find that their volunteers don't stick around for long. And, at a deeper level, being involved in a grassroots, community effort should allow you to make a little room for the community to participate meaningfully.

Get Help From Volunteer Matching Organizations

Various programs match or recruit and place volunteers with nonprofits, especially through the Internet. (Studies show that the Internet has become second only to word of mouth in its effectiveness at bringing in volunteers.) Such volunteers might be useful in your development office or to substitute for paid positions in other parts of your organization. Some national sites worth looking into include:

- **The Clearinghouse for Volunteer Accounting Services (CVAS), at www.cvasusa.org.** This group matches accountants with nonprofits in need of their professional services.
- **Idealist and Action Without Borders, at www.idealist.org.** Nonprofits can enter their own profile and update it to mention events and volunteer opportunities.
- **Jesuit Volunteer Corps, at www.jesuitvolunteers.org.** The JVC's long-term volunteers, mostly recent college grads, accept one- or two-year placements where they can provide direct services to economically poor or socially marginalized people. (Your organization doesn't have to be Catholic or religious to use JVC volunteers.) The program pays travel costs and provides some other support, while your organization pays for screening and placement fees, food, a monthly stipend, daily transportation, housing, and medical insurance—typically up to $18,000 a year.
- **Make a Difference Day, at www.usaweekend.com/section/MDDAY.** This is an annual (October) event sponsored by *USA WEEKEND* magazine. Volunteers seek out projects for one-time work. Nonprofits as well as individuals can register project ideas.
- **Taproot Foundation, at www.taprootfoundation.org.** This organization's pro bono project finds professional volunteers with expertise in information technology, marketing, design, finance, strategic planning, and human resources and places teams of them in nonprofits in major U.S. cities that have successfully gone through a service grant application process. Grant applications are reviewed quarterly.
- **Volunteer Match, at www.volunteermatch.org.** This site is the largest online network of nonprofits recruiting volunteers.

If you're a development staffer, some, much, or even all the work of recruiting volunteers may fall to you. This makes some sense—your mailings and publicity may ask for donations of time as well as money. You'll soon realize that this is one of those tasks that can turn into a full-time job. If your organization really does plan to rely on volunteers in a big way, you might want to create the position of volunteer coordinator. Because foundations are always interested in leveraging their grant money into maximum results, you may be able to attract the financial support necessary to make this a paid position. Or, if you find a person with lots of energy, time, and savvy, you may find yourself in the happy position of having someone volunteer to be your volunteer coordinator.

Fortunately, there are a number of relatively simple ways to satisfy volunteers' needs and interests. Asking them at the outset what they'd like to get from their experience is a good way to start! But be prepared to talk with them individually (or to save time, in small groups) about what you can and can't involve them in. Emphasize that volunteers are most likely to construct useful, fulfilling roles with the organization if they commit to sticking around long enough to allow you to help each of them find a good fit. Another great approach, if you have regular volunteers, is to try to schedule them so that they overlap and can talk with each other. Especially if your organization uses volunteers in nondevelopment roles, arrange for volunteers to split their time between the development office and other work, for variety's sake.

To help with development tasks, you might capitalize on the fact that some volunteers are primarily interested in learning high-level job skills—writing or marketing, for example—which means that they might be interested in interning with your office for an extended time period. Local business schools are likely sources for this kind of help. And don't think only about the classic development office tasks, such as proposal writing and mailings; also look at the tasks you might otherwise hire out, such as photography, illustration, or designing a newsletter or an annual report.

Volunteer Training and Commitment

A formal training process, in which you explain the work of the organization and the volunteer's place in it, will make the experience more satisfactory for all concerned. If the volunteer is willing to help in the development office, briefly go over the annual budget and the fundraising plan. Explain the importance of seemingly mundane tasks, such as writing thank-you letters or entering data. Discuss what you normally expect volunteers to do, and what more interesting tasks they might "graduate" to after proven good work. You might also want to create a volunteer manual, something like an employee manual, explaining:

- what you expect of volunteers (in terms of hours, calling when they'll be late or absent, and the like)
- your commitment to making the volunteer experience a positive opportunity for community involvement, and
- basic office policies, such as personal use of the phones and photocopiers.

Unless you are recruiting the volunteer for a one-time effort, ask for a commitment to a certain number of hours per week or month. Be prepared to make this flexible, however. With changes in the U.S. economy and work environment, the number of people who work traditional 9-to-5 jobs is declining. Your best source of daytime volunteers may be freelancers who have spare time—but not always at the same time each week.

Be ready to provide feedback on how your volunteers are doing: constructive criticism as well as positive reinforcement. Volunteers who are trying to develop job skills, or will eventually ask you to serve as a reference, need to know how they are really doing. Your feedback will be taken best if you tell the volunteer during the initial training that you'll periodically sit down for a performance review—and if you make clear that the volunteer will then have a chance to give you feedback on the volunteer experience and what would make it better.

Make Volunteering Convenient

If the very mechanics of volunteering for your office are difficult—for example, if the volunteer has to call someone on your staff who's hard to reach—it creates another reason for the volunteer to drop the obligation.

Let's look at how a school literacy program in Oakland developed a volunteer program that's convenient for all concerned. The program is in a public school, in an area with numerous senior care centers. Seniors and others are encouraged to spend one hour a week reading to schoolchildren. No experience is required. To participate, they simply call one of the volunteer coordinators and say they'll be there that week. The coordinators prefer it if the volunteers can make a long-term commitment, but it's not required. For weeks when the program is short on volunteers, it has a list of backup people to call. And, to make sure the program doesn't become too much of a burden for any of the volunteer coordinators, each of them is in charge of managing one day a week.

This literacy program has run smoothly—and succeeded in boosting the children's interest in reading. It creates a system in which no one feels overwhelmed by the amount of work, and people with more or fewer hours to spend can commit accordingly. It also has the virtue that volunteers perform the same task every time, to reduce the amount of oversight needed. This won't always be possible in your office, but it's something to bear in mind.

> **TIP**
>
> **Do they really need to come into your office?** Online volunteering is on the rise, by people who have just enough time to sit down at their computer. Take advantage of this trend, for example by posting online volunteering opportunities at national websites, such as www.volunteermatch.org or www.idealist.org.

Make Volunteering Fun

Although the volunteers are there to help you—and you don't have time to make it a party for them—they won't come back unless they can share in some way in your organization's sense of purpose. One of the most common requests volunteers make is to work directly with the people (or plants, animals, or environment) being served. If they're working in the development office, that won't always be possible. However, there are other activities that will allow them to work with the public, including:

- canvassing
- asking local businesses for raffle donations
- calling donors to express thanks, and
- participating in telethons.

> **CAUTION**
>
> **Your volunteers are the face of your organization.** Be choosy about who you let interact with the public on behalf of your group. If the only human contact a supporter has with your organization is a grouchy high schooler doing mandatory volunteer service and not well versed in your program, you'll turn the supporter off. (Not that all high school kids are grouchy—some of them are developing interests in community service that will last a lifetime, so giving them interesting and appropriate volunteer tasks is a community service in itself.)

Once your organization starts thinking innovatively about what volunteers can do, you may find that your volunteers breathe new life into your programs—thereby attracting more attention from funders and supporters.

Show Appreciation

Every volunteer wants to know that he or she is making a difference and advancing the cause. Especially when working with highly effective volunteers, it's important to say thank you early and often. For example, I fondly remember volunteering for a school garden tour committee that hardly ever let me walk out empty-handed—I was given a school T-shirt, a pair of gardening gloves, a poster from last year's tour, tomato seeds, and more. I was momentarily embarrassed by their generosity, but I got the message—they appreciated the help. And, most important from the school's point of view, I kept going back to do more.

Try also to plan some organized volunteer appreciation activities. An annual volunteer party, for example, is guaranteed to be well attended. Inviting volunteers to your nonprofit's other events, such as a holiday party, a lecture, or an annual dinner, is also an excellent way to show your thanks. Don't forget to take advantage of a well-attended occasion by giving a little speech about how much particular volunteers have done for your organization—which you can accompany with awards or certificates.

Outside Consultants and Contractors

To supplement your salaried development staff, it can be useful to hire consultants and contractors. Be warned, however—the hourly rates of well-established writers, designers, accountants, and others may dwarf your own salary. But independent contractors start to look more affordable when you realize that you don't pay for their health insurance or office space, and you don't have to find a way to pay their salaries year-round. You can assign them to a limited task and tightly control the hours they spend on it. Consultants and contractors are probably available in your area for just about every task a development office does, from grant writing to direct mailings to individual solicitations to leading board seminars or retreats. Ask other nonprofits for recommendations, or go to www.idealist.org, where you can post requests for volunteer consultants or search for and read profiles of consultants for hire.

While outside workers can provide valuable expertise and take the pressure off when numerous deadlines loom, you'll want to avoid three common problems. First, start by making sure you remain the "boss" in this relationship, and don't end up unsuccessfully trying to manage an opinionated and balky consultant. Second, carefully define in advance exactly what the contractor will do on your behalf, when the job will be completed, and how much it will cost. Third, be sure that the services to be completed according to the contract are ethical, honest, and follow fundraising approaches with which you are comfortable.

You've probably heard of scandals where hired fundraisers go out and solicit money (by telephone, for example), then take a healthy chunk for their own salaries and "costs" before turning the remainder over to the nonprofit. Although the nonprofit isn't directly at fault for depriving donors of money that doesn't go where they thought it would, the nonprofit won't emerge unscathed from any resulting negative publicity. In addition, some states' laws address nonprofits' use of professional fundraisers, for example, by requiring the fundraisers to disclose their status to the people being asked to donate. Whatever you do, don't hire outside contractors on a commission basis—that is widely viewed as unethical and, in some states, is even illegal.

Can You Pitch Your Nonprofit in the Space of an Elevator Ride?

As part of your personal skill building, it's important to be able to quickly engage others about what your organization does, and why it's important. According to Mona Lisa Wallace, an attorney and nonprofit expert, "It's amazing how even some established organizations can't describe what they do—I'll hear vague statements like, 'We're sort of a homeless organization.' But what people really want to hear is who and where your organization is, what you're all about, where you're heading, and how you plan to get there. So, for example, a good elevator pitch might be, 'Our homeless-families support network provides temporary housing and support services to parents and children with no place to go. We help them get back on their feet and find a stable, long-term home. We may never be able to eliminate homelessness altogether, but we're going to keep trying to reduce it, one family at a time.'"

Oakland housing activist Randolph Belle recommends taking out a stopwatch, and practicing saying what you need to in 30 seconds or less. He suggests practicing succinct answers to follow-up questions, such as:

- "What would you do with $10,000?"
- "Tell me about the needs of your constituency."
- "Who are the other service providers in your field and what makes you special?"
- "Tell me about the composition of your board of directors."
- "What made you get into this field?"

CAUTION

Don't inadvertently turn a contractor into an employee. If you treat contractors or consultants like employees (by requiring them to keep regular office hours and closely supervising them, for example), you're headed for legal trouble. The IRS, as well as state tax and employment authorities, may claim that you should have paid the same taxes and benefits as you would for ordinary employees. For easy-to-access, free information about the legal differences between employees and contractors, see the independent contractor materials on Nolo's website at www. nolo.com. For more detailed information, including a wide selection of sample contracts, see *Working With Independent Contractors*, by Stephen Fishman (Nolo).

Fundraising Skills

This section briefly covers the most important personal characteristics and skills a good fundraiser needs. Of course, there's no one perfect way to raise money—a variety of approaches and styles can work well, depending on your audience, personality, and so forth. Some of these skills may be hard to develop if you weren't born with them, so be patient with yourself, and concentrate on bringing out the things you do best. This section will also help you evaluate prospective new staff, volunteers, and/or board members. It covers:

- interpersonal skills
- writing ability, and
- profiles of various people who have made a career of fundraising.

Interest in Other People

You've probably heard the saying that "people give to people, not to causes." While that may be a bit of an exaggeration, it contains an important message: A fundraiser's ability to relate positively to his or her fellow human beings is crucial to that person's long-term success. Unless your fundraising office has so many staffers that a few can sit in the back room and write grants all day, every one should enjoy the idea of interacting with outsiders, be they donors, foundation funders, board members, or others.

If you're interviewing a prospective new development staffer, and the consensus is, "We're not crazy about his personality, but he's smart, writes well, and knows our work," proceed with extreme caution. Your supporters and funders may have the same tepid reaction.

Networking with other fundraisers is also an important part of this job. It's worthwhile for development professionals to join national or local groups such as the Association of Fundraising Professionals (www.afpnet.org).

Writing Ability

The ability to write effectively plays an important role in nearly every aspect of fundraising, whether it's drafting a thank-you letter, an email appeal, or a grant proposal. If you're more of a people person, who would rather swallow frogs than devote a few days to a writing project, you'll probably be very effective at some aspects of development work. However, if you hope to run a development office, you'll need to learn some new skills.

Top Five Tips for Effective Writing

- **Write like you talk.** Or better yet, write like you're on the phone with your Aunt Millie, who's a little deaf and wishes you'd get to the point. Too many people think that using long words and convoluted sentences makes them sound professional and authoritative. They're wrong. Turn your writing into a conversation with the reader. Reading your written work aloud is a good way to put it to the test. If the voice you hear doesn't sound friendly, straightforward, and passionate about the cause, try again.

- **Find out what makes your own writing flow.** With all due respect to high school writing teachers, many of them propounded rules that can hinder your subconscious writer—like the one about creating an exhaustive outline before setting pen to paper. I know many excellent writers who simply can't write that way—people who instead begin by writing in bursts, only later weaving them together to discover a structure. In short, if you have your own style of getting your thoughts out, go with what works for you.

- **Be your own editor.** No one I know can produce a finished writing job in fewer than three drafts, and important tasks often take far more. So, when you are finished writing something, read it over with a critical eye. Look for issues like:

  - **overlong sentences.** Any sentence that runs on for more than two lines can probably be chopped.

  - **boring or extraneous words.** Eliminate every word that's not necessary to the sentence. See whether a tired word can be replaced with a more expressive alternative. For example, instead of using "difficult" three times in a paragraph, try "thorny," "obstinate," or "tough." Give your thesaurus a workout.

  - **potentially misleading word order.** We all love to laugh at signs that say "Half Baked Chicken, $7.99!"—but some of your supporters may be less amused if you announce that "Volunteers help burn victim's family."

  - **passive voice.** The passive voice is well named; it sounds as if the writer wearied of the cause long ago. Just say "no" to phrases like "it is of concern that" and "a donation of $xx was received." Instead, use active statements that explain who did what, like "our counselors are worried that" and "the Family Foundation generously donated $xx."

Top Five Tips for Effective Writing (continued)

- **Never, ever send anything out without a final read through.** Mistakes and typos can lurk in any document—even one that's been read a dozen times. Ask someone you trust to give your written work a careful going over. Also, if you can, put every document aside for a few hours or days before you finalize it. You'll be amazed at what pops out at you—or what new inspirations arise—with a fresh reading.

- **Lose the lingo.** After you've written a few grant proposals and attended some United Way trainings, your head will be full of terms like "outcomes," "mission statement," and "service-driven." And your organization's own area of expertise is probably jargon laden, too. You'll have to learn the jargon and use it when funders or others won't be happy hearing any other terms—but don't let it take over your entire vocabulary. Even funders fall asleep when they read too much jargony stuff.

TIP

There may be a movement afoot to make the language of philanthropy more readable. Here's what The California Wellness Foundation had to say about the matter: "We also try to avoid the 'philanthropy speak,' which has been a nasty habit for too long in our field. ... If you think about it, philanthropic communications should be painless, as enjoyable as reading a good book."

RESOURCE

More on the jargon of giving. For a humorous deciphering of some of the most prevalent jargon found in the philanthropic world—terms like "at-risk," "capacity building," "empowerment," and "leverage"—see Tony Proscio's book, *Bad Words for Good*. Proscio will make you think twice about some of the words that may have been slipping off your tongue.

Fundraising Equipment and Technology

Though good equipment can be pricey, the inefficiencies that result from trying to raise money with tools and technology from the horse-and-buggy era will cost far more. Of particular importance are:

- adequate office space and equipment
- effective telecommunications equipment
- computer technology, and
- credit card capabilities.

Office Space and Equipment

If you're a development director or other high-level development staff-person, it should go without saying that you need a private office, a desk, and a phone to do effective fundraising work. Unfortunately, many a fundraising professional has had to make do with a table in the corner of the reception area or the ED's office. In case anyone in your office needs reminding, explain that you'll be placing important and sensitive phone calls to supporters and funders, so you'll need some quiet and privacy. Preparing proposals and mailings are also tasks for which you need adequate space to collect and organize your documents. For example, if you ever have to prepare a grant proposal for the federal government, you may end up with a five-inch-high stack of forms, reports, statistics, and more. If you don't have enough room to sort and organize your paperwork, you might lose track of important documents or leave something out.

> RESOURCE
>
> **Need more information on office space for fundraising?** For an eloquent and detailed exposition of a development office's needs, see Kim Klein's *Fundraising for the Long Haul* (Jossey-Bass).

Effective Telecommunications Equipment

Although you may not have much say in the type and condition of your office's telephone system, you should emphasize the important role communications play in your work. People must be able to reach you easily. To accomplish this, you'll want a wired phone system with a direct line to your desk and a mobile phone you can use to stay in touch when you are out of the office. Ideally, that should be a smartphone—not only because of what it does, but because of what it teaches you about a prospective donor's experience. Donors may be looking at your nonprofit's website, Facebook page, and more through their smartphones—by early 2014, usage of the mobile Web is predicted to surpass desktop. The only way to be sure your sites don't look awful on a smartphone—and to track that device's ever-changing technological capabilities—is to own one yourself.

Put yourself in the shoes of a major donor or foundation officer who is trying to reach you. Can the caller make his or her way through your reception or voicemail system quickly and easily? What if the caller doesn't know or can't remember your last name or your direct line or extension number? If you have a live receptionist, he or she can easily handle these kinds of contingencies. As a back-up, your website should also make clear how to both email and call the development office.

Computers and Software

Computer technology becomes obsolete quickly, and it's probably inevitable that many budget-challenged nonprofits are using yesterday's equipment, complete with software that was state-of-the-art last decade.

Unfortunately, because you have to communicate with people in the for-profit sector (and in foundation and government work), relying on seriously inadequate technology risks leaving you quite literally out of touch.

The good news is that you're not alone. Because inadequate computer systems are so endemic in the nonprofit sector—and money for upgrades is so short—you'll find classes at your local nonprofit support center, written materials specifically directed at nonprofits, and foundations offering grants and consulting to help you bridge the technology gap. All of these can help you meet your basic needs, such as:

- computer equipment
- a donor and finance database
- a client-tracking database, and
- a website and email access.

Computers

Buying your own equipment allows you to avoid the common trap that many strapped nonprofits fall into: accepting used computers from corporate offices. (They unload these dinosaurs and get a tax deduction; more often than not, you get junk.) Assessing donated equipment and fixing problems or adjusting it to fit your office's needs is often more trouble than it's worth, unless you have a staffperson or volunteer who's adept at information technology. Or, you might ask the donor to send a tech person to get everything up and running. With new equipment, the odds are better that you'll reach a helpful person when problems arise.

RESOURCE

Need technical assistance? For consulting on computer equipment and technology needs, talk to:

- **TechSoup,** a San Francisco–based nonprofit specializing in technology planning, implementation, and support for community-based organizations and schools, at www.TechSoup.org, or
- **NPower,** a New York nonprofit that provides free or low-cost technology assistance to nonprofits and schools, at www.npower.org.

Donor and Finance Database

A high-quality database that keeps track of individual donors' names, other information, and gifts can be one of the best investments your organization makes. If you're still working with a homemade database that only you know how to use, lose it now.

New databases are getting progressively faster, cheaper, and easier to use. They offer wonderful opportunities to segment donors into categories for special attention and produce reports showing patterns you might never have dreamed of. They can also save you huge amounts of time—a mailing list that might take you two weeks to put together by hand can be generated in 15 minutes or less using a database.

Get Your Donor Records in Order First

A database is only as good as the information that goes into it. Whether you are two days or two years away from getting a sleek new database, now is the time to make sure you won't be feeding it garbage. In her work as a database management consultant, Lauren Williams has seen it all in terms of donor record quality—including organizations whose records were in such poor shape that she had to reconstruct donor information from Christmas cards and bank accounts. Lauren offers the following tips for a grassroots organization still working its way towards a database:

- **Keep every last scrap of paper.** "If your office is still very low tech, it's safest not to throw out anything relevant to your donors, because you never know what you'll need later."

- **Write a date on everything.** "For example, if you've got someone's business card, but no one remembers having received it, it doesn't do much good unless a written date shows you how recent it is."

- **Write down your sources for information.** "For example, if your files contain a scrap of paper saying 'Donor may be opening a new business— partnership possibilities?' but the scrap doesn't say who mentioned the possible new business or who took the notes, it won't do your records much good a year or two later."

- **Write down the context in which you gathered information.** "For example, with a business card, don't just date it and sign it; write down the circumstances in which you received the card, and a note about the conversation you had with the person. A collection of thousands of names and addresses, each without context, is useless."

TIP

Get free advice or even funding for your investment in a database. For example, a funder may be willing to offer a grant toward this. Or some organizations may help you locate free or discounted software, such as:

- **Idealware,** at www.idealware.org, with many articles on donor management systems

- **TechSoup,** offering free and discounted software to nonprofits, at www.techsoup.org
- **ebase,** which provides free ebase software; see www.ebase.org, and
- **Technology Grant News,** a subscription-based service that tracks technology funding opportunities, at www.technologygrantnews.com.

There are literally dozens of software programs available to handle your supporter database (and other technology needs). Many can be downloaded via the Internet, making upgrades automatic and information accessible to all your office locations.

If possible, team up with your accounting staff when investigating databases and setting up your website. Many packages include accounting functions (thereby ensuring that donor gifts are tracked smoothly from the mailbox to the bank) and can handle the credit card portion of your website. In any case, make sure any software you choose will interface easily with your other information systems.

Instead of driving yourself crazy with research, talk to your colleagues at other nonprofits. As M. Eliza Dexter, former development director of Oakland, California–based Save The Bay, says, "The smartest thing we did when choosing a database was to call around, ask what others are using, and ask what they've been disappointed in." You might even visit other offices and watch how they use their database—see if you can intuitively understand how they move between screens and whether the visual layout appeals to you. Also ask your colleagues how much they're actually taking advantage of the various bells and whistles—many software packages promise a world of reports, tracking features, and more, but users find the features too hard to use or irrelevant to the organization's needs. (That's why another piece of advice is important—don't let your tech geek choose the software!)

Once you've got some recommendations, look closer at:

- **Cost.** Prices for fundraising software packages can vary from zero (especially for introductory periods) to $250,000. Some companies charge a flat fee, others a monthly one as well. Some customize the software to the user's needs and charge accordingly, others assess a per-user (or per-concurrent-user) fee. Even if your nonprofit is as tiny as it is financially challenged, you're likely to find a product that meets your needs. The prevailing rule of thumb is to spend 0.25% to 0.50% of your annual budget on this.

- **What's included.** Depending on your office's needs, you'll want to see some combination of:
  - transferability of your existing data
  - interface with your website
  - office management, including task deadline reminders or "ticklers"
  - information-keeping capability, with extensive biographical and gift records (with sophisticated tracking for different kinds of gifts, whether cash or in-kind), the ability to segment populations of supporters—and any other constituents—based on various biographical or gift criteria, the ability to link files on couples or related donors, and a hopefully unlimited ability to enter contact information on individual donors
  - mail merge and production of labels
  - automated or prepackaged reports (including charts and graphs) that draw together the information in the database, such as multiyear support trends, tracking of grants (when they're received, how much is received, and when reports are due), successes of particular mailings or campaigns, and detailed information on donors (how and when they've given, groupings by gift amount, and other criteria)
  - automated mail-merged production of receipts, thank-you letters, pledge reminders, and renewal requests
  - easy generation of personalized correspondence (by letter or email)
  - specialized modules for planned giving, special events, and more, and
  - the ability to import and export data to *Word* and *Excel* programs.
- **Possibilities for customization.** The automated reports mentioned above can be great, but what if you need your information collected and presented in a different way? Look for a database that lets you create your own reports (without having to be a tech wizard). Then again, the more the software meets your group's needs "out of the box," the cheaper it will be to buy and maintain.
- **Record capacity.** Unless your organization is small and has no plans to grow, make sure the database can accommodate plenty of

individual records. They all promise this, of course, but some don't deliver. For example, if the vendor's definition of a "record" is every single gift entered, your database will quickly fill to bursting. You want every record to represent one donor, with unlimited capacity to enter relevant information.

- **Training.** Find out how much (if any) training is necessary. Some software packages are advertised as being so easy to use that you don't need training. (Check out this claim with current users.) If, as is common with more sophisticated programs, some training is needed (somewhere between three days' and two weeks' worth), find out how much, if any, you'll receive for free and where classes will take place. Some companies conduct trainings only at their headquarters, which may put the software out of your price range if you have to fly staffers across the country.

- **Ongoing technical support.** Installation and support costs can mount if you're not careful. Ask whether the support contract runs out after a time (usually a period of months) and if so, how much it will cost to receive support after that.

- **The company's future.** You don't want to buy a product from a company that's about to be sold, go bankrupt, or discontinue the product line you're interested in. Unfortunately, this happens frequently, with the result that loads of nonprofits end up with "orphaned" software that will not be supported or updated. Even the shakiest company will claim to have a rosy future, but doing a little outside research (for example, a simple Google search of the company's name) often turns up interesting information.

- **Ease of use.** Here is another reason to ask friends for recommendations. A program that looked easy to use when the salesperson demonstrated it may turn into a nightmare when you're alone staring at a mystery screen. Another excellent approach is to ask for a demonstration model before you purchase the product. Challenge it and yourself to doing something difficult. Also, see how easy (or impossible) it is to recover if the program fails. Finally, think about how hard this system will be for an office volunteer to learn to use quickly.

- **Upgrade frequency.** Does the company periodically publish newer versions, and will you receive these for free, or at a price? If you must pay for them, how well will the company continue to support the old version?
- **Remote access.** Look for systems that allow you to get or enter information from your smartphone or in the cloud.

> ⊘ CAUTION
>
> **Pay careful attention to the database's available security measures—and use them.** The accuracy of your data is critical—so protecting it from accidental deletions or alterations, perhaps by inexperienced users, should be a first priority. Most software provides some protective measures, such as a backup system, but you may need to take an active role in implementing these measures. Find out what kind of security measures various programs offer before you decide which one to buy.

Service-Tracking Database

In addition to the donor database described above, you'll also want to consider a database that collects information on your outcomes or provision of services. Why is this a fundraising issue? Because your organization will have to send detailed reports to foundations and others on how their money was spent. If you're a development director or another development professional, it will likely be your job to review these reports. And if they're not up to snuff, you're obviously going to have a tough time approaching the same funder for more support next year.

Unfortunately, advancements in data collection software tend to lag behind donor software. This is in large part because the developers who profit by creating standardized software find that service provision is anything but standard. Even among nonprofits providing the same type of service—for instance, shelters for the homeless—one shelter might be accustomed to measuring success based on the number of beds filled, while another might measure the number of hours spent housing or counseling each client. In fact, many software companies throw up their hands, leaving nonprofits to try to develop their own databases.

Although this may seem like a daunting task, it's important that you tackle it. Foundations and other donors increasingly want access to up-to-the-minute information—and many want to know how you're collecting it. They're tired of seeing the ad hoc, often questionable data that many nonprofits throw together at reporting time. To set your nonprofit apart, find or develop a database that makes tracking and reporting simple and accurate. Once you've done that, loudly advertise that fact to every foundation or other funder with whom you're in contact.

Website and Email

Time has proved wrong the optimist's predictions that people would meander the Web looking for places to give their money.

But for people who have already heard of your group, a website is the first place they will go to learn more about it and obtain key contact information. It will also become the "home base" for your social networking activities.

Email has not eliminated the need for "snail mail" marketing, but it is an easy and affordable method of communicating with existing supporters who have demonstrated an interest in hearing from you. Show your group's professionalism by paying to have staff email accounts with a ".org" handle, derived from your group's name—as opposed to using free Hotmail or Gmail account handles. The cost is minimal.

While you're at it, be sure that the designer—or redesigner—of your website, blog, and e-newsletter (if any) ensures that they can be viewed on smartphones and other mobile devices.

You'll find more on creating a website that effectively supplements your fundraising goals in Chapter 12. Chapter 5 explains how email can fit into your overall fundraising strategy.

Credit Card Capabilities

One of the mantras of every fundraiser should be, "Make it easy for supporters to give." To this end, allowing people to donate—or even make recurring donations—by credit card can be crucial. A person who doesn't feel like writing a check—or even thinking about his or her account balance—may be happy to give you his or her credit card number, whether on a reply card, at an event, or online. And the good news for you is credit card payments don't bounce.

> **TIP**
> **Credit card donors give more.** Numerous studies have shown that people paying by credit card give more, on average, than those paying by check.

To set up a credit card system, talk to a few banks or a third-party provider such as PayPal (www.paypal.com). You'll be asking to either open your "merchant banking account" or, if you use a service like Pay Pal to have a third-party merchant accept payments on your behalf. Various services are geared especially for nonprofits, such as DonateNow, which handles processing of online donations and allows you to create a customized donation page that matches your website; BlackbaudNow which, in tandem with PayPal, charges no setup or monthly fees; and DonorPerfect (within its suite of fundraising management products).

You'll likely have to pay a start-up fee (usually no more than $200), a monthly or an annual fee (usually no more than $15 per month or $150 per year—avoid banks that charge both), and a charge per transaction (usually either 1.5% to 15% of the amount of the transaction, or a flat fee of 10 cents to 75 cents, or a combination of the two). Transactional fees are usually higher in cases where you aren't given the actual card to swipe, as with a telephone or an Internet donation.

Shop around for an intermediary that charges low fees and whose overall fee structure isn't so complicated that you find yourself paying high fees without knowing what you did "wrong." It's possible to find ones that waive some of the fees, or return a portion of the percentage normally charged, in recognition of your nonprofit status.

Developing Your Fundraising Plan

Every worthwhile endeavor starts with a plan, and your annual fundraising efforts should be no exception. If I could give you a simple formula, such as "spend ____% of your time proposal writing, ____% on donors, and the rest on special events and planned giving in order to raise $____," I certainly would. But, because every nonprofit has its own strengths and unique position within the community it serves, no such generic fundraising plan exists. It's up to you to create your plan, based on the work you need to accomplish and the financial support you can reasonably hope to attract.

It's okay if you've been operating for a while without a plan—it often makes sense for a new group to focus on the cause first and the funds second. Still, no matter how busy you are now, it's absolutely crucial to your long-term viability that you take some time to develop a coherent fundraising plan. Don't worry that coming up with a plan will be all drudgery and paper pushing: This can be an exciting chance to reaffirm what works and rethink what doesn't, set goals, and make a commitment to keeping an eye on the big picture.

Take care, however, to fit your fundraising planning into the other types of planning that your nonprofit (hopefully) engages in—strategic planning, program planning, and budgeting, in particular. Every organization needs to make time to plan—and dream—without always viewing things through the lens of, "But how are we going to pay for this tomorrow?"

Here are the key tasks you'll have to tackle to create your fundraising plan for the next one to five years:

- Determine a reasonable dollar goal to work toward.
- Evaluate your organization's greatest fundraising assets.
- Create a strategy that uses these assets to most effectively reach potential funding sources.
- Write down your strategy in a short, easy-to-understand document to keep everyone on plan in the future.

The Broader World of Strategic and Business Planning

To keep your priorities in order, your organization should look at broad planning issues before focusing on fundraising. Done right, this planning process should include researching, collecting community input, and coming to decisions about:

- the current concerns—and needs—of the community you serve
- whether your organization's original mission is still relevant and appropriate or needs to be modified
- whether your programs, products, or policies still represent the best ways to go forward
- whether the community is sufficiently aware of your organization's existence, and, if not, whether further marketing is needed, or if so, whether it supports—or continues to support—your mission and goals
- whether your organization is paying enough attention to its own infrastructure, future viability, and the needs of its management and staff
- the risks and benefits of contracting or expanding your programs
- your overall financial situation, and
- putting this all together, where your organization should focus its energy and fundraising resources in the coming year or years.

Various resources are available to help: See, for example, www.bridgespan.org (under "Publications & Tools," choose "Strategic Planning").

Getting Started: Set Your Fundraising Goal

Every nonprofit should produce an annual budget. When you begin, this may be done informally, with the founding members chipping in a few dollars as needed. But certainly by your second year, the process of creating an annual budget should be institutionalized. Ideally, it should be a collaborative process, overseen by the executive director with input from the board, the accounting staff, and any relevant program managers or other staffers. The resulting budget will reflect all of the income that the organization brings in and all of the expenses it foresees paying out.

> ⚡ TIP
>
> **Try to create a small reserve fund.** Too many nonprofits create a budget in which the total income exactly equals the total expenses. Given the shoestring on which most nonprofits operate, this isn't surprising—but it's still risky. If unavoidable extra expenses arise, the nonprofit may be pushed into the red. Setting aside even a small amount each year—preferably out of donor funds or fees for services—can significantly enhance your organization's stability and limit the chances of a time-wasting midyear financial emergency. Depending on the size of your organization and how quickly it's expanding, it makes sense to create a cash reserve that will keep your organization going for a full 90 to 180 days.

Of course, it would be nice if someone could just tell you how much money you'll need to raise each year. But in the real world, arriving at your total income figure is—and should be—a complex process, in which planners typically look at:

- how much money would be needed in an ideal world to develop programs and infrastructure
- how much money was raised last year (probably a lot less)
- how much more can reasonably be raised this year
- how much the organization's programs and infrastructure can *really* get by on, with appropriate penny-pinching
- whether the reduced figure looks more realistic in terms of fundraising,
- and so on.

Without our examining the entire budget process, we'll look in this section at the particular and limited role that a development director and other development staff can and should play in developing a budget. This role may include:

- creating the development department's budget
- helping to arrive at accurate and reasonable income projections
- monitoring the percentage of the overall budget that is going to administrative overhead, that is, to nonprogram staff and activities
- identifying places where the group may be able to raise more by better marketing its services, and
- considering whether expensive equipment or services can be obtained via donations, rather than by paying for them.

> CAUTION
> **Don't arrive at your fundraising goal by ratcheting up last year's income.** Some nonprofits come up with their fundraising targets by simply increasing the previous year's number by a set percentage or amount—for example, by deciding that a fundraising effort that raised $100,000 last year can raise $120,00 this year. But fundraising involves too many variables for this kind of approach to be accurate. And if major grants aren't renewed, or other known income sources drop out of the picture, an ambitious goal like this could end up crippling the organization, as expenses keep mounting. Look at every revenue source and make a reasonable projection as to how much you're likely to receive this year to arrive at an informed total.

Create a Budget for Development Activities

At some point in the growth of your organization, the development staff may be asked to draft a separate subbudget for their own activities. How, a first-timer might wonder, can you estimate how much money you will spend on photocopying or travel for an entire year? You aren't even sure what events you will have, whether many of your donors will suddenly prefer a full lunch over coffee, or whether the economy will hit a period of inflation.

At the beginning, you'll have to rely largely on your instincts and your careful review of past years' budgets or records of expenditures. Try some simple budgeting exercises. Go through an entire day or week, noticing what supplies you use, how many photocopies you make, how many faxes or letters you send out, and so forth. Then estimate the costs of these items and add up what they'd cost for a month, then a year. Also think about the things you're pretty sure you'll do over the course of the year—send out a certain number of mailings, hold an annual event, and so on—and add up their costs. Though unscientific, these exercises can be revealing, showing that some costs add up faster than you'd think and others are less significant.

Next, look at any budgets or fundraising-expense records from past years. The first thing you'll probably notice is that your biggest expenses are not for incidental items, but for employee salaries and overhead (taxes and benefits, plus the costs of the office space and utilities). You'll see other fixed or regular costs, too; perhaps phone or Internet fees, which give a certain predictability to any budget, year to year. (It also explains why, in tough times, all the cost cutting in the world can't necessarily forestall the need for layoffs).

Also look at what fundraising activities your organization undertook in past years, how much they cost, and whether these activities will likely be reduced, repeated, or expanded. Of course, this kind of analysis creates a chicken-and-egg problem—you can't know for sure whether you'll be doing more mailings and fewer grant proposals, or vice versa, until you've developed your fundraising plan. But you can at least get a sense of your operating constraints and, with experience, learn to balance the budget and planning possibilities more naturally.

If you've already been involved with the organization for a year or more, think about what will (or should) change this year. Was there enough money last year to order appropriate stationery and office supplies? Did you have a large one-time expense, such as the cost of renting a hall for a special fundraising event that won't be repeated?

After going through these various exercises and reviewing past budgets, you should be able to fill out the sample cost analysis below (and online, see Appendix B for the link). There's a column for "notes," where you might write down the costs you're uncertain about, what might affect them, and the like. For example, if salaries are changing, you'll need to talk to your accounting department about how much the associated employment taxes and benefits will be.

Obviously, no budget will reflect future expenditures with 100% accuracy. That's why, over the course of each fiscal year, it's important to keep an eye on what your development department or staff actually spends, to get a sense of what is normal and reasonable and to figure out where your estimates could use a little fine-tuning. Your accounting staff—or at least the volunteer who keeps the books—can help here, by putting together regular reports on actual versus budgeted expenditures. If this isn't practical in your organization, it will be up to you to make sure that you either stay within budget or receive permission from the powers that be to deviate from it.

Fundraising Worksheet 1: Sample Cost Analysis

Item	Cost per year	Notes
Salaries and benefits	$ _____	_____ _____
Fees to independent contractors and consultants	$ _____	_____ _____
Travel (trainings, donor visits)	$ _____	_____ _____
Office supplies	$ _____	_____ _____
Graphic design/printing	$ _____	_____ _____
Dues and publications	$ _____	_____ _____
Staff trainings and networking events	$ _____	_____ _____
Web, database, and other technical support	$ _____	_____ _____
Telephone and Internet	$ _____	_____ _____
Postage	$ _____	_____ _____
Food (such as coffee or meals with donors)	$ _____	_____ _____
Special event costs	$ _____	_____ _____
Other special program costs	$ _____	_____ _____
Total	$ _____	

Check Your Income Projections

The income side of your organization's proposed annual budget should include known or projected income from reliable sources such as ongoing grants, annual member renewals, and income that your fundraising efforts will almost surely bring in. For example, if a particular fundraising event has raised between $22,000 and $26,000 for three years running, it's probably safe to assume that it will raise at least $20,000 this year. You may even want to use a slightly higher number.

Your most important budgeting task is to make sure that the known income figures are accurate. Check to make sure that all of the grants will continue as the budget says they will, and that they don't run out in the middle of next year. Your treasurer or paid accounting staff should be tracking this too, but mistakes can be made.

> CAUTION
> **Be particularly careful when your fiscal year and a grant year are different.** If, for example, half of the grant will be received in one fiscal year, and the other half in the next, you'll need to allocate income and expenses accordingly.

Also look at the estimated amount of member donations. Most budget planners estimate this figure based on recent years' results, with adjustments for any known or likely changes. In your review, you will need to consider whether these estimates and adjustments are appropriate. Obviously, you don't have a crystal ball. But, if you have a regular base of members who are encouraged to renew annually, and you can review this history of renewals, you've got a good starting point for your predictions. You can also estimate how many interim mailings or appeals you'll send out to existing members or supporters, and make a realistic assessment of how much these will bring in.

Be sure to consider any unusual circumstances that affected recent years' giving patterns. If you know, for example, that individual donations hit a spike last year because of a particular hot issue or disaster, you'll need to make sure that this figure is revised downward. By the same token, if your development office was unusually short-staffed last December and sent out no holiday email appeals, you can assume that individual donations will be at least a little higher this year (allowing for those lost donors whose loyalties shifted in the meantime). A planned hike in your membership dues will also affect your likely income.

The income projections probably will, and should, have a separate line for the amount of major donations you're likely to solicit. If your group is typical, at least a few people will contribute more—sometimes far more than any annual dues. You can put any existing estimates through the tests described above—what will be different this year? Was there anything unusual about last year or recent years, like a lapse in stewardship of major donors, a huge one-time gift, or a change in the tax laws, that affected your major donations?

Another thing to consider is how certain the various anticipated income items are. Identify the areas of greatest vulnerability—where would your organization be hurt the most if money you've included in the budget doesn't come through? You might want to develop a worst-case scenario budget, and think ahead about how you would adjust your organizations fundraising plan accordingly.

> EXAMPLE: Save the Banana Slugs (SBS), an Oregon-based nonprofit, has always received half its budget—$25,000 out of its annual $50,000—from a local timber company trying to better its reputation. The company has indicated a willingness to renew that support. However, SBS has heard rumors that the company will be sold to a multinational conglomerate whose motto is "Cut the trees down and get out of town." SBS therefore creates two budgets—one including the projected $25,000 in corporate support, and another that omits the $25,000 (and cuts certain staff and programs to make up the difference).

Administrative Overhead

Your public relations needs can have a major impact on your budget planning. Every nonprofit must pay careful attention to how much it spends on actual services and programs, versus how much goes to administrative costs—the salaries, equipment, and supplies for people and activities behind the scenes, such as management, accounting, and fundraising. Your grant makers and individual supporters will be keeping an eye on the ratio between these two amounts and will cast a wary eye whenever more than 35% to 50% of your total budget is spent on administration.

This doesn't mean that your organization absolutely cannot spend more than 50% on administrative costs. Not only is there no law against it, but for some organizations, it might even be appropriate. A new nonprofit, for example, might sensibly spend large portions of its budget on administration while building the very programs, and reaching the very size, at which maximum effectiveness and efficiency become possible. The percentage of the budget allocated to administrative costs will then drop quickly.

But you'll have to recognize—and make sure your group's leaders understand—that high administrative costs will make your job as a fundraiser harder. Not only do some foundations and corporate funders limit the amounts of their grants that can be spent on administration, but they may also simply refuse to support any group that spends too much on administrative overhead in general. When you submit a proposed budget with a grant proposal to one of these funders, you'll have to allot an artificially small figure to administrative overhead in order to get the grant.

If you have a shortfall like this, the pressure will be on the development staff to make up the difference elsewhere—probably from individual supporters, but you'll also have to explain to them why such a high percentage of their dollars is going right back into fundraising and other nonprogram functions. If you're stuck in this situation, at least make sure that your departmental budget allows for sufficient staff and other resources with which to ramp up an individual donor program.

TIP

Grow your nonprofit slowly. Most nonprofits begin with volunteers doing much or all of the work, including fundraising, which all but ensures that administrative overhead and fundraising costs are a tiny percentage of the budget. To avoid tipping the balance, grow your paid staff slowly, only as you really need and can justify it. Resist trying to jump-start growth by engaging in expensive fundraising campaigns.

Look for Places Where Your Organization Sells Itself Short

Nonprofits obviously exist to help others, not to profit from doing so. That means any fees that you charge for services to clients or others should be fair. But many nonprofits have taken "fairness" too far: They significantly undercharge for their services and end up exploiting their own underpaid staffers. This is a losing strategy—especially when you consider that to succeed in the long run, you'll have to count on those same staffers to stick around and help build your organization.

Client fees have been studied and agonized over in all sorts of contexts, but one conclusion comes through loud and clear: Except when you are dealing with the truly indigent, it's better to charge fees for services than to give them away. For one thing, clients tend to think more highly of services they've paid for. Things gotten for free are seen as throwaways—as evidenced by the phrase I and others heard while providing immigration law advice at a free clinic, "Thanks, but do you think I need a *real* lawyer now?" Later, I learned another valuable lesson: Clients who have paid even a modest fee are more likely to keep their appointments and actively participate in problem solving.

Both your organization's mission and budget will benefit if you charge reasonably for your services. If you've never charged fees before, start by figuring out how much each service really costs you to provide, then survey your client population to consider how much they can reasonably pay. Often, you'll find that people's incomes are spread across a wider range than you at first imagined, which means that a sliding fee schedule may be a good approach. Finally, you'll have to let your clients know why you're imposing fees (especially if you have provided free services in the past) and what you are doing with the money.

Also take a close look at other areas where your organization might be able to charge a reasonable fee for services or benefits it's currently giving away:

- Are you letting a local group use your space at no charge?
- Are you taking members of the public on educational tours or outings that also happen to be fun or much sought after?

- Are you providing speakers for other organizations' events (for-profit or nonprofit) where they're charging the attendees money? Ask them to share!
- Are you providing services to private businesses that could afford to pay for them? For example, if you are picking up surplus food from local restaurants to feed the homeless and prominently listing the restaurants as program sponsors, you may actually be providing them with economic benefits (a lower garbage bill and free promotion). If you explain these benefits to the restaurants, they may agree to chip in for the salary of the person who does the food pickup and delivery.

Noncash Contributions

Before rushing out to raise every dollar that your organization needs, consider whether you can supplement your fundraising with:

- in-kind donations of goods, or
- donations of professional services.

You've no doubt seen "wish lists" that other organizations place in their newsletters, event programs, and the like. They're usually for major items of equipment, such as a new or used laser printer, car, or costume for an event. These lists work. Though you can't count on receiving every item on your list, you'll get some of them—and quite possibly from supporters who wouldn't have given money.

An alternative to the wish list is to ask local businesses for equipment or supplies, new or used (but still serviceable). Nonprofits routinely receive donations of everything from computers and desks to flowers for their front entrance by following this approach. The key is usually to contact the owner of the business directly, and be ready to provide the owner with written materials—and, if needed, references—establishing your credibility. Also be sure to highlight any place that the business will be publicly thanked, such as in your newsletter, website, or event program. If your organization or its key members are regular customers mention that, too.

Berkeley Repertory Theatre's Wish List

Few organizations have as wide and varied material needs as a theatre, and the Berkeley Repertory Theatre, in Berkeley, California, is no exception. As an award-winning, professional company that stages everything from modern world premieres to ancient Greek drama, their props alone fill a warehouse. In addition to paying a good-sized staff, the theater has all sorts of additional expenses, such as apartments for visiting actors and directors, which need furniture, cooking equipment, and more. So, Berkeley Rep posts a wish list in its programs and on its website (www.berkeleyrep.org). You might spot such items on their list as scooters, tumbling mats, a bedazzler, and low-cost physician's services, to name but a few.

I asked Lynn Eve Komaromi, Berkeley Rep's director of development, how well the wish list has worked: "It's been very successful—sometimes too successful! We occasionally have to refuse gifts, such as clothing. But we've been helped a lot by gifts of washers and dryers, as well as computers. The most common gift we receive is furniture, which we use for the artists' apartments. Someone also once donated a Volvo, so that became the car that our visiting directors used—much better than the old beater we could offer them before.

"We make sure to give donors receipts for their contributions. We also list the names of those who gave high-value gifts within the donor list in our theatre programs, with an asterisk indicating that they're 'in-kind' contributors.

"Although we name specific items on our list, I try to be open to whatever comes along. The most interesting unsolicited gift we got was a live, miniature horse. Not exactly something we could put in our prop warehouse until the right play came along! Fortunately, we had an auction coming up at one of our special events, and someone bought the little horse. We heard later that the buyer had been a bit swept up in the moment, and the next morning had some doubts about what he'd do with his new acquisition. But he had a good friend with a farm, who was delighted to receive the horse, so things worked out happily all around."

Soliciting in-kind donations is an excellent task for board members and other volunteers, particularly in preparation for an auction or a raffle. It's an especially fitting task for those who find asking for objects easier than asking for money.

Your organization should always be looking for ways to get volunteers involved, as covered in more depth in Chapter 2. As you look at the budget, see whether any discrete new possibilities emerge, particularly for professional services. If a new program is being created, ask whether the planners considered ways to involve volunteers—including whether any needed positions could be filled by a quasi-volunteer who receives a stipend from another program, such as a Jesuit volunteer (see Chapter 2).

Professionals customarily donate all kinds of services—everything from consulting to proposal writing to graphic or Web design to legal and accounting advice. Considering that their hourly rates may look staggering next to your nonprofit's budget, soliciting such donations can be useful and necessary. Be aware, however, that there are a couple of downsides to accepting such donated services: Your volunteers may not maintain their commitment over time or may not have the time and energy to meet deadlines. Donated services usually involve a series of commitments by the donors—meetings, initial proposals, drafts, and final results. These commitments may be hard for donors to keep. For example, some use volunteering as a way to launch their businesses or establish their reputations. If their paying customers start filling their time, you may find your project pushed to the back burner.

Also be careful about accepting free services that the provider wants to leverage into a paid relationship. Unless you're clear at the outset about how much you'll pay and for what services, you could find yourself drawn into an overly expensive or otherwise problematic arrangement. To guard against this, lay out your agreement and mutual expectations in a written letter at the start of the relationship.

Evaluate Your Nonprofit's Fundraising Assets

Every nonprofit's mission, property, program, and history are different, which helps explain why there's no one-size-fits-all fundraising plan. Beyond this, however, different organizations also have different fundraising strengths, both tangible and intangible. This section explains how to evaluate your existing assets, with an eye toward strategically deploying them as part of your overall fundraising plan.

Identify Your Assets

An organization's assets come in all shapes and sizes. The reputation you build by running an effective and well-known program is an asset, as is a building or a truck. Skills, people, and experience can also be assets.

Some of your assets would hardly be noticed by outsiders looking at your organization—for example, low employee turnover. With such hidden assets, it becomes even more important for you to identify them and, if and when appropriate, use them to attract supporters or funders.

Although not all assets are suited to every type of fundraising, think creatively about what types of assets would best attract your different audiences, among them foundations, corporations, and individual donors. Take, for example, TechSoup, a San Francisco nonprofit that provides technical support for other nonprofits' computing needs. As much as TechSoup might like to recruit a long list of individual contributors, that may not be possible in a world where baby seals, hungry children, and disaster victims are the first to capture donors' hearts. A far more realistic strategy has been for TechSoup to focus energy on foundation grants. This allows it to play to its real strengths, such as providing a hugely needed service to hundreds of other organizations that might otherwise grind to a halt.

Your organization might be in the opposite situation. If you have a program that individual donors can readily understand—such as advocating for urban bike paths or supporting the arts in area schools—but your program doesn't happen to fit neatly into any foundation's niche, you'll want to concentrate on individual and, perhaps, small business donors.

Some organizations have unusual assets or fundraising advantages. A community radio station, for example, has the airwaves—and can request donations from anyone willing to listen during its pledge drives. The International Institute of Buffalo, New York, resides in a classic 19th-century mansion, the gift of a long-ago donor—which it rents out for meetings and parties. The Berkeley Repertory Theatre, after its annual clean-out of its props and costume warehouse, holds a sale of all the items it doesn't think it will need for a future production. Lynn Eve Komaromi explains, "We get lots of folks who like to shop for Burning Man—they find costumes and bits and pieces for their art displays. It's a win-win."

The people within your organization—your staff, board, and volunteers—may well be its most important assets. Consider people's skills and personalities without being either overly judgmental or overly optimistic. Thinking to yourself, "I'm sure Sarita will finally make time for fundraising this year," or "If I can just talk Jay out of his shyness, he'd be great with major donors," is not likely to make the cash register ring. Instead, identify specific and proven strengths, such as:

- personal connections with particular communities (for example, ethnic, political, or interest-based groups) or potential major donors
- personal connections with foundation staff members or potential corporate donors
- good people skills
- reputation—or even fame
- writing or marketing skills
- artistic skills
- event-coordinating skills
- Internet or computer skills
- ownership of or access to a nice home, club or boat or another facility
- eagerness to participate in a certain type of fundraising (for example, someone who hates to phone potential donors may delight in running an annual silent auction), and
- any other special skills and interests.

Face—And Embrace—Your Organization's Weaknesses

In the course of considering what makes your organization and its people great, you'll have to also consider what it lacks—gaps or weaknesses, personal or organizational, that might undermine the use of a particular fundraising strategy.

If, for example, you've got a great writer on your team, foundation support might be an obvious fundraising choice—but if you know that you've already tapped every possible foundation, you'll probably have to find some other uses for your writer's talents. Or, let's say there's a famous person on your board who could be the keynote speaker at a fundraising event—but that person is controversial or, even worse, disliked by a significant number of your supporters. It will be of little long-term benefit to run a successful event that alienates a significant part of your constituency.

Rather than writing off the people or fundraising methods you had in mind, consider how to turn supposed negatives into positives. Such creative thinking has been a central theme in the fundraising work of Lupe Gallegos-Diaz, who teaches fundraising courses at UC Berkeley and once worked with a national Chicano studies organization. That group had a large membership, but most—about 80%—were financially challenged undergraduates, with the remaining 20% mostly underpaid faculty members. Because this population was not ripe for major gifts, the group instituted a campaign asking members for donations of at least $1. They educated every donor about the importance of giving even a little. Although they didn't bring in big dollars the first year, they got people into the habit of giving, thus laying the groundwork for continued—and larger—gifts in the future.

Another example Lupe cites is of a group whose members were mostly stay-at-home mothers. Because they were neither socially prominent nor affluent, they didn't feel ready to reach out to rich and powerful donors. But they did know plenty of people in their own community who would enjoy a good meal. To start their fundraising, they held a series of in-house dinners, hosted by their own members, with everyone helping prepare food and sell tickets. Later, they used the goodwill they'd developed through these small events to put on a bigger, more elaborate dinner event—by which time the prospective guests knew each other and were eager to attend. The group raised significant funds and educated many people in the community about their excellent work.

List Your Assets

As soon as you're ready, take a piece of paper and write, in a column, all the relevant assets—whether people, property, or abstract qualities—that you can identify within your organization. When it comes to people, you might want to mention individuals by name, and give each a separate line. Next to each asset or strength, list the types of fundraising it could support.

The worksheet below (and online; see Appendix B for the link) will help you create a list of your nonprofit's assets and their possible fundraising applications. Don't just fill this out on your own and put it in a drawer. Take a blank version of the chart and meet with staff, board members, and other stakeholders. Ask them to brainstorm and record their ideas on it. Remind them about the various tasks and activities involved in fundraising, and ask them to think specifically about what and whose skills and advantages might be helpful. Explain the reasons behind some of the items on the list—for example, under "physical facilities," a boat could be used for a special event, or a weekend at someone's lakeside vacation home could be offered up during a silent auction. Your brainstormers may come up with something you didn't think of—or didn't even know about. For example, a board member might say, "You know, my brother's wife is part of a famous band that sings about social justice issues—I bet they'd do a benefit concert for us!"

After you've collected input from others, create a master chart of your organization's assets and their fundraising applications (using the same format as before). You'll use this to develop your fundraising strategy, as described next. You'll also probably want to refer to this chart again during next year's planning process.

> **CAUTION**
> **Special events aren't always so special.** When you get volunteers together to think "fundraising," you'll often see most of the excitement and ideas generated around proposals for special events. "Hey, we could do a carnival, with a dunking booth, and I'll bake 1,000 cookies ... it'll be great!" In part, this tendency is natural: Most people have more experience with events, from bake sales and raffles to silent auctions and wine tastings, than with any other kind of fundraising. And who wouldn't rather plan a party than write a grant proposal or call ten major donors? Too bad that when you figure all the time and energy that goes into them, special events are, on average, the least profitable form of fundraising (though they have their other benefits; see Chapter 8 for more information). Try to keep your brainstormers focused on the overall goal, the full breadth of fundraising methods needed to meet it, and the assets that might support those methods.

Fundraising Worksheet 2: Fundraising Assets

Asset Type	Asset Description	Possible Fundraising Use
Organization's mission		
Organization's programs		
Organization's reputation or history with certain foundations or individuals		
Organization's access to certain members of community		
Organization's physical facilities or resources		
Physical facilities or resources owned or accessible by board, staff, or volunteers		
Executive director		
Development director		
Development assistant		
Other development staff		
Board members		
Board fundraising committee		
Particularly active individual volunteers		
Volunteer program generally		
Other friends of your organization		

Develop Your Fundraising Strategy

Now that you know how much income you'll need for the coming year's activities and you know your organization's fundraising strengths and weaknesses, it's time to figure out how you'll get the money.

Start by calculating how much money you'll have to raise. From the total needed for the coming year, subtract the amount that you can count on receiving, such as committed grants and fees for services you're fairly sure to provide. The number that's left is the amount you'll actually need to raise.

You're now ready to decide on a fundraising strategy—that is, to identify which of the fundraising techniques or sources described in this book can be tapped for maximum advantage. You'll have to consider some general tactical issues, such as what your core assets are and how much you'll need to diversify your funding sources. Then consider how your assets match up with the possible range of fundraising methods. Finally, make sure the board and key staffers are enthusiastically behind the final plan.

Tactical Considerations

Your fundraising strategy should depend, in part, on your organization's purpose and goals. Stick with fundraising activities that are time-tested or core to your organization's identity; stay within the boundaries of your organization's strategic plan and mission; and otherwise try to diversify your funding sources and activities.

Although you should engage in an open-ended planning process, that doesn't mean that your whole fundraising strategy has to change. If certain fundraising activities have worked well for your organization in the past, you'll probably want to continue to use them. There's no point in junking a well-run individual member program (ever) or a much-loved annual event (unless it's truly draining other resources or you feel you've gotten into a rut). In fact, donors appreciate a certain degree of consistency. Just as with fast food restaurants, there's a certain value in letting people know what to expect in terms of offerings and quality. Some supporters may even mentally plan around your traditional fundraisers, thinking "I'll buy my greeting cards from X organization again this year, and take my friend

Cynthia to its annual auction." If you bounce between an auction one year, a holiday tree sale the next, and a walkathon the year after, you may confuse and frustrate your most loyal supporters.

Fundraising isn't tangential to an organization's work; indeed, to be truly effective, fundraising must be an expression of a group's philosophy and identity. For example, the Mayflower Historical Society would probably not do too well with a rock concert, and the West Flatbush Neighborhood Improvement Association might concentrate on getting new individual members who live in and care about the neighborhood, not on soliciting large donations from celebrities.

> **TIP**
>
> **Focus on individual donors.** No matter how else you plan to raise money, virtually every nonprofit should be trying to increase the number of people who support it each year and the amount of money each of these individual donors gives. Not only does increasing member support send an important signal about your organization's vitality to larger donors, it's also an important hedge against economic hard times.

You should also try for a certain level of diversity among funding streams—we all know the risks of putting all your eggs in one basket. It's sad to watch all the work and energy that goes into building or developing a program go down the drain because the funding faucet gets turned off. And sometimes the staff who get laid off are the lucky ones—the remainder have to pick up the workloads they left behind, because of promises made to the remaining funders.

At the same time, you'll want to diversify thoughtfully. Having numerous baskets each holding one egg can be problematic, too. If you have too many separate sources of funds, each with its own time, staffing, and reporting requirements, you'll be pulled in too many directions to be effective. Maybe that's why a study of the nation's largest nonprofits—with revenues over $50 million —came to the surprising conclusion that concentrating on just a few funding sources helped their success. The National Wild Turkey Federation, for example, has found hunters to be its biggest and best funding source. (See "How Nonprofits Get Really Big," by William Foster and Gail Fine, *Stanford Social Innovation Review,* Spring 2007.)

EXAMPLE: Nonprofit X had built a successful track record at providing overnight shelter and job training to the city's homeless population. The city and county governments knew that the agency's work directly improved conditions in their area, so they were willing to pony up a few thousand dollars when asked. There was just one problem. Nonprofit X had never built up much of an individual donor base. Meanwhile, the city and county money was restricted to program activities—little or none of it was allowed to go toward administrative overhead costs. That meant it was always a scramble to pay the ED and accounting staff's salaries, and hiring a development director was out of the question. Less and less time was devoted to soliciting individual—and unrestricted—donations, and the financial picture got progressively worse. Everyone knew that the loss of any one of the main funders could bring down the entire agency.

Instead of trying to diversify the funding, the ED kept applying for more grants from local governments, hoping to pool enough overhead funding from the contracts to make up the shortfall. Unfortunately, with every grant came new requirements—to provide more beds and more trainings, which required more staff time.

The funding situation finally hit a crisis point—when the over-worked staff members (those who didn't quit) were ready to mutiny. The board, which had been reluctant to acknowledge how critical the situation was, finally couldn't stand idly by. A new fundraising plan was developed, which focused on outreach to individual donors and foundations. A new ED was also brought in—with a firm mandate to implement the new plan and end the agency's overreliance on restricted funds.

The ideal is to have a manageably sized mix of stable sources providing the bulk of your budget, with some additional sources to provide balance, create future potential, and fill in the fundraising gaps. Author and expert Kim Klein recommends that no more than 20% of your total funding come from any one person or source. (See *Fundraising in Times of Crisis*, from Jossey-Bass.) She also recommends that no more than 20% to 30% of your total budget come from foundation or government sources, because foundation money tends to dry up after a year or two, and government funding is notoriously affected by recessions and elections.

RELATED TOPIC

Information on developing donor diversity. Diversity among the race, ethnicity, and lifestyles of your donors is also worth striving for. Refer to Chapter 4 for information on developing such diversity.

Spread Out Fundraising Responsibilities Among Your Staff

The goal of diversifying applies not only to your fundraising sources—where the money is coming from—but also to the people who go after it. If you've ever worked in an organization where the ED or development director quit, and all development efforts went stagnant for a few months because no one else had any idea what was planned or underway, you know all too well what this principle means. There are similar dangers in having one person who reigns over development efforts and guards his or her territory from others' input and participation like a jealous Gollum in *Lord of the Rings*.

If you are unable to hire a large development staff, it's even more important that various members of your board, as well as other volunteers, are committed to your fundraising program. There may even be times when you want to build activities into your fundraising program specifically to keep certain board members enthusiastic and involved—sort of like writing the script to fit the actors.

Your First Draft Plan

Now it's time to make some important decisions about your future fundraising activities. This is not a task to handle alone; instead, bring in some combination of the ED, development staff, and key board members (depending on your organization's size and number of paid staff).

Pick up your final version of Worksheet 2, showing organizational assets and possible fundraising applications. You'll use it to create another chart, shown below, in which you choose the best fundraising activities for your organization and make sure that these activities will help you reach your goal without draining your budget.

Fundraising Worksheet 3: Fundraising Strategy Chart

Activity or Funding Source	Amount It Should Raise	New or Unusual Expenses	Total Amount (Column 2 minus Column 3)
_____	$ _____	$ _____	$ _____
_____	$ _____	$ _____	$ _____
_____	$ _____	$ _____	$ _____
_____	$ _____	$ _____	$ _____
_____	$ _____	$ _____	$ _____
_____	$ _____	$ _____	$ _____
_____	$ _____	$ _____	$ _____
		Grand Total:	$ _____

Using this chart (also available online; see Appendix B for the link), play around with various scenarios. Start by choosing a promising fundraising activity, such as "proposals to foundations," in Column 1. Estimate how much you'll be able to raise through that activity in Column 2. Then estimate any new or unusual costs the fundraising activity will require in Column 3 (which is there to make sure you don't render your departmental budget irrelevant). Particularly if you're shifting course toward a strategy that requires a high up-front investment, such as a new direct mail program or special event, you'll need to estimate the added costs carefully and make sure that they aren't going to break the bank. Subtract the amount entered in Column 3 from the amount in Column 2, and enter the result in the fourth and final columns.

As you go, keep a running total of the amounts entered in Column 4, until the Grand Total equals (or preferably exceeds!) the amount you need to fundraise for that year. (To get even more scientific about this, you might go back to your department budget to see if there are any costs you won't be incurring because you've shifted strategy away from the activities with which those costs were associated.)

Let's say, for example, that your organization is a clinic. Its greatest asset may be satisfied ex-patients and their family members, who already support a successful major donor program. The major donor program is no doubt worth continuing—or better yet, increasing at a realistic rate. Enter the likely fundraising proceeds in Column 2 (and, if you're expanding, any new costs in Column 3).

However, even an expanded major donor program probably doesn't cover all of your monetary needs. Moving on down your assets chart, you may see that you have a volunteer who is willing and able to take patients' artwork and turn it into greeting cards and another volunteer willing and able to market the cards. This may, however, require some up-front investment (unless the cardstock and printing are donated). Enter the amount this strategy could realistically raise in Column 2, being sure to estimate the new expenses in Column 3.

Check your running total from Column 4 to see how much that leaves to be raised from other funding sources. Grant proposals to foundations, corporations, or government are a likely prospect for most nonprofits. In the clinic's case, submitting proposals would be particularly appropriate if the organization's assets include a good reputation, any history of foundation support, current board or staff members with inside contacts, and someone who can write up a compelling proposal.

Keep matching up your organization's greatest strengths and their corresponding fundraising uses, being sure not to assign more tasks to any one person than he or she can handle.

Also remember that your department will have to take on responsibilities that don't raise money directly. You'll need to decide what tasks the development office will carry out that won't have an immediate payback, such as preparing an annual report, setting up a new database, or planning donor forums or appreciation events. Make sure you've left time for someone to take care of these activities, too. Play around until you've found a way to raise all the needed money.

Finding a balance that seems to work is incredibly satisfying—but it's no cause for complacency. In fundraising, as in everything else in life, things can and will go wrong. Pick up that chart one last time, and ask, "What if?" For example, what if several major donors don't contribute this year? What if your board member with the party yacht takes it on a yearlong trip to New Zealand? What if donations to your silent auction aren't as generous as in past years? Focus only on the greatest, foreseeable risks—there's no point in obsessing over plagues, floods, or pestilence. But now that you're scared a little, modify your plan so that you have an adequate financial cushion if things go wrong.

Strategize With—And Seek Buy-In From— A Larger Group

Creating a fundraising plan involves estimating how much help, and what type of help, you'll get from the people involved in your organization. Before chiseling your plan in stone, make sure that all these folks will happily support it. You should have already enlisted their voices at the brainstorming stage—now it's time to go back to them at the commitment stage. Draft your preliminary fundraising plan and present it to staff and board members, at the same or separate meetings. If there are key volunteers outside the board, meet with them separately.

You have three principal objectives in holding these meetings. First, you want to give people a clear idea of what it will take to raise a particular amount of money. Second, you want to give them an opportunity to be heard, so that you can, if necessary, adjust the plan based on their ideas. Third, you want to be sure that they buy into the plan and will commit to doing the necessary work.

To facilitate this process, create a final version of your fundraising strategy chart. Distribute copies, labeled "Draft," to everyone in attendance. Go through each intended fundraising activity one by one, explaining whose help will be needed, how much work will be asked of them, how much up-front investment the organization will be adding, and the risks of failure. If there are any alternate plans you considered and rejected, or are still considering, describe these as well.

Then it's time to sit back and listen as open-mindedly as possible. There is no need to be defensive—if your ideas are excellent, others will come to see that. One effective strategy for doing this is to start by writing down everyone's ideas on a whiteboard or an easel-mounted pad. It's best to use just a few words for each, saving discussion for later. Once this is done, come back to those ideas, one by one, to consider them as a group. Be clear, however, about who will make the final decision on the fundraising plan.

If you are hearing major resistance to a particular element of the plan—especially if it's from the very people on whom you're relying to carry it out—it may be time to rethink. Try to gauge the level of resistance. If you're hearing embarrassed laughter about the prospect of soliciting in-person donations, then a pep talk or training may be all that's needed to tip the balance. If, however, you've got a room full of stone-faced board members who think that starting a car donation program is the worst idea they've ever heard of, it's time to reconsider—unless you want a parking lot full of used cars and no one to deal with them but yourself.

If, at the end of this planning process, you realize you don't have enough staff or volunteers to raise the needed funds, talk with the leaders of your organization. You may need to invest time and resources in finding this help before setting your budgetary or fundraising goals. In the worst-case scenario, your organization may have to scale down its programs or ambitions or look into merging with another organization. These can be painful decisions, but ones that will be better in the long run than hobbling along without sufficient staff or funding.

Create the Final Plan

You'll want to write your fundraising plan down, so that you and others can remember what you decided and refer to it later. But this isn't like school, where more pages get you a higher grade. A document that's padded with lofty expositions of your goals, spreadsheets, and long-winded analyses will intimidate everyone and undermine its very purpose. Keep it simple and usable.

Choose a format that will work for you and your staff—one that everyone will intuitively understand and want to look at. Some helpful components to include in your plan are:

- **An indication of the time duration of the plan.** One year is the standard, but it can also be helpful to include less detailed projections for the next few years.
- **A narrative description of your various goals.** For example, if the plan is to continue on your current course, say so—or if it's to reduce donor mailings by a certain number in favor of spending time on special events, describe that. And again, include goals that support fundraising indirectly, such as staff training, projects involving your Web presence, and the like.
- **A calendar showing what you'll work on month by month.** This should including mailings, grant proposals, events, and whatever else you've decided on.
- **A breakdown of responsibilities.** Describe who will lead each task, who else will be involved, and if appropriate, approximately how much time the person will devote to this task. For staff persons, this can be expressed as a percentage of overall time.
- **How you'll measure interim success over the year or years.** Plan on revisiting your plan at least quarterly, to see how reality is measuring up to your projections.
- **Descriptions of backup plans if particularly risky strategies don't pan out as hoped.** The picture is sure to change over the course of the year,

and having a Plan B is a great way to minimize any shock or need for new planning meetings.

Once you've written the plan down, make copies for the appropriate people and slip these into colorful folders. Also post the plan on your internal server if your computers are networked, and do whatever else it takes to make sure that everyone can find it. Emphasize your commitment to making this a living document by bringing it to board or management meetings, reporting back on progress toward its various goals, and asking for feedback on what's working and what isn't. (And realistically, plan on issuing some individual reminders of tasks to be done.)

Don't forget to draw up a new plan when the old one runs out. Preparing a detailed fundraising plan once a year is a good idea. This doesn't mean reinventing the wheel or overturning your strategy every year—it will get easier each time. Part of your organization's goal should be to develop an annual cycle of fundraising, in which you develop years-long relationships with donors and funders. The more systematic you get about this, the easier it will become.

Fundraising Pros Start With a Plan

With 30-plus years of development experience, Christine Grumm of the Women's Funding Network has come to appreciate the importance of planning ahead. "People go wrong by not having a plan—they start out assuming that they should simply write a grant or ask for money. But they've forgotten to do the up-front work of understanding the various possibilities. It's a very systematic process. You can't just look at a grid of fundraising techniques and say, 'I'll do some of this and some of that.' Unless there's a connect between the financial need and the assets that you have to support that need—such as a board contact, or interest on the part of foundations—it's not going to happen."

Attracting Individual Supporters

The day-to-day work of a nonprofit can feel isolated. Your staff may be toiling away on research projects, meeting one-on-one with low-income clients that society seems to have forgotten, or worrying about an indigenous population a continent away. However, you have a nearby constituency and a support network you may never see: your donors and dues-paying members. I'll call them "supporters" or "donors." Some people also use the term "investors."

Think about organizations that you have given money to—didn't you feel that you personally were helping to clean up a waterway, save a dog or cat from being euthanized, or release a political prisoner? Until every member of your staff realizes that these unseen supporters are a vital part of your work and learns to communicate with and actively solicit more of them, your organization will be heading towards stagnation.

Why Not Call Them "Members"?

In some states, the word "member" has a specific legal meaning in the nonprofit setting: It indicates a person with legal rights to participate in and sometimes vote on important organizational decisions, such as appointments to the board of directors, amendments to the articles and bylaws, the sale of certain assets, or mergers with other nonprofits. Most organizations don't want this many people involved in such decisions. Therefore, they go without a formal membership structure (stating this in their articles and bylaws), and avoid using the term. For more information, including state-by-state summaries of membership rules, see Anthony Mancuso's *How to Form a Nonprofit Corporation* (Nolo).

From a practical standpoint, recruiting individual supporters is particularly worthwhile, because their donations come with very few strings attached. While a grant from a foundation or the government may yield your organization a lump sum of tens or even hundreds of thousands of dollars, such grants can come with enough restrictions to significantly hamper your work—and paperwork requirements that gobble up precious staff time. Many foundations insist, for example, that an unreasonably low figure be allotted to the costs of managing your organization or pressure you to prove immediate success in settings where it can't be realistically measured. New or smaller nonprofits may have difficulty attracting grant money in the first place. Also, a grant may be here one year and gone the next.

When fundraising professionals are asked about their strategy during economic downturns, they almost inevitably say, "We're looking to our individual donors." In fact, a 2009 survey by Bridgespan found that while fundraising from every source got harder due to the recession, fewer nonprofits lost money from individual donors than from other sources. And approximately 33% of the organizations surveyed reported that certain funders (both individuals and organizations) had actually increased their support as a result of the downturn. (See www.bridgespan.org; click "Managing Through Tough Times," then "Managing in Tough Times Survey.")

No matter how bad the economy gets, goodhearted people will part with a small amount of cash. In fact, individual donors typically account for over 75% of all funds raised by nonprofits. Even better, you can generally use this money as you wish, to fund programs, compensate your staff, or simply pay the rent.

The question for most nonprofits is not whether to solicit funds from individuals, but how to go about doing it. This chapter will address both subtle and more direct approaches to attracting new supporters, including:

- demonstrating that your organization can meet individual supporters' increasingly high expectations
- understanding why people give—and what will encourage them to give to your organization, and
- using direct mail, email, and other techniques to solicit new supporters.

Make Your Organization Look Support Worthy

Individual supporters don't normally attach conditions to their donations, but that doesn't mean they don't have expectations. Just the opposite—a number of forces are driving them to expect more and more from nonprofits in terms of efficiency, results, and reporting—and to be suspicious if they don't get this information. Of course, your supporters don't have the time or energy to poke around behind the scenes to see whether your nonprofit is really what it claims to be. They'll have to rely on more external indicators, such as your publications and media coverage. This doesn't let you off the hook—the true quality of an organization's work and people becomes known in the community one way or another, and its reputation eventually affects its ability to attract financial support.

Although there are a number of metrics by which nonprofit performance can be evaluated, most everyone has their eyes on one ratio: the proportion of funds being recycled into administration and fundraising instead of fueling the core work of your organization. A ratio of more than 50% of your funds going to administrative costs is generally considered too high. And the Better Business Bureau (BBB)'s Wise Giving Alliance (which many look to as a leader in this area) recommends that no more than 35% of total funds raised be churned back into fundraising—and that 65% of a nonprofit's budget be spent on program activities.

RESOURCE

More information on the Wise Giving Alliance's recommendations.
To access its latest standards, go to www.give.org and click "Charity Accountability Standards."

You probably realize how widespread the public's concern over nonprofits' misuse of funds has become. Studies show that the average donor considers a nonprofit's costs of fundraising and administration in making a decision about whether to send a gift. And, tellingly, one study of wealthy individuals found that 56% said they would give "a great deal more" to charity if they knew that the organizations were effectively managed. So, while financial accountability and organizational efficiency aren't components of fundraising, they are the cornerstone upon which your fundraising hopes and plans must be built.

Of course, taking the time to build a support-worthy organization is easier said than done. I know firsthand the frustration of having outsiders fussing about your so-called "efficiency" when you're putting in long hours with bare-bones staffing, antiquated equipment, and the world's least ergonomic chairs. And while there is much truth in the prevailing wisdom that the majority of organizational resources should be spent on direct services or programs, it's also true that no organization can succeed over the long term without adequately supporting an appropriate managerial staff. People who can carry out fundraising and other managerial activities are absolutely necessary to keep an organization running; at a minimum, someone has to be there to comply with the various demands for reports and other accountability measures!

What has led to this current fashion for intense nonprofit scrutiny? In large part, it stems from the media's age-old interest in scandal, and its investigative reports on the United Way, the Red Cross, and many far more culpable groups. Hardly a month seems to go by without another nonprofit becoming the subject of a media "exposé" or even a Congressional inquiry.

Another contributing factor is the increasing entrepreneurial savvy among financially successful donors, particularly those who made their own money through high-tech, biotech, or other start-up efforts. Many of them believe (sometimes naively) that the principles that made their businesses successful should be applied in the nonprofit sector as well—though perhaps forgetting that you can't reach optimal levels of efficiency without a certain size and level of infrastructure.

In addition, many foundations have adopted and loudly advertise their own efficiency and accountability demands on the nonprofits that they fund. When you put it all together, you may start to feel like you are working in a petri dish, under maximum magnification.

The bottom line is that your organization should try to meet or exceed generally accepted guidelines measuring nonprofit efficiency. Even if your organization is a start-up with few resources, you'll need to do your best to keep the administrative side of your operations lean and channel as many funds as possible to the program/services side. This may require you to have volunteers perform some administrative functions longer than you would like, but there is nevertheless a significant bright side to this lean and hungry approach. As your organization grows, careful attention to financial procedures and reporting should help you guard against sloppiness, self-dealing, or worse, embezzlement by a bad apple on your own staff. For example, developing good financial tracking systems will quickly alert you to instances where you're spending more money than is appropriate. And knowing that you can back up your assertions about well-spent donations will make you and your volunteers more confident when it's time to raise funds.

Once you have taken steps to ensure that you are spending donated money responsibly and well, how can you make that apparent to your supporters? This section discusses four ways to demonstrate your financial bona fides:

- Deliver accurate, up-to-date reports to foundations, the IRS, and other watchdogs.
- Open your books and be willing to share financial information with individual supporters.
- Be courteous and efficient in your dealings with supporters.
- Set realistic but visible benchmarks for success.

Responsible Reporting to Foundations and Government

Running a nonprofit means dealing with a mountain of paperwork. At a minimum, you'll be required to submit reports to your grantors, to the federal government (the IRS), and possibly to your state and local government throughout the year.

Whenever you get a grant, whether from a foundation or the government, you'll likely be asked to write a report, in a very specific format, detailing how you spent the money. These reports may be due once a month, once a year, or somewhere in between. Some funders even require you to provide a financial report before they write a check. While some of the material you provide in the report will be general and narrative, you'll also have to supply an up-to-date accounting of actual costs and expenditures.

For the IRS, your organization will probably need to fill out a Form 990 annually (an informational form, used to assess compliance with the tax laws). Organizations with receipts normally less than $25,000 can e-file a short form or "e-postcard" called a 990-N, while those with gross receipts between $25,000 and $999,000 can use a simplified "990-EZ." Select types of organizations can avoid the 990-filing requirement altogether, including faith-based organizations, subsidiaries of larger nonprofits, foreign nonprofits, nonprofits not registered with the IRS, federal corporations and state institutions, and private foundations. (For details, see *Every Nonprofit's Tax Guide: How to Keep Your Tax-Exempt Status & Avoid IRS Problems*, by attorney Stephen Fishman (Nolo).)

On your Form 990, you'll need to supply information about where your revenues came from and where they were spent. The Form 990 then becomes a public record. You're obligated to give a copy to anyone who asks for it or to post it on the Web.

> ○ **TIP**
>
> **Fill out your Form 990 with an eye to marketing.** Most nonprofits enter minimal information on their Form 990s, just enough to satisfy the IRS and no more. However, the form—in particular, Part III—offers an opportunity to toot your own horn. Part III asks your nonprofit to describe its accomplishments. Why not add some colorful description of your programs, activities, and successes? Though space is tight, there's nothing to stop you from adding a supplementary schedule, telling the story as you want the world to hear it. Some potential supporters will review this information when deciding whether to give. Even nonprofits that aren't required to fill out the full Form 990 might wish to do so, in order to take advantage of this marketing avenue.

Some state governments also monitor nonprofit finances. Most states now require registration by nonprofits that solicit money from individuals there. A few states also require financial reports in connection with nonprofits' regular reregistration. All of these reports may become public information. Most states now publish the nonprofits' reports in some form—including on the Internet. For more information, see Anthony Mancuso's *How to Form a Nonprofit Corporation* (Nolo).

Apart from these registration requirements, many states also require registered nonprofits to submit reports (annually or in connection with each fundraising campaign) detailing how much they spent on fundraising activities in order to bring in a certain amount of donations. These states also tend to require that, along with any request for support, the fundraising organization disclose to prospective supporters the percentage of their donations that will be used for fundraising purposes.

Will your individual donors ever see these various reports? Probably not, unless they're savvy enough to look up your Form 990. But that doesn't mean the information won't come to them by other means. For example, investigative reporters doggedly check out Form 990s, always looking for the latest, hottest nonprofit ripoff. And a number of groups now evaluate and compile data on nonprofits, using the Form 990s and other reports. Potential donors can view the results on the Internet, on websites such as:

- **www.charitywatch.org,** by the American Institute of Philanthropy, which provides grades on selected nonprofits based on their financial practices
- **www.charitynavigator.org,** which rates nonprofits on a four-star system based on their financial health, accountability, and transparency
- **www.give.org,** by the Better Business Bureau Wise Giving Alliance, which provides reports and information on nonprofits, reviews them against a list of 20 standards, and posts complaints about U.S. nonprofits, and
- **www.guidestar.org,** by Philanthropic Research, Inc., which gathers 990s and other information on virtually every nonprofit in the United States, creates reports, and allows nonprofits to register and post information about themselves.

I highly recommend that you have a look at these websites. Search for a few organizations that you know, and see how well—or poorly—they appear onscreen. Ask yourself whether you would continue to support an organization whose expenses appear disproportionately high. Also notice how half-hearted it looks when a nonprofit has an opportunity to register on a site (which usually involves merely filling in a few blanks) but doesn't—and vow never to make the same mistake.

Share Financial Information With Supporters

Your organization has to compile financial reports and statistics for funders and the government, and there's no reason not to make this information available to individual supporters. You'll enhance your credibility—and convey that your organization is committed to good planning, wise spending, and rigorous oversight practices—by presenting the information up front. (In many instances, this may require your fundraising staff to keep in regular contact with your accounting staff—always a good idea.)

There's no need to overwhelm your supporters with facts and figures. Instead, concentrate on clearly and concisely providing the key financial metrics that will allow them to judge whether you are meeting your goals in a cost-efficient way. The data they are most likely to want are the spending ratios described above, as well as your budgets for particular projects. It's also helpful to your donors—and very effective for fundraising—to break down expenses on a per-unit basis, such as "every $4 allows us to feed one hungry person for a day."

Your website is an excellent place to post this sort of information. Why stop at posting a PDF of your annual report? For an example, check out the website of the Global Fund for Women (at www.globalfundforwomen.org). In early 2013, if you went to the "Who We Are" tab and clicked "Financial Highlights," you would have found easy-to-read bullets and graphics concerning costs and revenues for their most recent fiscal year.

You should also include financial information in any newsletter you regularly send to supporters, perhaps in an article entitled "Where Your Money Goes" or "How Your Gifts Support Our Services." Important tidbits of financial information can also be incorporated into articles on other topics. For example, if you're discussing a particular program, you might discuss the challenges of raising funds when "bus rentals to transport the children cost $250 alone." Specific dollar figures catch people's eyes and make them better understand why you're tackling an ambitious financial goal.

If you don't have a newsletter or website (and many new or struggling organizations don't), consider preparing an annual statement of your finances. Send it along with a mailing, or simply make it available to interested supporters. You should also include financial and budgetary information in any written material you present in individual meetings with potential major supporters, as discussed in Chapter 6.

Be Professional in All Contacts With Supporters

Supporters will see every interaction with your organization as a reflection of how well you actually deliver services or fulfill your mission. A donor who gets a thank-you letter from your marine mammal protection organization three months after contributing probably won't think, "Oh, they must have been too busy saving the whales to get to my letter"; instead, he or she will probably wonder, "Hmm, if this place can't get its act together to answer one little letter, how are they going to save a whole whale?"

Of course, thanking supporters promptly is just one of the ways your organization can demonstrate its good management and interest in donors. Other ways include good writing and careful editing of letters, newsletters, and website content; returning phone calls courteously and promptly; handling supporters' checks and credit card pledges responsibly; and demonstrating an obvious desire to treat supporters as both friends and, at some level, customers.

Knowing that you're under this kind of scrutiny can raise your stress levels—but it can also give you a sense of purpose as you engage in the tedious tasks of printing out supporter acknowledgments, checking your supporter database for mistakes and duplications, entering new data quickly, and so on. Make sure your staff and volunteers understand the importance of such tasks—and be sure to thank them profusely when they do them well.

> **TIP**
>
> **Respond to donors' questions quickly.** When a donor or prospective donor asks anyone in your organization a question, whether in person or online, it's a golden opportunity to engage that person. Don't pass it up. Promptly pick up the phone, put fingers to keyboard, or even better, arrange to meet for coffee.

Focus on Your Successes

Focusing the public's perception on the great work that your organization is doing can defuse the concern over ratios. Who's going to quibble about how much you're spending on services if it's clear that you're getting a giant bang for your buck? To convey this enormously positive and effective message, fundraisers need to sit down with program staff and look hard at what you're really achieving. Try to break things down—look not only at your long-term goals, but at the step-by-step or indirect successes that you achieve along the way.

EXAMPLE: A youth project runs an after-school program that gives kids who might otherwise join gangs an opportunity to build friendships and leadership skills and to learn about their ethnic heritage. One of their funders has asked them to prove that they've measurably changed society and reduced teen violence. Because it's hard to prove this kind of major impact, the group is understandably nervous. However, when they sit down to consider successes they can share with the funder, they come up with the following:

- the number of students who voluntarily join their program each year
- the percentage of students who regularly attend the program
- the number of students who have voluntarily met with counselors on a long-term basis
- the improvement in their students' grades relative to the rest of the students in their school, and
- the community service projects that the students have successfully completed.

All of these are legitimate successes. If their program wasn't really providing a valuable service, the kids wouldn't be coming, improving their grades, and giving something back to their community.

Part of your job as a fundraiser is to identify these successes and communicate them effectively to your supporters and the public.

Understand What Motivates Your Supporters

The question of what motivates donors has been examined in excruciating detail, but at some level, this discipline will probably always be in its infancy. After all, understanding givers' motivations doesn't directly lead to knowledge of which fundraising techniques will tap into those motivations. Almost as soon as a particular technique achieves outsize returns, it becomes overused.

Still, it helps to have some understanding about what leads people to give, and especially to give to one type of cause over another. This section looks first at the more abstract, altruistic reasons for giving, then at the more tangible benefits you might offer donors in return for their support.

Why People Give

Evidence is mounting that humankind possesses a sense of altruism, and gives to charity accordingly. Some sociologists even claim that an instinct to help others is hardwired into the human race, as a way of ensuring group survival. The statistics certainly look good. Though the U.S. economy has its ups and downs, Americans tend to be generous in their giving: An average of 65% of households give some money to some causes. And total giving remained near record-high levels of nearly $298 billion in 2011.

With numbers like that, you may already be realizing that it's not just the rich who give—in fact, studies consistently find that the typical donor is middle or lower income. So you should feel comfortable approaching people with the sense that their hearts and minds may be generally open to giving. It's just a matter of finding the supporters who will give to your organization.

Why Altruistic People Choose One Cause Over Another

People's motivations for giving become clearer when you look at how they decide how much to give and how they choose between the various good causes seeking their support. People seem to give when they feel they will get something in return—in most cases, something that satisfies them at a deeply personal level. Although the giveaway baseball cap or coffee mug might tip the balance for a few, most are looking for something loftier, but no less tangible. These rewards might include, for example:

- feeling good about themselves
- returning a favor, if they or their family has been helped by a particular organization
- getting a tax deduction
- helping solve a social, environmental, political, or medical problem that they find personally important or that has affected their friends or family
- sending a message about their beliefs
- receiving quality information about a topic that interests them
- aligning themselves with friends, peers, or a community, or
- bringing about justice, or even vengeance, in an area where they or their loved ones have been hurt.

If the length of this list surprises you, remember that people are complex and often have more than one reason for giving. For example, you might give to your college alumni association because giving makes you feel good, because you get a tax deduction, because you feel that supporting quality education will help society, and on top of this because your alumni friends asked you to give! But, by the same token, if you get a letter from an organization within which you have no prior friends or contacts, which supports a cause that has never touched you or your family personally (say, the restoration of a landmark in a city you've never visited), about which you have no interest in reading a newsletter, and whose message you might agree with in the abstract but don't feel strongly about, you're unlikely to support it. (Simply feeling good and getting a tax deduction don't seem to be enough to persuade someone to give to an organization.)

TIP

Guess who's telling the men to give? A 2009 survey by the Fidelity Charitable Gift Fund found that over 90% of men cited their spouses as their primary influence in deciding which charities to support and how much to give. The women surveyed named a broader range of influences, including extended family, friends, and coworkers.

Understanding your supporters' motivations can help you devise ways to interact with them. You're looking for a way to hook into each supporter's personal interests—to make him or her realize that your organization has been competently and effectively working on issues close to his or her heart all this time and is a natural match for the person's support.

Of course, it's always a good idea to look first for readily identifiable people who are closely affected by the issue you are trying to address. For example, if you're working on a campaign to block the construction of a shopping mall, you could rush out and buy mailing lists of people who are against shopping malls in general, but a better bet is to start by simply contacting people who live in nearby neighborhoods.

Although some people's links to an organization will be obvious—for example, they are former patients of your clinic—others can only be accounted for by the vagaries of personal taste. Just as some people like chocolate ice cream better than vanilla, some people will be drawn toward environmental causes, not human rights issues. There's not much you can do to convert people on such fundamental matters (those who prefer chocolate can be pretty adamant about it). But you can learn more about the general characteristics of the type of supporter your own organization will attract.

> **TIP**
>
> **People may choose one group over another based on its marketing.** Particularly in major cities, you'll often find a number of groups addressing the same cause or issue. In such cases, people may choose the group with the best reputation, or the one in which they know people, or simply the one that got to them first. Virtually all of the advice in this book is intended to help you distinguish yourself from the competition.

Don't Expect Everyone to Give

You'll save yourself some grief by realizing that people whose interests don't line up with your organization's mission aren't going to donate, no matter how strong your message. Finding supporters isn't like winning an argument—you'll rarely convince someone to part with some cash against his or her early inclinations. The bottom line is that no one has an obligation to support you, no matter how great your work.

If you're nodding your head, or saying "I knew that already," reflect on how easy it is for an organization to give the wrong impression. You've probably seen newsletters whose stridency implied that everyone should support them now, or feel bad if they didn't. I've even heard nonprofit staff shrilly proclaim that all wealthy people should feel guilty about their relative comfort, and therefore give money to their causes. The unfortunate truth is that most affluent people either don't realize how good they've got it, aren't listening, or are already major nonprofit donors. In none of these instances will a guilt-based pitch help—and it might end up breeding resentment.

TIP

How much money in the bank does someone need to feel financially secure? A study by sociologist Paul Schervish asked this of people with a net worth of at least $25 million. The answer: $20 million! Good thing philanthropic giving appears not to be just something people do with their spare cash—"Gosh, I've got an extra million; wonder where I should put it?"—but is motivated by complex and deeper sentiments.

Find Out Why Your Supporters Give

Within the big picture of why people give in general, or give to particular causes, you'll want to focus on why people choose to give to your organization. Such exploration should lead to both useful information and surprises—all of which will help you predict where you might find additional supporters.

As an obvious example, your research might show that most of the people who support your battered women's shelter are women—no surprise there. But you might additionally find that a number of your supporters are the fathers of women who have been abused by their spouses or partners. Or, if your organization works on an age-related illness, such as Alzheimer's or macular degeneration, you might not be surprised to find that most of your supporters are in the over-55 age range—but your research might also unexpectedly reveal that a significant number of your supporters are in the medical profession.

Your first step in this exploration is to develop a "donor profile." This is much like the market research that any business does to learn how and where to sell its product. For example, you might gather the following information about your existing donors:

- household income
- educational level
- job or profession
- neighborhood of residence
- family status (for example, whether they have children or are caretakers for elderly parents)

- experience with social or medical issues that your organization addresses, and
- recreational activities and hobbies.

Once you decide what you want to know, there are a number of ways to gather the information. The simplest is to survey your existing donors. You can collect information from them along with their pledges of support; call them to say thanks after you receive a contribution and chat a bit about who they are and why they're interested; or email a request to take an online survey. Negative information can also be useful—you may occasionally wish to survey lapsed donors, asking for their honest input on how they felt about your organization's performance and why they elected to end their support.

At a more personal level, some organizations set up focus groups, in which a selected group of supporters gathers to talk for an hour or two about why they care enough about your organization to support it financially. This kind of research can serve a double purpose—not only does it help your efforts to fundraise from individuals, but the information you gather about community needs and concerns can help you update your mission, design your programs, and approach foundations and corporate funders for support (covered in Chapter 10). If you have a website with a tracking system, this, too, can provide useful information. You can follow which pages viewers visit the most and whether these viewers go on to become donors.

RESOURCE

Want more information on surveys? See Eric Leland's article, "A Few Good Online Survey Tools," at www.idealware.org.

If your organization can afford it, you can hire outside experts to do your donor profiling. Plenty of consultants will analyze organizations' existing donor pools, as well as their goals and subject areas, and match these with descriptions of potential new supporters. This matching will become particularly important if you embark on a program of finding donors through the mail, as discussed later in this chapter.

Once you develop a feel for why people give to your organization, it will help inform many aspects of your fundraising efforts, including your personal interactions with donors, the information you choose to convey via newsletters or written appeals, and the steps you take to more actively involve them in your work.

What Donors Gain: Tax Deductions and Gifts

Although receiving tax deductions and freebies aren't the main reasons that people give, they're on the list. This section will help you work these considerations into your fundraising strategies.

Tax Deductions

As a nonprofit corporation organized under Section 501(c)(3) of the Internal Revenue Code, you are eligible to offer tax deductions to those who give you cash or certain other gifts. Many nonprofits throw the word "tax deductible" around when asking for gifts, but not all of them have a clear idea of what this means for the supporter. And even those that do often speak in generalities instead of providing specific information. Here is some basic information that will help you make the issues clear to your donors.

Not every donor can make use of the tax deduction for charitable contributions—only those who itemize their deductions using Schedule A. This means that their itemized deductions must be higher than the standard deduction available to all taxpayers. This benefit isn't lost on potential donors, especially the affluent ones: Itemizing households tend to give more than nonitemizing households. However, because people who contribute to nonprofits aren't necessarily the wealthiest in our society, you cannot assume that all your supporters will itemize their deductions. Those who don't itemize have no use for a tax deduction and get no tax benefit from donating to your group.

For those who can use the tax deduction, however, the benefits can be substantial. Taxpayers are allowed to deduct the full amount of their charitable contributions, up to 50% of their adjusted gross income. This helps explain why charitable giving goes up so much in December. People realize that it's their last chance to top up their deductions for the year.

Exactly how much a particular donation will be worth in tax deductions depends first on what type of tax return the donor will file (single, married, and so on) and then on which tax bracket the donor falls into. (The tax bracket is the percentage of income a taxpayer must pay in tax; those who earn more fall into a higher bracket and, therefore, must pay a higher percentage of each dollar they earn in income tax.) For every dollar contributed to a charitable group, the donor will save what he or she would have had to pay in tax on that dollar—and because wealthier taxpayers pay more tax on the dollar, they also save more tax by taking tax deductions.

> **EXAMPLE:** Maria, a single woman, earns $29,000 a year in taxable income. That puts her into the 15% tax bracket (at 2012 tax rates). If Maria donates $100 to charity, she will actually be out only 85 cents for every dollar, (one dollar minus 15 cents), because she'll pay less at tax time. Her total expenditure will come out to $85. In other words, she'll be able to reduce her taxes by 15% of the $100, or $15.
>
> If Maria's taxable income were to rise to $36,000, she'd be in the 25% tax bracket. Now, every dollar she donates would cost her only 75 cents (one dollar minus 25 cents). That means her out-of-pocket costs are only $75 for a $100 contribution.
>
> Should Maria's fortunes improve even more in the next few years, and her taxable income rise to $86,000, she'd be in the 28% tax bracket. Every dollar she contributes will cost her only 72 cents, and her $100 contribution will cost her only $72.

Donors in even higher tax brackets than used in the example above benefit as well, but the calculations become more complex, and are beyond the scope of this book.

Donations of property. Donors may deduct gifts of both cash and property (land or personal property). However, special rules apply to setting a value on property, as described in IRS Publication 561, *Determining the Value of Donated Property* (which explains how to value anything from used clothing to Old Master paintings). If you're planning a vehicle donation program, be sure to see Publication 4302, *A Charity's Guide to Vehicle Donations*; you'll need to tell the donor the eventual sales price for tax purposes.

Supporters have a particular incentive to donate property that has gone up in value since they bought it, such as stock. If they sold the property for cash, they might have to pay capital gains tax, thereby reducing the amount of cash they had available to give to charity. By donating the property directly to charity, however, they can deduct the full, current fair market value of the donated item, without worrying about the capital gains tax.

EXAMPLE: Arif bought stock 12 years ago for $100. The stock is now worth $2,000. By donating the stock directly to the charity of his choice, Arif can take a $2,000 tax deduction. If he sold it instead, he would owe tax on his $1,900 profit.

Quid pro quo contributions. The value of a donation of cash or property must be reduced, for tax purposes, by the market value of anything substantial the donor receives in return. And, if the gift was worth $75 or more, you must send the donor a written statement with your good-faith estimate of how much he or she can deduct, after subtracting the fair market value of the item. For example, if a supporter sends you an $80 check that entitles her to a calendar with a fair market value (the amount it normally sells for) of $15, her contribution is valued at $65. It doesn't matter whether your organization paid anything at all for the item—the donor must subtract the value of what he or she receives.

EXAMPLE: A soup kitchen holds a silent auction to raise money. One of its board members donates a weekend at her cabin. Roger and Allison put in the winning bid, at $60. They're excited, because this is a bargain—weekends at cabins in this area usually go for at least $150. However, if they were also hoping for a tax deduction, they're going to be disappointed. Because they didn't pay anything over and above the fair market value of what they received in return, they cannot claim a charitable donation.

Token or low-cost items, like stickers or bookmarks, need not be subtracted from the donation. (For 2013, a "token" item's cost to your organization could be no more than $10.20 and the contribution received must have been at least $51. Token items must also bear your organization's name or logo. To qualify as "low-cost," the items must either have a fair market value of $102 or less, or be worth 2% or less of the donor's payment, whichever is lower. But the cost of raffle, bingo, or lottery tickets is never tax deductible (perhaps because every buyer is hoping for the grand prize). For more information, see IRS Publication 557, *Tax-Exempt Status for Your Organization,* and IRS Publication 1771, *Charitable Contributions: Substantiation and Disclosure Requirements.*

> RESOURCE
>
> **Need more information on tax rules?** IRS publications are available at any local IRS office, or can be easily downloaded at www.irs.gov. If you have further questions, the IRS provides an information line for tax-exempt organizations, at 877-829-5500. Also see *Every Nonprofit's Tax Guide*, by Stephen Fishman (Nolo).

Volunteer work. Separate tax rules apply to people who volunteer their services. The market value of the services themselves is not tax deductible. So, for example, if a licensed massage therapist donates services at your health clinic, or a lawyer gives your organization a free consultation, neither can claim a tax deduction. They can, however, deduct the costs of their unreimbursed expenses, including the use of their cars on behalf of your organization (gas, oil, parking, and tolls), incidentals (such as treats with which to help train a shelter animal or art supplies brought to teach a Sunday school class), and travel expenses if they're away from home (transportation, meals, and lodging).

When receipts are required. You're required to send donors a receipt for any gift valued at $250 or more, for them to keep in their tax files in case they're audited. But as a matter of good donor stewardship, you should send thank-you letters that also serve as receipts for all gifts. The receipt can simply be a letter, or even an email, but should always specify the value of the gift. (See Chapter 5 for more about thanking and providing receipts to donors.) For more information, see IRS Publication 526, *Charitable Contributions*.

Freebies

People don't give to good causes solely because of the promotional items they commonly get in return—but they might act faster or more decisively because of them. For example, if you were planning to give to your favorite public radio station anyway, but by pledging within the next hour you'll get a Bulgarian music CD that you can't get anywhere else, you might just get out of your chair and pick up the phone. And, because so many of us procrastinate, this might make the difference between the station's receiving your gift right now—or never.

Many organizations offer promotional items in return for donations, particularly when they're asking for an annual renewal of support. The lowest level of donation usually receives a token item (such as a poster) or nothing at all, but each higher level of donation comes with a gift of higher value. It's customary to list the gift premiums on the reply card right next to the suggested dollar amounts. Make sure to include a box to check if the person doesn't want the gift (perhaps because they want to maximize the amount of their donation going toward services or they want the full tax deduction).

From your standpoint, the best promotions are the ones that don't cost anything to produce. For example, those radio station gifts are usually solicited in advance from publishers, stores, and restaurants, which realize that they'll get free advertising in return for giving the station some free or reduced-price products. Some organizations create their own low-cost gifts—for example, artworks or greeting cards with images drawn or photographed by their clients.

> ! CAUTION
>
> **Be prepared to market any homegrown items separately.** The costs of producing items like bumper stickers, mugs, or T-shirts usually mean that you're best off creating a large number at once. However, these could end up in a stack on your floor if not enough supporters respond to your appeal. See Chapter 9 for more on marketing and selling goods for your organization.

Bring in New Supporters

In the early days of your organization's life, finding supporters will usually be a grassroots effort—friends, fellow activists, fellow community members outraged by the prospect of a new, local supermall or the like, relatives, and people you meet on the street while getting petition signatures are among those who might be inspired to help. These early supporters might, in fact, be some of your most loyal ones, because they will feel a stake in an organization they helped found and a deep personal connection to your issue or cause.

As your organization grows, however, donations from the cookie jars of your founders' mothers and neighbors won't be enough to pay the rent. You'll need to look toward building a broader base of support, among people with whom much of your communication may be by mail. And you'll need to realize that this is an ongoing task—there will never come a day when you can safely say, "That's enough, we have all the supporters we need to keep us going."

The sad truth of the matter is that most of your rank and file supporters probably won't stick around for more than two to three years. That may have nothing to do with the quality of your nonprofit; it's just an average based on other nonprofits' experience of people's giving patterns. In part, it's because many people who give to charity actually prefer to spread their giving around and will deliberately withdraw their support when they think it's someone else's turn. It's also partly because many nonprofits do a mediocre job at donor retention!

Your goal should always be to turn every casual supporter into someone who will stick with you over the long haul (see Chapters 5 and 6 for more on them). Treat every supporter as a potential major donor in the making.

But it's also important to be realistic. As your organization grows and your relationship with supporters becomes more distant, so does their level of loyalty. Even in a healthy organization, the majority of your supporters will be of the "here today, gone tomorrow" variety. Yet their existence remains critical to your organization just the same.

Where do you find the new supporters who will replace those who move, die, or just have a short attention span? Here are some possibilities:

- individuals contacted personally by your board members, volunteers, and staff
- overlooked ethnic, racial, and other diverse communities
- the people your organization serves, their caregivers, or others in close contact with them
- people you meet in face-to-face solicitations
- people who hear about your organization through the media
- people you bring in through special events, and
- people you locate through direct mail solicitations.

TIP

Don't limit yourself to these techniques. Converting new donors to your cause is an area where tapping your own creativity is key. And your entire staff, not only your fundraisers, should be encouraged to speak out positively about the work of your organization (including in their online social networks) and to collect the names, addresses, and other contact information of people who might want to help.

Your Circle of Friends

The most likely people to take an interest in your organization are those you already know, who may be living in the same community, dealing with or personally interested in the same social, political, health, environmental, or other concerns, or perhaps just moved by hearing you talk about your cause. And don't forget people who were once part of your community, but have moved on. Alumni of a school, class, or performance arts group are the most obvious example. Less obvious examples are people who have moved away in search of better opportunities, perhaps from a low-income or rural community. Such people may still feel the tug of their roots, and be willing to help—and their local friends and family are the ones likely to know how to reach them. Even if the leaders of your organization tapped into their own friends early on, remember that as your nonprofit continues and grows, there will be additions and rotations among staff and board members.

It should be a regular policy of your office to ask for names and contact information of potential prospects. If this sounds like a lot of work for a few names, remember that the most effective way to raise money is through personal contacts. For an example of how one organization put this theory into practice, see "Zen Hospice Project Mobilizes Volunteers," below.

The name givers shouldn't have to worry that you'll hassle their buddies. You can approach potential new prospects with anything from a simple letter to an in-person meeting, depending on what seems appropriate. For further information on personal meetings with potential major donors, see Chapter 6.

Your circle of contacts also includes anyone who volunteers for your organization—even if it's just a one-shot deal. If, for example, a local company sends a crew of its employees to paint your building, staff a telethon, or provide other services, don't just say "thanks" and "goodbye"— get names and contact information from each and every person who arrives, then put them on your mailing list. (Studies show that people who spend time volunteering are almost 40% more likely to donate to a cause than those who don't.) Your first mailing should start with individual thank-you letters, then add brochures and other information on how they can become further involved.

Zen Hospice Project Mobilizes Volunteers

The Zen Hospice Project, a San Francisco organization whose collaborative services include residential hospice care, volunteer programs, and educational efforts to foster wisdom and compassion in service, was facing a common challenge: The economy was down, individual donors were feeling exhausted by desperate appeals, and every nonprofit in town was trying to drum up new support. Lisa Ruth Elliott, then–development manager, described how Zen Hospice conducted one of its most successful campaigns ever:

"Mailing is generally a good strategy for us, since our organization touches people in a very personal way. However, we decided to take this approach one step further. We really engaged our volunteer caregiver corps—about 150 of them. These are people who ordinarily spend their time in the residential care part of our hospice, interacting on a weekly basis with terminally ill patients. Now, we asked them for their help in taking their stories to their communities, meditation groups, families, and friends and obtain their support. We put together fundraising packets for them that included talking points, newsletters, brochures, a sample fundraising letter, and a reply envelope. Some of the volunteer caregivers crafted letters based on their own experience— these were particularly effective.

"There was a bit of resistance at first. Some volunteer caregivers said things like, 'This is not something we should have to do,' or 'I'm scared; I can't fundraise.' However, we gave them a lot of support and the opportunity to ask questions as the campaign went along. Once they started to see the generosity of their communities, they got excited about the process. The results were impressive—the volunteer caregivers raised over $35,000 and contributed about $18,000 among themselves."

New Friends in Diverse Communities

Some people think that you can raise substantial amounts of money only from society's traditional string-of-pearls elites. It isn't necessarily so: Diversifying one's donor base makes ample sense in a country where minorities are soon to be the majority (and an increasingly affluent majority, to boot). Today, achieving real representative community involvement means we can't all go chasing after the same old donor groups until final bequest do us part.

There's been much study lately on how to increase donor diversity—not only ethnic and racial diversity, but also diversity of lifestyle, age, gender, and physical ability. What the emerging findings show is that you may have to throw some of your old fundraising practices out the window in order to succeed with diverse donor groups.

When it comes to certain ethnic minorities, for example, research shows that their altruism is traditionally directed at groups other than mainstream nonprofits, often staying closer to home with family, church, and community groups. And contributions are often made in forms that fly under the traditional fundraising radar, such as collecting clothing or food for distribution to recent immigrants, or making small cash contributions directly to friends or community groups. Some of the supposedly tried-and-true methods of attracting new members, such as the direct mail approach we'll describe below, may seem distant and cold—and, therefore, may not be effective.

Where and how you focus your diversification efforts obviously depends on the community in which you're located as well as the clients or constituencies you're serving. If this is a new outreach effort for your organization, you have a lot of learning to do and shouldn't expect overnight success. You'll need to think carefully about who your most likely allies are and incorporate a long-term strategy to attract them into your fundraising plan. As part of this effort, you'll need to identify ways to increase the relevant community's trust in your organization, such as visibly participating in ethnic and community festivals and celebrations, advertising your job openings or special events in ethnic or group-based media, and recruiting diverse staff and board members. In other words, you need to get out and make friends before you can start turning people into donors.

A nonprofit whose own staff and board aren't representative of those from whom they seek support may have a tough time establishing credibility within a new group. Without a history of working together, you may encounter understandable suspicion that you're not "one of them" and are hoping only for a quick new cash source. The most natural way to break through this perception is by strengthening preexisting, natural relationships among your staff, board, and community members. This, too, will have to involve long-term planning—you can't just fire and replace your trusted staff and board members.

RESOURCE

Need information on donor diversity? See The Association of Fundraising Professionals' "Diversity Essays," found via the Resource Center links at www.afpnet.org.

People Your Organization Serves

You may already be overlooking some of your most obvious supporters.

> **EXAMPLE:** An agency that helps immigrants and refugees opens its phone lines once a week for questions from the public. A woman calls, identifies herself as Kathy, and expresses concern that her children's nanny, who is from El Salvador, has been waiting years to hear whether she'll be granted political asylum. The nanny has a work permit, but nothing more. The staff lawyer explains that this is a normal delay and describes how to send the immigration authorities an inquiry just in case. Kathy is relieved, says, "Thank you, I couldn't seem to find this information anywhere else," and they politely end the call.

You can probably guess what went wrong in this example. The lawyer completely missed an opportunity to make Kathy, an already concerned citizen, an active supporter of the organization. It's an understandable mistake—the lawyer is focused on providing direct services to the public, the next caller is already waiting, and the lawyer probably thinks fundraising is "not her department." But it would have been quite simple for the lawyer to get Kathy's full name and address, explain that thousands of people are in her nanny's position, and ask whether she could send Kathy some more information about the organization. That's one more name on the database and at least one more potential check in the mail.

Look at your own organization's procedures and contacts with the public—are there people with whom you're missing a chance to connect? Not just your own clients, but people who call or visit your organization for information, buy a craft article at a fair, or even bring their kids trick-or-treating at your front office can all be given information and an opportunity to become supporters. Also, think broadly about your beneficiaries—for example, if you provide child care training services, the parents who hire your graduates are also benefiting from your organization, and should be given an opportunity to support your work. You're not twisting their arms; they can always say no.

What if your organization provides direct services to low-income clients who you believe can't possibly support you now, either by paying fees or making donations? Don't underestimate their value as supporters. For example, if you provide great services for homeless people, who knows better than they the value of your organization? They may even enjoy seeing the endeavor as a team effort in which they have a role to play. In fact, some organizations have found that, until they got better at telling their clients about their fundraising needs, the clients just assumed the money flowed from the government or other source on high—and may have wondered why their service providers often seem frazzled and overbooked.

Even if they are truly penniless, your existing clients may provide help as volunteers, particularly on one-time projects, such as painting your facilities or participating in a special event. Longer term, it's possible that their economic and life circumstances may improve. (That may well be part of your goal in helping them.) Though keeping in touch after the immediate crisis is over can be difficult, try your best.

There's no need to send current clients every fundraising solicitation, but an occasional newsletter may increase their sense of pride in the work that you did together—and result in real contributions down the road. In an immigrants' services organization with which I worked, one of the staunchest supporters was a man from the Sudan whom the organization had helped gain political asylum. He happened to be a highly educated professional; once he got on his feet, he become a board member and tireless advocate.

What if your organization doesn't provide direct services at all and, so, doesn't have a client base to mobilize? There may still be ways in which you benefit a sector of the public that doesn't even realize it. Your job is to find those people while they're getting the benefit at issue. An organization in Utah, for example, was working to save an unprotected canyonland from mining and other development. While it relied on some of the traditional techniques for garnering interest and members—such as publicity and mailings—it realized that loads of potential supporters would probably never hear about its existence. To help reach them, the organization took the simple but brilliant step of posting volunteers outside the entrance to one of the area's existing parks. The volunteers briefly explained to people coming to enjoy the park what the future might hold and asked for financial and other support. In this way, they reached visitors from far and wide who might never have seen or responded to their local efforts—but who were concerned enough to support the cause.

Looking Beyond Your Client Base

Fundraising guru Tony Poderis tells the following story, which aptly illustrates how a little creative thinking can turn up potential supporters based on their existing links to your organization. (Check out his website at www.raise-funds.com.)

"One of the first organizations I ever worked with was Big Brothers of Greater Cleveland. At the time, it served more than 500 boys who did not have fathers at home. The boys' mothers weren't able to give much, but we did a little research and discovered that more than 10% of the women were employees of a local utility. Our funding request to the utility pointed this out and came complete with endorsements from many of those employees. The gift we got was far larger than the utility's usual contribution."

Grassroots Methods of Reaching Out to Supporters

The value of person-to-person contact is being hailed anew—and rightfully so, especially as potential donors become tired of the barrage of indistinguishable emails, direct mail letters, and intrusions by professional telemarketers. In this climate, meeting an enthusiastic volunteer outside a grocery store or coffee shop can seem like a breath of fresh air. (But if the person is pushy or not well-trained, it can seem like an annoyance.)

Another grassroots technique that shouldn't be forgotten is leafleting. A simple one-page explanation of the issue at hand, what your organization is doing about it, and how people can get involved may be all you need — particularly for urgent or local issues, such as a pending development, a movement to restore a local landmark, or a need to support a local team or school. Don't forget to distribute your leaflets to local business owners, particularly if it's an issue in which they have a vested interest, such as neighborhood aesthetics.

If sending volunteers to wander outdoors seems a bit random, try more targeted presentations. Ask your board and staff whether their church, service organization, or other club would be open to a presentation from your organization. Make your presentation colorful and fun, then tell people how they can join in your exciting efforts through volunteering or donating. People's workplaces are also potential venues for such presentations, particularly if there's a thematic tie-in. For example, I was first introduced to immigration law while sitting around a conference table in a corporate law firm, listening to how nonprofit lawyers whose time was spent helping people who'd fled persecution presented their political asylum cases to judges. Like many corporate law firms, mine then allowed me to spend numerous hours helping these clients for no fee.

Supporters From Traditional and Social Media Outreach

Getting your name into the public's eye can have both direct and indirect fundraising benefits. Hopefully, at least a few of the people who watch an online video or read a news story about your work will be moved to contact you afterwards and offer financial support or volunteer help.

Young people in particular are most likely to first connect with your organization via social media— and to throw the snail mail letter described later in this chapter into the trash.

At an indirect level, the more exposure people have to your organization's good name, the more credibility they'll attach to it if and when you solicit them individually.

Because social media and other outreach are such important tools for reaching many types of funding sources (not just individual supporters), it's addressed separately, in Chapter 13.

Crowdfunding Campaigns

Tell people you're trying to raise money for your nonprofit, and they're likely to ask, "Have you tried Kickstarter?" (Or Fundraise.com, CauseVox, Fundly, Razoo, indiegogo, or some other crowdfunding site.) Such sites are getting lots of buzz—and they've raised plenty of money for the nonprofits (as well as artists, filmmakers, and businesses) that know how to use them. But they're tools, not magic wands.

For one thing, crowdfunding is not meant for ongoing fundraising. The usual idea is that after you've paid some combination of fees for setup, monthly use, and transaction processing, you get to post a page on one of these websites saying, in essence, "Hey, we're trying to raise $X by X date to do X-and-such, can you all pitch in? Also *according to the rules of some sites*, you'll get X as a thank-you gift or "perk," and if we don't raise the needed amount, you'll get your money back!"

Users donate online, and if all goes well, the site transfers the proceeds to you at the end of this minicampaign.

Don't be intimidated by the tradition of giving perks to people who donate. The "Let's Build a Goddamn Tesla Museum" indiegogo campaign of 2012, for example, gave out glossy photos of Nikola Tesla in return for donations of $25; and to donors of between $3 and $25, it said, "If [Tesla] were alive today he'd totally high-five you and compliment your haircut and/or mustache." (Did I mention that humor helps in the crowdfunding world?) The goal was $850,000, but with an average of $145,000 coming in per day from people in over 100 countries, the organizers surpassed that number easily, reaching a whopping $1,370,461.

As for giving money back if you don't reach your goal, that's so far the norm only on Kickstarter; and you need only *offer* the money back. (Many people would probably allow you to keep it.) On indiegogo, you choose in advance whether or not to keep all the proceeds; though if you choose that arrangement, you'll have to pay a higher commission to the site.

A bigger issue is that, unless your campaign is hugely lucky and instantly goes viral, you've largely got to find your own "crowd." Depending on which site you use, you may not only be competing with other nonprofits, but with savvy artists and entrepreneurs, all trying to attract the same bunch of people. It's not easy to make your voice heard or to come up with an idea that will take off. Unless your nonprofit already has significant online contacts through your email list, website, and social media, and a good sense of how to create compelling online content, it may not be ready for crowdfunding.

With that reality check in mind, there are situations where a crowdfunding effort might work, namely where your nonprofit:

- has a particular, tangible goal in mind—such as a new piece of equipment, a trip to a project site, medical care for one individual, or production of a film; or a time-delimited concept around which to fundraise, such as a matching grant or the birthday of a celebrity supporter who makes a personal request for donations

- can confidently predict that the goal is sufficiently exciting, moving, or fun that your existing supporters and social media contacts will tell their friends about it and they, despite knowing little to nothing about your organization, will be moved to pitch in

- has the skills to present the idea in an attractive way, preferably complete with photos, graphics, and video, and

- has loyal supporters who will create tangential pages connected to your nonprofit's master page (as is allowed on some sites), on which they ask friends and connections to give.

By the way, it doesn't necessarily have to be your nonprofit that sets up an original crowdfunding page. Any of your supporters may do so, if they are motivated and have a wide personal network to tap into. Of course, you'll do best to provide advice and support for such efforts.

To learn more about and choose from among the various crowdfunding sites, visit them yourself. Pretend you're a potential donor, and have a look at the various projects and campaigns vying for funding. The "most popular" projects will give you a sense of whether yours might measure up. Look at the less popular ones, too. You'll probably notice things to avoid, such as the tendency of nonprofits to simply say, "Please support our work; our mission is this." Such messages lack any sense of urgency, and appear dull by comparison to the others.

Also take a careful look at each crowdfunding site's features, fees, ease of use, terms, and level of success being achieved by other nonprofits.

Supporters Through Special Events

Any event that you hold or participate in—whether it be an arts or entertainment event, lecture, crafts fair, walkathon, petition drive, or annual dinner—is an opportunity for you to inspire and bring in new donors. Because special events are an important fundraising tool of their own, and not merely useful for bringing in new supporters, they're covered in detail in Chapter 8. But now is a good time to remind yourself that every special event provides a great opportunity to collect the names and contact information of potential new supporters.

There are various ways to collect this information without seeming intrusive. For example, I once attended a concert given by a nonprofit musical society, at which attendees were invited to enter their names and addresses into a raffle for free tickets to a future concert. Not too surprisingly, I've been receiving newsletters and fundraising appeals from them ever since. (An alternative raffle prize might be items donated by local businesses.) I fell for a similar technique at a theater event recently, in which audience members were invited to "vote" on the outcome of the plot. The ballots asked for our name and address and also offered a raffle prize. And yes, I'm on yet another mailing list.

Also remember that personal checks you receive from ticket buyers and others usually have addresses on them. Don't cash them without first making a photocopy, so that you can enter the information into your database. (But keep such copies in a secured file.)

Be sure to make people aware of your organization's name at any event. I've attended a number of benefit concerts where the charitable organizations never made it clear who they were and what they planned to do with the money raised. Perhaps they just weren't very efficient, they assumed that most attendees were long-time supporters, or they were shy about intruding on people's "pure" enjoyment of the event. But, in fact, many audience members' enjoyment is enhanced by hearing that they are helping a good cause.

If there's an intermission, the opening of the second half is a good time to have a representative of your organization speak briefly but directly about its work and how donations help. Also make clear where people can pick up brochures or learn more, and put out a clipboard so people can, if they so desire, sign up to be on your mailing list. A collection basket by the ticket desk doesn't hurt, either. And, of course, the event program should mention your organization's name, website, and other contact information and give a brief blurb on the activities the benefit is helping fund. Many people bring these programs home!

Donors Through Direct Mail

Even if you, your staff, and your board members have used all the techniques described in the earlier sections to attract supporters—personal contacts, media publicity, and special events—you still may not have the numbers of supporters you need or want. And because your budget probably doesn't allow you to buy commercial air time during the Super Bowl, you may consider a direct mail campaign.

Soliciting new supporters by mail is a small subset of all the types of mail your organization will send out, which include brochures, newsletters, or appeal letters you send your existing supporters. A direct mail, new supporter solicitation is one in which you beg, borrow, trade, or buy a mailing list that comes from another organization or a marketing specialist. You then send letters to all the names on the list—or to a test sample (usually 1,000 to 10,000 names) from that list—explaining the work of your organization and asking for support.

In theory, you could do the same thing via email, rather than U.S. mail—and of course, do it much cheaper. However, because of the backlash against spam and everything that could be interpreted as spam, I neither recommend nor cover email solicitation of new donors. Unless your nonprofit has a highly reputable name that everyone will recognize on the sender line, it will likely be impossible for recipients to separate your message from the hundreds that offer cures for baldness and bad debts.

Because Internet rules and courtesies are ever developing, however, keep your eyes on the nonprofit journals, and keep talking to your colleagues— eventually a way may be found to use email for new donor solicitation. Also remember that this chapter addresses only finding new donors. When it comes to communicating with your existing supporters, email can be a fantastic and timesaving resource, as discussed in Chapter 5. And, as explained in that chapter, you can use your emails to existing supporters to encourage them to get their friends involved in your cause—by forwarding your email to others who might be interested.

! CAUTION
Don't misuse membership rosters. Many professional, social, and alumni groups publish lists of their members, with contact information—and it can be awfully tempting to borrow one. However, read the fine print: Many such rosters specifically warn the members that letting the list be used without permission will be frowned upon, or worse. And even if they don't, you are implicitly invading people's privacy—something that is sooner or later (probably sooner) going to anger key supporters.

Most everyone has mixed feelings about direct mail fundraising. We all receive too much of it, and we're increasingly hip to all the tricks—the "urgent" stamps on the outside, the seemingly handwritten envelopes, the promises of free gifts inside, the little see-through windows trying to fool us into thinking it's a check. It's all starting to look like it was produced by the same band of consultants.

Even if the letters your organization sends out are understated and honest, the majority will be thrown in the trash. You'll be lucky to break even on your first mailing, and you'll probably have to invest a few years in trying out various lists and refining your methods before you see a return in immediate and long-term support.

Despite all this, however, direct mail can still be a cost-effective way to reach donors who might not hear of your organization by any other means. If you've designed your letters well and sent them to the appropriate recipients, a certain percentage of them will be opened and read. One percent is considered a respectable number, and 0.8% is more normal. While these immediate returns may seem negligible, look at the longer term. Small-time supporters whom you initially find via direct mail may turn into your long-time contributors and major donors—and all for the initial cost of some staff time, some paper, and a stamp.

CAUTION

Don't start a direct mail campaign until you're ready for major donors. This discussion assumes that you're in a position to handle donor steward-ship and major donor solicitation. If you're not, be wary about investing heavily in direct mail now. If you back out halfway, those initial letter and stamp costs will have been wasted—and they add up fast.

Direct mail solicitation involves much more than simply sending out a bunch of letters. You'll have to choose the right mailing lists, design and write an attractive appeal—or two, if you want to test out different approaches—have them printed and packaged, and deal with arcane postal regulations if you send the letters bulk mail. Then comes opening the return letters, cashing the checks or running the credit card donations, entering the results into a database, sending out thank-you letters—and just when you think you're ready for a rest, starting all over with another list.

RESOURCE

Want more information on direct mail? This section covers the basics, but you might want to consult some additional resources, like these:

- **The website and products of consultant Mal Warwick** (the self-created guru of direct mail fundraising), at www. malwarwick.com, and
- *Fundraising for Social Change,* by Kim Klein (Chardon Press Series/Jossey-Bass). Kim Klein's entire book is a must read, being eminently practical.

Create or Choose a Mailing List

One of your first steps is to find a mailing list and decide how many people to solicit. In some situations, you can create your own list. For example, if you've just held a special event and you have the names of the ticket buyers, they should go on your list. Similarly, names collected from board members and other volunteers can be added to a mailing list. You can also cull your organization's old records for the names of donors who haven't given for a few years and have thus been dropped from recent mailings.

Your next best bet is to trade lists with another nonprofit organization. Though that may sound entirely counterintuitive—like everyone trying to take bites out of the same cookie—studies have shown that many supporters give to more than one organization anyway. There's usually no direct harm in revealing the names of your supporters to others, or vice versa. That said, you may sensibly conclude that you want to avoid direct competition with a very similar group. Your best bet is to look for an organization whose work is complementary to yours in a way that reflects underlying affinities to your donors. For example, an ethnic arts organization and an immigrants' rights organization might be logical trades, or a women's musical group and a women's political group.

After a little testing, you can expand your list trading to groups whose members have less obvious affinities to your members. The concept of affinity is both psychologically simple and ultimately unpredictable. Your goal is no more and no less than to locate lists of people who are most like your typical donors—whose hearts are not only in the right place (because they give to charity) but are in similar places when it comes to choosing a charity. With enough testing, you're likely to find affinities you wouldn't have expected. For example, Project Open Hand, a Bay Area organization that provides home-delivered, hot, nutritious meals to homebound people with critical illnesses, has found that donor lists from arts and environmental organizations yield particularly good results for them.

> **CAUTION**
>
> **Watch out for duplicate names.** If you're combining lists to get to the number you want, some names may appear more than once. You may want to run what's called a merge/purge to identify and delete the duplicates.

If you've already run through these options, your primary remaining avenue is to rent a mailing list. Sometimes this is loosely referred to as "buying" a mailing list. However, mailing lists are valuable property— you probably couldn't afford to buy the whole thing for keeps. But many are made available for a one-time rental, from sources including other nonprofits, magazines, businesses, museums, schools, and many more. Again, you should be looking for lists of people with likely affinities to your group, but who are preferably not already donors of organizations nearly identical to yours.

Mailing lists vary widely in price, because they vary in quality. The closer the list is to what you need, the more you're likely to pay for it! Before agreeing to rent any list, ask questions to assure yourself of its quality, such as when it was last updated, and whether qualified professionals do the data entry.

To prevent you from copying the list, you will probably never actually get your hands on it—the list will be handled by a go-between. Even if you are given direct access to it, however, most organizations plant a couple of "seed" names into their lists, addressed to their own staff or board members, so that they catch anyone who tries to use their entire lists a second time. When your organization gets around to trading or renting your list, you should implement the same security measures.

CAUTION

Your own list is a commodity, too. As your own list of supporters develops, you'll naturally feel very protective of it. You should be—never just give your list away for free. But also consider this: You've got a commodity that can bring in rental fees, and such a source of revenue shouldn't be ignored. You definitely don't want to rent the list out too frequently—both because you'll anger your supporters, and because a less-frequently rented list has a higher value. But with some careful thought, and screening of the list renters to ensure that they are appropriate and not too competitive with your own organization, industry expert Mike Maxwell explains, "You should feel comfortable doing list exchanges—it's how the fundraising business is done." For the sake of your supporters, be sure to honor any of their requests that you not include their names on any shared mailing lists.

The result of the one-time use practice is that you've got only one chance to turn the names on any one list into supporters. But once a mail recipient responds to your mailing, you're free to continue the relationship. You can see why direct mail solicitation is an ongoing process: You'll need to keep trying out various lists, homing in on the categories of recipients that seem to produce good results, and so on.

Working With a List Broker

In the typical scenario, you never meet the actual list owner—your broker acts as the intermediary from start to finish. It's best to start by providing the broker with some written materials, including a sample of the mailing you intend to send (it can be a mock-up or an idea, not the completed version) and a summary of what you're hoping for. This summary should include your:

- **Target audience.** This can be as broad as "people who like animals" or as narrow as "biology teachers at private schools along the Eastern seaboard."
- **Rental budget.** Consult with the broker before putting down a figure. There's certainly no upper limit on what you can spend—prices vary depending on who's selling the list and how narrowly you've defined your target audience.
- **Timing.** Explain how soon you need a list and how soon you expect to send out your mailing.
- **Desired results.** State how many names you're hoping to rent.

The broker will then shop around and get you some list options, telling you each list's rental fee, the date the list was last updated, the spending power of the list members as a whole, and your selection options within that list. Some lists will be too expensive—remember that you're competing with big for-profit businesses who are willing to spend more than you are. You'll pick any that look like good prospects. If none seem right, you can reformulate your proposal, perhaps broadening or narrowing the target audience. After a bit of back and forth, you and the broker will arrive at your final choice or choices.

But the broker's role isn't over yet. Once you've arranged the list rental, the broker also helps you access the list—without ever actually letting you lay hands on it. If, for example, you use a printer or a mail house to send out the final piece, the broker would send the mail house the list—and the mail house or printer would be duty bound to destroy the information or send the list back to the broker when you're done with it.

Finding a mailing list to rent is a less mysterious process than you might think (although, because of the costs and level of effort, it's probably not appropriate for newer, low-budget organizations). In fact, a whole profession has grown up around matching nonprofits and other businesses with mailing lists, known as "list brokers." Ask your colleagues at other nonprofits for recommendations of good brokers who specialize in working with nonprofits, or look for ads in the *Nonprofit Times* and *Chronicle of Philanthropy*. The great thing is, you not only save time and gain the list broker's expertise about what works, but you don't usually pay the broker directly for his or her services (though you'll pay for the rental of the lists themselves). The broker is ordinarily paid by arrangement with the organization that rents you the list. For more details on this process (when you're ready for it), see "Working With a List Broker," above.

How large a list should you start out with? That depends mostly on the size of your organization and how much you're willing to invest in initial test mailings. However, the prevailing wisdom is that an initial mailing should include no fewer than 2,000 names and as many as 500,000.

Prepare the Letter and Remainder of the Mailing

Now you have to come up with something to send to this select group. The standard direct mail package comprises four or possibly five parts, including:

- outer envelope
- letter
- reply device
- envelope in which to send the reply back, and
- insert (optional).

TIP

There's no magic formula—testing is the key. Below, you'll find various suggestions for how to draft and design compelling parts of a direct mail package. But, particularly because every added element can also add expense, you've got to set aside any assumptions and test to see what works on your own donors. As your direct mail program develops, this will literally mean dividing every mailing list in two and sending your basic, tried-and-true "control" package to half the list, and a "test" package containing anything new to the other half. Or, divide your list into thirds if you're mailing one control and two test packages. As an example, says Mike Maxwell, "I've seen compelling teasers and photos on outer envelopes work extremely well, but I've also seen instances where they depressed the response rate. Test to see which works best—you may be surprised by the results."

The outer envelope. Most people—and some say *all* young people— will take one look at your mail package, decide, "Oh, it's just a request for money," and toss it into the trash unopened. So consider how your outer envelope can induce recipients to actually open it. Printing a photo or a few words about your cause may be helpful. But keep it simple—splashing too much text and imagery across the envelope reminds people of cheap commercial marketing.

The letter. The central item should be a letter, on your organization's stationery, between one and four pages long. Exactly how long is best continues to be debated by fundraisers. Some say one-pagers are better for today's attention-deficient readers (particularly the young ones), while others say that only the heft of a four-page letter conveys authority and substance. If you're going to go for a four-pager, however, it had better be a real page turner (or start out so strong that only a few people will feel the need to keep reading before donating). Mike Maxwell, drawing on his 20-plus years of direct mail experience, reiterates: "I've seen donor solicitation packages get simpler and shorter. Years ago, you could send long letters with multiple inserts and people responded. Today, there's greater competition in the mailbox for donor dollars. Many donors seem to appreciate you getting to the point in an honest and succinct fashion. Every page or component that you add may unnecessarily raise your production costs. While you should always invest enough in your mailing to build a compelling case for support, you may find that a two-page letter raises—or at least nets—just as much money as a six-page letter, perhaps more. What's most important is that you test these assumptions over time."

Even if you're getting help from a direct mail professional, it's best to keep control of the process, by writing the initial draft of the letter yourself or suggesting detailed material for it.

Before you even get to the text, you've got to figure out who your letter will be addressed to. In fact, you might get hung up on the "Dear So and So." If you've got the technology, it's best to use the person's name rather than "Dear Friend." Here's the first reason why it's important to use a quality mailing list, however. People whose names are misspelled may toss the letter right then and there. ("Dear Friend" sounds far better than "Dear Mr. Carolyn Reeeed.")

A number of nonprofits don't even wait for the "Dear" line to launch into their story, but capture people's attention with a "teaser" paragraph, known as a "Johnson box." It's usually in a different font, in the upper-right area of the letter. See, for example, the below sample from the ASPCA, with a photo of an abused dog, beaten by his owner and left to suffer. The letter then picks up the story from there.

💡 **TIP**

Make the letter from "me" to "you." This is a personal letter, not a college essay or an academic paper—so make liberal use of personal pronouns and ditch any overly long words or flowery language! The letter should address the reader as "you," and be written in the honest voice of the "I" who will sign it. That helps emphasize the personal connection between the two of you. Any other personal links you can mention—even simple statements like, "I know you share our concern for urban creek protection," will also help to draw the reader in.

With or without a Johnson box, the opening paragraph of your letter can be the hardest to write. Nonprofits have tried every catchy opening in the book. However, the type that seems to draw people in the most effectively is a personal story. This isn't just a quirk among people who donate to charity—human nature makes us all particularly interested in other humans (or animals). If your organization doesn't work directly

His body was limp. His legs and hips were battered and broken. His rib was cracked. DaVinci had been severely beaten by his owner and left to suffer.

with living creatures, don't worry—there's always a way to connect it to something alive. For example, one of your volunteers could describe why she has devoted every Saturday afternoon for the last several years to your cause. Personal quotes, either from clients or others participating in your work, are also a powerful way to remind people that you're not just making this stuff up.

In the rest of the letter, you'll want to build on the opening story, so that the reader comes to appreciate:

- the scope of the problem
- why your organization is well placed to help solve that problem
- why this should capture the reader's heart or mind, and
- how the reader can help, primarily financially, but possibly with volunteer and other opportunities as well.

In a way, your letter is like a mininovel. There's a conflict, or perhaps a person in distress. (That someone should be your clients or the cause you serve, not your own organization—potential failure doesn't sell well.) Then there's a duo of heroes—your organization and the person you're reaching out to. The plot you are constructing should also point to the prospect of a happy resolution. This is particularly important, because people's usual reasons for giving often include a healthy dose of self-interest—they want their voices to be heard, and to help create a world that's more in tune with their values and dreams.

Unlike a novel, however, your letter's reader is not going to be curled up in a chair with a cup of hot cocoa. More likely, he or she will be ripping open the envelope while shedding coat, bag, and groceries after a long day's work. Your main points need to stand out strong and stand out fast.

Some helpful tools for this are old-fashioned underlining and bullet points. You can underline a few key important words or phrases, such as "While our theatre productions are ever more popular, ticket sales cover only 60% of our annual expenses." (But don't overdo it!)

Also avoid one of the most common mistakes made by fundraising letter writers: loading the text down with big, thick paragraphs (particularly in a small font). Eliminate extra words, and break these into shorter, even single-sentence paragraphs so that the eye has somewhere to move. Or, if an important list of items is buried in a long string or separated by many commas, think about using bullets to highlight them. For example:

"Instead of having nothing to do after school, youth in our program can:
- participate in our basketball team
- volunteer in community activities, or
- receive one-on-one support from trained counselors."

> **TIP**
>
> **If your letter is good enough, you can use it more than once.** There's no need to rewrite your letter every time. Once you hit on a content and presentation that inspires donations, keep using the letter—or its basic structure, with some freshening up—for as long as it's effective. Some respected organizations have been using the same letter for years! But also keep testing out alternatives, so that you can retire the letter after you've outdone it with an even more effective one.

At the end of the letter, there's no need to be subtle. The reader probably already guessed you were going to ask for money. Come straight out and say something like, "We hope you'll help us with your contribution," or "Now we are asking you to make a tax-deductible donation," or "Every $_____ you give will put a meal onto the table of a housebound senior."

In the past, there was much brow knitting on the subject of who should sign these solicitation letters, with nonprofits frantically looking for a famous person to lend his or her name. However, the consensus that has developed is that your executive director or a board member is the most natural signer and will get as good a response as anyone else. The exception is if a famous person is intimately involved with your organization and eager to speak out about it.

Most organizations end their letters with postscripts. They do it for a reason: It adds a sense of up-to-the-minute urgency that the rest of the letter doesn't have. And because of that, it often gets read first. For example, your PS might say "Every gift that we receive before [_date_] will be matched by a gift from the _____ Foundation," or "Eighty percent of every dollar you give goes straight to helping people in need."

Even better is to organize your volunteers to come in and handwrite personal notes as PSs—though this will preclude you from using bulk mail, because all the letters will no longer be identical. The personal touch may be worth a first class stamp, however.

> ⊘ **CAUTION**
> **You may have to run your letter past a local government body.** Check with your lawyer, board members, or other organizations for more information.

The reply device. To make the giving easy, you should include a reply card, on which the person indicates how much they're giving and by what means (check, credit card, monthly installments, or whatever you're prepared to offer). You've seen a thousand of these reply cards before—by now, the format is fairly standard. The card should be attractive and self-contained—some people toss the letter, but keep the reply card around in case they decide to donate.

If you have a website, be sure to list its URL on the reply card and indicate whether supporters can donate online. This will be the preference of many donors, particularly the young ones. So if at all possible, make sure your website is a welcoming place for first-time visitors; highlights the same topics as mentioned in the letter; and provides a quick path to a donation page. For more on making your website attractive to donors, see Chapter 12.

The biggest decision you'll make is simply what gift amounts to suggest (for example, "☐ $25 ☐ $50 ☐ $100 ☐ Other"). Starting out with too low an amount may encourage people to take advantage of that option. On the other hand, I know of an organization that suggested $1, simply as a way of building their membership, in accordance with a strategy of approaching foundations with a strong showing of community support. You'll need to choose suggested donation levels based on your sense of your potential supporters' giving capacities and your ability to credibly ask for high amounts.

Some organizations like to attach names to the various giving levels, such as "bronze," "silver," and "gold." This helps inspire people toward higher gifts and allows you to group donors' names in publications such as your annual report. Naming the giving levels can, however, be tricky. Each giving level needs to sound appropriately recognized, with no one falling into a category like "tin" or "aluminum alloy." The Aurora Theatre in Berkeley, for example, in its printed program, ranks its $50 to $199 donors as "stars," then advances donors up the stratosphere, from "novas," "constellations," "supernovas," "nebulae," "quasars," "pulsars," and "cosmos" to—what else?— "the big bang" (at $100,000 and up). It's probably safe to say that most donors wouldn't be offended at being called a pulsar rather than a nebula.

Some groups get around the ranking problem by assigning value-neutral names. Bryn Mawr College, for example, names its "donor societies" after historic college buildings, such as Cloisters, Pembroke Arch, and Goodhart. Yet another alternative is to give a quick summation of what each gift level will fund, as in "☐ $500 (funds one student fellowship for four weeks)"

If people will receive something in return for different gift levels (a fleece vest or baseball cap, for example), your suggested amounts should of course bear some proportional relation to the value of this return gift.

The reply envelope. The reply card should fit neatly into a reply envelope (which has to be small enough to fit into your cover envelope). Your address should, of course, be printed on the front of the envelope. But should you provide return postage or not? Fortunately, most people willing to donate to your organization are also willing to put their own stamp on the letter. You'll add a lot to your costs if you put first-class stamps on the envelopes. Organizations with higher budgets and more experience at direct mail may wish to send preprinted, business reply envelopes (with those postal seals that say "No Postage Necessary If Mailed in the United States"). But believe it or not, the postage on these is actually higher than a first-class stamp, though your overall costs should be lower because you only pay for those envelopes that donors actually mail back to you.

Optional inserts. There are also optional items you can include in your direct mail package—a Post-it® note with an urgent or "late-breaking" message, a relevant news clipping, or a "freebie" such as return address stamps or a bumper sticker. All of these will, of course, add to the costs of your package. If you're new to direct mail, you might as well go without them—particularly the freebies, which are getting so common that people feel less and less obligated to give anything in return. You can always try adding such extras later.

Eventually, however, you may find that certain types of extras are very effective. For example, Rachel Rubin, Director of Annual Giving at Project Open Hand, a Bay Area nonprofit that provides nourishing meals to seniors and people living with AIDS and other serious illnesses, says: "Our response rates go up by 7% when we include 'meal certificates' with our acquisition mailings. They're actually a combination of reply device and insert. Donors choose an amount to give to a person in need of food, such as $35 for 'Certificate Good for 1 Week's Worth of Meals.' The certificates are pretty expensive to produce, adding 2% to our overall costs. But with their high return, they're clearly worth it. I think they feel tangible to people, who can see that they're giving something specific." (See a sample of Project Open Hand's meal certificates and accompanying donor acquisition letter below and at the end of this chapter.)

CAUTION

Don't add extras to some letters and not others. If you're planning to mail via bulk mail, the U.S. Postal Service (USPS) demands that each of your letters be of the same weight.

Meal Certificates From Project Open Hand

Reprinted with permission

Make the final product look professional. Can you prepare a mailing without a professional designer or printer? If you're on a low budget, sure. Simply print a bunch of letters on your organization's letterhead, go to a local copy store to have reply cards printed and cut, and send it all out using first-class stamps. The letter should be single-spaced, but with short paragraphs and wide margins so that the pages have plenty of white space. (If your budget is extremely low, however, remember that investing in direct mail solicitation may not be the right thing for you at this time, given that its payoff may take a few years.)

How many colors of ink get the best results? Some nonprofits say only two, others say four.

I know people who've given to organizations in part because the solicitation letter was so obviously homespun rather than slick. As long as your content is intelligent and doesn't seem hysterical or slapdash, your readers will be pleased to hear a "true" voice. (But homespun letters are not a strategy you can use forever—people may start wondering why you can't get your operation off the ground.)

With new technology and in-house publishing programs, however, assembling professional-looking packages on your own is getting easier. A staff or board member who has photographic or artistic abilities (not just amateur) may come in handy to add visuals to the package. A compelling picture can be worth pages of explanations.

If you'll be using a professional printer or mail house, get recommendations from other nonprofits. Some printers specialize in working with nonprofits and will help you figure out ways to keep down costs and produce something in line with your own values. For example, an environmental organization might want to use obviously recycled paper—but still have the mailing package look classy and be affordable.

Whether you'll be using a professional or printing in house, make sure to proofread everything several times. You'd be amazed at the mistakes that crop up. Professional printing is not like photocopying; a word that you typed perfectly in your version can suddenly transmute into something else through the "miracles" of scanning or program conversions. And don't forget to be alert for sins of omission—for example, the one board member whose name was left off or a photo without explanatory text.

The Mechanics of Mailing

Getting a mailing out creates a busy time at a nonprofit, whether you're handling it in-house or through a printer and/or mail house. No matter which, you'll want to give everything one last looking over—or two. Then have everyone—including volunteers and possibly staff members who don't normally participate in development activities—ready to kick into high gear.

If someone at your organization or from your board is going to personally sign the letter, make sure he or she won't be on vacation that week, and can spare an hour or two. Someday, of course, your group will use printed signatures, though it makes the letter one step less personal.

If you're doing the mailing in-house, several boxes of paper will arrive from the printer, and you'll need to have staff and volunteers lined up to deal with them. Depending on what services you ordered, you may need to have volunteers fold the letters and combine them with the reply cards and envelopes before placing them in the mailing envelope. Give your workers a clean space, miles away from any coffee or snacks. Carefully train everyone in the assembly process. Letters should be neatly folded and placed in the envelope so that the greeting is the first thing the reader sees upon opening it, with the other inserts behind.

As a nonprofit, you can take advantage of the USPS bulk mail rates if you're sending 200 or more identical pieces of standard mail (same size and weight, up to 15.999 ounces). You'll need to plan for this in advance, first by getting a permit, using USPS Form 3624, *Application to Mail at Nonprofit Standard Mail Rates*. (Your permit will lapse, and you'll need to reapply if you don't use it at least every two years.) The exact rates will vary, depending on the size of your letter and the rate for which you qualify. Be warned, however, that the bulk mail regulations are tricky. In fact, people usually attend trainings just to find out how to organize and prepare mail in a way that meets the postal service's requirements. And you can't just go to any post office once you're done—you'll have to work through one of the special Network Distribution Centers. (On the usps.com site, search for Network Distribution Centers for a list.)

Various software programs (either within your fundraising database program or separate) can make preparing your bulk mailing—in particular, the envelopes and labels—easier. Nevertheless, mail houses are the choice of many nonprofits, despite the added costs. As Lisa Ruth Elliott (formerly of Zen Hospice) points out, "With a mail house, there's less chance of the process dragging on. You can ask them to have it done within a certain length of time. If you do the mailing in-house, the paper can build up and consume your office. At least make sure to have a number of experienced volunteers on hand if you go this route."

After assessing and comparing the time and costs of a mail house and of learning to use and handling bulk mail yourself, you may discover that first-class stamps are actually your most cost-effective option. This isn't a cop-out—many organizations decide the same thing (take a look in your mailbox and see). First-class mail can also be forwarded if the addressee has moved; bulk mail doesn't offer this advantage.

> **RESOURCE**
>
> **Want more detailed information on bulk mailing?** Take a look at these resources:
>
> - The U.S. Postal Service's website at www.usps.com. Be careful, however—many of the links lead you to for-profit business bulk mail rules, which are different. Look for Publication 417, *Nonprofit Standard Mail Eligibility*, by clicking "Forms and Publications" on the bottom of the home page.
> - The Alliance of Nonprofit Mailers. See www.nonprofitmailers.org.

Follow Up

After your mailing goes out, you can collapse—for no more than ten days, however, because with any luck at all, replies will be rolling in steadily by then.

I don't need to tell you to rip open those first envelopes quickly. But you'll also have to keep up a steady pace, carrying out these critical follow-up tasks:

1. Photocopy the checks and forward these and all credit card information to your accounting department.
2. Enter the supporter information and gift amounts in your database.
3. Send thank-you letters (discussed in detail in Chapter 5).

Each of these should be done within 24 hours to two days of receiving the replies (the sooner the better). For one thing, some people don't balance their checkbooks and will keep drawing out money until it's gone, unless you get there first. For another, developing an up-to-date system of data entry is crucial at every stage of your organization's activities; once you start getting behind on this, you may never catch up. And third, supporters who aren't thanked immediately can take it personally.

> ⓘ **CAUTION**
>
> **Quick thank-you letters are that important.** I once heard a radio show debate over whether a charity-based bicycle event had become too corporate. One person called in for the sole purpose of announcing that she'd stopped her support because it took the event organizers two months to send her a thank-you letter. It's easy to understand how this might have happened: Events take up staff time, the data entry person perhaps quits and is replaced by a part-time temp, and the reply cards pile up in a corner with the most recent tossed on the top as the bottom ones molder. But the supporter in this example doesn't know about all this, nor should she. She simply views a thank-you letter as an indication of how much an organization needs and appreciates her support.

If you don't think you can handle rapid follow-up, either hire a professional, or delay soliciting supporters by direct mail until your organization is better prepared for the aftermath. You can inspire even greater donor loyalty by combining a thank-you phone call with the letter.

Most supporters will send their replies within about the first month after you sent the mailing (though some people will literally add them to a pile that they'll hold for their end-of-year decision making). Wait until your replies have fallen to a mere trickle, then evaluate the success of your mailing by filling out the form below.

For **Item B,** include not only the costs of printing, postage, and materials, but also any special staff or professionals hired to help. You don't, however, need to include the hours put in by development staff who would be working anyway. For **Item F,** don't be surprised at a low percentage—a 1% response rate is considered successful. Hopefully, **Item G** will be a positive number, indicating that the mailing at least broke even. But if it isn't, focus your (and your board's) attention on the number of new supporters. With proper cultivation and renewal efforts, one of them could turn into your next $10,000 donor.

Fundraising Worksheet 4: Mailing Evaluation

For mailing sent [*date*], consisting of:

_____

_____

_____

_____

Describe appeal and any special enclosures:

_____

_____

_____

A. Number of letters sent out   _____

B. Total expenses of mailing $ _____

C. Number of new supporters   _____

D. Total amount of donations $ _____

E. Usual donation amount $ _____

F. Percentage of response (C divided by A)   _____ %

G. Net profit (D minus B) $ _____

H. Cost of acquiring each new supporter (B divided by C) $ _____

Comments:

_____

_____

_____

_____

_____

Sample Solicitation Letter From Project Open Hand

Project Open Hand
meals with love

> "A young neighbor of mine died last week. But during the last, and what must have been the most poignant part of his life, you fed him. Such a simple act. Such a humbling lesson."

Dear Friend:

There are few things more basic than feeding someone who's hungry and ill. Project Open Hand has been feeding people who are sick and in need every day for over 25 years. And every day we learn the same, humbling lesson: a hand extended to someone in need never comes back empty.

I'm writing to ask your help in our mission—meals with love—because we truly cannot accomplish it without generous gifts from people like you.

My name is Julie Wasem, and for the last 12 years I have been responsible for the team of volunteers and staff that prepares and cooks the nourishing meals we serve to thousands of people each day...every day of the week, 52 weeks a year.

I started working here because I was impressed with Project Open Hand's commitment to providing only the freshest and healthiest food for people battling serious illness.

You may already be familiar with the story of Project Open Hand's beginnings—how Ruth Brinker, a retired grandmother, started it all in 1985, by delivering meals she cooked herself to seven people who were suffering as much from isolation and malnutrition as from AIDS.

Back then, no one could have foreseen how devastating the AIDS epidemic would become, or how many other people would join those first seven clients.

(over, please)

730 Polk St., San Francisco, CA 94109 • (415) 447-2419 • www.openhand.org

Sample Solicitation Letter From Project Open Hand (cont'd)

That was the start of Project Open Hand and it has been our work for over 25 years: <u>life-saving and healing meals prepared with love for people who are seriously ill and homebound, or elderly and alone.</u>

In all the years of feeding people—over 17 million meals—we've never had to turn down a request for help. That, I think you will agree, is nothing short of miraculous. <u>And it's because of the caring and commitment of people—people just like you—from all over the Bay Area that we've been able to do it.</u>

One of the things we're most proud of is that since the very beginning—despite an unprecedented epidemic, a major earthquake, fires, bad weather and many other obstacles thrown in our way—<u>we've never missed a day for the people who depend on the life sustaining nutrition Project Open Hand delivers.</u> We grew to meet the demands of an unprecedented and growing AIDS crisis over the years...then modified our services to make <u>bags of nutritious groceries</u> available to those who benefited from new AIDS drugs and could prepare their own meals.

In 1998, we decided to put all the good systems we had in place to work for others who would benefit from what Project Open Hand knew how to do. That's when we started providing <u>warm, nourishing meals to elderly people</u> who are too often isolated and alone. Then, several years later we extended our nutrition programs to <u>women with breast cancer, people with heart disease and other seriously ill people</u> who didn't have the strength or the resources to feed themselves.

Almost daily we get notes from people like Richard, who wrote to say,

"Your meals have meant the difference! The difference between eating and not eating. When you started bringing meals to me, I had lost over 30 pounds. I had just come home from the hospital and was in no shape to cook. In the last month, thanks to your 'open hearts' (the meals too), I can now get around and have started to put on weight."

(next page, please)

Sample Solicitation Letter From Project Open Hand (cont'd)

Kristine is another client who thinks Project Open Hand is a lifesaver. She lives alone and has a degenerative condition that is crippling her. Some days she can walk with the help of canes, but her disease has gotten so bad that she is unable to shop or stand up in the kitchen to prepare meals for herself. Before a social worker put her in touch with Project Open Hand, she actually went several days without eating because she couldn't get any help.

Doctors say she will soon be in a wheelchair, but Kristine is determined to keep her independence. She thinks she'll be able to do that with Project Open Hand's home-delivered meals. She says that "someone stopping by to check in on me with a hot, delicious meal and a smile is a wonderful thing."

Richard and Kristine are only two of the people who receive daily nourishment from Project Open Hand because of the generosity of caring individuals like your-

self. <u>To someone who is alone and frightened, this caring and love are sometimes as healing as the nutritious food we provide</u>. With your help, we'll be able to provide meals with love to even more who are in need and alone.

Many times over the years it seemed like there just would not be enough food to go around. But we've found that whenever we've asked for help, compassionate and caring people have always stepped forward to lend a hand.

I'm urging you to do just that. Will you help feed those who need the proper nourishment to fight their illness, keep up their spirits and better tolerate often drastic medical treatments?

Fortunately, because of the volunteer efforts of so many, the donations of food and time, and the efficiency of everyone involved with Project Open Hand, we can still serve a person in need a nourishing meal for just about $5 a day.

(over, please)

Sample Solicitation Letter from Project Open Hand (cont'd)

A donation of $35 will feed a person living with a serious illness a nourishing meal prepared with love for seven days. A gift of $150 will feed someone for a month. Your gift will send a message of life—life-giving nourishment to someone who is sick and in need.

Please know that whatever you can give will go a long way—and it will be very special because you cared to give it.

With your help, we can fulfill our promise that every day of the year, rain or shine, the men and women who face so many uncertainties will know one thing for sure: Project Open Hand will always be there with a smile, a word of encouragement, and a hot, nutritious meal.

Thank you,

Julie Wasem
Director of Programs
Project Open Hand

P.S. Please consider what your gift can mean to a person who is homebound and depends on us each day for nourishing food. Send the most generous gift you can today in the enclosed reply envelope. Or if you prefer to give online, go to **www.openhand.org/donate**

How to Keep the Givers Giving

A first-time donation is an opportunity, not a fait accompli. Typically, it means that the person was momentarily persuaded to contribute, by one or another of your organization's fundraising efforts. Unfortunately, without your creative intervention, the donor's impulse may well turn out to be fleeting. In fact, studies of lapsed supporters have found that a significant number couldn't remember having supported the particular organization in the first place! Given the high cost of finding a first-time supporter, this is not what you want from your own supporters. Retaining a supporter costs only one fifth of what you'll spend to attract him or her in the first place, which makes donor retention a relatively low-cost source of untapped potential for many organizations.

This chapter will help you figure out how to keep your donors giving. From the moment your supporters first contact your organization, you need to give them a sense of personal identification with your group and its mission. Over time, this initial rapport can turn into a sense of true belonging, encouraging your supporters not only to continue their donations and involvement, but to increase their support over the years.

Some people refer to this progressive process as moving supporters up a giving ladder, or bringing them closer and closer within concentric circles of engagement. Eventually, your most committed supporters should see that your organization is the most effective instrument by which they can carry out their hopes to improve at least a little corner of the world. Currying this relationship with donors is known as "stewardship."

To inspire this type of commitment, you'll have to carry out the core work of your organization well. But no one is going to know about the great things your organization does unless someone tells them. That's why the most effective strategies for keeping supporters—and drawing them into an increased sense of engagement with your organization—include:

- thanking them for gifts, immediately and appropriately
- communicating with donors frequently, through regular mailings, newsletters, and annual reports (covered in Chapter 11), and social media and other outreach (covered in Chapter 13)
- offering them other ways to contribute to your work
- periodically analyzing your donor base to look for trends, groupings, and weaknesses, and
- calling supporters on the telephone.

Thank Your Supporters
(and Help Them Satisfy the IRS)

The IRS requires nonprofits to send receipts for any donations of $250 or more. But really, anyone who makes more than a token pledge or gift to your organization should receive a prompt—ideally, handwritten—thank-you letter. The letter should go out no later than within 24 hours or a few days.

For smaller gifts—say, $15 or under—an email or postcard is sufficient or even preferable to a formal letter; you don't want the donor to feel like you spent the entire gift on return postage. For example, see the postcard sent by the San Francisco Mime Troupe (a theater group that performs political satire in the parks of the Bay Area and beyond) reproduced here. According to Peggy Rose, former general manager of the San Francisco Mime Troupe, "It's important to thank people, but we don't want to waste the resources they've just provided us with. People want to see that you're using their resources in the best way you can. Plus, the postcards are colorful and fun."

Reprinted with permission

Your thank-you letter serves two important functions:

- It lets the supporter know the gift was important to you.
- It gives your supporter written proof of the gift in case an IRS auditor ever pays your supporter a visit (especially important if he or she gave cash).

The letter should be personal in style—it need not look like a receipt or follow any special format. In fact, you're encouraged to make your thank-you letters interesting, for example by using handmade cards crafted by your clients. Treat the letter as an opportunity to reiterate how the gift is helping your organization do its work. It's also compelling if you can tell the donors something they haven't heard before— like how many other donors have joined in on this recent effort, what progress is already underway on the project to which they gave, or what upcoming projects and events you have planned.

No matter what else you say in your letter, however, include the following information in order to meet the IRS's requirements:

- your organization's name
- the amount of the donation
- whether the donor received anything in return in cases where the gift was $75 or more; if nothing, "No goods or services were exchanged for your donation"
- no mention of token items of insubstantial value (such as a membership sticker, pen, or refrigerator magnet that cost your organization $10.20 or less if the contribution received was $51 or more; or if the item's value is either up to $102 or 2% of the amount of the contribution, whichever is less) or a membership privilege worth less than $75 a year (such as event tickets or free parking at events), and
- in cases where the giver received something substantial in return ("substantial" meaning it has a fair market value of $96 or more, or exceeded 2% of the amount of the donation, whichever is less), a good-faith estimate of its value and notification that the donor will need to reduce his or her tax deduction by the value of what was received.

If the gift was very large, you'll want to take extra steps to thank and otherwise recognize the donor, as discussed in Chapter 6.

Below is a sample thank-you letter from a fictional organization.

TIP

"Our board and staff members call and personally thank everyone who's made a contribution of $100 or more," says Peter Pearson, president of The Friends of the Saint Paul Public Library in Minnesota. "It's a great way to nurture donor relationships. They're so happy to hear from us, and often say things like, 'Yours is the only organization that's ever called me!'"

Sample Thank You Letter

Sand Dune Restoration Project
5432 Beachside Way
Oceanside, LA 12345
123-555-1212
www.ladunes.org

Mary Doane-Orr
2345 First St.
Oceanside, LA 12345

Dear Mary Doane-Orr:

We were delighted to open today's mail and find your generous gift of $80. Your support will help our staff and volunteers bring native plant life back to Oceanside's sand dunes for the enjoyment of present and future generations. Community support for this phase of the restoration project has been very encouraging—already we've received gifts from 120 people.

And, there's exciting news to report: Just yesterday one of our volunteers spotted some new shoots of one of the native flowers that once dominated these dunes—but have recently been threatened with extinction due to development and other problems. Our staff and volunteers will continue their efforts to weed out nonnative species and put protective cages around the new, native growth.

Please save this letter, which will serve as your receipt for tax purposes. [*Alternatively, depending on circumstances:*]

To comply with Internal Revenue Service regulations, this letter also confirms that you are receiving no goods or services in return for your contribution.

[*or*]

We'll be sending you the sand sculpture that you requested as a recognition gift, by separate mail. For tax purposes, your contribution must be reduced by $10.00, the value of this sculpture.

Again, thank you. We hope you'll come see the difference your gift has made, at our celebratory evening ceremony this June 25th—on the beach, of course! Look for more details in an upcoming mailing or on our website at www.ladunes.org.

Very truly yours,

Rocky Beech

Rocky Beech
Executive Director
Sand Dune Restoration Project

Follow-up Communications

In an age when we're being barraged by information, you'll have to send powerful, directed communications to remind donors of the great work your organization is doing—hopefully without joining the ranks of the bombardiers. A number of different methods are available to convey these important messages. Some are discussed in other chapters of this book, including newsletters and annual reports, covered in Chapter 11, and social networking and other media outreach, covered in Chapter 13.

This section covers the mail, both traditional "snail mail" and email. It will help you develop a strategy for mailing communications to existing donors over the course of your funding year, covering:

- how often to send mailings
- crafting your annual appeal
- designing special appeals
- what to say—and what not to say—in an appeal letter
- special considerations for sending email, and
- when to stop mailing to unresponsive donors.

How Often to Mail

There's much professional disagreement about how often your supporters should hear from you—especially because you will often be asking for money. A number of direct mail devotees recommend coming up with a reason to solicit funds every two to three months—and suggest that if you hold back, other organizations' more frequent mailings will get all the attention. Others contend that when donors are asked for money too often, they are likely to feel as though the organization either forgot the fact that they just gave or is wasting paper and postage with repeated solicitations. And many donors—especially the most generous ones, whose names are likely to appear on a number of mailing lists—are getting legitimately irritated with the flood of fundraising letters swamping their mailboxes.

TIP

Give the donor control. The simplest approach is to ask donors their preferences about how often they'll receive mailings. For example, you might tell donors at the outset that you'll typically contact them once a year to renew their annual membership, and twice more for targeted solicitations—then give them a chance to elect to hear from you less often. If asking seems like too big a risk, at least respect and follow the wishes of donors who speak up and request fewer mailings.

A Peeved Donor Story

Trisha had been a dues-paying member of a national nonprofit for several years. The mailings went to her parents' house in Portland, continuing on while she was away at college. She'd find a pile of them waiting for her when she came home on break. Not only did she start feeling confused about how often she was expected to "renew" in order to get her newsletter, but given the huge pile, she wondered if she would actually save the organization money by ceasing to send her $25 per year. After college, she moved to California, volunteered at the organization's local office, and signed up for a membership from there. She kept getting renewal letters at her parents' Portland address, but figured these would drop off eventually. They didn't. Then she let her California membership lapse. The organization called her, and she agreed to renew her membership—on the condition that they remove her Portland address from their database. "Sure, no problem," Trisha was told. She made the renewal gift.

The next time Trisha was home in Portland, she found an even larger pile of renewal letters and solicitations. She hasn't donated to this organization since.

You may also want to experiment a bit in order to develop the most effective possible mailing calendar. Retaining supporters has been shown to depend in large part on their sense that you've remained accountable and told them how your organization spent their gifts—and the results you've achieved through their continued support. This means you'll have to balance your need to keep in touch against the danger of wearing out your supporters' goodwill.

TIP

Follow your snail mailings with email reminders. Your emails can be shorter than your letter, though even this proposition is worth testing on your donors. The emails should remind the donor of the situation described in the letter, but provide enough information to satisfy anyone who threw the letter away. They should also provide links to your group's website and donation page. Two or three follow-up emails is appropriate at most times of the year, but even daily emails are acceptable at the end of the year. (As with all rules, however, rethink this one if it seems to fall flat or draws complaints from your donors.)

Annual Renewal Letters

Of course, you'll want to send at least one letter per year asking for a "renewal" of support. This is a good time to remind donors of their long-term commitment to your organization and about the vital work that you continue to do. Whether or not you have a formal membership program, try to style your appeal as a renewal of their alliance with your group—and of any membership benefits they receive. Remind them that their newsletter subscription and any other benefits will expire on a certain date, and let them know what other benefits would come with an increased gift.

For a sample of a persuasive, upbeat, and ultimately successful renewal letter, see the one below from Project Open Hand.

According to Rachel Rubin, the organization's Director of Annual Giving, "We sent this letter, like all our renewals, in the month of January, to everyone active on our list (about 24,000 people). I was skeptical about this schedule when I first started at Project Open Hand—here we were, asking people to renew their support one month after many of them had made end-of-year donations and regardless of the date of their original gift. But it works! I think people have a general sense of renewal in the new year, and our letter usually talks about success and makes them feel like they're part of a winning team. To set the stage for the renewal letter, we also try to frame all our November/December asks as special holiday gifts. The renewal then gives us a chance to thank people for their ongoing giving and let them know their total giving amount the previous year, in hopes of anchoring them to that bigger number—in other words, getting them used to the idea that, even if their usual gifts throughout the year were of a

Sample Renewal Letter

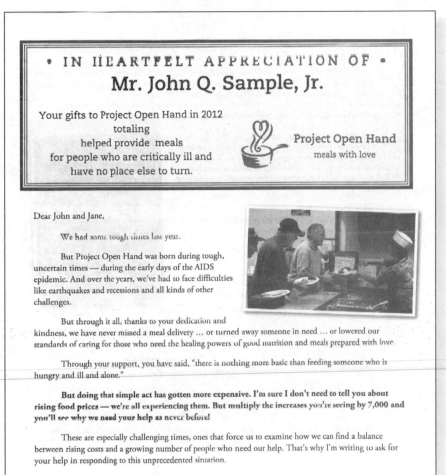

• IN HEARTFELT APPRECIATION OF •

Mr. John Q. Sample, Jr.

Your gifts to Project Open Hand in 2012
totaling
helped provide meals
for people who are critically ill and
have no place else to turn.

Project Open Hand
meals with love

Dear John and Jane,

We had some tough times last year.

But Project Open Hand was born during tough, uncertain times — during the early days of the AIDS epidemic. And over the years, we've had to face difficulties like earthquakes and recessions and all kinds of other challenges.

But through it all, thanks to your dedication and kindness, we have never missed a meal delivery ... or turned away someone in need ... or lowered our standards of caring for those who need the healing powers of good nutrition and meals prepared with love.

Through your support, you have said, "there is nothing more basic than feeding someone who is hungry and ill and alone."

But doing that simple act has gotten more expensive. I'm sure I don't need to tell you about rising food prices — we're all experiencing them. But multiply the increases you're seeing by 7,000 and you'll see why we need your help as never before!

These are especially challenging times, ones that force us to examine how we can find a balance between rising costs and a growing number of people who need our help. That's why I'm writing to ask for your help in responding to this unprecedented situation.

Can you renew your commitment to the people who depend on Project Open Hand for sustenance and caring to fight their disease, heal their bodies and find companionship and nutrition through the meals we provide?

So much of what we do is directly proportional to the generosity of you and others who become good neighbors to someone who is critically ill or elderly and without comfort ...

(over, please)

Project Open Hand • 730 Polk Street • San Francisco, CA 94109 • (415) 447-2419 • www.openhand.org

Reprinted with permission

Sample Renewal Letter (continued)

Page Two

Many of our supporters are often most generous during the holidays and while the spirit of that is especially appreciated, we know that our clients and neighbors depend on us all year long. The need for a warm meal and loving smile does not diminish when the holiday season is over.

A lot has changed since we were facing the early days of the AIDS epidemic but the constant factor has been **people reaching out to others in loving compassion** — whether by chopping vegetables, packing groceries, delivering hot meals or donating needed resources: all acts that bring healing as surely as nourishing food does.

We can be proud of how our community responded to a crisis almost 30 years ago, and it gives me great hope that we will do the same during these current tough times. I know we can with your help.

Will you help us meet the challenges of 2013 by renewing your commitment to Project Open Hand in this new year?

On behalf of all who turn to us in their time of greatest need, thank you for all you have done and all you continue to do.

Sincerely,

Kevin Winge
Executive Director

P.S.   It's not often we'll ask you to make a smaller gift but if you're considering a contribution of $100, consider instead $10 a month. When you sign up with The Supper Club, our monthly giving program, your entire contribution goes directly to providing food for those most in need. Learn more about The Supper Club in the enclosed note.

modest amount, they comfortably reached a total giving level that's higher than they perhaps realized."

TIP

Make renewal appeals obvious. Some nonprofits send out so many fundraising appeals every year that donors have no idea when they're due for an actual renewal. Try to protect the integrity of the renewal cycle by clearly indicating that other solicitations are special-purpose appeals. Also, it's a great idea to tell donors the date their last gift was made and how much it was, or better yet, set forth their giving history over the last few years; studies show that most donors mistakenly believe that they gave more recently than they actually did.

Be prepared to send some follow-up letters or emails, as well. It can take four or five communications before a past supporter is moved or remembers to renew. It rarely pays to send more than eight or ten renewal requests; better to put these donors in the "lapsed" section of your database and wait a decent interval before trying them again. But if your lapsed supporter received a newsletter or another benefit as part of his or her membership, make sure to cut it off when you said you would.

Appeal Letters and Special Communications

One good way to avoid overwhelming your donors is to vary the tone of your communications. A supporter who gets a letter every two months that says, in effect, "The situation is critical! Send money!" will almost surely tire of your tone of perpetual desperation.

However, the same donor may be interested in reading a newsletter or an emailed notice discussing late-breaking news. For example, if your group is raising money to protect a particular estuary, supporters may be fascinated to know about a new study of the area's previously underappreciated biodiversity. And this, in turn, may be a powerful trigger for future gifts. Meanwhile, when a true emergency comes along, your supporters will be more open to hearing about it and responding.

Tailoring your communications to different segments of donors, and to different donor interests, is another good way to make sure your mail is read with interest. For example, you could customize letters or send entirely different letters based on characteristics like gender, age, socioeconomic class, original connection to your organization (for example, people who attended an event as opposed to those who follow you on a social media site), or behavioral criteria, such as typical amount donated or frequency of giving. This segmentation may affect not only the substance of the appeal, but also how much you ask for. At Berkeley Repertory Theatre, for example, Director of Development Lynn Eve Komaromi says, "Why send out emails asking everyone for a $100 donation when, for example, we can ask members of our audience who always buy the best seats in the house for a higher amount, and ask the bargain-seat buyers for an amount closer to their range of comfort?" Or, you can tailor letters to different donors by asking board members to write personal notes on the letters.

Many organizations send an informational newsletter two to four times a year and an annual report near the end of the year. (Newsletters and annual reports are discussed in Chapter 11.) Be sure to keep the newsletter and annual report schedule in mind as you plan your other mailings. It's usually counterproductive for people to receive these items just days before or after an appeal by letter—build in a break of at least four weeks.

TIP

Create a gift donation program. More and more families are substituting gifts to nonprofits for yet another round of holiday gifts. And it's becoming popular to ask guests at weddings and other celebratory events to make a gift to a designated charity instead of to the people being honored. (This is especially true for second marriages, when the allure of all those new toasters may have worn off.) Savvy nonprofits let their supporters know that they are happy to establish special-occasion gift programs. Don't forget to send acknowledgment letters to both the donors and the people who inspired these gifts.

What Goes Into an Appeal Letter

In drafting an appeal letter, some of the tools you used for your initial solicitation letter (described in Chapter 4) will be helpful. However, you shouldn't speak to the reader as if he or she has never heard of your organization. Opening with a reference to your organization's recent history and the important role of your supporters is one way to set an appropriate tone: for example, "As we enter our second theater season, we know that you're as excited as we are by these rave reviews …" or "It has truly been a time for celebration, as support from you and many others has allowed us to move into our new space."

The most important elements to include in your letter are:

- **A defined project or event.** This is your reason for writing. For example, a holiday gift drive, in which you collect and wrap gifts for low-income children, would both make for a good story and provide an understandable reason for sending this separate letter. Even if you're asking for help to fund ongoing activities, find some new, seasonal, or otherwise special concern to highlight.

- **A personal story or hook.** Personal stories that illustrate how your group makes a difference are always good for drawing people in. For example, if your group is collecting and organizing lightly used sports uniforms and equipment in the United States, and then transporting and distributing them to children in South American villages, you might feature accounts, quotes, and even before-and-after pictures of a particular low-income Peruvian team.

- **The financial challenge you're facing.** Be clear about the costs associated with the project and how people's donations can make a difference.

- **A reminder of your organization's overall mission and how your current appeal fits into it.** Make sure to tie your appeal to your group's purpose and goals. When you ask for a contribution at the end of the letter, it will be in the spirit of asking the donor to reaffirm his or her support for your underlying mission.

- **A request for a donation (as well as for volunteer help, if appropriate).** Always be direct in telling people what they can do to make this project or event happen. Depending on your organization's technological capacities, you may want to refer specifically to the amount of the supporter's last gift and ask him or her to increase it by a certain amount. Don't make the mistake that one San Francisco organization did, however, and simply ask all supporters to give the difference between their previous donation and a predetermined amount (in this case, $1,000). Someone who'd donated a mere $25 to the organization got a letter saying, "Won't

Sample Appeal Letter

TVNewsMonitor
1234 Fifth St. NW
Washington, DC 20000
www.tvnewsmonitor.org
(212) 555-1212

Dear Friend:

Were you as outraged as we were about the television news' recent coverage of our state election? Once again, issues were ignored in favor of gossip, and voters were left with little to go on except the candidates' misleading attack ads.

With your support, however, we at TVNewsMonitor were able to turn our collective outrage into positive action. In keeping with our mission of increasing viewer awareness and applying pressure to the television media, we:

- sponsored well-attended voter forums for presentation and discussion of the issues in nine cities

- mobilized nearly 2,000 viewers to send critical letters to television news outlets

- disseminated critiques of dozens of news shows with suggestions on how to do better, and

- prepared a list of ten important, overlooked news stories and overlooked resource suggestions and sent them to producers at 31 alternative media outlets.

Now, we are at a critical juncture. Our research has shown that in order to get our media reform message to a broad cross-section of people, we will need to buy advertising space on a cable television channel—at a cost of several thousand dollars per airing.

Will you be part of taking this exciting next step? Already, one of our longtime members has pledged $25,000 in seed money. We know we can raise the remaining $100,000 with the help of supporters like you, who realize that the longer we wait, the less accountable our media will become—at an incalculable cost to our free society. Every $50 tax-deductible gift will buy two seconds of airtime. It may not sound like much, but working together we can make those seconds add up to a powerful pro-democracy message.

Thank you, and be sure to check our website for the latest news critiques and reports on TVNewsMonitor's activities.

With best regards,

Warfield Watcher

Warfield Watcher
Executive Director

P.S. As a special thank you, all donors who increase their past gifts by $35 or more will receive free passes to our next showing of "Collected Worst News Clips"; and all who donate $75 or more will receive a video of this hilarious and horrifying collection.

you increase your donation by $975?" She thought it was a good joke, but the letter clearly didn't add to her sense of personal connection with the organization.

For a sample of how all these strands can be woven into a complete—and not overly long—letter, see above.

> **TIP**
>
> **Any holiday can create a basis for appeal letters.** At the end of the year, people really do seem to experience a spirit of giving. However, this needn't be the only seasonal event to which you tie your appeals—especially given that every other nonprofit in town is also sending end-of-year appeals. Check the calendar for other holidays whose theme is linked to your nonprofit's work; for example, a gay marriage project might send out a June letter discussing this month of weddings, an African-American studies group might send a letter around Martin Luther King Day, or a comedy troupe might have fun with an April Fool's Day letter.

After every mailing, tally up your returns and compare them with past mailings of the same type. Also keep track of any comments you get from recipients, to help you assess how well you did with the content and presentation of each mailing. Of course, events beyond your control may play a role in your returns—a month of bad weather or a disaster such as an earthquake, a war, or a terrorist attack can focus people's giving sympathies elsewhere.

Email: Appeals and Other Messages

Email messages are an increasingly important way for organizations to communicate meaningfully with their supporters. Although it's not well suited to the standard, two-plus-page appeal letter, plenty of organizations successfully email out shorter appeals—especially during the end-of-year push.

Email is also good (as is, in many instances, your Facebook page, Twitter feed, or other social network account) for the below:

- **quick updates,** such as news or a link to a video about how all of the eagle chicks whose rescue was the subject of your previous appeal letter survived and were released

- **follow-up to an appeal letter,** for example containing a similar message about a campaign or an issue, as a subtle reminder and a way of making payment easy, with links to your website
- **member surveys**—for example, requesting input on whether to shift toward providing mental health services to only the most complex psychiatric cases, which would necessitate serving fewer people, or to continue to provide more services to less critical cases
- **newsletters** (usually as attachments or via a Web link) discussing recent projects and achievements
- **alerts on issues requiring member action,** such as attending an upcoming vigil or demonstration or to sign a petition and
- **requests and reminders for volunteer help, upcoming special events, and more.**

> ⓘ **CAUTION**
> **But will people read your emails?** The statistics don't look good. According to the 2013 eNonprofit Benchmarks Study, average "open" rates of nonprofit emails are at about 14%, and response rates have dropped precipitously, down to .07% for fundraising appeals. Ouch. Perhaps this was partly due to the 2012 elections, and perhaps the response rates look worse because nonprofits are failing to weed out nonresponsive recipients from their lists, but nevertheless, you'll want to work extra hard at making your emails stand out. Also be sure to include newsletters and other advocacy pieces in the email mix—these get opened more than straight fundraising appeals.

Check out what other nonprofits are doing with email. This is easy enough—just sign up for their email services.

Many of the types of email described above don't directly ask for money. However, they may bring in potential donors and involve them in your work—which, as you already know, is critical to bringing them up the giving ladder. And, there's no harm in adding a "how you can help" link within the message, taking readers back to your website's donation page.

Here are a few guidelines to remember when sending messages via email:

- **Confine your mailings to existing supporters who have either expressed an interest in receiving email communications ("opted in") or who are given a chance, in every message, to opt out.** (And make sure to process opt-out requests immediately.) As you collect email addresses from supporters, let them know your policy on sharing that address with others. The policy most likely to please your supporters is to never rent out your email lists unless you've gotten people's advance permission.

- **Personalize the "sender."** Readers are much more likely to open an email that comes from, "Ilona Bray, Fix Everything Foundation" than the name of the organization alone. That sense of personal communication should be carried throughout the message. Use different staff names for different types of messages or different segments of donors, as appropriate. Even better is if you can incorporate the sender's photo and a graphic of his or her signature into the message.

- **Make your subject line brief and catchy, yet specific and clear.** Even existing supporters have to be convinced to open a message. A bland heading like "News From Our Nonprofit" can turn off the many people who've had enough doses of reality for one day. An overly general title like "What's New" may sound like spam. Create interest or excitement with something like "Otter Born in Captivity," or "Invitation to KidsOrg's 10th Anniversary."

- **Don't get caught in a spam filter.** First, be careful about subject line words or phrases that might trigger content filters. These are set to prescreen the spammers' latest favorite words or tricks. Though these are ever changing, surefire trouble words are any that sound remotely sexual (watch out for double entendres), strings of capital letters or punctuation marks, mentions of debt, baldness, or popular health remedies, and even the words "free," "limited time," or "opportunity." Second, try to avoid volume filters—that is, filters that interpret all messages sent to large numbers of people as spam. Talk to your email provider to make sure it has negotiated an exemption for your organization with the major Internet service providers.

- **If a particular message is likely to resonate with a wide audience** (for example, a development that impacts a popular national park), encourage recipients to forward the email to friends. But be sure to date the message, and to tell people about any deadlines for action. You don't want your email to bounce around the Web for years.

- **Include enough information within the message that someone who has never heard of your organization will see who you are and understand what you do.** Remember, your email may be forwarded beyond your immediate supporters. And it never hurts to remind donors exactly what their contributions are funding.

- **Informality doesn't mean sloppiness.** Typos look just as bad in an email as in a letter. And, IMHO (in my humble opinion), there's no need to use smiley faces or cute abbreviations.

- **Keep messages short and readable.** A few paragraphs, with lots of bullet points, is plenty. If you have the capacity to put the message in HTML format, great. If not, make sure to use a large font, put spaces between paragraphs, and review the text from the viewpoint of someone who will open it and give it a few seconds' quick scanning.

- **Be ready for two-way communication.** Your readers are only a click away from the "reply" button. They may have questions or concerns, or wish to respond to your requests for information or help. The speed of email creates an expectation that someone at the other end will answer right away. Make sure you've got someone lined up—if not with a full answer, then at least with a note saying "Thank you for your [comments, concerns, *or* offer]. I'll look into this and get back to you within the week."

- **Encourage readers to click through to your website or Facebook page.** While your email message should be interesting on its own, it can also legitimately act as a "teaser," compelling people to learn more.

- **Don't send emails encouraging donations unless your website is equipped to handle credit card transactions.** If you have to add to potential donors' workloads by asking them to write a check and put it in the mail, you'll irritate the very ones who are most accustomed to doing things at the speed of email.

Another way to use email to your benefit is to send messages to segmented groups from your mailing list. For example, if you'll be posting a press release on your website that you know will appeal to a particular subset of supporters, alert them by email and provide a link to this Web page. Or, you might share a quick success story with donors or volunteers who recently helped with a project. This won't prevent you from fleshing out the full story in a letter, a newsletter, or another communication later.

When to Give Up on a Donor

As you continue corresponding with supporters, you'll notice that very few of them respond to every single mailing with a gift. Some will inevitably start to drop off. After a year has gone by without any response, you may start to wonder whether it's worth keeping them on your list at all.

At what point do you give up? If you encourage supporters to think of themselves as members, then their lack of interest will become clear after your intense efforts at renewal fail. For those not on a renewal schedule, the dividing lines aren't so bright. Unless the supporter has died or joined an ascetic monastic order, you could choose to keep him or her on your list until you receive a request to remove his or her name. (Don't do this without analyzing your annual cost of mailing to lapsed donors, however.) The general rule is to continue regular correspondence until a year and a half has gone by, then take a rest.

> **CAUTION**
> **Be vigilant in removing deceased donors from your database.** Remember, someone still gets the letters, even if the former donor isn't around to read them. A friend of mine who was responsible for tying up her deceased aunt's affairs wrote letters—for 20 years!—asking a charitable organization to take her aunt off its mailing list. The organization's appeal letters kept on coming. The bad news for the organization is that my friend had formerly been a donor too—but, as she said, "Even if they're a good organization otherwise, how can I support them when they're wasting so much money sending letters to dead people?"

Some supporters shouldn't be relegated to the "lapsed" file even after a year or two has gone by. In particular, try to stay engaged with supporters who have:

- **made large gifts.** Donors who've made gifts of hundreds of dollars or more have felt strongly about your organization's work at some point. Perhaps more mailings aren't the best strategy—try a phone call or an invitation to a lunch, meeting, or small event.
- **given for a long time.** If the donor has given to your organization for five years or more—regardless of the amount given—don't give up hastily. The donor may be a little worn out, but not necessarily

uninterested. You could reduce the number of appeal letters, but continue sending event-related mail, the annual report, and other pieces to reignite interest.

- **a personal tie to your organization.** Some people should be kept on your mailing list whether they give frequently or not. These might include former staff members, clients, or alumni. Again, you can tailor the type of communications to the person or group.

> ### CAUTION
> **Never call someone a "lapsed" donor.** Sounds like some sort of failure, doesn't it? Few people who haven't made a donation for a year or two would describe themselves as "lapsed"—especially those who don't subscribe to your belief that they should give early and often. Your correspondence can forever simply refer to its recipients as "members," "supporters," or whatever term you customarily use.

> ### RELATED TOPIC
> **Some supporters clearly have the interest or ability to give frequent or larger gifts.** These will require more than the occasional letter, as described in Chapter 6.

Invite Supporters to Get More Involved

Money may not be all that your supporters have to give, nor all that you want from them. In your various communications with supporters—thank-you letters, phone calls, emails, newsletters, and so on—be sure to describe other ways to support your organization's work. These could include volunteering, either on a regular basis or at a special event; participating in a campaign of writing letters or emailing congressional representatives; attending lectures and events that you sponsor; and more.

Author Kay Sprinkel Grace recommends contacting supporters twice with an invitation to get involved—perhaps to attend a lecture, tour, or reception—for every one time that you contact them for money. (See her book *Beyond Fundraising*, published by Wiley, for further suggestions on donor stewardship.)

Whether or not your supporters' participation in these activities helps your organization directly is not the point. It develops a relationship and makes them part of your inner circle. The more a supporter gets involved in your issue, with heart, mind, and body, the more the supporter will feel he or she "owns" it—and continue or increase support for your organization as a result. (See Chapter 2 for more on volunteer involvement and Chapter 8 for more on special events.)

Analyze and Segment Your Donor Base

As your base of support grows, you'll want to analyze your supporters' giving patterns and segment them into groups. The purpose is to tailor your appeals and stewardship accordingly. Most nonprofit organizations sort their supporters by financial levels. Some also create groupings based on particular interests or connections with the organization.

Segmenting Donors by Giving Level

Traditionally, grassroots nonprofits divide their donors into three financial categories:

- **regular donors,** who give less than $100, or who give less frequently than once every two years
- **midscale donors,** who give between $100 and $500, or who give once or twice a year, and
- **major donors,** who give more than the high end of your midscale donor category ($500), or who give several times a year. This category would also include people who have made your organization a beneficiary of their estates.

You don't have to create three tiers of donors or divide them along the dollar amounts suggested above—your groupings should depend on the giving levels among your organization's own supporters. You could also create a fourth category, perhaps of "top donors" whose gifts run to the thousands of dollars.

> ⓘ **CAUTION**
>
> **Never call someone a "minor donor"!** The terms by which you segment donors are, for obvious reasons, for internal purposes only.

In creating these segmentation lines, consider how your donors view their gifts. Research has shown that people see themselves as having made a major gift if they donate $500 to $1,000.

If you're lucky enough to have so many high-dollar donors that you've stopped thinking about the $500 givers as "major," you may need to think again. This year's $500 to $1,000 supporters are your most likely source of next year's larger gifts—but only if you've treated them with due respect along the way. Very few supporters leap directly from gifts of a few hundred to several thousand dollars. Donors usually inch their way toward the large gifts. To truly cultivate your donor base for next year's growth, and to keep your pool of givers full (as protection against slumps in the economy), keep a sharp eye on supporters who seem to be positioning themselves to become major donors.

Where you draw the dividing lines between supporters may depend on how much time you and your staff and volunteers can devote to communicating with them. Include as many people as you can handle within the midscale and major donor categories—even if their gifts were fairly modest—and then lavish attention on them to encourage their continued or increased support. You'll find information on how to do this in Chapter 6.

> ⓘ **CAUTION**
>
> **Are too many of your donors stuck at a certain giving level?** If your donors seem to be in a giving rut—particularly if it's at a low level of giving—you may need to look again at the message you're sending through your publications, marketing, and suggested gift levels. Make sure your communications encourage giving at higher levels—and explain exactly what these larger gifts will fund.

Segmenting Donors on Nonfinancial Bases

Giving levels are not the only possible distinctions you might draw among your donors. Equally important to your fundraising concerns are their subject matter interests. At an immigrant rights organization, for example, donors may be clustered into different ethnic groupings. At a musical or an arts organization, you might distinguish between audience members and present or past students or participants. At a health-related organization, patients and their families might form a separate and important grouping.

While these groups will no doubt share many interests, paying attention to their personal reasons for identifying with your organization can also increase your fundraising effectiveness. For an example of how one fundraiser identified and cultivated a nonobvious subgroup, see "Reunion of the Founders," below.

Reunion of the Founders

M. Eliza Dexter, then–development director at Save The Bay, relates the following: "We'd always known that an unusual number of our members had been around for 30 or 40 years, but we hadn't fully focused on what this meant. The more I got to know Save The Bay's donors, the more I realized that this group of early members was something special. They had been true environmental leaders in the '60s, when the movement was still in its fledgling stage. They were out there monitoring things, calling each other to say, 'Did you hear what they're going to do to this watershed?' or 'Let's organize something around that.'

"So, we decided to hold an event just for these 'founding members.' It was a tea party at the Berkeley Yacht Club, and included a speech by a former UC Berkeley Chancellor who had himself been a founding member of Save The Bay.

"I'll never forget watching people arrive—you would have thought it was a high school reunion. People were hugging each other. They were so excited to catch up and reflect on how far they and the organization had come together."

Also, keep an eye on trends within your donor base. Where are your new donors coming from? Is there a group that seems to be unmoved by your appeals? Such observations can help you tailor your publications and solicitations.

 RELATED TOPIC

Information on major donors. For more on working with midscale and major donors, see Chapter 6.

When to Call Your Supporters

Many nonprofits try to incorporate the telephone into their donor communication efforts—but most make a hash of it. We all know how irritating unwanted calls can be.

But there are ways you may be able to use the phone as an effective and inoffensive way to raise funds, including:

- to thank a donor for a gift
- in combination with a letter, and
- to follow up on an appeal.

FTC Efforts to Stop Telemarketing

In 2003, the Federal Trade Commission took steps to protect Americans from constant calls by telemarketers. It created a national "Do Not Call" list, for which people could register online or by phone (at www.donotcall.gov or 800-382-1222). The website and phone lines were swamped as soon as they opened—about 370,000 people registered within the first 12 hours.

What does this mean for nonprofits? The good news is that charities are not prohibited from calling people on the Do Not Call list. The bad news is that the public is clearly fed up with solicitors who intrude on their private life and space. Even if your group name shows up on their caller ID, many realize that this technology can be spoofed, too. The lesson is to use the phone judiciously—and hope that the FTC's actions will eventually create a world in which people no longer shrink from a ringing phone.

Thanking Donors by Phone

As discussed earlier, everyone who gives more than a token contribution should receive a written thank-you letter. In addition, for larger gifts, a phone call can be a nice, added personal touch. Chances are, the donor will remember your call long after the form letter is buried in his or her files.

If you can muster up the volunteer resources, calling everyone who sent in a reasonable-sized gift will yield results in terms of donor loyalty and potentially larger gifts later. However, a "big-name" person—such as the ED, development director, or a board officer—should always be the one to call the major donors.

> **TIP**
> **Voicemail can be your friend.** Chances are, the person you're calling won't pick up—in fact, he or she may be screening calls. This isn't necessarily a bad thing. If you're calling with a thank you or another simple message, leaving it as a recording is all that's necessary. Give the supporter a way to contact you, but make clear that calling back is entirely at his or her option. If your message requires a return call, at least you'll know that the donor will be calling at a time that's convenient for him or her.

Fundraising Calls Introduced by Letters or Email

A highly effective strategy to use with midscale donors (or donors not quite major enough to warrant a personal visit) is to send a brief letter or email explaining that you'll call to talk about how the donor can support an upcoming plan or project. This is known as a "lead letter." Studies have shown that this combo yields greater returns than either mail or telephone used alone.

Your letter should tell the donor approximately when to expect your call (in a few days or a week, most likely). The key, of course, is not to get too busy, because you must follow through on that promise to call!

This combination can also be done in reverse, by making phone calls alerting donors to expect a letter. This is slightly more sensitive, of course, because they aren't expecting the call. It's best to have a script that also includes a thank you for past gifts, and a quick word on what's new and interesting at your organization. You might also try calling when you know the person is unlikely to be available, with the intention of leaving a message!

Calls to Follow Up on Other Appeals

If you've mailed or emailed an appeal or sent a renewal request without results, it makes sense to follow up with a phone call. This is another good time to mobilize your volunteers, so you can reach as many people on your list as possible. Train them on the contents of your appeal. They should be ready to summarize the issue for the callers, and be willing and able to answer questions about it—or know who's available to handle any difficult questions or concerns.

It's best if your callers identify themselves (truthfully) as unpaid volunteers. This distinguishes them from the masses of telemarketers and makes the person on the other end more likely to stay on the line.

To give supporters an additional reason to donate when called, volunteers should remind them of what an early gift will mean—an immediate and needed boost for the project, and for the caller, freedom from future mailings on this issue! If you have a premium you can offer to the first several donors, all the better.

RESOURCE
Want to know more about fundraising by phone? See Mal Warwick's website—in particular the category of articles entitled "Raising Money by Phone," at www.malwarwick.com (click "Resources," then peruse "Articles").

Midscale and Major Donors

Chapters 4 and 5 discuss how best to appeal to a broad base of individual supporters, most of whom you hope will donate between $15 and $250. These donations add up. But the total probably won't be enough to support your growing organization. For most nonprofits, larger gifts—those in the range of $500 and up—are important pieces of their fundraising pies. So, where do you find someone who will give your organization thousands of dollars? Probably not from your regular appeal letters and other general outreach. Though you might dream of sending out a newsletter and getting a $10,000 check in next week's mail, that dream seems to come true only for the nonprofit across town.

To get donors to write big checks, you'll have to approach them individually. Most often, you'll be approaching existing supporters, asking them to upgrade their giving levels. In other cases, you may persuade people who haven't supported your organization in the past to give a large donation. Either way, to inspire gifts at this level, you will need to enter into a close personal relationship with each supporter. Fortunately, this won't require you to assume the role of a beggar. As any successful development professional will tell you, the donor-donee relationship that works most effectively can best be described as one of collaboration. You and the supporter work together, with shared excitement, toward the same goal: that of making a difference in the world. Your organization serves as simply a pass-through entity, through which the donor's generosity is transformed into social, educational, environmental, or other worthy change.

Still, you'll need to convince a good-sized group of major supporters that your organization is the best pass-through entity to achieve their goals. As discussed later in this chapter, an important part of doing this is showing the donor just how important his or her funding is to your results.

Even if this sounds frightening, or like hard work, it can also be a lot of fun. You probably didn't get involved in fundraising because you like counting money, but because you care about furthering a cause. Sharing your conviction and interest with other, like-minded people who can afford to help that cause can be a joy, not a chore. In fact, you generally shouldn't ask anyone for a major donation unless and until:

- The person is not a stranger, but a friend or someone with a demonstrated interest in your organization or the type of work it does.
- You know that the amount you request will be in line with the person's financial capacity or past giving history.

- You've laid enough groundwork so that the person won't be surprised, shocked, or offended by your request.
- You can convincingly explain exactly why the money is needed, how it will be spent, and what you hope to achieve.

The items on this list don't have to be accomplished in a day, week, or even a month. It's not unusual to spend two or three years cultivating a potential major donor until all of these conditions are in place.

So, if major donor fundraising is about building relationships, where do you begin? This chapter starts with the most comfortable and low-pressure parts of relationship building and works up to the more challenging. This gradual approach isn't for your comfort alone—studies of major donors have shown that when they feel rushed to give, they're more likely to say no. This chapter covers:

- doing background research on supporters
- getting to know your midscale and major supporters
- asking supporters for annual renewals
- designing special events for major supporters
- meeting with supporters one on one, and
- organizing a campaign in which you and your volunteers schedule numerous meetings with supporters.

Background Research

You've just walked into a nonprofit as a new development staffer. If you're lucky, you'll have a database of supporters, which you can use to print out a few reports. (If you don't have a database, look into getting one—see Chapter 2 for suggestions.) The most useful reports will tell you who the most generous and most frequent donors are. But the names may still be meaningless to you. Perhaps one of them sounds like an acquaintance from high school, and another has the same last name as a half-forgotten 18th-century author, but that's about it. You're going to need more information to figure out how best to approach the supporter in the future.

For example, learning more about a supporter will help you find common interests, personal connections, and shared history between that person and your staff and board members, which, in turn, should help you decide who in your organization the supporter should meet and which projects are most likely to interest him or her. In addition, doing background research will help you decide what size and type of gift to request, when the time comes.

Start your research in your own building, by talking to staff members. Ask them to name any supporters with whom they've had personal contact and to tell you their knowledge and impressions. Also check your development office and ED's records for notes on previous meetings with supporters, personal correspondence, and lists of people who participated significantly in special events or projects. Compile these notes for your database and files. Then put together a list of the hottest prospects, for further research and cultivation.

Now do the same thing with key board members (past as well as present, if possible), especially those who have been long connected to your organization or the community it serves. Board members probably haven't kept systematic records, but their friendships with major donors may be deeper. In fact, board members may have been responsible for bringing certain supporters into contact with your organization in the first place.

Even after tapping into your organization's knowledge base, your database reports may contain mystery names or supporters about whom you know little more than their names, addresses, and giving histories. Also, you may receive names of new prospects, from board members, for example. This is the time to do some independent research. To accomplish this, nonprofit fundraisers once had to spend many hours in the library or turn to outside consultants to compile biographies on supporters (and hiring consultants is still an option). However, the Internet has also made it possible to obtain surprising amounts of free information on someone.

For do-it-yourself research, see "Websites for Prospect Research," below, which contains a list provided by Lauren Brown Adams (a fundraising consultant with over 30 years' experience in working with major donors), to which I've added some commentary and a few more sites. Lauren describes this list as a "beginning," noting that you can delve much deeper using paid sites and other sources. The entries on this list will help you figure out everything from your prospect's business affiliations to his or her birthday, and help you estimate how much the person earns and paid for his or her house or boat, so it may be sufficiently comprehensive for your needs.

Although some of the sites on Lauren's list may seem unlikely to be of help—how often, for example, are you likely to be curious about a supporter's royalties from a hit record?—Lauren has, over the years, used all of them in surprising and valuable ways. Once, for example, while working on a school's fundraising campaign, she noticed that one child had the same last name as a famous Hollywood personality. By looking on www. imdb.com, a database of actors, directors, technicians, and producers, she was able to confirm the family relationship. Such clues help fill out the picture of a potential donor's life and background.

CAUTION

Don't be a snoop. While research on a donor's background is legitimate, invading his or her privacy clearly is not. For thoughts on where this sometimes wavering line should be drawn, see the Association of Professional Researchers for Advancement's Statement of Ethics, available at www.aprahome.org (click "APRA Community" then "Professional Standards"). One of their key guidelines suggests recording only information that is relevant to your fundraising effort. ("Getting caught up in reading about scandals is a waste of time anyway," reminds Lauren Brown Adams.) APRA also suggests never pretending to be someone else when seeking information and checking carefully to make sure that your sources and the information you glean from them are reliable.

RESOURCE

Subscriptions are available. If you'd rather pay someone to do the research for you, several Web-based services offer subscription packages— sometimes with free trial demonstrations using actual names from your database! For example, you might check out:

- **Target Analytics,** at www.blackbaud.com (click "Analytics" under "Nonprofit Solutions")
- **Wealthengine**, at www.wealthengine.com (under "Nonprofit," click "Research")
- **Nozasearch**, at www.nozasearch.com, also by Blackbaud (tells you what other charities particular individuals have contributed to), and
- **The Foundation Center**, at www.foundationcenter.org, whose subscription-based directory (free if you visit one of its libraries) will tell you if your prospect sits on the board of a grant-making foundation, in which case, you may quickly ascertain what causes that person believes most deserving (especially if it's a small, family board, and your prospect is the only member making grants in a particular geographic area).

Websites for Prospect Research

Here are Lauren Brown Adams's favorite starting points for research:

General Information and News:

- **www.google.com.** Even frequent Google searchers may not know all the things it can do. For example, if you type in a phone number, you might find out the name and address of the person or establishment it belongs to. This can be particularly useful if you have a work number and want to know where your prospect is employed. Or, if you enter the person's name and click on the "News" tab, you can pull up articles in which the person's name has appeared.

- **Wikipedia.com.** This publicly generated content should never be taken as the last word on anyone or anything—but it's a useful starting point, showing you what threads to follow.

- **Piplsearch.com.** By entering a name in the search box on the home page, you will get a list of the person's nearest relations.

- **www.hotbot.com.** This is another favorite search engine for research on prominent or newsworthy people. Because every search engine has its own formula for sifting through the massive amounts of information in cyberspace, you'll get different results from different services.

- **www.ibiblio.org.** ibiblio is a "library of libraries," containing a somewhat overwhelming array of Web links. However, by clicking "Collection Index," then (under the "Reference" heading) "Journalism," then "Newspaper Archives on the Web," you'll be brought to an archive of U.S. print news, some free and some available at a charge for articles or use. You can link to newspapers' websites and search for the name of the person or his or her company.

Business Information (for after you've discovered where a prospect works):

- **http://finance.yahoo.com.** This site will tell you most of what you might want to know about a publicly traded company, including who is on its board.

- **www.forbes.com.** Forbes keeps some irresistible lists, such as the 400 richest Americans and the top-earning CEOs. Your nonprofit is unlikely to know anyone on these these lists, but it is worth a look!

- **www.annualreports.com.** This offers a readily searchable database of the annual reports published by U.S. and international companies.

- **www.money.cnn.com.** This is another business site with a free search function of articles appearing in the print publications *Fortune* and *Money*.

Websites for Prospect Research (cont'd)

Profession-Specific Information:

- **www.linkedin.com.** This offers a great way to find out not only someone's professional position and history, but who he or she knows. However, be sure to hide your own identity when searching. (Go to "Settings," click "Select what others see when you've viewed their profile," and choose "totally anonymous." You'll probably want to switch back when you're done, however; otherwise, you give up the ability to see who's been viewing your profile.)

- **www.sacbee.com/statepay.** If you're researching people who work for any branch of the California government—including the university system—this allows you to search by their names and discover their salaries. Other states may have similar sites.

- **www.martindale.com.** This site compiles information on all practicing attorneys in the United States. By entering the name in its "Find Lawyers & Firms" function, you can find out where someone works, and whether he or she is an associate (usually a lawyer in the first six years of practice who earns a set salary) or a partner (entitled to a share of the firm's profits). To find out what salaries the firm pays associates, try the "Firm Salaries" section of FindLaw's career website at http://careers.findlaw.com, though this is most likely to yield results only for medium to large-size law firms. To find out what partners earn, try www.law.com and look for its survey of the profits earned per partner for 100 U.S. law firms.

- **www.ama-assn.org.** Click the "Patients" link to use the nationwide "Doctor Finder" function, which will tell you where a physician works and what type of medicine he or she practices. Then go to www.allied-physicians.com to learn the average reported incomes for various medical specialties.

- **www.imdb.com.** The film industry is the focus of this site. Using the search function, you can choose "Bios" from the pull-down menu, then enter a name and get detailed biographical information—sometimes including earnings information.

- **www.amazon.com.** If your prospect is an author, search his or her name to get a list of book titles—then look at the rankings to see how well the books are selling. While these rankings aren't scientific, any number under 1,000 means a book is selling very well, and the author is probably pulling in decent royalties.

Websites for Prospect Research (cont'd)

Salaries and Income:

In addition to the profession-specific salary information noted above, the following sites will help you figure out how much your prospect earns:

- **www.sec.gov/edgar.shtml.** Here, you can check companies' proxy statements (Form DEF 14A) to find out the executive compensation of officers and directors of publicly traded companies.
- **www.ascap.com/musicbiz/money-intro.html.** This site contains information about prospective music business profits.

Real Estate and Other Property:

- **Zillow.com** is a good option for information on real estate values.
- **www.boattradero.com.** Check out comparative prices of boats for sale here.
- **www.controller.com.** A prospect who owns an airplane is probably living well above the poverty line. But you might also like to know how much the plane costs. As long as you know the make and model, the answer is here.
- **www.askart.com.** If you noticed a Warhol or another work by a prominent American artist on your prospect's wall, find out its approximate value here.

Political Contributions:

- **www.opensecrets.org.** This well-titled website helps you discover how much a person has contributed to political campaigns or causes. The home page has a handy box with which to search by donors' names.

Birth and Death Records:

- **www.ancestry.com.** By clicking "Search Records" and entering a name, you can find birth and death dates in someone's family. This might tell you when it's appropriate to leave someone alone—or, depending on circumstances, when you might approach the family about a memorial gift.

Websites for Prospect Research (cont'd)

Fundraising Reference Lists:

- **www.indorgs.virginia.edu/portico.** If you haven't found a website to suit your search fancy on the list above, you may find it on this list of links to websites containing biographic, occupation, salary, and other relevant information.
- **www.specialissues.com/lol.** This site features a "list of lists," especially lists about top-ranked people and businesses. For example, if you choose "Arts, Entertainment and Recreation," the first thing to pop up is a list of the top 200 art collectors.

You may also want to research your donor's cultural background. Development pros are increasingly realizing that fundraising techniques that have been developed to reach upper-class persons of European descent don't work as well in a multicultural world. Particularly if your nonprofit is closely connected to an immigrant or a minority community, you will need to understand the relevant norms and social codes. Because these can be quite different even from one generation to the next, a potential donor's age may also directly impact your fundraising efforts.

Various books exist that purport to help bridge cultural divides. However, because most of these were written for people planning to do business abroad, they are mainly helpful in avoiding major gaffes (like showing up at a Lithuanian person's house bearing an even number of flowers, which would connote a funeral arrangement, or giving the thumbs-up sign to someone in one of the many cultures that interprets this as equivalent to raising one's middle finger). Beyond that, you'll get furthest by finding a friend who's savvy about the culture of the donors you'll be cultivating and who is willing to offer frank advice.

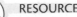 RESOURCE

Want more information on working with donors of different cultures? See the "Diversity Essays" section of the Association of Fundraising Professionals' website at www.afpnet.org (look at the links under "Resource Center").

Get to Know Your Existing Supporters

In a perfect world, you'd have time to meet and get to know all of your supporters, even those who send you only $10 carefully saved from their pension checks. Of course, that's probably not possible, particularly in growing organizations. The most practical alternative is to focus your personal attention on supporters who have given donations in the major and possibly midscale range.

To put your relationship with these supporters on a solid footing, and to identify personality matches between them and your board or staff members, look for meaningful ways to establish personal contact. Your early interactions should not involve a request for cash. Remember, you're trying to build a long-term relationship with a person whom you hope will contribute a tidy sum over many years, so it doesn't hurt to be patient at the start. Three good ways to foster your relationship are:

- conveying your appreciation for a supporter's recent gift
- inviting supporters to get an inside peek at your organization, and
- creating forums where supporters can come together to share thoughts and ideas about your work.

> **TIP**
>
> **Know the names of your top supporters.** You (and others who interact with the public) need to be ready for spontaneous calls or visits. Imagine your embarrassment if someone who's steadily given substantial gifts to your organization calls or stops by, and hears, "Sorry, what exactly can we help you with? Could you repeat your name? How do you spell that?" Far better to say "Wonderful to hear from you, Mrs. So-and-So. Your support is helping the kids already." Make up a list of these top supporters and put copies where you, your receptionist, and other people in regular contact with the public can access them when they pick up the phone (but keep them out of public view). Of course, you should also be friendly to anyone who calls, but time probably won't allow you to memorize all of their names.

Express Appreciation for Recent Gifts

What better time to get to know a midscale or major supporter than when he or she has just made a gift? You know that your organization is already on the supporter's mind, and you don't need to do anything more elaborate than show your thanks. Make sure your database and office procedures are set up to let you know when an unsolicited midscale or major gift arrives.

Midscale gifts in particular may arrive without personal contact, perhaps through a mailed appeal or an event, or as a result of positive publicity. But you can make the contact personal by simply picking up the phone—preferably on the very day when you receive the gift. Thank the donor graciously, then follow up with a few friendly questions, such as, "What got you interested in our organization?"; "Is there a particular branch of our work that interests you more than others?"; and "What type of work would you like to see us do more of?"

> 💡 **TIP**
>
> **Read your file before you reach for the phone.** Although it may sound obvious, study all the information you already have on the donor before you call. And don't forget to review the reply card that came with the donation. It could tip you off to an important fact—for example, that the donor recently moved and changed her last name (as would be common for a woman after a divorce). In the words of development professional M. Eliza Dexter, "I read through everything I've got on a donor before I pick up the phone, even for a simple thank-you call. It's common for them to ask questions, or to refer to something, like 'I remember that great coastal walk with David [the ED].' The last thing I want is to sound surprised!"

Asking the supporter for his or her thoughts may bring inspired suggestions. But even if you don't learn anything earthshaking, it will give you valuable insights into the supporter's personality and motivation for supporting your organization. And depending on how the conversation goes, you might slip in some relevant personal questions, such as "Are you an artist yourself?" or "Do you spend time hiking in our state parks?"

At the end of the call, you'll probably want to suggest further involvement with your organization, again without asking for money. For example: "I'm sure you'll enjoy the information in our next newsletter, coming out in two weeks—if you'd like to help with any of the volunteer activities, give me a call and I'll connect you to the coordinator."

If you receive a solicited gift after a personal meeting or other direct contact, then your phone call obviously need not dwell on these preliminaries. Simply pick up where your last conversation left off, perhaps with an update on the project you sought funding for. For starters, however, the person who solicited the gift should absolutely follow up with a personal thank you (in writing or by phone) when the gift arrives. For example, if your ED inspired the gift after making a talk at a local service club, the ED should be the first to convey thanks.

Especially if your organization receives many donations, you may, if you're a development staff person, want to handle the follow-up on only the most promising donors yourself, delegating the task of thanking others to a board member or savvy volunteer. Be sure to use volunteers who have a pleasant manner and good interpersonal skills. This may be the first human contact some supporters have with your organization.

TIP

Train your volunteers. They might need a word or two on proper phone manners. For example, remind them to ask, "Do you have a moment to talk?" before launching into the conversation. Also explain what issues or recent achievements the supporter might want to hear about. If the gift was made in response to a mailed appeal, for example, volunteers should expect questions about how you're progressing on the issues described in the appeal letter. And listen to the volunteer's first few calls to make sure he or she doesn't sound like someone merely reading a canned speech.

When a thank-you conversation is concluded, make sure the volunteer enters detailed notes on the donor's interests and background into your database or the donor's file. And don't forget to record the name of the person who made the call.

Other Special Ways to Thank Supporters

Any time that you can reach out and show appreciation to a supporter, you increase his or her sense of connection to your organization. For example, if the supporter has mentioned his or her birthday to you, a card can be a nice gesture. If you're on a business trip or vacation in another city, check your database to see whether any major supporters live there. I don't recommend completely giving over your personal time to your work, but you might enjoy squeezing in one lunch with a major donor. (Use it as an excuse to take a long lunch with a friend when you're back at work.)

The year-end holiday season is also a good time for general supporter appreciation. For example, the Allerton Estate in Illinois (a historical home and park) celebrated the end of one year by sending select donors jars of honey made by local bees, together with handwritten notes from the group's development director. Many organizations send selected supporters cards or nicely printed one-page letters recapping the highlights of the past year. If you send a card, make sure the cover image represents a universal theme, such as snow, candlelight, or family togetherness, not a holiday image associated with a particular religion (which your supporter may not share).

Invite Donors to Watch Your Organization at Work

Once you've made your thank-you call, the next step is to broaden and deepen this personal contact. (This is also appropriate even if you've had no opportunity to place a call.)

Fundraisers often rack their brains for the perfect way to excite donors about their organizations, when the answer is right under their noses: Invite a donor to watch what your organization does. Makes sense, doesn't it? If you were a donor, would you rather see glossy marketing materials and a staged event, or the real people or places that the organization is working to help? One of the best examples I've heard of is Save The Bay, which invites major donors (and foundation staff members) to get into canoes and see the watersheds they're working to preserve. (For more on that, see "Giving Donors a Canoe's-Eye View," below.) But you don't need a boat or a view of the Golden Gate Bridge to interest people: Activities involving children, nature, or animals tend to be popular for such donor invitations. If your group teaches foster parents how to raise good kids, the graduation ceremony from one of your courses is likely to be a similarly inspiring moment.

Of course, if you work with a think tank where people sit at computers all day, or at a hospice or shelter where visitors aren't allowed, this strategy may be harder to implement. But keep it in mind just the same. If, for example, your researchers receive an award and you'll be filling a table at the ceremony, see if you can make room for a supporter or two.

Inviting potential major donors to an event requires some forethought. For example, if you're planning a trip or an outing, don't invite more than a few new supporters along. The focus should be on keeping things real and reasonably intimate. Also, you don't want the supporter to feel out of place, or like he or she has interrupted something. Be sure that staff members and others in attendance know who your guests are and behave or reach out appropriately.

Giving Donors a Canoe's-Eye View

Save The Bay works to restore and protect the San Francisco Bay and Sacramento-San Joaquin Delta Estuary. Founded in 1961, the organization has spent more than 50 years fighting to stop unnecessary fill, unwise construction, toxic chemical dumping, and invasive plant and animal life. To further that mission, Save The Bay has acquired a fleet of canoes, which it uses to create "outdoor classrooms." Adults take tours, children learn to take water samples, and teachers attend institutes where they get ideas for bringing water ecology concepts into the formal classroom.

All of this offers a prime opportunity to get supporters interested. Save The Bay arranges to bring donors, as well as foundation staff members, along on its educational tours. Or, sometimes it will create special outings just for donors—including short coastal walks for those who don't feel up to canoeing. M. Eliza Dexter, former development director at Save The Bay, remembers one donor who took a canoe tour and shortly afterward gave a higher donation than ever before—but said, "I'm not giving this just because you took me on a canoe trip!" The way Eliza figures it, the canoe trip probably helped the donor "get" why Save The Bay's work was important and increased her sense of connectedness to the organization—even if she didn't realize it!

Because most real events—whether it be a morning at a clinic, listening in on a course, or helping at a shelter—won't offer you and the potential major donor much opportunity for one-on-one conversation, it's not the best time to ask for specific support. If the donor is asking financial questions, however, by all means give the answers, and tell the donor what a difference financial help could make. Being too nonchalant may give the impression that financing is the last thing on your mind.

Create Donor Forums

In addition to inviting potential donors to see the good work your group does, you may want to involve them more systematically, by creating small meeting or discussion groups, either on a one-time or an ongoing basis. For example, The Women's Foundation in San Francisco, created donor circles—small groups focused on grant making in issue-based areas, such as race, gender, and human rights. Each member of the circle makes a commitment of both time and money. Circle members educate themselves about the chosen topic and decide what they'd like to support with their pooled contributions.

Although your organization probably doesn't make grants, there's no reason not to adapt this model to your own purposes. You might, for example, create a donor group around a particular project, such as a community outreach effort or an arts event. The important thing is to give the group members the freedom to make some real choices—in other words, don't just tell them to round up money for a health awareness campaign, but ask them to research and discuss what type of campaign they would be willing to support.

Annual Renewals of Support

Your organization may or may not have formal "memberships," in which supporters receive annual benefits—such as a newsletter or gift—for certain levels of support. Regardless, the one-year anniversary of a gift is usually an excellent time to ask for a renewal of support. When it comes to midlevel and major donors, you'll be talking to people who have already demonstrated a willingness to make substantial contributions—and an entire year may have passed since their last contributions.

A good database will tell you when supporters will reach their one-year anniversary, or you can check your records each month.

Once you've figured out who to ask for support renewal, you'll have to decide how to ask. A letter is okay for rank-and-file supporters, but for your midscale and major supporters, a more personalized request is appropriate.

The midscale supporters should receive, at a minimum, a personalized letter, signed by the executive director and mentioning relevant personal details such as, "We'd love to hear more about your trip to Kenya," or "The summer program that you helped sponsor is attracting record numbers of participants." At the end of the letter, ask for continued support and suggest that, if possible, the person raise his or her donation amount. One good technique is to suggest an appropriate percentage increase above the last gift. But do the math, and tell the supporter what the new amount would be (rounding the number to the nearest sensible amount). Include a reply envelope just as you would with an ordinary mailing. If you don't hear from the supporter, a personal phone call is typically in order.

For major supporters, send a similar letter, but also suggest a personal meeting—perhaps over lunch—to discuss the supporter's renewal. Say that you'll call in a week, and then be sure to do so. The supporter may well renew before the lunch date or meeting. But if he or she instead schedules a meeting with you, it's still a good sign; it shows the supporter's potential interest and gives you an opportunity to reignite that interest and increase the supporter's involvement with your organization. For tips on conducting such a meeting, see One-on-One Meetings, below.

(!) **CAUTION**

Beware the holiday rush. You may find that a number of your supporters' giving anniversaries fall towards the end of the year. Try your best to plan ahead and schedule meetings as early in the season as possible. With this flurry of activity, it is also especially important that gift information is entered into your database immediately. The last thing you want is to telephone a supporter asking for a renewal when the check has already arrived.

Lectures, Small Events, and Parties for Major Supporters

If you don't have ready-made opportunities for donors to see what you do, then why not arrange one? Some organizations sponsor supporter appreciation events, such as a complimentary "major supporters only" dinner preceding a publicly open fundraising lecture or performance. You could also take a donor or small group of donors to lunch, invite them to a reception with your actors, artists, researchers or others, or do something else that resonates with your organization's mission or shows off its work. Note that we're now transitioning into occasions at which it can be appropriate to issue a general request for financial gifts.

For example, an immigrants' rights organization with which I worked invited about 20 major donors and board members to an informal luncheon at the organization's own office. The group selected well-spoken clients to join the group, including a Guatemalan who had survived a massacre and was receiving help to apply for political asylum, and a Laotian student participating in an after-school program that offered a positive alternative to gang membership. Both spoke briefly about their personal circumstances and how they'd been helped by the organization. There was also time during the meal for chatting and getting to know one another personally. When the executive director stood up at the end, thanked everyone for participating, and asked for financial support, one impressed donor wrote a $10,000 check on the spot.

TIP

Lunches don't have to drain the budget. There's no need to pay big bucks for catering or even restaurant take-out. The prevalence of partly prepared gourmet food has made it easy to serve a classy meal without breaking the bank.

Lectures or talks by prominent people associated with your organization can be another effective technique to build support. These can be of any size, from an intimate discussion with a small group of supporters to an event at a larger venue, perhaps even open to the public. Because you will be inviting people who already contribute to your organization, it's usually best to keep these events free or donation based. Look upon a lecture as a vehicle for educating people about a specific topic and how your organization plays a critical role in it. If you do this graciously and well, your guests will find plenty of ways to support you in the future. For example, the San Francisco Girls Chorus, prior to staging "It Is the Silence," based on the diary of Anne Frank, invited major donors to a lecture by the work's composer, Linda Tutas Haugen. (For more about large lectures as special events, see Chapter 8.)

Another popular type of event is what's known in the fundraising trade as a house party. Such an event is usually held at the home of a board member, preferably one who has a fair amount of space and is comfortable playing host (and ideally, paying for the food and drink). Between ten and 40 midscale to major supporters are invited. However, there are many terrific variations on this theme, including holding the event at a gallery or private venue that would otherwise be closed to the public. Nevertheless, as Morrie Warshawski points out in his helpful and compact book *The Fundraising Houseparty*, "There is significance and symbolic power to crossing the portal into someone's private home."

Commonly, many of the invitees are midlevel donors suggested by your development staff. But they should also include friends of the host or of key board members whom you hope to recruit as significant donors. A few representatives of your organization should also attend—some combination of ED, board, and staff members. The object is to create a mostly social evening, in which supporters connect with old friends (don't be surprised at getting lots of "Who else will be there?" questions), get to know new ones, and learn more about the organization. Food (usually hors d'oeuvres or dessert rather than a full meal) and drinks are served. The event should feature remarks by your ED and/or board president about your current programs and why you need more financial support.

CAUTION

The invitation should make the purpose of the event clear. Your guests will resent it if you play a "bait and switch" game, pretending that the party is an ordinary social event when it's actually part fundraiser. Also, you want to make sure that your guests bring their checkbooks or credit cards.

A house party can also include a prominent guest speaker, short video presentation, or similar "extra," but it's not really necessary. Believe it or not, people will be pleased to simply meet the people who run your organization and do its day-to-day work. And because they already care about your cause, it shouldn't be difficult to further inspire them with your enthusiasm, dedication, and stories of struggles and successes. Still, if someone in your organization has a contact with a famous artist, author, or other prominent person whom people would be eager to meet in an intimate setting, don't hesitate to build a house party around this person.

Depending on how much the host will be involved in the food preparation and how experienced he or she is with staging a house party, you may want to do some menu consultation. Food is a powerful symbol. It offers opportunities for your organization to show its personality—whether formal or easygoing, regionally focused, vegetarian, or otherwise. If your organization has an ethnic link, then food prepared in appropriate style is all but essential. The party planners should also make sure the menu doesn't contradict any of the organization's principles. An obvious example would be that a dolphin protection organization probably shouldn't serve tuna.

Plan in advance exactly who will address the group and when this will occur. After the party has gained momentum, but before anyone is thinking of leaving, the host should ask for everyone's attention. If some people are standing, it's often best to ask them to sit in prearranged chairs.

After welcoming everyone and acknowledging the people who helped plan the event, the host should introduce the board chair or ED, who can provide a brief overview of the organization's current plans, upcoming projects, and recent successes. Then someone (usually not the host) whom the partygoers respect and think of as a peer should claim the floor to talk about money. One effective technique is to mention a specific dollar figure the organization needs to fund the projects the ED discussed. For example, "To buy cages and medicines for the rescued birds we'll need to raise $45,000." If you've already raised some seed money (no pun intended), let people know. This shows that others have confidence in the project.

Another effective technique is for the person making "the ask" to state how much they have already given to the project. For example, I recently attended an alumni event at which a classmate of mine was handed the microphone and said, "My husband and I have been steadily giving to various charities over the years, but this year we've agreed to make the biggest gift we've ever given, period, to the college." You can bet that caused some audience members' eyes to widen. I, for one, was thinking, "Gee, if she can do it...."

Finally, the speaker should make a polite but very direct request, such as, "I'm hoping everyone here can help us with $1,000."

Creating Donor Recognition Opportunities

Though a few donors wish to remain anonymous, they tend to be in the minority. At the other end of the spectrum are a few donors for whom heightening their reputations as philanthropists, impressing their peers, or being part of a "club" of high-level supporters is a major motivation for giving.

At a minimum, use your annual report to list the names of all major donors, and as many other donors as space will allow. Newsletters or event programs are also good places to thank groups of donors by name, or perhaps to focus on a particular gift and what it helped to fund. Beyond this, you should talk to individual donors to come up with a way to publicly recognize their contributions (while realizing that not every gift merits a building with the donor's name on it).

Your organization should develop options that allow you to recognize substantial numbers of donors without having to come up with a fresh and creative approach for each one. A wall of tiles or walkway of bricks at your front entrance, each bearing the name of a donor, is one simple yet effective method. Donors don't seem to tire of having their names inscribed in this way—just look around you, at places like the Pike Place Market in Seattle or the beach boardwalk outside Asilomar State Park in California. If a gift went toward a particular use, such as a new piece of playground equipment, a small metal plaque saying "Gift of So-and-So, 20xx" can be affixed to it. For especially large gifts, media coverage may also be a possibility (see Chapter 13).

After making the request, you may want to pass a hat. But it's probably more appropriate to carry on with the party, making it clear where checks and pledges will be collected. Putting a couple of attractive boxes or jars in obvious places in the room works, or you could have certain people designated to receive checks or pledge cards. Those people should wear obvious hats or flowers on their lapels and avoid standing behind any large potted plants. If you'll be accepting credit cards and have a machine that swipes the cards, the money taker should be seated at a table—preferably near the front door.

> ### TIP
> **A pledge is better than a promise.** Some guests will tell you they'll send in a check soon. This is fine, but to help underline the seriousness of this promise, ask them to fill out a pledge card for your records (and as a basis for subsequent reminders). Also, be sure to give the donor an envelope in which to send their check or a sheet of paper with the URL and instructions for giving online.

One-on-One Meetings

Once you've gained experience with midscale and major supporters and gotten to know some of them personally, you'll be ready to take the next step: asking for a large gift. And you'll also be ready to request gifts from people who haven't previously supported your organization.

Because the techniques for approaching existing and new midlevel and major donors are quite similar, they're discussed together in this section, which covers:

- deciding who to ask
- arranging the meeting
- preparing for the meeting
- assembling materials for the meeting
- the psychology of making a request
- holding the meeting, and
- following up with the donor.

Who to Ask to Meet

For your existing donors, the question of who to ask will be partly answered by their personalities and giving histories. A major donor who gave last year should be asked again, and probably asked for more. An enthusiastic midscale donor who has been giving regular gifts—say, of $100 or $200—should be personally asked to take a step up in giving.

There is no reason to be shy about asking people who already support you. Very few contributors start out as major donors—instead, they work their way up from smaller gifts. Signs that they are ready to make a bigger commitment included repeated gifts of a good size and progressively larger gifts.

Another good sign that someone is ready and able to give more is that they're making large gifts to other organizations. You can find this out by keeping an eye on other organizations' annual reports and other publications, or by doing background research on your midscale donors.

CAUTION

There is no "average supporter." Even when this book cites a general rule—for example, that most donors work their way up to large gifts—there are plenty of people who don't fit this mold. Think of the news stories you hear about people who save their pennies for years and then give a million to their alma maters—or to poetry magazines—in their wills. People have different thresholds at which they feel financially secure, and react to suggestions that they increase their support in different ways. If your donor avoids or resists your efforts to coax him or her to write a bigger check, back off on asking for money, but keep doing appropriate things to build the relationship. You never know—the big check you hope for may show up just when you've given up hope.

Finding potential major donors who aren't current supporters of your organization will require a little more research. The best prospective supporters are people who have a known interest in your cause or a similar one, a financial ability to give, and a history of giving to other organizations. Prospects who match only one of these criteria might not be worth a personal visit, but should certainly be added to your database for a mail appeal. Prospects who match two or three of these criteria are probably worth pursuing in person.

TIP
Your board members may be major-gift prospects. Or some of them, at least. In the words of Tony Poderis, development consultant and author, "... a board that does not have members of sufficient wealth or influence to deliver major gifts is not a well-balanced board." The board president should be the one who approaches other board members for major gifts.

Keep your eyes and ears open to find out who the generous members of your community are. One easy place to find their names is at the back of programs from the theatre, symphony, and special events held by other organizations. You can even read the inscribed bricks on other organizations' walls. (It may feel like spying, but everyone does it.) Though you may not know the person, someone on your board or staff may have a link with them, because they are alumni of the same college or members of the same church or other group, for example.

> **EXAMPLE:** Alan, the development director of a school for autistic children, notices that Tedward Goldstein is listed as a major donor by both a local children's hospital and a homeless shelter that focuses on helping families. After research indicates that Goldstein is a retired family court judge with a long history of personal involvement with children's issues, Alan gets on the Internet and finds out Judge Goldstein's college, temple, and other affiliations. One of the school's board members belongs to the same temple. That weekend, the board member casually approaches Judge Goldstein, describes the school's activities, and asks whether he's interested in more information. The judge is intrigued, they invite him to a lecture event, and through careful cultivation, he eventually becomes a major donor.

Focus your research on people with a history of giving. Though you might dream of finding that quiet rich person who, by some miracle, hasn't been approached by any other group, such dreams rarely come true. For one thing, being rich isn't enough by itself—the wealthy widow who spends half her year shopping and the other half traveling to trendy resorts probably is not going to engage in her first act of generosity as a result of your phone call. Remember, statistics show that it's not the upper strata of U.S. society who give the most; members of the middle class—especially those who have become borderline affluent in middle age—are probably your best bets, even for major gifts.

No matter who you ask, find out whether he or she is part of a couple. If you arrange to meet with someone who doesn't make decisions without his or her other half, then you won't get a decision on the day you meet—and may have to either schedule a second meeting or risk having the partner veto a gift without hearing what you have to say. Be ready to meet on an evening or weekend if that's the only time that works for both.

Arranging the Meeting

Once you've identified a likely prospect, it's time to call him, her, or them and suggest a meeting. (You might also send a letter in advance of your phone call, particularly if you're cultivating someone who doesn't know the organization well.) This shouldn't be a stealth mission—simply tell the person that you'd like to discuss the work of your organization and how he or she might support it. Exactly how you phrase this will depend on how well you know the person and how sophisticated he or she is about philanthropy. For the experienced giver, it's enough to say, "We have a project we'd like to share with you, and we could use your help." For someone who's newer to charitable giving (and might think you're just going to ask for an opinion or a batch of brownies for your bake sale), try something more specific, like, "We're trying to fund scholarships for our kids, and I'd like to talk to you about supporting this effort."

You might worry that such an initial phone call would cause any sane person to laugh or hang up, but you'd be wrong. First, almost no one is offended by such a request—you're paying the person a compliment, implying that you believe he or she has a good heart and is successful enough to be able to share. Second, you've given the person enough information to allow him or her to say no. You've been clear and straightforward, which means no one needs to feel uncomfortable.

Many will say no. But don't assume the relationship is over. Six months or a year from now, the person may be receptive to your call—or may even call you. Remember, you're calling someone whom you've already identified as inclined to give money to a good cause. (Some of the truly wealthy philanthropists say that they'd like to give more money away if only they could find causes good enough!) A surprising number of people will say yes to your request to meet. With that simple, short phone call, you've taken a huge step forward.

If you're calling someone who has no previous connection with your organization, the initial phone call will have to be slightly longer. Be ready to tell the person where you got his or her name (particularly if it was through a friend) and why you think your organization might be of particular interest. Sum up what your organization stands for and what it does in a few sentences. (Even if you sent an advance letter, it may now reside in the circular file.) It's particularly effective if you have a specific need in mind, something urgent enough to justify meeting soon (and without cultivating the donor more gradually). Here's a sample script:

> Hello Mr. Scarry, this is Ima Edie from the Society for Train Depot Restoration. We're working to restore the beautiful historic train depots in our community. We believe that, because of your interest in train history and in community improvement, you might be interested in supporting these efforts—particularly because the depot in your neighborhood is scheduled for demolition this summer. Could we meet at your convenience to talk this over?

At this point in the call, the prospective supporter will no doubt have questions, which you should take the time to answer in full. There's no harm in giving information that you will later repeat at a meeting (unless you tell the exact same "amusing anecdote" in the exact same words—it pays to have a good memory for these things when fundraising).

If the person agrees to meet, be ready to suggest a location, such as the donor's home or office, your organization's office, or a restaurant. If the person doesn't want to meet one-on-one but is willing to talk the matter over at further length by phone, go ahead and agree to this. In either case, plan on a minimum one-half-hour's meeting time.

After the phone call, quickly send out a confirmation letter (or email, depending on the person's preferences), mentioning:

- the purpose of the meeting
- the meeting time and location, and
- who will be at the meeting.

And to cover all your bases, call the prospect a day or two before the meeting to confirm.

To Lunch or Not to Lunch?

Professional fundraisers are of mixed minds about whether to meet with major supporters over lunch. On the plus side, it makes the event seem more social and gives you and the prospect a better chance to get to know each other through small talk before getting to the matter at hand. Also, assuming you make clear that you're hosting the lunch, it allows you to act magnanimous before asking the supporter to do the same—a sort of thanks for past support or thanks in advance for future support.

On the minus side, meeting at a restaurant guarantees not only that you'll use up more of your and the supporter's time, but also that the mechanics of ordering and paying will use up a good portion of that time. And you're leaving more up to chance—what if the food that day is terrible, the people at the next table have a screaming match, and the waiter spills the soup on your prepared materials? All of this helps explain why many fundraisers prefer meetings where food doesn't get in the way—such as your organization's offices or the donor's home or office.

If you invite a potential donor to a restaurant, don't pick the fanciest place in town. That might give the supporter some wrongheaded ideas about where his or her money will be going. This is especially likely to be true if the donor earned his or her own money rather than inheriting it—most wealthy people became wealthy by learning habits of frugality early in life.

Preparing for the Meeting

To prepare for your meeting, start by filling in any gaps in your research about the prospect. You'll also want to decide who will attend the meeting. If the supporter has a friend in your organization, that person should attend. Most development professionals prefer to bring a team of two, including some combination of the ED, development director or another gift officer, and any board members, staff, or volunteers who know the prospect or have mutual interests or backgrounds. Not only are two heads better than one, but if one of you leaves the organization, the personal relationship with that supporter won't be broken. Also keep in mind that the ED or someone on the policy side of the organization may be better able than the development director to speak with conviction about your programs and activities.

Use the results of your background research, along with other considerations such as the scope of the project and who else will be asked to contribute, to decide how much and what to request. You'll want to suggest a specific sum (or item, if you're looking for property). Open-ended requests make donors uncomfortable and lead to lowball offers. Obviously, you'll want to ask for an amount the person can afford. But no matter how much the person is worth, look into the person's giving history—to your organization and others—to figure out what gift level will feel right for him or her. Don't get fixated on your goals for this year or campaign—the donor might be more comfortable with a phased gift or one made via a will.

Also, notice whether the donor has typically made gifts of something other than cash, such as property or stock. And consider the larger social context for the gift. If the donor has friends in your organization, how much do they give? In *Fundraising for the Long Haul*, Kim Klein tells stories of donors who have, after discovering that they gave less than their friends or community peers, expressed annoyance that they were not asked for a higher sum.

Try to choose an amount that challenges the person to give a substantial percentage more than they've given before, but isn't off their personal scale. For example, if a donor has given $1,000 for the last couple of years, you might ask for $1,500 or $2,000 more for a special project.

TIP

Supply payment options. A cash gift need not be made in one lump sum. Many people think of their finances in monthly terms, in which case a monthly pledge might suit them. Or, if your prospective supporter has an entrepreneurial streak, suggest a "staged" gift—one that is given piece by piece, conditioned on your organization's success along the way. If you're starting a new program that looks like an uncertain proposition, this can also allay the supporter's fears of pouring money into a sinkhole.

Here's the big question: Who from organization is going to make the actual request for money? You can guess the probable result if you leave this vague—or worse yet, if both of you assume that the ask is the other person's job.

> ### TIP
>
> **Supporters may ask whether (and how much) your board members have given.** Wealthy people like to know that your board members believe in your efforts—and have backed up this conviction with financial contributions. Be ready with the most up-to-date, positive answer you can muster.

Assembling Materials for the Meeting

You may want to assemble or prepare some relevant written materials. This isn't always necessary, however. If the supporter has been involved in your organization for years, invites you to her house for tea, and prefers to think of the relationship as primarily social, showing up with a stack of brochures and budgets could ruin the atmosphere.

For other supporters, however, written information may be welcome and necessary to help clarify your request. In general, the more unusual or specific your request for support—for example, if it's around a new project or a capital campaign—the more appropriate it will be to bring written materials.

Make sure you have your organization's brochure and annual report on hand. Even if you've already sent the supporter an annual report, the person may not have read it carefully (or at all). If the person isn't very familiar with your organization, include some historical information and a detailed explanation of your mission. If you're talking to an existing supporter, you can just focus on what's new since you last met, and what's special about your current request for funds.

If you plan to ask for support for a particular big-deal purpose—a new transmitter for a public radio station, a new building for a school, or a new outreach program—it's a good idea to prepare a case statement:

a two- to five-page document outlining your request. Again, depending on your history with the supporter, this document might also describe your organization's history, mission, clientele and their needs, current goals, money needed to meet those goals, and ability to use the donor's gift effectively. The statement can be tailored to the donor's prospective giving level, explaining how gifts of particular amounts will meet specified needs—for example, "Every gift of $_____ can fund __ days of research into curing a medical condition," or "It will cost $1,200,000 to build a study annex onto our school's library. To start our campaign, we are seeking 20 founders' gifts of $25,000."

Bring any written materials discussing recognition opportunities for particular major gift levels; it's often easier to motivate donors to make large gifts if a brick, tile, or plaque will commemorate their contributions. And if your organization is lucky enough to have been the subject of any press coverage (positive, of course), bring copies of the articles or transcripts. These are great for adding credibility to your own materials.

Always bring a copy of your organization's budget, a specific project budget, and information about what percentage of every dollar you collect supports your organization's work. (See Chapter 4 for information about the importance of showing that contributions support your cause, not just further fundraising.) Not everyone will read a budget, although your supporter may take a keen interest in it if he or she has a background in business or finance. For those who don't enjoy interpreting balance sheets, however, be ready to explain the budget in plain English. In particular, note what parts of the budget represent growth or shifts in program focus.

Be sure to point out how much of your budget is made up of individual (as opposed to foundation or corporate) donations. Even if the percentage sounds less than impressive, you can put it in more realistic terms by saying, for example, that, "Without individual donations, we'd have to gut the entire educational portion of our program."

Some or all of your prepared materials should be assembled into a packet that you can leave with the donor after the meeting is over. Put it all together in a glossy folder. The packet shouldn't be overwhelming—the materials should all look professional and factual and be easy to read and understand.

Fundraising Worksheet 5: Meeting Checklist

Here's a summary of things to consider bringing to your donor meeting:

- ☐ Brochure
- ☐ Annual report
- ☐ Historical information
- ☐ Mission description
- ☐ Case statement
- ☐ Budget
- ☐ Plans for the future
- ☐ Publicity materials
- ☐ Copies of any recent newspaper articles
- ☐ Premiums and recognition opportunities
- ☐ Pledge card
- ☐ Return envelope or instructions for giving online
- ☐ Receipt book

The Psychology of Asking

To get yourself into a frame of mind that will allow you to survive—and even enjoy—the asking process, remember these simple rules:

- Be yourself.
- Be direct.
- Focus on the cause.
- Don't beg.
- Be ready to adjust to opinionated donors.

Be Yourself

Parts of this chapter suggest actual words to use and to avoid when requesting major gifts, so that you won't lie awake at night wondering what the "right" thing to say is. However, no canned script can give you the words to describe what excites you about your organization's work. Although your rehearsed lines may do a good job framing your message, ultimately you'll want to put them aside and speak from the heart.

In short, you need to have a "real" conversation with a real person. How you express things may be completely different from how another development person would. That's good—this is an area where, depending on the individual you are talking to and your own personality, there can be lots of right ways to do things.

Be Direct

You'll go a long way toward making yourself and your supporters comfortable by simply being direct. No matter how much you've done to ease into this relationship, there will come a time when you simply have to look the person in the eye and say, "A gift of $50,000 would provide a crucially important launch for this program." You can't back into it and you can't say it in code. But the wonderful thing is that once the words are out, the air becomes clear. Because you've shown that you're comfortable asking for a specific dollar amount, the prospect has the opportunity to respond with equal directness.

> CAUTION
> **A direct approach may not be appropriate in all cultures.** If you are working with people whose ethnic or cultural background requires or celebrates a more subtle approach, you'll need to adjust your style. In some communities, the potential donor—not you—should mention money first, so as to allow that person to maintain "face" or "honor" if now is not a good time to give.

Focus on the Cause

You'll be more persuasive (and more comfortable) if you can mentally remove yourself from the giver/recipient picture. You're not begging for money for yourself—you're asking the supporter to partner with your organization to achieve a mutually desirable result. Remember, this person has a history of giving either to your organization or others. People don't dip their toes into the major giving waters unless they really do understand that their giving can make a difference in the world.

It will also help if you remember that whether a person writes a big check or doesn't, this isn't about you, your career, or your sinking feeling that you should have signed up for more training seminars. You're simply the intermediary who guides the supporter toward the best path to make a difference. If you are able to paint a compelling picture of the job that needs to be done—the impoverished people who need AIDS medicine, the inner-city child who can grow via your music program, or the sea turtles endangered by a proposed oil refinery—you've done your job.

> **TIP**
>
> **Ever made a major gift yourself?** Then you can mentally picture yourself on the same side of the table as the donor—and if the gift was made to your organization, assure him or her that you've made the same commitment that you're asking for. Also remember what doubts or concerns you had before making the gift and how you overcame them.

Don't Beg

Even with your eye on the cause, it's easy to slip into phrases like, "Could you help us with," "We'd be so grateful if," and "I hope it's not asking too much if …." People who humbly importune a potential donor to make a gift are more likely to get stepped on than they are to get a big check. That's because begging is almost always a sure turnoff. The supporter may wonder whether you lack other community support or are in such dire straits that the money may just plug a leaking hole and nothing more. The supporter may also buy into your own accidental message and think he or she is being asked to support your organization's need as opposed to a greater good. Better to show your excitement about what results the donor's gift could lead to.

Be Ready to Adjust to the Donor's Interests

Plenty of major donors are just plain opinionated. They may have worked hard for their money, and they sometimes want to decide exactly how it will be spent. You may hear things like, "No, I won't give one penny to your group to provide extra funding for area public schools—the whole system is a mess—but I might fund a totally different approach, such as a small school demonstration project, focused on parental involvement."

At times like these, you'll have to be quick on your feet. If the donor's suggestion is closer to your proposal than the donor at first realizes, then it may be worth steering his or her attention back to the proposal on the table. If it's not, however, then it is usually best to express sincere interest in the donor's ideas, explain that you will present them to the decision makers in your organization, and get back to the donor afterward.

Holding the Meeting

Now, all you have to do is meet! Some people wonder at first how they'll have enough to say to fill a whole meeting's worth of conversation. But filling the time is rarely a problem, especially if two people from your organization attend the meeting. And remember, you've got two fascinating subjects to keep you busy: the supporter (practically everyone likes to yak about their background, interests, opinions, and current activities) and your organization.

If it helps you to think about the meeting sequentially, here's the usual play-by-play: You and your teammate should meet a few minutes in advance to share any last-minute information and, if necessary, discuss what you'll talk about as an icebreaker. Once you have all assembled, start with introductions. Remind the supporter that you're there to talk about a specific need or new program your organization is embarking upon, the critical importance of financial support, and how long you expect to spend in this meeting. Work in a little fun small talk, with the idea of engaging the supporter.

The best fundraisers say that if possible, they like to spend the majority—say, around 75%—of any meeting just listening to the supporter. This isn't idle or phony listening. You'll not only be learning more about the supporter's interests and passions, but also refining your understanding of how and why he or she might give. In fact, if the donor is savvy about your field, you may learn information vital to your organization's successful growth.

Journalists will tell you that the best way to interview someone is to ask open-ended questions—questions that don't show off your expertise or imply a conclusion, but simply invite the other person to educate you. Depending on your nonprofit's work, you might ask such questions as: "What do you think are the most important components of a child's education?" "Which of our shows did you like best this season?" or "How do you think our project could be improved?" Find out about the donor's other interests, hobbies, and work. Ask what other organizations the supporter is actively involved in and what he or she likes about volunteering or other experiences there.

At some point, bring the discussion back to the purpose of the meeting. If you've brought written or visual materials, present these in a well-organized fashion. Lay out what your organization is up to and why its work, or a particular project or program, is worth investing in.

But don't get too buried in your written materials. Always remember the things that get you personally excited about the organization. Draw on these and the inspiring conversations you've had with other staff and volunteers to build the supporter's interest. Your enthusiasm for the cause will usually be more convincing than a briefcase full of budgets and brochures. Also try to incorporate specific details, to distinguish your organization from the many others doing good work. Which of the following two statements would you find more persuasive?

- "Our program of reading aloud to children in shelters has been shown in statistical studies to make a significant difference to their psychological well-being and produced measurable improvements in their school performance."

- "I'll never forget the first time I participated in our program to teach at-risk kids to read. I was sitting on a mat on the floor at the back of the shelter on 17th Street with a homeless six-year-old whom I had been working with for a month. When one day she picked up a book and read 'Spot saw a cat,' I literally had tears in my eyes."

The first sentence is relevant, and might work (with a little paring down) in a grant proposal, or even as a subpoint in an annual report. But the second one tells your lunch companion what hooks you in, and will probably bring the work alive for him or her as well. It's all in the details.

Learning to Tell Donors About the San Francisco Girls Chorus

Sarah Clark, former development director at the San Francisco Girls Chorus, says she knew upon starting the position that she loved listening to the girls' performances—in fact, they sent chills up her spine. But to really develop her passion for the SFGC's programs, and to help her explain it to donors, the organization encouraged her to get even further involved.

Sarah took the time to attend an array of behind-the-scenes activities from rehearsals to outreach performances (at which the girls perform at schools in order to encourage budding singers to join) to the SFGC's annual summer music camp. She remembers, for example, an experience she had watching the Level 3 girls (ages 10 to 13) being coached by Judaline Swinkles Ryan: "I saw how the teaching emphasized discipline and excellence as well as musicality. Judaline was clear and direct with the girls about things like not coming in late, and paying attention—she'd say, 'Look at me!' And it made a difference. At the beginning of the half hour I spent watching, they sounded okay. But by the end, they were a tight, focused unit—and they sounded great!"

Through these activities, Sarah also got to know some of the girls who participated. She enjoyed seeing how they could be lounging on the stairs, eating junk food, and giggling together offstage, then turn into serious, poised, beautiful singers onstage. This is the stuff of which donor stories are made.

Before long, it will make perfect sense to start talking dollars. Candidly explain to the prospect exactly how much things will cost and how you arrived at that figure. Mention any in-kind donations that you've received, to show that you're trying to keep costs down, as well as any significant grants or other donations that have come in. This is a great way to tell your meeting companion that he or she isn't the only donor in town, but will join a respectable group of people who believe in your cause.

Finally, once the preliminaries are over, and you've built—or reinvigorated—the potential donor's interest in your case, look him or her in the eye and say something like, "We'd like you to consider a gift of $10,000, to bring us within a realistic distance of our goal." Or if you're asking for a slightly raised renewal of a past donation, you might simply say, "Can I put you down for a renewal at the $2,500 level?" or something similarly optimistic.

Then sit quietly and let the person have a chance to think. Try to look hopeful, while you resist the human urge to chatter or even apologize for a bold request. And make sure anyone who accompanies you respects the donor's need for time to think.

If the person agrees, say thank you and be enthusiastic, but keep your wits about you. You'll need to discuss when and how the payment will be made. For example, if the donor won't write one check, you'll want to explain various payment methods and ask the donor to commit to one. Also, offer a pledge card if the donor won't immediately be writing a check.

Now is also the time to talk about whether the donor is interested in any return gifts or recognition opportunities. But whether you're talking about a brick in a donors' wall, a listing in a program, or a name on the side of a building, you should put your recognition in terms of your desire to thank the donor, not as the donor's "payback" for giving. If the donor wants no recognition or wishes to remain anonymous, perhaps even in printed materials like your annual report, make a careful note of this and make sure your internal systems are geared to respect this wish. You don't want to be in your office the day someone who made an anonymous donation of $25,000 reads about it on your website.

If the person seems uncertain about whether to give, try to get to the heart of the ambivalence. Would he or she like more information about your organization? Does he or she need time to think about the purpose for your request or to consult with a key family member? Is there a slightly smaller gift amount the donor would be more comfortable with? At this point, your job is to try to learn what the person is thinking. Or put another way, you need to listen to the donor's concerns before you can sensibly respond to them.

But make sure you ultimately get a yes or no answer. As one experienced fundraiser told me, "I like to get to the point of hearing an actual 'yes' or 'no'—in fact, I'll follow up on a vague answer with a question like, 'Does that mean you can't make a donation at this time?' This makes it easier for the other person to respond directly, and allows us all to move on."

If the donor says no, don't take this as a flunking grade on your performance (unless you really did screw up the pitch, which is unlikely).

Remember, anyone affluent enough for you to approach has a world of things to consider—how much he or she has given to other causes lately, how his or her own investment portfolio is doing, his or her child's expensive scuba diving hobby, and the request for a major donation from another worthy nonprofit the donor received yesterday.

Also realize that it's not easy for many people to say no, so it's actually part of your long-term development task to make the donor feel better! You might say something like, "I'm sorry this didn't work for you, but I can certainly understand where you're coming from. Of course, we'll keep in touch, and I'll look forward to seeing you at our summer event. Would you mind if I contacted you again next year?"

Some experts recommend trying to negotiate after a "no" answer—for example, by suggesting a lower amount. Obviously, it depends on how the "no" was delivered—sometimes the donor's voice and body language suggest that it was really a maybe, and sometimes you'll get a clear signal that no means no. If you conclude that you really received a flat-out no, it's best not to torture yourself or the donor by trying to turn it around. Thank the person for his or her time, and focus both your attentions on the positive aspects of your time together—you perhaps had an enjoyable lunch or meeting, the other person learned more about your work, and you probably learned something about what ignites or dampens donors' interests. The lessons of that meeting may help you land an even larger gift from this person or someone else further down the road.

TIP

Is that your final answer? Take the advice of Sophie Lei Aldrich, President of the Fu Jen University Foundation, who says that she never thinks of any "no" as truly final. The "no" is just a reflection of the supporter's inclinations and financial situation on that day. Thinking along those lines gives her the freedom to graciously stop the money part of the conversation, while refocusing on fostering her long-term relationship with the supporter.

In the unlikely event that your meeting experience was truly horrible, just remember this: It will make a great story at your next professional fundraisers' gathering.

Follow Up After the Meeting

As soon as you get back to your office, draft a thank-you letter. And do this whether the answer was yes, no, or maybe. Also, promptly enter the pledge and other information into your database, and follow through on any other promises—for more written information or a meeting with another staff person, for example. And if a large gift was made, and you have either collected or put the process on automatic, don't forget to gather other staff and board members to celebrate your success.

Setting Up a Focused Major Gifts Campaign

Everything in life gets easier if you can share your tribulations and victories with others. That's why many organizations organize major gifts campaigns, in which staff and board members get together and schedule a series of gift solicitations. The basic task is the same as described in the previous sections: One or two members of your organization invite a prospect to a meeting or lunch, prepare supporting written materials, and ask for the gift. What's different, however, is that the campaign is time limited. While this typically sets you up for an intense fundraising push, it also lets you know in advance when the hard work will be over—something that can be very helpful when seeking to involve board and staff members. Most major gifts campaigns last for a few months, with each person going to approximately one meeting per week.

To organize all this activity, you'll want to:

- **Develop a list of potential donors.** Carefully go through your existing list of donors and prospects, and meet with board and staff members to identify new prospects, until you have a list of people that's sufficiently large and promising that their reasonably expected donations will be enough to meet your financial goal. Only about half of the people on even the most well-developed list are likely to give, so plan your goals accordingly.
- **Start off with a training.** Get all your participants together at the beginning for a rousing review of your organization's mission and work, any special goals involved in this campaign, and how to conduct themselves at the meetings. You could photocopy portions

of this book for them to review, or bring in an outside trainer. And don't forget that this isn't boot camp—your training should be inspiring enough that it also serves to remind the participants of what is really important about your work and why people will want to fund it. It often helps to bring in a client who's been helped by your organization's work, or a program staff person who can voice how it feels to see the results of the work. This will rev up your volunteers more than a dollar goal ever could (or should).

- **Distribute materials.** The materials you provide to your asking team should include an internal summary sheet describing the campaign and their roles in it, materials they'll take to meetings with prospective supporters, a contact list of participating volunteers, board, and key staff members, "visit record forms" to be filled out after every meeting for future reference, and stationery with envelopes to use for thank-you letters.

- **Assign donor meetings within the group.** As you plan who will visit each prospect, make sure participants are allowed plenty of input and at least a reasonable degree of choice. Be sure your tracking system is good enough to guard against embarrassing mistakes, like more than one participant's contacting the same supporter.

- **Schedule "check-back" meetings over the course of the campaign.** Every few weeks, participants should get together to compare notes, tally results, and exult over or complain about their experiences. This will allow you to fix anything that's impeding the effectiveness of your effort. For example, you might find that a tidbit of factual information was left out of the training, with the result that no one quite understands why a new piece of electronic equipment is absolutely necessary. Check-back meetings also prevent procrastination. And, they're great morale boosters. People who got large pledges help others realize it can be done; and people who had disastrous meetings feel better after turning it into an entertaining story for the group.

- **Tally up your results at the end.** Write up a summary of costs and expenses, a list of who participated and who was visited, and any notes about why the campaign succeeded or didn't meet expectations. Put this at the front of a file labeled "[*Date*] campaign," and include all the visit record forms and copies of other written materials that were used or distributed.

- **Celebrate.** Particularly if the campaign went well, have a final meeting or party in which participants hear the final tally, relax with some food or music, and have a last chance to boast about their fundraising prowess.

RESOURCE

Capital campaigns are slightly different. The campaign described above would be part of your annual fundraising program. This book doesn't cover larger-scale campaigns, including capital campaigns, in which your entire organization may mobilize around a particular project or monetary goal—often to fund something on a scale that dwarfs your normal fundraising activities, such as a new building.

What About Those Billionaires?

Even with slumps in the economy, many of the rich are getting richer—which means that the stock of big-time philanthropists should remain steady. And philanthropy has become chic, with stars advertising their affiliation with good causes, and rich businesspeople upping their "star quality" by being seen at gala fundraisers. The likes of Bill and Melinda Gates, the Waltons (of Wal-Mart), George Soros, and Warren and Susan Buffett have become actively interested in finding ways to use their wealth to change the world. The results are dramatic and visible.

So where's the trickle-down to your organization? Or better yet, the fat check? Many of these new philanthropists say that they'd give away more than they already do if they could only find a worthwhile cause. But don't get too excited until you hear the catch. If you think that foundations and average individual donors are demanding in terms of accountability and results, you ain't seen nothing yet. The philanthropist of today tends to be:

- highly attuned to business models and success strategies
- focused on personal involvement in a cause, either directly or through his or her foundation, and
- eager to see results within a lifetime.

Wealthy people tend to believe that their own skills and know-how accounted for much of their success. They reckon that the business models

What About Those Billionaires? (continued)

they used should be applied to charitable settings, to actually solve problems rather than to bandage them over. They speak of "investing" in programs, not "contributing" to them. The approach vaunted by investment banker Paul Tudor Jones's Robin Hood Foundation says it all: "Since 1988, Robin Hood has targeted poverty in New York City. By applying sound investment principles to philanthropy, we've helped the best programs save lives and change fates." (See www.robinhood.org.)

If the work of your organization involves a problem that's just not likely to go away anytime soon—at least, not without a total overhaul of the U.S. economic and social structure—you might be hard-pressed to attract the attention of these ambitious philanthropic capitalists. Sadly, feeding the homeless or providing shelters for victims of domestic violence might be seen as programs that don't "solve" an ongoing problem. You'll need to have a vision that's groundbreaking and can be implemented efficiently and effectively.

That probably means your organization will already have to be successful and stable—it's one of those classic "it takes money to make money" conundrums. The struggling nonprofit with inexperienced volunteers answering the phones, information scattered between various filing cabinets, and a website that was updated last year (if it exists at all) may inspire more scorn than interest. You may have better luck asking for support in the form of a loan or management advice, some of the alternative giving models that the new philanthropists are exploring.

You'll also find that many of the big-time philanthropists have moved beyond mere check writing and have started their own foundations (though some of them close these down as soon as they discover how much paperwork is involved). If a foundation has been established, you can approach it much like any other foundation—most likely with a formal grant application (see Chapter 10)—if it makes grants publicly available.

Many of these new foundations are trying to eliminate the middleman (that is, your organization) by directly funding grassroots projects (such as an overseas cooperative) or by starting programs of their own. For example, Eli Broad, founder of SunAmerica Inc. and KB Home, put $400 million toward his own educational reform strategy, helping train educational leaders and sponsoring a yearly competition among urban school districts to improve student performance—with a prize of $500,000 in scholarship money to the winning district. Or there's James E. Stowers, Jr., who founded American

What About Those Billionaires? (continued)

Century Services Corp., and pledged a whopping $1.5 billion toward the creation of a center to find a cure for cancer—a disease for which he, his wife, and one of their daughters have all been treated. Such philanthropists aren't content to sit back and write checks. They tend to believe that they've got methods or answers that haven't been tried before. In that sense, your organization's continued existence may be a strike against you. If you had figured out a way to solve the problem at issue, then you could have folded up your tent and gone home by now.

Still, as time goes by, some philanthropists are confessing to their own naiveté, noting the intractability of certain problems and the importance of experience at working a problem. We may yet see a swing back toward relying on existing organizations.

Funds From the Great Beyond: Bequests and Legacy Gifts

Your fundraising efforts with individual donors will doubtless focus on obtaining gifts out of their annual income. However, over the course of a donor's life, he or she may also accrue savings, property, and other assets—and eventually, the donor will have to decide how to dispose of these things at death. While bequests to spouses, children, and other close family members will almost always predominate, some people also plan to leave at least small slices of their estates to good causes. (Average gifts run between $35,000 and $70,000, according to Blackbaud.) And studies have shown that large numbers of other people, both regular donors to charity and not, would consider doing so if asked. This is where you come in.

By reminding donors about the importance of estate planning, and by explaining how their testamentary gifts can benefit your organization, you help everyone achieve their goals. It's a message that resonates particularly well with forty-somethings, even if they're not longtime donors. In fact, studies have shown that two-thirds of Americans age 40 and over already have wills, so you definitely don't want to reserve this message for your older donors.

Still, you'll want to start by letting potential donors know that if they fail to plan their estates, state law will direct that their property be distributed under a one-size-fits-all statutory formula (called intestate succession) that's unlikely to fully reflect their wishes. You'll also want to encourage them to include a charitable giving component within their larger estate plan—not only by demonstrating that your group will put their assets to good use, but also, for your wealthiest donors, by explaining how charitable bequests can reduce (or even eliminate) the amount of estate tax their beneficiaries will owe.

As your organization grows, and its development efforts become more sophisticated, you may want to offer donors a further giving incentive. Estate planning tools with names like "charitable gift annuities," "charitable remainder unitrusts," or simply "life income gifts" allow people to give assets to your organization for investment, but either continue to derive some income from those investments during their lifetime or give your organization the income but require you to return the principal to the donors or their heirs.

This chapter offers a primer on the rules and methods for making gifts through an estate—commonly called "legacy giving," "planned giving," "gift planning," or "deferred giving." However, because of the complex financial and tax concerns involved, this chapter will primarily cover the basics. Most organizations that are large and established either hire legacy giving specialists or attend intensive trainings when they're ready to move into this advanced area of fundraising. Nevertheless, this chapter will describe important steps that you can start taking right now, especially when it comes to accepting straightforward inheritance gifts. It's a time-efficient way to raise substantial gifts.

> CAUTION
>
> **Don't expect your planned giving program to be a quick fix for financial problems.** Because most supporters who include your organization in their estate plans will enjoy good health for many years to come, the typical planned giving program doesn't start yielding results for seven to ten years after its inception. And it may take even longer before you receive substantial income from these types of gifts. Once things get going, however, you should find that the return on your investment of time and effort far outweighs the return on any other sort of fundraising.

For some fundraisers, the most difficult part of developing a legacy giving campaign is to overcome the natural reticence to mention the word "death." Until about 20 years ago, fundraisers had a tendency to wait around politely, unwilling to broach the subject but hoping for a surprise call from someone's lawyer. However, the tide has now turned dramatically—requests for legacy gifts have become a normal part of fundraising requests, whether in person, in newsletters, or on websites.

But there's still more work to be done and plenty of opportunities to reach potential donors who haven't yet gotten the message. Research typically shows that a minority of U.S. residents have included charitable bequests in their wills, while another 14%, at least, would consider doing so.

To help you assess long-term legacy giving possibilities, this chapter addresses:

- what kinds of organizations can attract legacy gifts
- how virtually any organization can handle basic inheritance gifts
- how to roll out your legacy giving program smoothly and effectively, and
- the basics of soliciting and handling more complex life-income gifts.

How to Attract Legacy Gifts

Many people's aspirations to do something noteworthy—such as creating a work of art, making a scientific discovery, or helping to bring about peace in the world—are partly motivated by a desire to achieve at least a small measure of immortality. Of course, they know that they won't really live on through such acts. But, regardless of their religious beliefs, they may take comfort in thinking that their impact will be felt on this earth even after their death.

Your organization can play a role here, by becoming the vehicle through which otherwise ordinary folks can make a lasting difference. The emphasis here is on "lasting." Your goal should be to help donors achieve maximum impact (and recognition, if they want it) through their world-improving gifts. For example, bequests that include a plaque or an inscription with the deceased's name are quite popular (though plenty of givers are content to go without such recognition). Planting a tree in one's name has great symbolic significance. And other forms of remembrance—from published thanks to dedicating a building, program, or scholarship to the donor—are equally effective.

To be well positioned to receive bequests, your organization should have some or all of the following characteristics:

- **It will still be around when the donor's last will and testament is pulled out of the drawer.** This may be difficult for small or new organizations, as well as for those teetering on the edge of financial collapse. It will be impossible for organizations whose sole mission is to accomplish a certain goal and then close up, such as an organization created to build a bicycle trail or free a small group of political prisoners.

- **Your organization's mission, goals, and activities are momentous enough to appeal to someone's idea of a legacy.** For example, a donor would presumably rather imagine, "Upon my death, a new stretch of park will be purchased for my home city," than "My legacy will be to buy a year's worth of gasoline for the bowling league van." Most bequest givers choose nature or science, educational institutions, or arts and cultural organizations to leave money to.

- **Your organization can articulate how legacy gifts will be spent.** Most donors prefer to see that your organization has a clear spending plan in place—preferably applying their gifts toward something lasting, such as an endowment or a capital project, rather than toward covering general operating costs. If your organization has thought about how gifts will be used in advance, the donor will know that you won't spend a large gift carelessly.

- **Your organization offers meaningful recognition opportunities for those who are interested,** such as naming a creek, a building, or another long-lasting monument after the donor. Not every donor will want these, of course. As Audrey Yee, Director of Planned Gifts at the Golden Gate National Parks Conservancy (www.parksconservancy. org), puts it, "While many donors appreciate public recognition, others prefer low-key thanks and anonymity. The motivations of those preferring anonymity vary: Some are modest, some don't want other organizations to see their name and solicit them, and a few have delicate family situations—for example, estrangements where a person left out of the will might be upset at seeing that the money had gone to charity."

- **Your organization inspires enough respect and creates a sufficient sense of personal relationship with its donors,** that they trust you to use their gifts wisely—even though they won't be around to monitor your actions.

- **Your organization does its homework,** including internal education and discussion, so that relevant staff and board members can competently, confidently, and enthusiastically represent your legacy giving program.

- **When you start to offer more complex legacy giving options, such as gift annuities or charitable remainder trusts,** your financial management system will be in expert hands.

> **RELATED TOPIC**
>
> **Don't forget the qualities that bring regular donors to your organization.** For more on these characteristics—such as a timely and viable mission and a good reputation in the community—see Chapter 4.

To be sure, not every donor places "achieving immortality" as his or her primary motivation to make a legacy gift. Some longtime supporters will simply see a legacy gift as their final way of helping out. Those of more modest means may realize that it will be the first time they can make a gift of a substantial size. However, the characteristics described above are no less important to these people. After all, what donors really want to know is whether your organization can deliver maximum impact for their bucks.

Once you've identified the great opportunities to create a personal legacy that your organization can offer, don't be quiet about it. You can and should market your legacy giving options. At a subtler level, introduce messages into your mailed appeals, newsletter, website, or other communications materials that talk about your organization's long-term goals. An article, for example, on "How Our Work Will Affect Your Children's Lives" might allow you to offer some legacy giving information, in a way that more immediate articles (like "Summer Basketball Camp Opens Soon") don't. But you'll also want to approach people more directly, through mailings, seminars, and personal meetings, discussed below.

Handling Simple Inheritance Gifts

Here is some good news for the small, grassroots organizations not yet ready to handle the likes of annuities, remainder trusts, and other sophisticated estate planning devices: The vast majority of legacy gifts are made the old-fashioned way, through wills and simple probate-avoidance devices such as living trusts and beneficiary designations on IRAs, 401(k)s, and other financial and investment instruments.

Transfers of property made through wills and living trusts are known as "bequests." Fortunately, these legal devices are quite simple for a nonprofit to accept. When the will or trust maker dies, the person in charge of handling the estate (usually called an executor, administrator, or successor trustee) simply transfers the appropriate bequest to your organization.

It's perfectly reasonable for an organization to start a legacy giving program by focusing on attracting bequests, and not worry about the more complicated arrangements until the bequest program is up and thriving. In fact, such an approach is advisable, according to Greg Lassonde, owner of Legacy Giving Specialist: "My advice to people starting a legacy giving program is to keep it simple. You can start such a program with as little as 5% of your time—that's two hours a week. There's no point in getting too technical too fast."

Estate Tax Reductions Through Charitable Giving

Most of your donors (or, realistically speaking, their estates) probably won't end up owing any estate tax at all. The estate tax must be paid on the portion of a deceased person's estate that exceeds a statutory threshold—this threshold is often called the estate tax exemption. This exemption amount is very high, making most estates too small to owe estate tax. For deaths in 2013, a person can leave up to $5.25 million without owing the tax. Married couples can share their exemptions, leaving a combined estate worth up to $10.5 million tax free. These exemption amounts will rise with inflation in subsequent years.

Those with estates large enough to potentially owe estate tax will be eager to find ways to reduce their tax burdens—which is where you come in. All gifts to tax-exempt charitable organizations are exempt from estate tax, period. What's more, any amounts bequeathed or otherwise donated on death to charity are subtracted from the value of the estate to calculate the amount on which the estate will owe tax—and whether the estate will be subject to tax at all.

A sizable charitable contribution could significantly reduce the amount on which the estate must pay tax—or eliminate its tax bill altogether. For your wealthiest donors, these are very strong incentives to include some charitable gifts in their estate plans.

CAUTION

Don't cross the line into giving legal advice. The information in this section is intended to help you approach donors and explain how gifts can be made to your mutual benefit. Some of them might not know the first thing about estate planning. However, under no circumstances should you help your donors actually write a will or otherwise plan their estates. You could be held liable for practicing law without a license, and the gift could be invalidated if your overreaching looks like coercion. If your donors need specific advice, they should see a lawyer or financial professional. Also, for help writing a will and engaging in more sophisticated estate planning, Nolo offers highly rated self-help options, including *Quicken® WillMaker Plus* (software with explanatory text); *Nolo's Online Will*; and *Nolo's Online Living Trust*. You and donors can also get free information on wills and estate planning on Nolo's website, at www.nolo.com.

Gifts Made Through a Donor's Will or Living Trust

First, you'll need some basic information about wills and living trusts. A will is a document in which a person both specifies what is to be done with his or her property when he or she dies, and names an "executor" to oversee this process. The person writing a will is usually called a "testator," and those who will receive property are called "beneficiaries." Wills are also useful for taking care of some nonproperty concerns, such as naming a guardian for young children and stating who gets the pets.

A living trust does much the same thing as a will—that is, it allows someone to leave property to chosen beneficiaries. Instead of an executor, the trust maker (called a "trustor") names a "trustee." Usually the trustor chooses him- or herself as trustee until his or her death, when the named "successor trustee" takes over. The successor trustee will oversee transfer of trust property after the trustor's death.

The main technical difference between living trusts and wills is that the legal transfer of property ownership under a will happens only at the donor's death; with a living trust, this transfer happens during the trustor's lifetime. The trustor transfers his or her property into the trust, which technically owns the property, although, as the initial trustee, the trustor generally has the right to use trust property as he or she sees fit; to transfer property into and out of the trust; and even to dissolve the trust altogether.

Living trusts have become quite popular because property left though a living trust avoids probate. Probate is the court process for wrapping up an estate. It can be expensive, time-consuming, and of little benefit to beneficiaries. All property left through a will must go through probate, but property left through a trust skips probate and goes directly to beneficiaries. Also, certain complicated living trusts (such as an "AB trust," used by affluent couples) can help avoid estate tax. Even if they have living trusts, however, many people also write wills, to cover any property that they don't get around to transferring into their trusts before they die.

> ⓘ **CAUTION**
> **Bequests via wills can leave your group nothing.** A common problem that your group should be aware of occurs when donors leave a percentage of their "estate" to charity via their will—forgetting that hardly any of the estate will

Progress Report on Berkeley Repertory Theatre's Planned Giving Program

Berkeley Repertory Theatre, a 44-year-old professional resident theatre company based in Berkeley, California (www.berkeleyrep.org), could always count on getting a "surprise" bequest every year or so. However, around ten years ago, the theatre decided to institute a more formal planned giving program. Here's how Director of Development Lynn Eve Komaromi describes the program's first steps and subsequent developments:

"We rolled out our program with a brochure and an announcement, containing an invitation to join the Michael Leibert Society (named after our theatre's founder). We sent this package to our longest-time patrons; those who'd been with us for around 30 years. Our reasoning was that this group was not only loyal to the theatre, but likely getting to an age where estate planning was on their minds. A handful of people responded, as did some members of our board. You can't expect people to instantaneously put you into their wills. It's a thoughtful process, which typically requires meeting with an attorney and deciding on issues like which family members to take care of and what organizations to include.

"To acknowledge our Leibert Society members, we host a lunch once a year, at which they meet someone special, such as the artistic director. We also profile one or more of them in an article in our playbill at least once a year, in which they describe their decision to include the theatre in their estate plans. And we list each one of their names in every theatre program.

"That list of members keeps growing. Every season, some half dozen more people join. Some are, I think, encouraged by seeing their friends' names on the list. Others respond to the mail and email messages that we send annually to long-time donors and patrons. We also created a video, featuring personal interviews with patrons who've included Berkeley Rep in their estate plans.

"We do our best to find out who should be added to the Society list, by asking them to contact us or sign a letter of intent saying that they either plan to put us in their will or already have. With all of that, we still receive the occasional surprise gift!

"Everyone who has joined so far plans to make a gift through a will or living trust. We haven't engaged in any sophisticated planned giving instruments such as CRTs or gift annuities. The next question for us will be whether and how to accept gifts of real estate."

actually pass through probate. In other words, they've separately arranged to have so many major assets pass automatically to a named beneficiary (a joint owner of a house, perhaps, or a person designated on a payable-on-death account) that few assets remain within the will's control. If you're in conversation with donors about bequests, encourage them to speak to their lawyers or to separately name your group as a beneficiary of a particular asset. The "nothing's left" problem can be easily avoided once it's been identified.

Neither a will nor a living trust needs to be written in legalese, and neither requires the help of a lawyer. Your donor should have no trouble naming your organization as one of the will or trust beneficiaries. The primary issue is simply making sure that whoever is handling the estate can clearly understand which of the world's many charities the deceased person had in mind to receive the property. Whether the donor uses a will or a living trust (or both), all the donor needs to do to leave your organization a gift is to:

- accurately state the full legal name of your charitable organization (for clarity, it helps to include your tax ID number, but this isn't required)
- state your organization's location (again, for clarity, it's good to state the address, but city and state are enough), and
- describe the gift, as well as what the donor expects you to do with it.

To help donors assemble the information listed in the first two bullet points above, prominently display it on your website, your newsletters, and any brochures or other communications related to planned giving. (A donor who is preparing an online will at 11 p.m. and can't find key information on your website may decide to skip the gift.)

CAUTION

Be ready for surprise gifts. The donor can do everything necessary to leave your organization a gift without your involvement—which means that you may not know about the intended bequest, or know how much it is worth, until after the donor has died. Studies show that this is exactly what happens in one out of three cases. I'll explain how to encourage donors to advise you ahead of time.

Types of Gifts

Money is hardly the only asset transferred through wills or living trusts. Most people accumulate copious amounts of other property, far more than they themselves are aware of—everything from clothing to cars to jewelry to childhood journals. Therefore, when a person sits down to draft a will, he or she will have to find a logical way to distribute both the money and the property. The options for types of gifts that the donor might make to you or others include:

- cash of a particular dollar amount (called a "general bequest")
- a percentage of the total value of the donor's estate (a particular type of general bequest called a "percentage bequest")
- a particular item of property, such as real property (land), personal property, such as a car, painting, or refrigerator, or a financial instrument, such as stock certificates (called a "specific bequest")
- a remainder of the donor's estate, after all the other gifts have been made to other beneficiaries, and all debts and taxes have been paid (called a "residual bequest"), or
- a portion of the estate that will go to your organization only if the originally intended beneficiary dies before the donor (called a "contingent bequest").

Restrictions on How Your Organization May Use the Gift

After deciding what type of gift to give your organization, the donor's next task is to specify how the gift must be used. For your purposes, it's best if the donor chooses the broadest possible drafting language, stating, for example, that the gift is "to be used for its [your organization's] general purposes." This is what's called an "unrestricted gift."

Unrestricted gifts can be put toward any uses your organization thinks appropriate, within its mission. But few people will be willing to give you what amounts to a blank check. Instead, you'll have to respect the fact that many donors will specify purposes toward which the gift must be put (called a "restricted gift"). For example, the donor might state that the gift is to go toward your organization's endowment; that it can be used only for a particular program; or that even more conditions must be met, such as "to be used only for support of hatha-style yoga during the summer children's program."

You're legally bound to follow the restrictions stated in the donor's will to the extent possible and to track the gift funds carefully within your organization's accounting system. I don't need to tell you, however, how frustrated your organization might feel when trying to follow a detailed set of restrictions or conditions, especially if some of them are inappropriate or incoherent. In the yoga example above, for example, suppose you no longer offer yoga? Or, suppose you do offer yoga, but have replaced your hatha program with Iyengar yoga? Although your organization may have some flexibility in cases where carrying out the donor's wishes would truly be impossible, you'll nevertheless need to consult a lawyer about any significant changes in how you use the gift.

If you have a chance to talk to the donor about his or her intention to leave you a restricted gift, it makes sense to remind the donor of the potential difficulties of too narrowly describing the gift's intended purposes. Explain that while you'll do everything possible to respect the donor's wishes, hopefully many years will pass before the gift is actualized, and binding your organization to something that may no longer be important won't honor either your organization's needs or the donor's intentions.

Obviously you can't write the donor's will for him or her, but as an alternative, you might suggest tying the gift to more general purposes that the donor will nevertheless be excited about supporting. Another approach is for the donor to tie a gift to narrowly defined purposes, but ameliorate it by adding a sentence along the lines of, "If the gift cannot be used for these intended purposes, it may be put toward such purposes as the board of directors or trustees decides."

You can also encourage the donor to make a nonspecific gift to your organization while at the same time writing a separate letter, outside the will, in which the donor expresses his or her wishes for how the gift is to be used. While this type of letter isn't legally binding, it should help the donor feel that his or her voice will be heard by your group's board when the gift is received.

! CAUTION
Update your database or mailing list when a bequest donor has died.
The last thing you want is for family members, who no doubt know of the donor's generosity to your organization, to receive one of your regular mailings, addressed to the dead person, requesting more funds.

Can You Count on Receiving This Gift?

Even if you have been told that a donor has included your organization in his or her will or living trust, don't forget that—as in those Hollywood scenes, where shocked family members sit around the table while a lawyer delivers the bad news—both wills and living trusts can be, and often are, changed. If, over the course of the donor's long life, the donor becomes bored or disappointed with your group, or simply shifts focus to another group, he or she might rewrite the will or living trust without telling you. Fortunately, such changes are relatively rare, especially because many donors make bequests to more than one charity in the first place.

Another concern often expressed by nonprofit fundraisers is that disgruntled family members might go to court and contest the will. Rest assured that contested wills are also rare, particularly because the family member would probably have to prove either that the donor was mentally incompetent when writing the will or living trust, or that your organization used fraud or exerted "undue influence" on the donor. Both of these are presumably unlikely scenarios.

While chances are reasonably good that you'll get any legacy gifts that donors have told you about, you can't count on them until they are sitting on your desk (or in your parking lot). Above all, don't enter such gifts into your organization's budget, break ground for the intended new building, or otherwise change your organization's plans in anticipation of a particular legacy gift.

Gifts Made Outside a Donor's Will or Living Trust

Wills and living trusts are not the only methods by which estate gifts can be transferred. The simplest probate-avoidance technique is to name a person or an organization as the beneficiary, upon death, of specified property, such as a bank account, life insurance policy, or retirement plan. These financial instruments usually require the naming of a beneficiary, so the donor doesn't have to take any extra steps—except perhaps to fill out a change of beneficiary form—to choose your organization.

First Steps Toward Attracting Inheritance Gifts

Your organization could just go about its business, never planning for the certainty that key donors will eventually die, and hoping for surprise windfalls. Although you may receive the occasional gift this way, you'll be much more successful if you ask donors to actually consider including your organization in their estate plans.

Get Your Legacy Giving House in Order

Your first step is to create a plan to attract bequests. Hold a meeting among your board, ED, and development staff to reach agreement on the following issues:

- **Your organization's ability to attract significant amounts of inheritance gifts.** Determine whether your organization has the characteristics that legacy donors are seeking.
- **Your organization's ability to actively solicit and appropriately handle inheritance gifts.** Also consider how far you want to go with your program: Will it be limited to simple inheritance gifts, or is your eventual goal to offer your donors more complex giving arrangements, such as life income gifts?
- **The types of gifts you're willing to accept.** Cash gifts are a no-brainer, but what about gifts of stock in a private corporation, interests in a limited partnership, or other financial instruments? Unless you have a board member or staff person competent to deal with these types of arrangements, you could end up squandering a potentially valuable gift. Gifts of property are an even iffier proposition. Real property (land or houses) can certainly be valuable—but such gifts can also create problems and even substantial liabilities if they come with environmental problems, long-term tenants, or other baggage that makes a quick sale impractical. (Some nonprofits attempt to reduce their risk by limiting gifts to "marketable" property, but remember that donors may not realize the potential liability problems.) And, gifts of personal property can simply be a hassle, if

you have to arrange for the property to be sold or hold an estate sale yourself.

- **How your organization will use inheritance gifts.** Remember, the donors will be eager to hear that their gifts will have a deep and lasting impact.
- **Your initial budget for staff time and training, explanatory brochures, volunteer mobilization.** Consider these and other costs of instituting the program and communicating with donors.

Plant a Seed in Your Donors' Minds

Step Two is communicating your bequest giving plan to your donors. Some of them might need a reminder to plan their estates (though probably not your older donors—a whole industry exists to remind them). But you do need to remind your donors how satisfying it will feel to leave a world-improving legacy, via your organization.

At this point, you should be talking to all of your donors, not just the affluent ones. In fact, your low- to moderate-income donors might be eager to leave you a bequest gift, in part to offset their inability to make larger annual gifts from their income. As Audrey Yee of the Golden Gate National Parks Conservancy explains it, "I think of planned giving as a hybrid of the other individual giving models. You have your annual gifts, your major gifts, and your planned gifts, and you can view each in some respects as a subset of the other, or all of them as intersecting circles. For example, an annual giver might become a planned giver without ever becoming a major donor. This is especially common when an annual giver needs the money during his or her lifetime, but is sufficiently interested in your organization to want to help as soon as he or she can."

Greg Lassonde echoes this analysis: "I'd estimate that only about 10% to 20% of legacy gifts come from major donors. That makes legacy gifts special—so much thought goes into them, by people who may have never before had the means or opportunity to make a substantial gift."

The simplest way to start conveying estate planning information is within your existing newsletter, brochure, or website. Make sure that any section that discusses general giving also mentions inheritance gifts. Many organizations simply insert a shaded box into every newsletter, containing the central message and key information, including:

- a reminder of the importance of estate planning
- a suggestion that supporters consider planned gifts
- the great uses to which their gifts would be put
- any recognition or naming programs
- your organization's legal name, and
- who to contact for more information.

Others add a checkbox to their donation reply cards, saying something on the order of "Please send me information on how I can make a bequest gift to your organization through my will or living trust," or "I have included your organization in my will or living trust."

> **CAUTION**
>
> **Terms like "legacy giving" and "planned giving" may mean little to your donors.** Although these are common terms in fundraising circles, your donors may have no idea what they mean. Therefore, your communications materials should avoid headings like, "Have you considered a planned gift?" Better to stick to plain English, with headings like, "You can leave a living legacy," or "Please consider including [*name of your organization*] in your will or living trust."

Another great form of encouragement is to tell stories of other donors. Save the Redwoods League uses this strategy nicely, as shown in the example from its newsletter below. Sharon Rabichow at Save the Redwoods League, says, "Our work really comes alive when it's told through people. The stories about why our members make planned gifts stir similar emotions in our other donors, motivating them to leave a legacy as well."

Again, such stories could go in your newsletter, on your website with links from your Facebook page, or even in your annual report. They can be anything from lengthy profiles to small boxes with photos and mentions of the intended gift (particularly appropriate for your website, in the section describing donation possibilities). You'll need the donor's permission, of course, or that of his or her family if the donor has already died. But there's no need to wait until the donor is gone to celebrate a planned posthumous gift—many donors will be pleased to get credit for their generosity while they're still around to appreciate it.

Your anecdotes should briefly highlight each donor's personality, special interests, and values during his or her lifetime, and explain how the gift

A Commitment as Great as the Redwoods

Debra and Rich Whitall fell for the redwoods — and each other — as students at Humboldt State University in Arcata, California. They love redwoods so much that Debra changed her major to forest hydrology so she could help protect the forests, and Rich worked his way through college as a forest firefighter throughout the redwoods' range. They were even married in a redwood grove before they graduated in 1984. Fifteen years later, they showed their commitment to the redwoods again, by including Save the Redwoods League in their estate plan.

"It just made sense to start considering who is really doing the kind of long-term work that we value," said Rich, referring to their estate beneficiaries.

Debra and Rich Whitall made a commitment to include the League in their estate plan.

"The ancient groves are such a powerful reminder that we humans have a huge responsibility to honor and preserve the remaining wild places," said Debra, a social scientist with the U.S. Forest Service in Washington, DC.

For information on including the League in your estate plan, visit savetheredwoods.org/development/planned-giving.shtml, or contact Sharon Rabichow, Major and Planned Gifts Associate, at (888) 836-0005 ext. 828 or srabichow@SaveTheRedwoods.org

Reprinted with permission

allowed, or will allow, these interests and values to be furthered. Make clear how your organization has made excellent use of the gift (if it has already been received), and that it will have a lasting impact. Positive quotes from family members are also reassuring to donors fearful of disappointing their rightful heirs.

Be Ready to Respond to Interested Donors

After you start putting the word out, you're bound to get some responses from interested donors. This is where some organizations fall down on the job. Perhaps because they never believed in the possibility of success, they fail to put together materials or a plan in advance. The result is that donors may feel alienated and/or lose interest in the whole enterprise.

The appropriate plan for your organization depends partly on the types of overtures you made in your marketing materials. For example, if people checked a box saying "Please send me more information," then of course you'll want to have an explanatory brochure or other information at the ready. (The same information should be available on your website.) If you've asked people to check a box saying they'd like to be contacted to discuss this matter, then you'll want call right away to offer more information—whether it be immediate details over the phone, written materials, or a sit-down meeting to further explore the possibilities. Try to make personal contact if at all possible.

Approach Prospective Legacy Donors Who Haven't Expressed Interest

Consider how and whether to approach the topic of inheritance gifts with appropriate long-term or major donors who haven't spoken up, perhaps because your newsletter and other messages haven't made an impression on them. As with any major gift request, scheduling a personal meeting may be appropriate. (See Chapter 6 for more on arranging and holding personal meetings with donors.)

Legacy giving isn't a topic about which you'll be scheduling a separate meeting with every donor, or even with every major donor. Ideally, you should approach donors whom you, or one of your board members, know well enough to comfortably offer this giving option. If you keep your ears open, you may pick up verbal clues. For example, Berkeley Repertory Theatre's Lynn Eve Komaromi remembers talking to a donor who light-heartedly said of her annual gift, "Well, I guess I'll keep doing this for as long as I live!" That gave Lynn Eve an opening to suggest that the donor think about giving even after she is gone—and they immediately scheduled a meeting to discuss it further.

Beyond the donors whom you're close to personally, the most likely ones to approach are those who fall into at least one of the following categories:

- **Committed supporters of your organization.** These may be major donors, with whom your organization has built a solid and warm relationship. Also look for longtime volunteers and donors who've been making gifts for years, even if only $10 a year.
- **Donors age 45 and older.** This is the age at which most people write at least a basic will or living trust. And the younger they are, the more likely they are to include a charitable donation. (But not everyone will be ready for will writing; statistically, people at age 45 can expect to live from 40 to 45 more years, and many won't yet be interested.)

- **Donors of any age who are childless or widowed.** Such folks are more likely to have considered their lack of natural heirs and the prospect of a planned gift.
- **Donors with wealthy children.** The reason is obvious.
- **Younger donors who work in a field like law, accounting, or medicine.** These professionals are conditioned to be realistic about preparing for their death (although they may still be procrastinating about writing a will).
- **Homeowners.** Something about buying a house spurs people to write a will. And longtime homeowners in urban areas may be living in an appreciated asset, and so have a good-sized estate to plan around, regardless of their current income level.

As with all donor interactions, success in attracting legacy gifts comes down to doing your research and understanding each donor's individual interests.

> **TIP**
>
> **Meeting with prospective planned givers may jump-start their annual giving.** According to planned giving professional Linda Solow Jaffe (currently with Special Olympics Northern California), "I've had many experiences where I've helped a donor who had never once made a major gift look into our planned giving options—and, as a result of the conversation, the donor's level of excitement about our organization rose so much that he or she began increasing the level of his or her annual gifts, as well! The lesson is to make every donor aware of your planned giving program, if only through a mention in your newsletter or website."

In preparation for any legacy donor meeting, write up a statement explaining how your organization will use a significant gift. Be specific about how the gift will be applied toward an important, lasting goal (such as opening a new wing to your clinic or saving a beach from development) or will support the donor's favorite programs and activities (such as a literacy program that will help bring reading to future generations). Your written statement should also briefly explain what sorts of gifts your organization is in a position to accept (or can't accept, such as real property). If your organization offers more complicated giving vehicles, explain these possibilities.

The end of a conversation about a posthumous gift is quite different from one about a current major donation, since the donor won't open up his or her checkbook on the spot. A good way to close the discussion is to ask anyone making a planned gift to stay in touch as he or she takes the various practical steps required, so that your organization can appropriately recognize the planned bequest. To be even more proactive, ask whether you can follow up with any program material tailored to the person's interests (particularly if he or she seems inclined to make a directed gift), and offer to send your nonprofit's IRS exemption letter and other tax-related information for the donor's lawyer or estate planner.

Software programs can generate expected income amount for annuity based on life expectancy at various ages.

And, after your program has a significant number of participants, you may also want to invite them to join in events or groups geared toward honoring planned gift donors.

> **TIP**
>
> **Get your board on board.** As committed members of your organization, your board members are good prospects for planned gifts. One effective way to enlist them is for one member to take the floor at a meeting, and say, "I've included this organization in my will—who else is willing to commit to this?" Assuming the eventual answer is quite a few, you'll want to ask board members to help recruit others. After all, a pitch that begins with the fundraiser's own story of setting up a planned gift to your organization stands a better chance of success.

Develop Meaningful Ways to Recognize Legacy Donors

Now that you've gotten your donors thinking about the benefits of leaving your organization gift through their wills or other transfer devices, you need to find ways to thank them. It's an interesting situation, because the gift hasn't been made yet, and you may not know for sure how large it will be—yet waiting until the donor's death to recognize his or her generosity would be nonsensical.

First, you need to find out what inheritance gifts lie in store for your organization (whether from major donors or others). The only way to get this information is to actively solicit it. (A minority of donors proactively advise the nonprofit of their planned gifts.) For example, your reply cards for fundraising appeals might include a box to check, saying, "I have included your organization in my will or estate planning arrangements." Follow up on those who check "yes," by calling to thank them and ask whether they'd like to discuss the uses to which their gift might be put and recognition opportunities. Your newsletter or website might also ask your donors to advise you if they've named your organization in their will or other estate planning arrangements.

Be Ready for Memorial Gifts

If a donor who cared deeply about your organization dies, his or her family members may ask friends to make a charitable memorial gift in lieu of sending flowers. Memorial gifts not only require special handling, but you'll also need to be ready to spring into action quickly. Be prepared to:

- Provide the donors a specially designed card that they or you can immediately mail to family members, offering condolences and advising that they have made a gift in memory of their loved one.
- On your website, for those wishing to donate online, add a box for donors to check indicating a memorial gift, followed by a space where they can fill in the deceased person's name.
- In addition to sending the usual thank-you letters to the actual donors, notify family members of the amount of each gift made in memory of the deceased.
- List memorial gifts under the name of the deceased in your annual report, newsletter, and website, as appropriate.
- If the deceased person was well-known and the gift pool may be large, be ready to quickly establish an ongoing special fund in the deceased's name.

You might send memorial gift donors a brochure with your acknowledgment letter and add them to your mailing list, at least for a year or two. Even if they weren't interested in your cause before, their departed friend's commitment to it may inspire their interest. And they'd probably be interested in receiving your newsletters for a while, to see how their gift was spent. But don't be surprised if their gift was just a one-time deal—and be sure to remove them from your mailing list if they show no interest after a reasonable period of time.

Next, you need to find special ways to thank your bequest donors. Many of the familiar ways remain appropriate, including a thank-you letter or lunch invitation after you first hear about the bequest and a mention in your annual report or event program. (Names can be removed a year or two after the gift is actually made.) However, you should also consider how to give unique recognition to this group. After all, they haven't merely given you a slice of their income; they've promised you a potentially substantial amount of their worldly goods, as one of their last acts on this earth.

TIP

How should you treat contingent bequests? Some donors—for example, married persons with no children—may name your organization as a "backup" beneficiary in case their spouse or another primary beneficiary dies before or at the same time they do. It's wonderful that they're doing so, but given the unlikelihood that you'll ever receive the gift, do they really deserve a place at your legacy luncheon table? According to Greg Lassonde, "You'll obviously want to thank the donor if you find out about such a contingent bequest, but most organizations don't go beyond this when it comes to recognition."

CAUTION

Distinguish the living from the dead when creating your recognition lists. If your annual report, newsletter, program, or website lists legacy donors by name, be sure to asterisk those who are already deceased, and explain this in a footnote. (Otherwise, some people may assume everyone on the list is dead, a potentially very disturbing miscommunication.)

For gifts that are particularly large and might inspire future gifts, you might create a fund bearing the donor's name, dedicated to a particular purpose—the Warner Scholarship or the Guerin Endowment, for example. To ensure the posterity of the gift, it's possible (after some internal planning and policy decisions) to make it an "endowed gift." With an endowed gift, your organization invests the gift, and uses only a portion of the interest earned to carry out the gift's purposes. Creating a named fund or endowment not only gives posterity to the donor's name, but also allows you to leverage the donor's gift, by using it to attract others.

For the larger pool of more modest gifts, some organizations create a special "society," with an honorary name.

What Should You Name Your Society?

For the unimaginative, a host of generic names are possible, like "legacy society" or "heritage club." It's far more compelling, however, if you follow the lead of those organizations that name their group after an honored person, such as one of the organization's founders, like Berkeley Repertory Theatre's "Michael Leibert Society." (This so-called "society" isn't a separate legal entity; it's just a way to name a segment of your donors.) An added advantage to naming your group after a known person is that some people treat this as akin to a memorial gift, and make bequests in the named person's honor.

Other organizations choose a name that's inspiring for other reasons: as with the Golden Gate National Parks Conservancy's "Silver Lupine Circle," named after its successful efforts to replant the silver lupine in order to create a habitat for the endangered Mission blue butterfly.

Once you have your society in place—and even if you don't institute an actual society—consider these additional ways to honor your legacy gift donors:

- Invite them to an annual thank-you lunch, tea, or dinner, just for society members (the San Francisco Symphony, for example, holds an annual lunch at which the members listen to chamber music, meet the musicians, and receive a small gift such as a chocolate musical note).
- Invite them to volunteer events (the Golden Gate National Parks Conservancy, for example, has invited its legacy donors to spend a morning at one of their native plant nurseries in the parks, and serves them an organic box lunch).
- Create bonding opportunities (the Golden Gate National Parks Conservancy holds fireside chats, evenings around a campfire, and invites legacy as well as major donors to watch Fourth of July fireworks together from a local park).
- Establish a walkway, a wall, or another place where society members' names can be inscribed.

- Have your ED or a board member visit society members occasionally, especially those whose health doesn't permit them to attend events.
- Send regular letter reports or greeting cards with news of your organization's doings, and perhaps a small gift, such as a pin commemorating their society membership.

You should also, of course, include your legacy society donors in the same activities and opportunities as your other donors, such as tours of your facilities and holiday parties. If, however, certain donors have made restricted gifts, try to tailor your efforts to their interests. For example, if the donor has promised a bequest for the free meals portion of your homeless services, make sure he or she is invited to attend during one of these meals.

Preview of Other Legacy Giving Arrangements

As you've seen, gifts made via wills or living trusts require very little action from your organization. Most of the hard work is done by the donor, possibly (but not necessarily) with the help of a lawyer. After the donor's death, the estate's executor, administrator, or successor trustee will ensure that your organization receives its due.

Life income gifts are another matter. Most of them are designed to take advantage of favorable but complicated tax laws. Typically, they involve a donor gifting money or property to your group in exchange for your commitment to pay the donor regular interest income for life. You'll need the help of a professional, either an in-house staff person, or an outside consultant or bank, to set up and run this kind of program. For this reason, this section will simply give you a taste of the possibilities.

TIP

Your local community foundation may be willing to handle life income funds on your behalf. Many are already accustomed to creating pools of donor funds and handling complex financial arrangements for small nonprofits. Talk to the larger foundations in your area to find out what they have to offer.

Below are the main types of life income arrangements and their close cousins. Which one is best for any particular donor depends on the donor's current level of assets, need for predictable future income, and various income tax and capital gains tax considerations.

Charitable gift annuity. During his or her lifetime, the donor gives the nonprofit either cash or another asset (often real property), and the nonprofit in return pays the donor (or another beneficiary) an annual, fixed income (an "annuity") for life. The amount of the annuity is negotiated at the outset between the donor and the nonprofit. To produce the income that will hopefully cover the amount of the annuity, the nonprofit invests the assets or proceeds from the sale of property (or, in the case of real property with tenants, may manage and continue to rent out the space). When the donor (or another beneficiary) dies, the nonprofit becomes sole owner of the assets and can use them for its charitable purposes.

Deferred payment gift annuity. This is much like the charitable gift annuity described above, except that the donor decides not to start receiving annual annuity payments until a later date, usually at a specified age. This option is most often chosen for tax reasons, particularly by younger donors (who can claim a tax deduction in the year the gift is made, but don't have to worry about paying tax on the annuity payments until they are older—and presumably in a lower tax bracket).

Charitable remainder annuity trust. The donor gives assets over to a trust, and a trustee manages and invests the assets, then makes payments to the donor (or another beneficiary or beneficiaries) out of the trust's income and, if necessary, out of its assets. This continues for either a specified number of years or for the rest of the donor's life. The amount and rate of payments are established when the trust is set up. When the term of years ends or the donor dies, the nonprofit gets what's left in the trust. Though very similar to the charitable gift annuity, the charitable remainder annuity trust is preferred by some donors for capital gains tax reasons. (In particular, with gifts of securities or other property that a donor purchased a year or more ago and that have appreciated in value, transferring them to a trust completely bypasses the capital gains tax system. Contrast this with a donor who transfers appreciated securities to a nonprofit for a charitable gift annuity and will still have to pay tax on a portion of their value.)

Charitable remainder unitrust. A donor gives assets over to a trust, and the trustee manages and invests the assets, then pays the donor an annual percentage of the trust's current value (meaning that the amount the donor receives may go up and down over the years, depending on how the investments are doing). After the donor dies, remaining assets go to the nonprofit. This has capital gains tax advantages similar to the charitable remainder annuity trust. The unitrust is also good for donors who aren't as interested in a fixed income, but are willing to gamble that the value of the trust will go up, and that their payments will therefore increase.

Charitable lead trust. This is sometimes called a reverse charitable remainder trust, and for good reason. The donor creates a trust, out of which payments are made to the nonprofit for a specified number of years or until the donor's death. When those years are up or the donor dies, the principal assets are returned to the donor or whoever else the donor has named as a beneficiary. Donors enjoy the same capital gains benefits as with other trusts, as well as estate tax benefits when the property is transferred to their heirs. A charitable lead trust is especially appealing to those donors who want to leave a particular piece of property to their heirs, but also want to put it to use both philanthropically and for tax purposes in the meantime.

Pooled income fund. A group of donors contributes assets to a particular fund at a nonprofit, and the nonprofit invests the pooled assets and pays out the earnings to the donors. When each donor dies, the nonprofit may withdraw that donor's share of the fund for its own charitable use. This is a good option for schools, hospitals, and other nonprofits whose donor base doesn't include many people with enough money to warrant setting up an individual charitable gift annuity.

Retained life interest. The donor transfers ownership of a piece of real property, such as a home or farm, to the nonprofit, but retains the right to live there for life.

RESOURCE

Need to keep up to date on laws and practices concerning bequests and other forms of legacy giving? See the following resources:

- the website of the Partnership for Philanthropic Planning, at www.pppnet. org. This is the standard-setting organization in this field, and it publishes an online magazine called *The Journal of Gift Planning*.

- the website of consultant Phil Murphy, at www.plannedgivingcoach.com. This site contains free information, including sample letters to prospects regarding both bequests and life income gifts.

- *Planned Giving Today,* a monthly newsletter written in plain English with a marketing focus, available by subscription at www.liebertpub.com/pgt.

Special Events

A sk any professional fundraiser to name best or worst fundraising memories, and you're likely to hear about special events. Special events can be the highlight of your fundraising year—grand occasions that mobilize volunteers, bring you into direct contact with your friends and supporters, and create a festive atmosphere for everyone involved. Unfortunately, special events can also set the stage for huge public embarrassments and spectacular losses of money. I know one fundraiser who still shudders when she thinks about the 600-person picnic where the person with the one and only restroom key disappeared.

Special events come in all shapes and sizes. Their common denominator is that, by definition, they are occasions outside your nonprofit's usual activities, where your membership and/or the public is invited to attend and support your work, usually by paying an admission fee or buying things once they get there. The more common special events include dinners, auctions, fairs and festivals, lectures, benefit concerts, home and garden tours, tournaments, contests, sporting events, walkathons, garage sales, and bake sales. Whole books have been dedicated to exploring the array of possible special events—and they still don't cover everything that an innovative mind might envision.

Rather than attempting to describe how to plan and put on every possible type of special event, this chapter focuses on how to make your special event serve the focus of this book: raising money. This is an important distinction, because not all special events are intended to serve primarily as fundraisers. One of the first questions that experienced development pros ask when considering a potential special event is, "Will this be a fundraiser or a friendraiser?" It's an especially legitimate question given a report by Charity Navigator, a watchdog group, finding that special events are an inefficient way to raise money, bringing in an average of $1 for every $1.33 spent on them, and generating only 15% of total individual contributions. The exceptions are often large groups with well-connected boards and compelling causes.

Events that don't bring in any actual profits can still be valuable, particularly if they bring visibility to your organization, mobilize and expand its donor base, or highlight a particular issue of special importance to your members and/or clients. An open house, for example, when you invite your membership—and possibly a few prospective new members—to come see what you do and meet your staff, might serve important purposes beyond raising money for your group.

No matter the purpose of your event, it's important to stay focused on your goals—especially during economically tough times, when it may make sense to rethink or even drop certain events because they tend to absorb so much valuable staff time and energy. With careful budgeting and planning, however, you may be able to turn a potential break-even event into a true fundraiser.

This chapter covers:

- types of special events and the fundraising potential of each
- choosing an event that suits your organization
- planning the event with respect for the climate and environment
- creating a realistic budget
- creating a schedule of activities before and during the event
- protecting your organization from legal and financial liability
- tips for making your event go smoothly, and
- following up after the event.

TIP

Get their names. No matter what type of special event you choose, you'll have an opportunity to put your organization's name and work in front of new eyes—which means you'll want to be organized about getting people's names and addresses (including email) for your mailing list. If you won't know in advance who will be attending, create a sign-in sheet. But to make sure people don't breeze right past your registration table, professional events planner Laurie J. Earp (based in Oakland, California—see www.earpevents.com) suggests an even more effective tactic: "I like to create a door prize, requiring people to fill out their name and contact information or provide a business card. I've found that this brings in not just a few more names, but many times more names than I'd get with just a sign-in sheet." Also, be sure to have a table or another location featuring brochures, photos, and other demonstrations of your organization's work, so that new people realize that the event serves goals beyond their own pleasure.

Other Reasons to Hold a Special Event

Although this chapter focuses on the fundraising potential of special events, there are a number of other good reasons to hold one, such as to:

- **raise visibility**—the promotional activities surrounding the event, as well as the new contacts you make with people who attend, will be of lasting benefit
- **improve your organization's relationship with the public,** such as the residential neighbors around your shelter, or with a particular group of influential people (if you're a children's education group, for example, you might hold a reception for faculty members of the education departments of local colleges)
- **mobilize volunteers**—and bring in new ones
- **celebrate milestones and achievements,** such as your organization's anniversary, approval for a large grant, a staff or board member's departure, or the graduation of a group of students or trainees (though these can easily be turned into effective fundraisers)
- **thank dedicated people who have helped your organization,** or
- **kick off a membership or fundraising campaign** (although the larger purpose here is to raise money, the event itself may be primarily a consciousness raiser).

Survey of Special Events

This section takes a quick ride through the special events landscape, looking at the most common types of events, the major costs associated with them, and the keys to making yours a financial success. Bear in mind that the biggest predictor of any event's success is the quality and energy of the people who work on it, as well as the size and dedication of your group's core roster of supporters.

TIP

Watch the calendar. Keep tabs on events being held by other organizations in your area. This is important both to collect creative ideas and to make sure you don't duplicate something already happening nearby or at the same time. Also, keep an eye on important dates—you don't want to schedule an event on a Jewish or Muslim holiday, for example, particularly if you have members from these faiths.

Lunches, Dinners, and Other Food Events

The most common special event is the annual or special celebratory dinner. And, of course, luncheon, tea, or cocktail hour events are also fine. There are numerous variations on the meal theme—your basic hotel or restaurant sitdown meal (most often with your organization paying the costs, though some restaurants will cut you a discount as a donation); a small food or drink event at the home of a supporter; a meal for which your clients or supporters make the food, such as a themed or an ethnic buffet; a staged event where participants go to different houses or restaurants for drinks, appetizers, a main meal, and dessert; and a "tasting," where you arrange for local vendors, such as restaurants, wineries, or ice cream manufacturers, to send a representative offering samples (free advertising for them, free food for you).

Most meal events also try to incorporate some sort of entertainment or education, such as a speaker, musical performance, video presentation, or showcase of clients' talents or activities. If your organization doesn't regularly hold an annual dinner, then other effective event themes might include its anniversary or the retirement of a longtime ED or board member—especially because such occasions tend to bring back long lost supporters who want to share memories or honor a favorite person.

The key to making a dinner event profitable is to understand that its main proceeds won't come from ticket sales. (In fact, "banquet fatigue" is an increasingly common complaint among philanthropic types.) Although important, the money you take in from ticket sales almost never catches up with the event's costs. Instead, you must make the event serve as a rallying point for a broader effort to collect individual and corporate donations. For example, a local business that might not give you a cash donation to support your programs might instead be willing to donate in-kind to your annual dinner, especially with your assurances that the event will receive press coverage and that the business will be appropriately (and prominently) thanked in the printed event program.

Many dinner events also incorporate another moneymaking activity, such as an auction, a raffle, or a series of booths with items for sale. Involving a well-liked celebrity is also a good way to boost your dinner's fundraising potential—it will both elevate ticket sales and allow you to charge more for the tickets.

> **TIP**
>
> **Seek donations of necessary items.** Of course, it's always best to receive cash in hand, but you can also fund your event with donated contributions of time and materials. With these items covered, you can more confidently approach potential donors about your surefire-success event. Because there's no limit to your imagination, there's also no limit on what you can request—flowers, balloons, other decorations, costumes for the waitstaff, music or other entertainment, a sound system, printing services, transportation for your keynote speaker, and more. It all depends on your organization's connections and the energy of your staff and volunteers.

On the expense side of the ledger, you'll need to make sure your dreams for the event don't degenerate into a bucket of red ink. Food and catering costs alone can add up fast. One option is to have volunteers prepare the meal, but you'll probably have to bring down your ticket prices for a more homespun event like this. Also, you'll find that feeding large numbers of people requires special equipment, such as warming trays and coffee urns, not to mention space, tables, and chairs, that you may have to rent. After adding up all the extras, some organizations find it more cost-effective to hire professionals.

Renting a private hall and hiring a caterer is usually cheaper than con-tracting with a hotel—the latter are famous for charging five bucks for a mediocre cup of coffee. If a hotel seems like your best option, you can bring down the costs by asking to include some separately donated items on the menu, such as wine or chocolates.

The Virtues of Combo-Platter Events

To maximize both fun and profits during an event, it's worth considering whether mini-events can be dovetailed into the main one—combining, for example, a raffle with an open house, an auction with a dinner, or booths of food vendors at a sports tournament. As long as you're mobilizing your volunteers anyway, you may as well offer them alternative directions in which to channel their fundraising energies.

You'll be surprised, too, at how often the very same donors are willing to spend money on a variety of things, even if they wouldn't have been willing to write one big check. (No one who arrived at your event willing to spend more should leave unsatisfied! At the very least, a booth where you sell your organization's T-shirts might be profitable.)

Also, combining activities often increases participants' enjoyment. At a dinner event, for example, many people will be too shy to mingle with strangers on the open floor, but will happily chat with them as they view the silent auction tables.

There are, however, two potential drawbacks to consider when combining events. First, if your event is already complex, and your pool of volunteers stretched thin, you can easily overdo it by piling on more responsibilities. (In any case, make sure your various activities don't get into one another's way—keep them to a strict schedule, and make sure, for example, that a silent auction ends before dinner starts.)

A second possible drawback is that combining fundraising activities might exclude potential donors. For example, a friend of mine volunteers at her children's school, where a gala fundraising dinner was formerly combined with a raffle. However, the development committee realized that, because many of the parents are low-income, they couldn't afford the relatively expensive dinner tickets—but would have been quite willing to buy raffle tickets. So, the two events were split apart, and overall parental donations increased as a result.

> **TIP**
>
> **Good food is critical.** Participants will remember overcooked pasta or tiny portions years later. Worse yet, I heard of one event where a group tried to cook dinner for 500 people—who waited hungrily until 10:45 in the evening to be fed. If you're doing your own cooking, at least consult with a professional about how to pull it off. If not, try to sample all menu items before the event. Ask the hotel, restaurant, or other food preparer to prepare you the exact same meal as your guests will be served. Make sure the meal fills you up and tastes good—but isn't so decadent that health-conscious diners will stick to the parsley garnish. Also try to arrange options for people with special diet needs, such as vegetarian or kosher. Because of the variety of diets and allergies, it's usually easiest just to give your guests the name of a chef or another food-planning person to contact directly, and let them work out the details.

Auctions

An auction, whether silent or live, can be a stand-alone event or a part of another event, such as an annual dinner. (Even online auctions, discussed under "How to Hold an Online Auction," below, can be incorporated into live events.) A silent auction is one where people write their bids on a sheet of paper, usually in an area where the items up for auction are displayed, with little time pressure. People can go back to see whether they've been outbid, and then write in a higher bid if they wish. At an appointed time, you close the bidding, and later announce the winners or let people check for their names on the bidding sheets.

A live auction, of course, is one where an auctioneer (preferably a professional) is at the helm, and people call out (or otherwise indicate) their bids. Which one you choose may simply be a matter of practicality—an important advantage to a silent auction, for example, is that it can be conducted quietly, without disturbing any other simultaneous activities (such as speakers or cocktail hour conversation).

If your choice between a silent or live auction will be based on which is more profitable, go with a live auction. Silent auctions usually bring in about half the market value of the items auctioned, while live auctions tend to bring in bids closer to or exceeding an item's market value. The reason may be that more excitement, or even frenzy, develops as people compete out loud. People may start out looking for a bargain, but end up saying, "Well, at least it was for a good cause."

How to Hold an Online Auction

An online auction is one in which the nonprofit displays photographs of items up for bidding on an auction website such as MissionFish (a 501(c)3 nonprofit that has an exclusive relationship with eBay), IDonateToCharity.org (which offers a flat-fee payment structure rather than taking a commission on items sold), or Bidding for Good (formerly known as cMarket). Would-be bidders register, enter credit card information (meaning guaranteed payment from the winning bidders), and then place their bids within a set period of time, typically one to three weeks, after which your nonprofit sends the winners the goods.

Online auctions offer many advantages over live events. You don't have to fill a room with people, they're open to members who are spread out geographically (or to the whole world if you wish), bidders can participate at any time of the day or night without leaving home, you won't need volunteers for setup (though you will need some for the shipping or delivery), and you won't have to deal with the risk of displaying fragile or high-value items.

The online auction method isn't free; you'll have to pay the hosting website or auction service provider. Someone will also need to pay for shipping, but you can specify ahead of time whether it's the buyer or the organization.

The preparatory steps to holding an online fundraising auction are much like those for a regular auction. You'll solicit goods, set starting bids, and present goods in an attractive light to bidders—which in this case, means taking good photos and/or writing up enticing yet accurate descriptions.

An online auction can also be combined with a live auction. You'd allow online bidding to begin first, with the highest online bid serving as the live auction starting bid. Or, you let online bidders enter a maximum dollar amount for an item ahead of time, which is told only to a volunteer proxy who bids on that person's behalf. Another option is to hold an online auction after your live or silent auction, to deal with items you didn't have room for or that didn't sell.

For more detailed information on all types of fundraising auctions, see *The Volunteers' Guide to Fundraising*, by Ilona Bray (Nolo).

No matter which kind of auction you hold, your overall profits will also depend on your audience. In the words of events planner Laurie Earp, "You have to know who your guests are going to be. Are they looking for a good bargain, or are they looking for a good bidding war, and willing to pay more than the retail value of the items? It's best to have a combination of both." Part of this will depend on whether your guests are existing organization members or donors, or are simply members of the community who attend for their own pleasure. If it's the latter, you may be able to tweak their consciousnesses and further open their wallets by reminding them of the purpose of the event—and by setting minimum bids higher than bargain basement levels.

> **TIP**
>
> **Numerical rules of thumb for auctions.** Experienced fundraisers suggest making sure you'll have a minimum of 25 people in the bidding audience, with at least two people for every item to be auctioned. And, to reach a certain dollar goal—for example, if you're hoping to raise $8,000—get donated items whose worth is at least double that amount, or $16,000.

Silent and live auctions can both be highly profitable fundraisers because, of course, you'll be auctioning off donated goods. Many businesses understand that donating something to an auction brings them publicity. They probably paid wholesale prices for the goods, while you will bring in something closer to their retail cost. You can also minimize how much you ask of any one business (and have fun to boot) by creating packages—the classic one being plane tickets to a holiday destination like Hawaii, with a week's stay at a hotel (or supporter's home), and meals at nice restaurants. Package deals don't have to be on such a grand scale, however—you could also create an auction package offering "A Day on the Avenue," and ask merchants along a popular commercial street to donate certificates for a spa visit or massage, lunch, movie tickets, and a latte. Or, you might create a food basket, with every item carrying a tag from its donor.

Some of the best donations come from your own board members or other supporters—for example, a ride on someone's sailboat, dinner at someone's home, a foursome at a private golf club, use of a vacation home, or use of professional services from chiropractic to accounting to hairdressing. A friend of mine who happens to be a highly ranked chess player offered a free chess lesson as an auction donation. The most interesting auction I've attended was one selling paintings made by elephants—abstract paintings, of course. These particular elephants were on an animal preserve in Thailand, and the auction helped to raise money for their care. See the website of the Asian Elephant Art and Conservation Project, at www.elephantart.com.

The drawback to auctions is that they take an enormous amount of time to prepare. Every merchant or other donor needs to be approached, the items need to be picked up, certificates may need to be created for the winners of intangible items such as dinner at a board member's house, packages need to be put together, and thank-you letters need to be sent out to every gift giver. Obviously, these tasks are ideal for board members and other volunteers—but you'll need to set some parameters first, on the types of items you want and the potential sponsors or donors who should be approached. You don't want volunteers showing up at your office with donated kittens, or worse yet, carloads of used goods.

Coordinate your volunteers so that the same donor isn't approached twice. Also make sure that all volunteers are armed with brochures describing your organization and a "Dear Friend" letter explaining the event and the recognition the donor will receive for making a contribution.

TIP

Raffles are a close cousin to auctions. Though they're not really "events," raffles are a great way to earn between $2,000 and $10,000. The principles of lining up donated goods are the same. You simply set a raffle ticket price that seems fair (and sufficient to make it worth your investment of time), create tickets with a stub for the buyer and a portion for you where the buyer fills in his or her name, address, and email and then sell the tickets. Having kids sell raffle tickets is a surefire way to get things going. I have a friend who says, "All you need is three kids and a mountain bike." The concept is that you arrange with a sports store to buy the bike at cost, then post the kids (and the bike) outside the store or at another popular location, such as a coffee shop. They sell raffle tickets until they've earned enough to cover the bike plus a healthy profit, then some lucky ticket holder pedals off into the sunset.

The names and addresses you collect from your raffle tickets are yet another source of potential new members for your mailing and email lists. A caution, however: Some states separately regulate raffles—for example, by limiting the number you can have per year or the value or type of items you can raffle, or by requiring you to file a report when you're holding a raffle. Check with your state nonprofit-regulating agency for more information.

Fairs and Festivals

This category encompasses events like crafts fairs, carnivals, Renaissance fairs, music festivals, and other occasions that showcase a variety of vendors or talents. Some organizations invent their own theme festivals—for example, the International Crane Foundation, a Wisconsin-based center for the study and preservation of cranes (www.savingcranes.org) has held a Crane Fest, featuring bird-related activities like guided hikes, origami crane folding, bird-feeder building, and a performance of the play "Sadako and the Thousand Cranes." The key is to create an occasion where people can access things that they might not ordinarily find all in one place—or attract people who are simply looking for something to do.

But don't try to undertake a large-scale fair or festival until you've had experience with other or smaller special events. For example, if you hold an ethnic culture fair at a local church, no one is going to expect miles and miles of booths. You might increase profits by combining it with a silent auction. Make sure your publicity materials don't exaggerate what you'll be offering, of course. If you feel you

Announcement for KPFA Annual Crafts Fair

must start on a larger scale, it may be worth hiring a professional—not only an events coordinator, but perhaps also someone with experience in the particular industry you'll be featuring, such as music or arts. If you work with a professional outside the nonprofit world, be prepared for him or her to charge a substantial fee, or to take a percentage of the proceeds.

As the scale of your event gets larger, you can charge rent to both the exhibitors and the people who attend. Also, because a fair or festival is already a variety program, it offers you great opportunity to mix in other fundraising methods, such as raffles, bake sales, and the like. And, although costs start to go up as you look at larger venues and more equipment, the greater community benefit you'll be providing increases your chances of getting help from sources such as your city government (for example, with waived parking fees) or local businesses (for example, with loans of equipment). For a more detailed account of the process of shepherding a crafts fair from infancy to large-scale success, see "KPFA Annual Crafts and Music Fair," below.

Benefit Concerts, Lectures, and Other Presentations

Here's where your organization's personal contacts come in handy. If you know a celebrity, author, expert, or musical group that will offer to perform or speak for free or at a discount, and if the public would be interested enough to pay money for it, you've got yourself an event. It's crucial, of course, that the person or group be interesting or high profile enough to inspire high tickets sales. This is worth some research—at least ask your friends, or kids, to find out which names generate excitement. Someone you've never heard of may pack the house, while a famous old warhorse may barely fill the first five rows. (See Chapter 13 for suggestions on getting media publicity before the event.) Depending on how many seats you have to fill, however, realize that you may not have to look for someone of national interest. If a local band, for example, has a devoted following— even if it's mostly family and friends—it may be enough to pack a coffee shop that donates its space for the evening. Or, a well-regarded local pianist could perform in a board member's living room.

You can also approach people with whom you have no personal connection, although it's harder. Most celebrities and groups have

KPFA Annual Crafts and Music Fair

KPFA, a community radio station in Berkeley, California, has held an annual holiday crafts fair since 1970. The purpose of the event is manyfold—it helps put a human face on KPFA, raises money, and has become a favorite holiday tradition unto itself. The crafts fair now includes over 200 crafts and nonprofits booths and food vendors, all occupying a large San Francisco festival space. It usually brings in about $150,000—but before you get too excited, understand that all but about $30,000 or $40,000 of this goes to pay for the fair.

Jan Etre has been coordinating the KPFA crafts fair since 1988. It's a half-time job for her, along with a part-time assistant, who primarily handles publicity. Here's how Jan describes it: "As an organizer, my job is to make a party happen. But it's all the work done in the prior six months that makes the fair a comfortable place to be. My job starts slowly every year, requiring about ten hours a week, but builds to about 60 hours a week in the days and weeks before the fair happens. My tasks include things like screening the artists and craftspeople who will sell their wares, setting up the website, organizing the venue, organizing food, entertainment, security, and shuttle service to and from nearby BART (subway) stations, developing promotional materials and posters, and actually promoting the event. In fact publicity and promotions are well over half of my job.

"The best advice I have for someone starting a crafts fair is to start small, and put the artists first. If you try to put on a huge event and it fails, word will get out—and if you've made 200 artists unhappy, they'll tell their friends, and you'll have fewer quality artists to choose from next year. On the other hand, if you start with a small number of artists and focus on making sure they turn a profit and feel happy about your event (even if it means keeping your booth fees artificially low at first), they'll return. What's more, they will bring other high-quality artists with them, and your event will grow naturally.

"Sometimes our philosophy of putting the artists first means we have to make some counterintuitive decisions. For example, there's been some pressure to allow imported goods into the KPFA crafts fair. However, we've refused, because this would undermine the prices that our U.S.-based crafts-people can charge—and they're trying to make a living wage from their crafts.

"One last thing that I like to remember is that every year's event is also a dress rehearsal for next year. It's an opportunity to learn what might be done better—and I'm still learning!"

publicists who handle their bookings. The publicists are very experienced at diplomatically saying "no" to the many charitable organizations that approach them. Your job is to convince the publicist that your event will be good publicity for the entertainer(s), that they will be well taken care of, and that they may even enjoy themselves.

If you don't have any personal contacts, the celebrities who are most likely to be interested in participating are those with something to sell—in particular, authors. Upon publishing a new book, a big-name author may go on a multicity publicity tour to visit bookstores, give media interviews, and make other public appearances. If there are any open spots in the author's calendar, the publicist will be eager to fill them—particularly if you can promise some time for the author to sit at a table and sell and sign books. By watching the local bookstores' speakers schedules, you may be able to figure out who's coming. Or, simply contact a publishing company whose works would be appreciated by your audience and ask to speak with one of its publicists. Explain your needs and approximate time frame and see what he or she can suggest.

> **TIP**
>
> **Avoid canned and rehashed speeches.** "I try to create an event that otherwise wouldn't have happened, and preferably won't ever happen again," says Bob Baldock, events coordinator at KPFA radio in Berkeley, California. "For example, I ask authors to not simply read from their book, but to talk about how they're apprehending the world at this time. Or, I'll try to put together an interesting pair— or even a small group—of people. With enough ingenuity, you can create an event that will basically promote itself."

Although most arrangements for this type of event can be handled through letters back and forth, there are circumstances in which you'll want to protect your organization's interests by signing a contract. This is particularly true if you'll be covering a number of costs, such as transportation, hotel, room service, and the like. Your contract should clearly specify and limit the costs you'll cover, so that you won't be surprised by a bill for your celebrity's personal assistant's three-hour massage at the hotel spa after the event.

Benefit events can be reasonably good moneymakers, because you can control your expenses, including the cost of space, promotion and publicity, a sound system (always expensive, but not something you should compromise on), and refreshments. Expenses can mount quickly, however, if you're bringing in out-of-town performers—the cost of transportation and accommodations for your performers and their entourage can be especially high.

> **RESOURCE**
>
> **Want to read more about events with celebrities?** For a well-written, engaging guide with lots of information—and horror stories—about celebrity events, as well as sample contracts, see *Black Tie Optional: A Complete Special Events Resource for Nonprofit Organizations,* by Harry A. Freedman and Karen Feldman (Wiley).

Walkathons, Tournaments, Contests, and Sporting Events

Not every special event has to require a suit and tie; consider the many possible special events that get people out sweating or competing. Such events are particularly appropriate for organizations that have young memberships or are concerned with health issues. The various "a-thons" (walkathons, bike-a-thons, swim-a-thons, 10Ks, and the like) are among the simplest ways to fundraise, because your primary needs include only a route or pool, some paper for participants to use as sponsor sign-up sheets, refreshments to hand out along the way, and a few prizes for those who finish first and/or collect the most in sponsorship money. Of course, larger events will need to incorporate more, including medical assistance, bike mechanics, and other support goods or services.

You should also try to solicit corporate sponsors. Fortunately, people are so accustomed to seeing corporate logos associated with sports events that you can prominently exhibit these without fearing that folks will think your nonprofit has sold out. The sponsors will probably ask for their logo to be displayed on your promotional brochure and Web ads, on banners at the event, and possibly on participant T-shirts.

One problem with these various "a-thons" is their very popularity. The public is getting tired of participating, especially in the more boring ones. Some really do lack imagination—I remember participating in a walkathon as a teenager, and thinking at approximately Mile 16 that they couldn't have chosen a less interesting stretch of paved-over Seattle suburb for us to drag our feet through. Our energy would have been much better spent volunteering for the cause—and in fact, some groups now organize volunteer-a-thons, along those very lines. For example, the Nakomis Healthy Seniors Program, in Minneapolis, Minnesota, holds a Clean-a-Thon, in which volunteers spend a weekend morning doing yard work and heavy scrubbing at the homes of neighborhood seniors.

However, there are times when a walkathon can be just the right fundraiser for an organization. Schools and other organizations with lots of kids and families, for example, find that they are a good way to tap into this donor group (with the added benefit that you start children on a tradition of philanthropy). Walkathons and their ilk are also a good fit for organizations in low-income areas, where small amounts can be solicited from a large number of donors. And the press can be surprisingly interested in events like walkathons, which could lead to increased visibility for a fledgling organization.

Organizations that do best with these events make it an inspiring experience for participants. For instance, the AIDS/LifeCycle is a bicycling event in which participants, some of whom are HIV+, train hard enough to ride all the way from San Francisco to Los Angeles. People camp side by side along the route, develop friendships, and get lots of support and cheering from route bystanders. Of course, this event takes place on a much larger scale than your average nonprofit is prepared to handle.

Before you decide to do a walk-, swim-, or bike-a-thon, consider whether the people who would go out and seek sponsors could be utilized in more effective ways—for example, by canvassing for new members as described in Chapter 4, or approaching potential major donors, as described in Chapter 6. If a recreational event really is the best way to use your potential participants' time, be sure to put some imagination into your event.

A close cousin to walkathons are sports tournaments and contests, in which you raise funds either by charging an entry fee, relying on individual sponsorships, or both. You should also line up corporate sponsors. Groups that successfully organize such specialized events are usually already associated with the activity, such as a horse, vintage car, or motorcycle club might be. The lesson here is that it's important to involve someone in the planning

Hill-Wide Garage Sale in San Francisco

ago, the senior services department of the Bernal Heights Neighborhood
(www.bhnc.org) decided to try a fairly traditional fundraising strategy:
ge sale. BHNC was already working to build community in this somewhat
e part of San Francisco, and had willing volunteers among the seniors it
d (with classes, congregate meals, and outings). This event has grown into an
-winning community tradition, involving as many as 120 registered garage
tes at locations spread throughout Bernal Heights, and attracting thousands
stomers, some from many miles away.

aren Garrison, former director of senior services with BHNC, described this
t: "Normally we have a large garage sale here at the Neighborhood Center, so
sort of the epicenter. Our volunteers also set up some food booths. People
e to the center and buy things at our sale, but they also pick up event maps,
ng them where other sales are being held throughout the neighborhood.
gives us a few seconds—because people are eager to get going—to tell the
ors about BHNC's work, and suggest a donation for the maps. The map is a
risingly important piece of the picture. People who want their garage sale
uded on our map pay us $30. The reverse side of the map contains narrative
rmation, including a reminder that the event is a fundraiser. Of course, some
ple don't stop for maps, and just drive around looking. The energy on the
eet is unbelievable—lots of people, lots of cars.

"We start planning about two months in advance, but once we get going,
very labor-intensive, about 200 staff hours, and many more volunteer hours.
ide from sending out invitations to potential participants (and guidelines,
er they sign up), coordinating volunteers, and creating the map, promotion
a big part of our preparation. We make use of all the community media
tlets' opportunities for free announcements, do outreach within our own
rvice network and at churches, and our volunteers place around 2,000
ers in local store windows, coffee shops, and the like." The catch, as Garrison
knowledges, is that the event doesn't make a lot of money—a little over $2,000
typical, most of that from the on-site garage sale (in addition to map fees and
ercentages of proceeds from other sales, which some people voluntarily pledge).
HNC has tried to attract corporate sponsors, but hasn't had much luck. But,
arrison adds, "What makes the event truly worthwhile is both the increased
isibility for BHNC and the fact that it creates wonderful community feeling."

process who truly knows and loves the sport or activity. You wouldn't want
to plan a Scrabble tournament only to discover you'd brought the wrong
kind of dictionary, for example, or plan a foot race on a route with significant air pollution.

> **TIP**
>
> **Contests make good media fodder.** There's always a winner and,
> particularly if you've got cute kids involved, some good photo opportunities.
> For example, a kids' pet show is almost sure to be covered by local media. See
> Chapter 13 for details on how to access and notify the appropriate media outlets.

Home and Garden Tours

Organizing a successful home and garden tour usually involves convincing
a group of private home or garden owners to open their space to members
of the public—who then buy tickets for the privilege of wandering through
these (hopefully) gorgeous inner sanctums. The themes can be refined almost
infinitely, from kitchen tours to Victorian home tours, sculpture garden tours,
or whatever else might fit the interests of your nonprofit—and sell tickets.

Tours are a wonderful way to make money from something you get for
free. The main costs are promotion (printing and advertising), supplies for
the day of the tour (such as banners and ticket tables outside the various
stopping points, and brochures describing the homes or gardens) and
anything else you add to the process (such as refreshments). Tours also
afford an opportunity to charge for extras, particularly if people will spend
any time at a central location. For example, Park Day School in Oakland,
California, holds an annual garden tour. Ticket holders start on the school
campus, where they (as well as the general public) can browse and buy
garden-related items, such as ceramic pots, tools, and starter plants, from
booths operated by local vendors. For an additional fee, participants may
buy box lunches.

The challenging part of putting on a home and garden tour is the
massive amount of organizing required. You've got to start well in advance
to find appropriate homes or gardens and negotiate with the owners to make
them available on the appropriate day. You'll also have to politely say no to

some eager people whose homes and gardens just aren't worthy of a tour stop. After identifying a set of homes or gardens, you'll need to gather information about them and write up descriptions for a brochure that visitors can carry with them on the tour. Unless you're lucky enough to identify homes and gardens within walking distance of each other, one of your volunteers will have to drive to every destination and write up clear directions. (Don't rely on Mapquest alone—it may not provide all the information your participants will need, such as landmarks to look for along the way, temporary detours, and suggested parking areas.) Also, you'll need to organize a large group of volunteers for the day of the tour, to handle tasks like checking tickets at each stop and standing at key points to answer questions and make sure visitors don't step on the tulips or pocket the silverware.

> **CAUTION**
> **Stay in touch with homeowners.** There's nothing worse than having someone withdraw a week before your event because they must jet off to Rome, Italy, or attend their grandson's kindergarten graduation. Staying in close touch with homeowners in the months and weeks before your tour will demonstrate how seriously you take their participation and help discourage last-minute defections.

Garage Sales, Bake Sales, Used Book Sales, and More

There's a reason why garage sales, bake sales, used book sales, car washes, and the like never go out of style. They don't require much time, money, or expertise to set up, and loads of people are happy to buy something at a reasonable price while simultaneously supporting a good cause. As a classic example, events planner Laurie Earp told me, "The third grade at our school spontaneously put together a garage sale in just over a week and made about $1,100. This was with incredibly minimal effort—imagine if they'd started earlier!" And, if you also hand out pamphlets and collect interested participants' names, you may also get some long-term donors out of the event.

Anyone who has been involved in one of these types of events knows how crazy things can get, with goods, cookies, or soap suds flying everywhere. The key to making it all work is organization, before, during, and after. Even if your event is small scale, it will probably take at least

twice the volunteer time that you imagi
to have an extra person on hand during
questions or requests. ("Can someone he
make sure they're all here?" or "Would y

Used goods sales: Here are some tips or
profitable. For starters, every item should
buyers don't have to find someone to ask.
Garrison, whose years of garage sale exper
Garage Sale in San Francisco," below, says
as a pricing czar. Otherwise, you'll have yo
around and saying, 'Oh no, I think it shoul
one will pay that,' or unilaterally dropping

Ideally, all donated merchandise for gara
reviewed in advance by an expert, who can
might be antiques or first editions and worth
at a higher price. If you know an antiques de
a used-book seller who will volunteer to take
Failing that, pick the most knowledgeable pe
don't want to sell a pair of once-worn Prada sl

Your experts can also help you identify wh
either be sold at a very low price or disposed of
recognize and deal with the junk well in advan
First, the worthless items tend to pull down the
property. Second, your trip to Goodwill or the
the day—an inevitable part of the event—will
than you'd anticipated.

> **CAUTION**
> **Accepting old clothing, household goods**
> IRS says that they must be in "good or better" conditio
> tax deduction. You can help donors by providing filled-
> products' condition, though few organizations have tim
> the donors themselves to take photographs of the good

Assuming you've priced things well, you'll prob
firm to those prices for at least the first half of your

that this is a fundraiser will help deflect persistent bargainers. Also decide in advance when to start dropping prices, to make sure you aren't left with too many unsold goods. For an all-day sale, late afternoon is usually an appropriate time to offer some bargains (allowing some discretion by your pricing czar, depending on how sales are going).

> **CAUTION**
>
> **Decide how you'll deal with earlybirds.** First, you'll have to consider whether to sell particular items to a professional antiques dealer or bookseller, particularly those who helped set your prices, and to your other volunteers who've no doubt been eyeing things they'd like, in advance of your sale—this might bring in guaranteed profits, but it also diminishes the public's perception of the quality of your sale. Next, you'll need to be ready to deal with the semiprofessional bargain-hunting community. They're likely to show up at your sale well before it is open, demand to start shopping, and scarf up all the good stuff before you've even begun (goodbye Prada shoes). The aggressive response is to put up ropes and post no-nonsense volunteers until you're ready to open; the lower-conflict but somewhat unsatisfying alternative is to warn your volunteers that they should plan to start the sale around 30 minutes before it's officially open!

Bake sales: Bake sales or other food sales are almost guaranteed to please a crowd. Even so, you've probably seen some of the problems that can reduce profitability—such as stingy or overgenerous portions or badly labeled items that are hard to identify. Also, with allergies and vegetarian or vegan diets increasingly on the minds of the American public, you need to be prepared for probing questions about what your food items contain. One good way to solve this is to have each of your food preparers list the ingredients in every item. Also, be sure to stock at least some items without the most common allergens, including nuts, eggs, peanuts, wheat, and milk products.

Car washes: Car washes are also a standby of grassroots nonprofit efforts. They can be particularly effective if you can put a hose or towel in the hands of a celebrity or two. One perennial tension, however, is that it takes a fair amount of time to wash a car well. This can mean either that the nonprofit doesn't make much money, or that the customers end up dissatisfied, as the soap bubbles dry into spots on their windshields. To keep things moving along, it's essential to use an appropriate space, preferably one loaned by a gas station or another place with lots of hose hookups. (In many areas, these are also environmentally friendlier, since they drain to the sewage treatment system rather than through the storm drains to local waterways.) Then, to ensure some quality control, practice car washing techniques with your volunteers, and explain to everyone what you expect. Volunteers should work in teams of four or five so cars move in and out quickly.

Choose the Right Event for Your Organization

The first step in deciding what type of special event to hold is the same as the first step in planning your annual fundraising strategy—examine your organization's assets. (Review Chapter 3 for a reminder of how this is done.)

If you've got a large physical facility, think about events that might attract a crowd. If you've got an unusually large volunteer corps, consider events that require large numbers of people to prepare or run, such as an auction, fair, festival, or home tour. If you've got access to celebrities or experts, consider lectures, benefit concerts, or major donor parties (see Chapter 6 for details).

> ⓘ CAUTION
>
> **Any special event should be grounded in your annual fundraising plan.** When a volunteer in a good mood offers up a beautiful house for a party or proposes some other unplanned event, it's easy to say "yes" without considering all the consequences. Unless you can truly mobilize volunteers who weren't serving any other fundraising purpose—a rare situation, and one that should cause you to question why those volunteers weren't otherwise occupied—your special event is likely to divert time and attention away from potentially more profitable fundraising activities. This doesn't mean that you should never seize an unexpected fundraising opportunity, but do so only if it doesn't unduly disrupt your plan.

After figuring out what types of events you could offer, think about who is likely to show up. Although "paying customers" are your first priority, remember that your event is also an opportunity to pick up new support, which means that you'll want to attract people who fit your donor profile.

For example, I once spoke with members of a suicide prevention group who started an annual golf tournament simply because one of the founders liked golf and could mobilize his friends—but its effectiveness sputtered out after a few years, as they realized that participants weren't interested in other donations or involvement.

Once you've got a brilliant event idea in mind, do some research to find out whether people will pay to attend (or pay for items once they're there). How much research you'll need to do depends on the size of your event. For a small event, it may require no more than talking informally to your major donors and other supporters. For events designed to bring in more members of the general public, however, you may have to find experts in the relevant area—such as the music business—to quiz about attendance estimates. Also talk to folks at other nonprofits that have done similar events (contact groups in comparable cities, if you're worried about being in competition with more local nonprofits).

How much time will an event take to organize and put on? Because you should be conceptualizing the event as part of your overall fundraising planning, answering this question—with regard to both staff and volunteer time—is critical. It's hard to exaggerate how much time a good-sized special event can take to organize! Multiply your initial estimate by three.

For a big event, hiring an outside consultant or events planner can be an efficient way of ensuring that your staff's daily work isn't greatly disrupted. Although this is likely to cost you several thousand dollars, a good, experienced events planner can often earn back his or her fee and then some, simply by drawing on longstanding relationships with graphic designers, printers, musicians, local businesses that are proven donors, and others to keep costs down and minimize delays. They can also help you make informed decisions about what works to draw in and satisfy the public, and how to maximize profits overall.

Just don't expect the events planner to do everything   in particular, soliciting donations from your own donors or even some local businesses is a task that should stay within your own staff and board, as part of your relationship-building efforts.

WORLD's Fashion Show Develops from HIV+ Clients' Personal Interests

WORLD (Women Organized to Respond to Life-Threatening Diseases) is an Oakland, California–based information and support network by, for, and about women living with HIV/AIDS (www.womenhiv.org). In recent years, a highlight of their traditional dinner event has been a fashion show put on by HIV-positive women and their children. This is no mere ode to fashion—the women, many of whom are low-income and dealing with AIDS-related illnesses or the side effects of medication, conceived of the event as a way to celebrate their lives and their bodies.

This fashion show provides an excellent example of the wisdom of planning your event around existing resources. As then-board co-chair Sonja Mackenzie told it, "Not only did the idea of the fashion show start organically within this group of HIV-positive women, but it so happened that in its first year at WORLD, our organization had a useful connection—one of our donors had friends within the fashion industry. She was able to line up loans of some incredibly fancy outfits for the women and children to wear, from notable designers such as Jessica McClintock. The women (and children) looked and felt beautiful.

"Audience reaction to the show was indescribable, incredibly powerful. I think the show really hit on the core elements around HIV and being a woman with HIV. The audience included medical providers, family members, and members of the pharmaceutical industry. They were both moved and impressed by seeing their family members/patients in a new, powerful role.

"The second year that we did the fashion show, we no longer had our fashion industry contact. That made the planning a lot trickier. In the end we found a more local contact, an Oakland-based designer of African clothing. We also divided the show into differently themed sections, such as 'On the beach,' 'My heritage,' and others. The emcee (a local television personality) read each woman's brief autobiography, such as 'This is so-and-so, a 35-year-old woman who's been living with HIV for ten years. The most important thing in her life is her son, whom she wants to see graduate from college. She's on the beach in Hawaii today, because one day she dreams that she will be able to live there.'

"In the end—and despite my initial misgivings—the show was another huge success, largely because it included such powerful personal narratives. Nevertheless, putting the show on was an enormous amount of work, more than any of us ever imagined."

Keep It Green

Whether your group's mission relates to preserving the natural environment or not, your upcoming special event shouldn't present an example of waste and excess. Attention to environmental goals when planning and implementing an event can boost attendance, audience excitement and participation, and media attention.

But where do you begin? Greening every aspect of your next event may not be a realistic goal. However, with some prioritizing, budgeting, and consideration of your nonprofit's core values, you may be able to choose and use many of the tips below.

Choose a Green Location

A country inn or your board member's vacation home may be a beautiful setting for a gala event—but is it the best choice from an environmental standpoint? Your choice of venue will literally set the stage for whether you can achieve a number of other green goals.

First, think about how many people will be driving many miles, and therefore consuming gas and emitting pollutants, to get to your chosen venue. If public transport is an option, one way to ameliorate the distance issue is to provide alternate directions to the event using public transport and bicycles (and to ensure the availability of safe bike racks or storage). Send this message loud and clear, or you'll find that most guests hop into their cars without thinking twice. If public transport is not a realistic option, you might coordinate and encourage (or even sponsor) carpools or shuttle services. Or perhaps a more centrally located facility (such as a downtown museum, hotel, or art gallery) will be your best bet.

Next, look into the venue's history of attention to and cooperation with environmental goals—and its willingness to sign a contract stating it will comply with your agreement regarding environmental matters. For example, a venue that agrees to use compostable plateware, but whose staff hasn't been trained to separate the bags of garbage when throwing them out, won't help your goals at all. Along with this, consider whether the place has ready access to a waste management server providing recycling. Some signs that a venue is already committed to environmental protection include that it uses energy-efficient lighting, low-flow toilets, and recycled paper materials, and places recycle bins next to the trash cans.

Many venues are taking the initiative and getting LEED certification (Leadership in Energy and Environmental Design) from the nonprofit U.S. Green Building Council, Inc. This certification means they've proven that their facility has been built, designed, and operated for improved environmental and human health performance. Also see the Green Venue Selection Guide published by the Building Council, which contains questions to ask venues that haven't yet obtained LEED certification (right down to the gallons per flush on their toilets). It's downloadable at www. usgbc.org; go to "Resources."

Create Environmentally Friendly Invitations

Sending "save the date" notifications by email is now completely appropriate and will save a lot of paper. For the invitations themselves, you (and your donors) may prefer traditional paper—but you can talk to a printer about how to minimize the size of the invitation and amount of paper used. One possibility is to issue a small invitation, or even a postcard, and then direct people to a page on your website for detailed program information and registration.

Also look into using recycled paper and soy-based inks (made from a renewable resource and far less toxic than regular inks, plus easier to wash off during the recycling process). The costs are close to comparable.

Avoid Creating Mountains of Wasted Paper Plates

If you'll be serving food, consider what you'll buy or use in the way of cups, plates, and serving ware. "Real" or reusable china and forks and knives, as well as cloth napkins, are obviously best. If these are impractical, a quick online search will bring up an array of environmentally conscious suppliers of serving products, so that you can comparison shop—but don't forget to prefer local vendors, so that the goods don't have to consume energy making one last trip across the country. Note that "compostable" is better than "biodegradable": It refers to something that breaks down as easily as paper and is nontoxic.

You can both save money and make an important environmental impact by the simple step of not serving water in individual plastic bottles. Instead, put out pitchers and reusable, or at least recycled-material cups.

If you'll be serving mainly appetizers or snacks, making sure that every bite can be eaten with one's fingers will save having to put out forks.

Don't Go Overboard on the Decorations

When planning flowers, decorations, and gifts, realize that less can be more. Now is not the time, for example, to plan a theme party with lots of plastic leis, disposable hats, and so forth. With a little creativity, you can save both money and the environment.

For example, how many of your board members have beautiful flowers or shrubs growing in their own garden that they'd be willing to clip from and bring to an event—even if you hire a professional to do the arranging? (And while your board members are at it, ask them to check their houses for spare vases. Almost everyone has a cheap one taking up space from their last floral delivery.) Another option for centerpieces is potted native plants, which can be reused or raffled off.

Other nonprofits may also have bought decorative items for events that you can borrow or swap for something from your last event.

Reduce Use of Other Materials

Start by investing in reusable nametag holders. You'll need to create paper inserts with people's names, then collect the badges at the end of the event for reuse.

Consider also how many handouts you need to provide. For disseminating general information, such as a map, can you post a few in highly visible places rather than putting a copy in everyone's folder? When handouts are necessary, create double-sided printouts when possible.

And don't feel you need to provide a tote bag! People have plenty of those already.

Serve Green Food

Your food choices for the event, and the way that the food is served, make an important statement about your environmental commitment.

Organic, seasonal, locally grown, and sustainable food sources should be your first choice whenever economically possible. Many caterers and restaurants specialize in such menus—and, as you know, some may be willing to offer you a nonprofit discount, particularly if you give them lots of good publicity. Be sure to offer vegetarian and vegan options.

Buffet service rather than individually boxed or served meals can reduce both food and packaging waste. Even when it comes to snacks, avoid individually packaged items in favor of trays of fruit, crackers, or trail mix. The same goes for condiments, cream, and sugar (to go with your fair-trade coffee).

What about the leftovers? Either arrange for guests to be able to take home doggie bags or contact a shelter ahead of time to set up a donation.

Develop a Realistic Budget

There's no great mystery to creating a special events budget: You list all your anticipated expenses in one column, then enumerate what you expect to bring in from various intended activities in the second. Finally, you subtract your expected revenues from your anticipated expenses to give you a total.

The trick, of course, is accurately projecting your expenses and income. Part of this involves taking your analysis to a micro level, so that you don't forget to budget for, say, paper napkins and microphone rentals. Another critical factor is how faithfully your volunteers follow through on certain activities. In other words, if you plan to keep expenses down by getting donated food and chairs, and to keep income high by getting corporate sponsorships, you've got to communicate this to whoever is in charge of doing these things, and make sure the tasks get done.

Every fundraising event creates financial risk. You'll have to cover most of your expenses before you know how much the event will bring in—or whether an unexpected snowstorm or other disaster will soak your balance in red ink. One great way to minimize risk is to stick to events that don't cost a lot to stage. Then, if anticipated revenues don't materialize for some reason, you haven't dug yourself a huge financial hole.

Estimate Expenses

There's no better way to understand the event budgeting process than to grab a pencil and paper. To make this easier, I've provided the expense worksheet below (and on www.nolo.com; see Appendix B for the exact URL). As you start to fill it out, you'll inevitably learn more about what you can afford, what key decisions need to be made (for example, how much you're willing to spend on advertising and promotion), and how many guests you'll need to attract. You'll also hopefully think up a few special items to add to the worksheet, based on whatever is unique about your event. And for every expense item, be sure to consider whether you can get needed items through donations, or cut the costs in some other way—by renting as opposed to buying, for example.

If you're new at this, assume that your final figure will be on the low side—some suggest adding at least 20% for unanticipated costs or occurrences. And always remember that staff time is a hidden cost—although it doesn't show up in the budget, it's a very important consideration. It's easy for staff to get pulled away from important development or program responsibilities by the whirl of activity leading up to a special event.

CAUTION
A cheap sound system can ruin your event. We've all been at events where the electronic feedback made our fillings ache or the speaker equipment was diabolically positioned to blast the VIP table. This isn't random bad luck—it can be overcome by paying a little more for your sound system. For example, in a large hall, it's best to connect speakers at points around the room rather than just line them up on the stage. Though paying more seems hard to justify at the abstract, budget-planning level, think of it as an investment against audience irritation or inattention.

Fundraising Worksheet 6: Projected Special Event Expenses

Expense Category	Projected Cost	Description of Reasoning or Assumptions, Particularly for Discount or Donated Items
Physical Space		
Room, building, outdoor space	$_____	_____
Chairs, tables, performance platform	$_____	_____
Site manager and other staff fees	$_____	_____
Heating or air conditioning	$_____	_____
Sound system, projector, screen, other equipment	$_____	_____
Municipal permits (traffic, etc.)	$_____	_____
Subtotal:	$_____	_____
Decorations		
Banners	$_____	_____
Lighting	$_____	_____
Flowers	$_____	_____
Candles	$_____	_____
Balloons	$_____	_____
Party favors, gifts, award plaques, and certificates	$_____	_____
Other	$_____	_____
Subtotal:	$_____	_____
Food and Drink		
Snacks or appetizers (for participants and volunteers)	$_____	_____
Main meal	$_____	_____
Extra catering or corkage fees	$_____	_____
Alcohol, other drinks, ice	$_____	_____
Plates, cups, napkins, cutlery	$_____	_____
Waiters and bar staff	$_____	_____
Subtotal:	$_____	_____

Fundraising Worksheet 6: Projected Special Event Expenses

Expense Category	Projected Cost	Description of Reasoning or Assumptions, Particularly for Discount or Donated Items
Performers/Speakers		
Performers' or auctioneer's fee or honorarium	$_____	_____
Transportation and parking (airfare, shuttle, rental car, cabs, or limousine)	$_____	_____
Hotel	$_____	_____
Meals	$_____	_____
Telephone and other extras	$_____	_____
Subtotal:	$_____	
Publicity		
Graphic designer and/or artist	$_____	_____
Printing (posters, programs, ad books, auction catalogs)	$_____	_____
Stationery, envelopes	$_____	_____
Postage (invitations, press releases, thank-yous)	$_____	_____
Professional mailing services	$_____	_____
Event photographer	$_____	_____
Subtotal:	$_____	
Miscellaneous		
Taxes on goods sold	$_____	_____
Photocopying	$_____	_____
Supplies for volunteer meetings and information packets	$_____	_____
Reimbursement of volunteers' expenses (i.e., gasoline, telephone)	$_____	_____
Name badges	$_____	_____
Insurance	$_____	_____
Unexpected or emergency expenses	$_____	_____
Subtotal:	$_____	
Total:	$_____	

Estimate Income

Correctly anticipating income is difficult, particularly in the first year or years of an event. Your crystal ball rarely reveals how many people will show up at an event, how much they'll buy, or how high their auction bids will go. Fill out the worksheet as best you can (available online; see Appendix B for the link), but protect yourself from risk by starting small and getting lots of advance support from major donors and corporate sponsors. If the event becomes a tradition for your organization, your projections will become more accurate, aided by your experience and by last year's records.

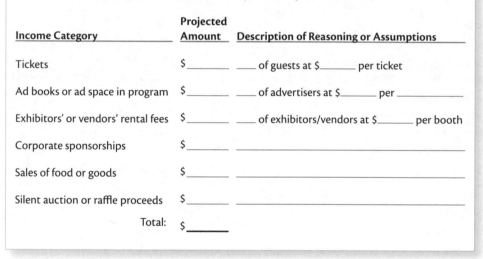

Fundraising Worksheet 7: Projected Special Event Income

Income Category	Projected Amount	Description of Reasoning or Assumptions
Tickets	$_____	____ of guests at $_____ per ticket
Ad books or ad space in program	$_____	____ of advertisers at $_____ per _____
Exhibitors' or vendors' rental fees	$_____	____ of exhibitors/vendors at $_____ per booth
Corporate sponsorships	$_____	_____
Sales of food or goods	$_____	_____
Silent auction or raffle proceeds	$_____	_____
Total:	$_____	

Compare Projected Expenses and Income

For a successful event, your income should exceed your expenses by a healthy margin. This is hard to quantify, but aim to earn at least five times your expenses—for example, kids selling a mountain bike worth $500 should attempt to bring in $2,500. Using this approach, even if you collect only $2,000 you're still doing pretty well. The actual dollar amount that you'll hope to earn depends, of course, on the size of your organization's budget and the size of the event. But if it's only a couple thousand dollars, think hard about how much staff time will be going into the event. Again, I didn't work this hidden cost into the budget worksheet, but when profits will already be low, staff time can make the difference between making and losing money.

Make sure your projected budget still shows a profit if things go wrong. For example, try running the numbers with a third of the attendees showing up, and see what happens to your income. Once you've swallowed that bitter pill, think about which of your expenses you can put off incurring until you're sure of attendance figures. Hotels, for example, will generally ask for a deposit up front, then require that you confirm attendance and pay for a set number of meals by a certain date. Make sure to set your ticket sales deadline before that date!

> CAUTION
> **Tell donors exactly how much of their ticket price or other payments to your organization during an event are tax deductible.** You and they must subtract the value of actual goods or services they received. You'll need to give each donor a dollar figure stating how much of his or her payment is tax deductible. For more information on tax deductibility of donations, see Chapter 4.

Plan and Pace Event Activities

The success of your event depends in large part on what goes on behind the scenes in the months or weeks leading up to it. Allow plenty of lead time—the "classic" special event, such as an annual dinner, a gala ball, or a benefit concert, normally takes between six months to a year to prepare. Giving yourself a realistic amount of time will not only save your sanity, but also save your organization money. For example, the costs of design and printing will go down if you give your designers and printers ample time to work the tasks into their schedules—and will go up just as easily if you ask for a rush job.

It's also important to get a head start on corporate sponsorships. Most companies make their decisions about sponsorships in either the last quarter of the preceding year or the first quarter of the year when the event will be held. This means that even for some fall events, you'll need to have gotten your sponsorship requests out in the previous year.

If you're working primarily with volunteers, however, it is often better not to really launch into preparations until six months before the event. If you give more lead time, people won't feel any time pressure—and some of them won't get over this feeling until a few weeks before the event. Be warned, too, that volunteers may be heavy on the good intentions and somewhat lighter on the follow-through, so having leaders who can motivate them (as well as do a little friendly monitoring) will help make sure tasks get done on time.

> **TIP**
>
> **Help motivate participants by creatively announcing your progress.** For example, the Bernal Heights Neighborhood Center marks its progress toward its community-wide garage sale (see "Hill-Wide Garage Sale in San Francisco," above) in terms of how many neighborhood residents have signed up to participate. They create a huge sign with the latest number and prominently hang the sign at the center for staff, volunteers, and passersby to see.

Some of the main preparatory tasks are covered below. However, when you've identified your event and outlined your goals regarding promotion and publicity, sponsorship, and the like, you may want to consult some more specialized resources. You'll find some listed at the end of this chapter.

Create a Calendar of Activities

The time-tested way to figure out what needs to be done by when is to work backward from the day of the event. What are the final steps—such as picking up rental chairs and flowers? By when do these need to be ordered? By when do decisions need to be made about how many chairs and what type of flowers? Who will be responsible for the decisions? When should this committee meet? Similarly, if you'll have a featured entertainer, when must you choose this person to make sure that his or her name will be announced in promotional materials? How much time before this should you allow to negotiate and sign a contract for this person's services? How many weeks in advance should be allotted for approaching different performers? When will the committee meet to select potential performers' names? You get the drift.

Once you've worked out what needs to be done and by when, create an actual calendar, whether online or on a giant poster (or both). Write in the dates on which you or one of your volunteers must start the various activities, not the dates by which they must be completed. For example, "Last day to choose menu" is not a helpful calendar entry unless it was preceded by one advising you to begin the selection process.

Working with the dates you've entered on the calendar, create checklists for yourself and your committees, itemizing every task that needs to be done. You or your committee leaders should review these checklists regularly, ticking off items as they are completed, and calling people to confirm that they have completed their assigned tasks by the required dates.

Define Committees and Assign Leaders

Every special event needs a central point person to coordinate volunteers and keep things moving according to schedule. But one person can't pull off an event alone. By looking at your budget and other planning materials, you should be able to identify all of the activities that need to be attended to. Then, create subject committees to match. For example, depending on the type of event you're planning, your committees might include some combination of the following:

- site planning
- meals or refreshments
- choosing exhibitors, performers, vendors, or home or garden tour destinations
- decorations
- transportation
- awards
- gathering auction or raffle donations
- obtaining corporate sponsorships
- event staffing and registration
- keeping it green
- promotion and publicity (including graphics and printing), and
- cleanup.

Some of these activities are discrete enough that they may require only a single person, or a committee of two or three. In fact, at times it's best not to assign too many people to a task, lest the abundance of people give committee members the idea that little is expected of them. The two most important considerations are these: First, everyone must understand his or her responsibilities, including what needs to be done, by what deadline, with what special considerations in mind (such as keeping the event green), and with whom to communicate about progress (or the lack thereof). Committee members should also understand the limits of their responsibilities. For example, if you want the food committee to come up with a potential menu, but the ED will actually have the final say on what is served, this needs to be made clear from the beginning.

Second, someone must monitor the situation conscientiously to make sure that all key tasks are really getting done.

> ⓘ CAUTION
>
> **Communication between committees and other leaders is key.** The more committees you've got, the greater the risks of miscommunication. As Sonja Mackenzie, then WORLD board co-chair, put it: "I'm a strong proponent of open group process, but you still need to be clear about who the point person is, and keep the communication channels open to that person. If you've got a lot going on— for example, in WORLD's case, we combined a fundraising dinner with a fashion show—you'll find that the questions start multiplying, such as who picks up the microphone, and whether the dinner planners remembered to rent a venue that will accommodate a fashion show stage."

The point person should plan to be in regular contact with all committee leaders. Depending on the timeline and number of people involved, scheduling regular meetings or conference calls, where everyone will report on their progress and any difficulties they're facing, may be worthwhile. To save on unnecessary meetings, periodic email check-ins can also be useful—perhaps once a week early on, moving up to daily in the last week.

In the name of good record keeping, the point person should ask for documentation of certain accomplishments, such as names of committed corporate sponsors or copies of press releases. Excessive politeness has been known to lead to situations where volunteers assert that everything is going great, when in fact little or nothing has actually been done.

> **TIP**
>
> **Time to get organized.** Your event point person should create a notebook or an equivalent system to help track important pieces of information and to ensure that nothing gets forgotten. Sections of the notebook, divided by easy-to-see tabs, should include your checklists, a month-by-month planning calendar, budgeting and finances, subject matter sections for each committee (containing important documents such as contracts or notes on decisions and accomplishments), a master contact list of all vendors, volunteers, and other participants, and anything else relevant to the particular event. The leader should also work with the committee heads to help them get similarly organized.

Plan Promotion and Publicity

If you're hoping to attract members of the public to your event, especially members who are not on your organization's mailing list, you'll need to pay particular attention to promotion and publicity. (Loosely speaking, promotion is advertising that you arrange or pay for yourself, such as posters and invitations; publicity is media reporting, usually in response to your press releases or other contacts.) In fact, because the success of an event like a garage sale or street fair rides upon people's hearing about and attending it, plan for promotional and publicity activities to consume the vast majority of your and your volunteers' prep time. It's helpful if you can enlist the services (preferably volunteer) of a professional public relations or marketing person.

Of course, Step One in promoting your event is to tell your members and supporters about it. Your social media feeds, newsletter, and website should start generating excitement months in advance, mentioning the date, location, and contact person for more information or volunteer opportunities. To make sure that people make room on their calendars (even before you're ready to sell tickets, if any), it's traditional to send a "save the date" postcard or email approximately three to five months before the event.

Invitations, or opportunities to buy tickets, should be sent or announced six weeks before the event. In addition to contacting your supporters, you might rent a mailing list of potentially interested people—for example, members of a musical society if you'll be holding a concert. (See Chapter 4 for more information on the process of acquiring mailing lists.) Collecting additional names is a separate and important task, one which you might assign to a committee. For example, all volunteers who get involved in the event should be given a piece of paper and asked to write the names, addresses, email addresses, and telephone numbers of any of their friends who they think might be interested in attending. Similarly, any featured speakers or honorees should be asked for the contact information of friends or relatives who might wish to attend. (You'll need to develop a policy in advance regarding how many complimentary tickets your speakers or honorees will be given—normally tickets for a spouse or significant other and minor children should do it.)

TIP

Each one bring ten. Sometimes the simplest and cheapest promotional methods work the best. If you have a good-sized local membership, you might charge each member with recruiting ten friends. Especially if you include a fun contest (the winning recruiter gets a weekend at a donated vacation home, for example), this can be an incredibly cost-effective way to spread the word.

Event posters should be created for any event to which the public at large will be invited. If pressed for cash, this is something you can do in black and white with your own photocopying machine, but don't try this if you plan to charge high ticket prices or attract high-income attendees. Usually the help of a graphic designer is required, unless you have particularly artistic folks involved in your effort. An attractive poster can be a sought-after item, so that coffee shops, stores, and other public places will be more than happy to display it. Putting up posters is a good task to assign to a large number of volunteers, making sure that each is assigned a separate geographical area. Watch out for local ordinances concerning placing posters in public spaces or on telephone poles.

Your promotion and publicity committee should also consider which newspapers, magazines, or websites are most likely to be seen by your potential ticket buyers. A fun site for all kinds of events is http://eventful.com, which provides a special page for "Fundraisers." Look for media outlets that offer free community calendars, and arrange for announcements within the newsletters of local churches or potentially interested groups, such as a bicycling or garden club.

The best advertising, however, is a positive media write up or in-depth coverage by electronic media. See Chapter 13 on how to generate media attention for your event.

> **TIP**
>
> **Take photos of this year's event for next year's promotion.** Even if your event won't be highly photogenic, good-quality pictures of key speakers or people enjoying themselves are great for your website and promotional materials. If you'll be sending out a press release immediately after the event, photos will also increase the chances that your story will be picked up.

Create Corporate Sponsorship Opportunities

Despite the fact that many events charge admission fees, event profitability often depends on garnering money from outside sources, such as corporate sponsors. Sometimes, getting corporate sponsorship can be as simple as encouraging your board members to ask their employers to buy a table's worth of tickets for an annual dinner event. Other times, you will want to look for more major sponsorship—for example, by asking a company to be the lead name on your 10K run or whale-watching tour, with its logo prominently displayed on your banners and publicity materials, in return for underwriting costs or supplying space, food, or other event necessities.

Either way, the important thing to remember is that a business doesn't ordinarily sponsor an organization unless it feels assured of gaining good publicity for the business itself. Be prepared to explain to any businesses that you approach:

- the nature of the event
- why it will suit their interests to be affiliated with it
- how many people you expect to attend, and
- what sort of publicity you're willing to give their businesses.

> 💡 **TIP**
>
> **Set up a system to display your sponsors' logos.** Although it's fine to have a lead sponsor who pays for this prominent position, you'll rarely want to depend on one sponsor alone, unless that business is truly willing to make a major financial commitment. Instead, set aside space for a number of corporate sponsors—and let them know that their names will be front and center at your event.

Advertisements in your event program or an ad book are other popular ways of getting corporate sponsorship. I know of one organization that earned $125,000 on its ad book alone, which was prepared in conjunction with an annual dinner.

An ad book is just what it sounds like—a small brochure that displays either traditional advertisements or small testimonials to the organization on behalf of the business or person buying the ad, such as "Bronze Medal Athletic Gear wishes to congratulate KidsClub for its 25 years of helping inner-city youth excel through physical activity and teamwork." Some sole proprietor or professional ad buyers, such as lawyers, accountants, or music teachers, will simply want a copies of their business cards in your ad book. Your graphic designer or printer should be able to help you set guidelines for planning and selling ad space.

Deal With Risks and Liability Issues

Because making your event profitable will require keeping costs down, you must consider any minor or major disasters that might befall your event—such as a child's getting injured on the site, a donor's drinking too much and causing an accident driving home, or a thief's taking your cash box or goods for sale. Because a special event is outside your usual course of business and may involve large numbers of people, you'll have to adjust your thinking to expect the unexpected—and plan to deal with the consequences.

There are three important steps you can take to forestall mishaps and disasters: First, make sure you've complied with all applicable laws and permit requirements; second, put your own sensible safety measures into place; and third, consider buying special insurance for the event.

For smaller events, accomplishing Steps One and Two would probably be enough, but for large-scale events attended by many people you don't know, buying insurance may also make sense. And some event sites may require you to carry a specified type and amount of coverage as a condition of using their facilities.

Comply With Laws and Permit Requirements

Whether your event is on your organization's own site or elsewhere, unusual attendance or activities may bring up legal issues. Large numbers of people impeding traffic flow or parking in one area may require advance discussions with your local police department. If you'll be serving liquor, you may be required to obtain a license or permit, usually from your city. Whoever will be serving the alcohol may also be required to go through special training (to make sure they understand how to check IDs and when to cut someone off). Auctions (particularly of luxury items) and gambling activities may also require licenses or permits.

As appropriate, talk to other nonprofits, your police department, or to a city official before proceeding. And, if you still have legal questions, look for a volunteer lawyer to help you find the answers.

Implement Appropriate Safety Measures

The best way to minimize damage is to avoid it in the first place, then create backup measures to deal with whatever can't be predicted or avoided. For starters, make sure that your event is well staffed and that every volunteer knows who to go to with a problem. The person in charge should carry a cell phone, and give every volunteer the number. Volunteers should wear something distinctive, so that members of the public know who to alert when the food has run out or they observe a burst pipe leaking in the direction of your sound system.

Also consider whether there are any rules that you want members of the public to observe. For example, if it wouldn't be appropriate to allow children below a certain age to participate, make this clear in your publicity materials, and be prepared to enforce it at the door. Similarly, if people shouldn't bring certain materials like alcoholic beverages or firearms, warn them in advance and be prepared to check for violations. This may require hiring a security person who is trained in dealing with such matters. I also suggest saying no to dogs, as well as to more exotic creatures—the cleanup problems are immense, and there's no upside unless it's an animal-centered event. (Working dogs, such as seeing-eye dogs, are of course an exception.)

Think carefully about who you're going to trust with sensitive tasks, such as handling money (never leave one person alone with it), serving alcohol, or transporting people by car or van. Don't forget that these people will need to take breaks or spend some time enjoying the event themselves, so schedule additional people to spell them from time to time. Ask to see the license of every driver, and if they'll be driving a large truck or bus, make sure they're specially licensed for this as well. All volunteers carrying out sensitive tasks such as cashiering should be told that they can't just hand their responsibilities over to someone else; by the same token, other volunteers should understand the limits of their roles and responsibilities.

If you anticipate large amounts of cash changing hands, make sure to have a foolproof system in place for tracking it and keeping it secure. For starters, tell your cash handlers to put all large bills, as well as all bills in excess of what are needed to make change, into a special place—either under a plate in the cash register or, better yet, into a locked and hard-to-move box. It is also sensible to schedule a two-person team to pick up cash at periodic points during the event. That team should keep records of exactly how much cash is taken from every cashier or box, in case questions arise later.

TIP

Take it to the bank. Picking up cash every hour or two solves one big problem, but creates another. Now you've got wads of money just waiting to be stolen or misplaced, with very little tracking as the day goes on. Instead of devising an elaborate security system, it's usually easier to simply deposit cash after every pickup.

Serving alcohol creates its own set of issues. You don't want to serve drinks to minors, you don't want people who've had too much to create a scene or a medical emergency, and you certainly don't want a drunk guest to injure someone driving home—who can then sue your organization for the damages you "caused." Even if your area doesn't require alcohol servers to be specially trained, servers should be ready to check IDs and tell patrons when they've had enough (or start mixing their drinks with nine parts soda). As the event winds down, someone should be stationed at the door to wish people farewell—and to offer a cab or other ride to anyone who seems to be staggering toward his or her car. To be extra cautious, you could arrange with a cab company to have a couple of taxis waiting for this purpose, though they'd probably charge you for this service. One way to deal with all the above issues is to restrict alcohol events to restaurants, hotels, and other venues with experienced staff on hand.

Disability access is an important consideration, too—and one to consider before contracting to use a particular physical space. Some buildings claim to have wheelchair accessibility, but it turns out to be a makeshift ramp at a precarious angle. Restroom accessibility is also an area where many physical spaces fall short. The last thing you want is a situation where helpful volunteers try to carry a disabled person up a set of stairs or into a bathroom.

These are just a few of the safety measures you can put into place. You may need to develop others based on the type of event, the number of people and type of activities people will be engaging in, any special needs that your guests are likely to have, and your own common sense.

Purchase Insurance

Ask your insurance broker or company to go over your policy with you, to explain how many of your activities will be covered. Chances are, there will be a number of gaps in your coverage. For example, someone who slips and falls while at your organization's office will probably be covered—but not if they slip while at a picnic in your local park. And injuries caused by staff members—for example, if your ED accidentally drops a case of wine on someone's foot—may be covered, while injuries caused by your volunteers may not be. Fortunately, event-specific insurance is available at a reasonable cost. Events in private homes may well be covered by homeowners' insurance. Realize, however, that almost no insurance policy is a substitute for detailed planning, and most won't cover harm caused by reckless or intentional acts (for example, if one of your volunteers drives a car filled with balloons at 90 m.p.h. and crashes or if a staff member gets into a wrestling match with a guest).

Last-Minute Tasks and Tips

The last days and hours leading up to the event are usually whirling-dervish time for even the most organized events planner or leader. Now you'll really want to put your checklists to work. Review them frequently and carefully, and double-check that all of your committee leaders are communicating with one another as needed. Here are some things no event planner should forget:

- **If you are the event leader, delegate shamelessly to make sure that your list of assignments for the actual day of the event is blank.** As Jan Etre, KPFA crafts fair organizer, says, "You should be completely available for answering questions and putting out fires. Someone will tap you on the shoulder, and you never know what's coming next—perhaps a lost child, or a parking problem." Sometimes just walking around your event can be important. One year, Karen Garrison took time out during the BHNC community-wide garage sale to walk the neighborhood, and discovered a number of "renegade" sites that hadn't paid for inclusion. After gently reminding them that this was organized as a fundraiser, she collected more fees.

- **Take a last look through your notebook, to make sure nothing got lost in the shuffle.** Make confirmation calls to any important speakers or vendors. Make sure that all money owed to you has been paid, and that you have paid all the appropriate vendors. You don't want to be signing checks and working out small disputes over financial matters during the event itself.

- **If you're having a sit-down lunch or dinner event, take your final list of ticket buyers and draft a seating chart.** Create an easy way for people to find their way to their tables, such as a number on a flag in the centerpieces. And be sure the registration staff know what to do if someone shows up without a ticket.

- **Pack any items that could possibly be useful in a pinch, such as adhesive tape, petty cash, a stapler, trashbags, paper towels, and first aid supplies.** Of course, you should also have created a checklist of—and started packing—those items you know you will need for the event, such as food and equipment.

- Buy snacks and goodies for your volunteers and water for everyone.
- **If you've rented space, make sure you'll be allowed to get in with enough advance time to set up, decorate, arrange silent auction items, and the like.** These tasks always take longer than you think they will—three to four hours is usually considered the minimum for a "typical" event.
- **Double-check that your registration tables will be adequately staffed and provided for.** A whole book could be written about the event registration process alone. Your goal is to have people registered and into the event within a few minutes of arriving. Depending on how many attendees you anticipate, this may require a whole bank of registration tables, with easily visible letters of the alphabet to divide people by name. Make sure all your volunteers know your policies on issues such as check acceptance and dealing with lost tickets.
- **Create handy contact lists of key people and vendors that you and other lead staff or volunteers can keep in their pockets or purses.** This will help reach someone in case he or she has forgotten something or you need emergency help.
- **Create a final list of who needs to be publicly thanked (hopefully, you kept a running list and will compare your final list against those of other event leaders).** At some point during the day, a key staff member or volunteer may have an opportunity to address the crowd. If so, that person should start by effusively thanking the people who did the most to bring about the event. Relying on memory has obvious dangers. If the names are too many to list one by one, refer to committees or groups, and make clear that there were many helpers who must remain unnamed.

TIP

You can't prepare for everything. Some final thoughts from events planner Laurie Earp: "Life happens, and you've just got to be ready for surprises—the caterer who doesn't show up, entertainers who bring lighting that's not bright enough to see them by, or equipment cables too short to reach electrical outlets. If you think on your feet, you'll find a way around the problem, and the event will be great in the end."

After the Event: Assessment and Follow-Up

A day or two after the event, you'll probably be dying to return to the other tasks you've been ignoring—all those unreturned voice messages and emails. However, if you don't tie up loose ends now and follow up with your new contacts, you may never get to these crucial tasks.

Send thank-you letters. You already know the importance of thank-you letters when dealing with individual donors, but after a special event, you'll have whole new lists of people to thank—and each one is critical. If you haven't already, send personalized thank-yous to every committee head, volunteer, sponsor, individual donor (including donors who bought things at auctions, because part of their payment was a contribution—but not including people who purchased items from independent vendors at craft or art fairs), and business donors. Remember to note the amount of any financial contribution, minus the value of anything received in return, for IRS purposes.

Issue press releases. If the story of what happened at your event is media worthy, then you should immediately send out a separate press release—for example, describing and quoting the contents of your famous speaker's presentation, complete with his or her photo, or announcing the winners of your bicycle race.

Reach out to participants. This step is one that too many nonprofit organizations skip. But with your organization fresh in the minds of everyone who came to your event—some of whom may be entirely new contacts—you'll be squandering some of your hard work if you don't implement some strategic follow-through.

For starters, you must immediately enter information on every person in the room into your database, so that they receive any emails, newsletters, or other communications that you're already preparing. Next, take a close look at the list of new contacts and consider (based on anything you know about them, such as who brought them), whether they are prospects for more targeted follow-up. If possible, have a board member or another volunteer call and thank everyone who isn't already closely affiliated with your organization for attending, find out more about what brought them to the event, and then discuss how they might get further involved.

Collect committee members' thoughts. Even if your event was a roaring success, there are no doubt many lessons to be learned from it. And, if there is any possibility that you might repeat this or a similar event, you'll want to collect all relevant information about what worked and what didn't. Assemble your committee leaders, and potentially the entire committees, to collect impressions of what they felt went well or could have been done better. Alternatively, you can simply distribute surveys asking what worked and what didn't. Remember to keep the focus positive. Although there will undoubtedly be touchy areas where people would love to shift or assign blame, the important thing is to constructively figure out how similar problems can be prevented in the future.

Prepare a final budget. One of your most important tasks is to draw up a final event budget and compare it to the original budget, to see how well your projections ultimately matched up with reality. After you've collected all your information, write up all of your narrative and budgetary conclusions, and put them into your event folder for future reference.

Update your notebook. Finally, imagine that this time next year, you and all your committee leaders will be enjoying Brie and baguettes at an undisclosed Parisian location. Meanwhile, back at the nonprofit, some poor soul will be trying to recreate your smashingly successful event. Will your notebook and files be enough to tell the whole story of how the event was done, who helped out (or flaked out), who was invited, who did the graphic design and printing, where to advertise, which media outlets were responsive, what other vendors to contract with, and the rest?

This is not an idle exercise—nonprofit turnover rates being what they are, you really could be somewhere else next year, or you might have simply forgotten all the details that seem so deeply burned into your brain right now. Go through your notebook and add any documents that are floating around elsewhere, making sure every section is complete and writing memos to explain important issues that aren't otherwise covered.

The Importance of Recognizing People's Special Efforts

Dr. H was a successful businessman with a comfortable cushion of inherited wealth. His family had a tradition of philanthropy, and he gave generously to a number of causes. When a local charity hosted a fundraising dinner, Dr. H bought tickets for an entire table, filled it with his friends, and made sure that his table set the evening's record for spending the most at the auction.

After the event was over, Dr. H promptly received a thank-you letter—but it was the same letter that everyone else involved in the event received. A form letter. It made no mention of the special efforts he'd made or the amount he and his friends had given. He felt sufficiently let down that he cut his contributions to that organization and has not attended any further events. He doesn't even return their phone calls—and they're still scratching their heads about it.

RESOURCE

Want more information on special events? The following are helpful, well-written guides offering further detail on the process of holding special events:

- *Event Planning: The Ultimate Guide to Successful Meetings, Corporate Events, Fundraising Galas, Conferences, Conventions, Incentives and Other Special Events,* by Judy Allen (Wiley)
- *Special Events: Proven Strategies for Nonprofit Fundraising,* by Alan L. Wendroff (Wiley)
- *The Business of Special Events: Fundraising Strategies for Changing Times,* by Harry A. Freedman and Karen Feldman (Pineapple Press), and
- *The Volunteers' Guide to Fundraising: Raise Money for Your School, Team, Library, or Community Group,* by Ilona Bray (Nolo).

Raising Money Through Business or Sales Activities

There have been times—usually late at night, when struggling over a grant proposal—when I've wondered whether it wouldn't be easier to just stand by the nearest bus stop and sell cookies. With all the time a fundraiser spends trying to engage people's hearts and minds, an anonymous transaction in which you engage little more than someone's taste buds can look like a welcome relief.

Of course, my idea isn't an original one. There is a time-honored non-profit tradition of hawking cookies, T-shirts, and tote bags, as well as conducting raffles, garage sales, and even car washes to augment other fundraising activities. Sometimes the only thing that stops a nonprofit from going into one of these or similar businesses is fear of the unknown—or of the IRS, which can investigate and ultimately shut down nonprofits that stray too far into the profit-seeking world.

On the other side of the coin, many nonprofits take a full plunge into commercial enterprise, by starting major side businesses, such as restaurants or retail shops, in some cases enlisting their clients' help, or entering into relationships with for-profit business ventures. Although some of these businesses have prospered or been spun off into successful subsidiaries, a daunting number have failed miserably, and a few have indeed dragged the nonprofits into trouble with the IRS.

TIP

Business is business, whatever the terminology. A lot of highfalutin terms have been coined to describe profit-making efforts by nonprofits, including "social entrepreneurship," "social-purpose enterprises," and "social enterprise." The trouble is, there is little agreement as to what these terms really mean. For example, "social-purpose enterprise" is sometimes used to describe a business staffed by clients to further the mission while at the same time raising money, while other times it's used to refer to any business run by a nonprofit. And "social entrepreneurship" is sometimes used to describe nonprofit business activities, but in other instances to describe philanthropists who "invest" their dollars in a social cause. To steer clear of all this semantic confusion, I'll simply refer to all of these activities as business ventures run by nonprofits.

It's impossible to draw a firm conclusion as to whether small-business ventures make sense for a particular nonprofit. There are just too many variables, and much depends on the skills, interests, and energy of the people involved—you might as well ask whether an ordinary person who wants to make money should open a business. Experience has shown that nonprofit-run ventures are no guaranteed pots of gold—even nonprofits that enjoy significant success in the business realm have to overcome major challenges, some of which inevitably take time and energy away from their altruistic concerns. But one generalization seems to hold true—starting a business is not a good strategy for a nonprofit that's desperate for cash, because a significant return on initial investment usually doesn't come for a few years at best.

On the other hand, for those nonprofits able to find a profitable market niche, their ability to draw funds from outside the usual donor pool can contribute mightily to their growth and long-term survival. The YMCA, for example, whose central mission remains to nurture young people, earns about 70% of its revenues from health club membership and other program fees—many paid by affluent adults who just want a good place to work out.

Business revenues offer entrepreneurial nonprofits a way to break out of heavy reliance on grant funding. And they can simultaneously make funders more excited about your operation's long-term growth prospects, and therefore more likely to fund you in the future. In fact, the prevailing belief among many funders is that the very process of starting and running a business venture can transform a nonprofit into a more effective and efficient operation.

Driven by these and other reasons, nonprofits are entering the business world like never before. Yet many of the start-ups one hears about seem to drop off the map after a year or two—it's a field that's littered with empty storefronts and dead Web links.

So, the question becomes, would marketing goods or services to the general public give your nonprofit a fresh way to bring in significant dollars from sources outside your donor base—better yet, funds with no strings attached? Or would it drag your staff into spending precious time on activities outside your core mission that end up producing little return— and may even lose money or jeopardize your tax-exempt status? This chapter will help you answer these questions, by considering:

- how much business activity the IRS permits without penalty
- lessons that can be learned from other nonprofits' business successes and failures
- how to come up with a business idea that's a good match for your nonprofit
- how to compare your business ideas with market realities
- how to create a business plan, and
- whether partnering with an existing business makes sense.

> (!) **CAUTION**
>
> **Is your accounting house in order?** Unless and until you've got a good in-house bookkeeper and an outside accountant, who have together successfully implemented a system for efficiently tracking your existing costs and cash flow, don't even think of launching a small business. The dollars will be flying around a lot faster once you start a business, and you'll need to be ready to keep up.

Tax Rules for Business Activities

Your organization was granted its 501(c)(3) status—and therefore allowed to avoid paying taxes—because its founders said that it would engage in charitable activities, not in for-profit business like the rest of the corporate sector. And the IRS will hold you to your promise, by taxing certain business activities and even revoking your tax-exempt status if you start to look more like a for-profit business than a charitable organization. But the prohibition against nonprofits' engaging in business is far from absolute. As long as a nonprofit stays away from ongoing profit-making activities that don't further its purposes and don't personally benefit any individual (other than a client), it's usually not at risk of losing its 501(c)(3) status. This means that a nonprofit can engage in one-time or irregular business activities, or business activities that fall squarely within its mission, as long as all profits go to the nonprofit and don't benefit insiders, such as staff or directors.

Sounds simple enough. But what understandably confuses many nonprofit managers about the federal tax law is the large gray area that exists between those activities that are absolutely prohibited and those that are clearly permissible. Much of this confusion stems from the fact that a nonprofit can, in some circumstances, engage in business activities beyond the limits of its tax-exempt mission or that are ongoing, without risking its existence as a nonprofit, as long as it pays corporate income tax on the business profits.

To understand how IRS rules might apply to your nonprofit's possible business ventures, it's helpful to separate business activities into the following categories:

- clearly allowable activities
- activities that raise income on which tax is assessed, but that nevertheless do not endanger the nonprofit's 501(c)(3) status, and
- business activities that the IRS considers excessive or inappropriate, and therefore undermine the group's very 501(c)(3) status.

> CAUTION
>
> **Never use nonprofit income for noncharitable purposes.** Though there's a lot of gray area in the tax rules regarding how money comes into your nonprofit, there's very little ambiguity about how it's supposed to be spent. Profits generated by a nonprofit business may not, repeat *not*, be used for the private benefit of any person or organization outside the charitable organization.

Activities That Will Never Raise IRS Eyebrows

Take a look around you—plenty of nonprofits are selling goods and services without so much as a peep from the IRS. Chances are that in storefronts near you, you'll find the Goodwill, Salvation Army, and perhaps a local church-run thrift shop. Your local museum or hospital may run both a cafeteria and gift shop. And, of course, you have the Girl Scouts selling cookies, your local public TV station peddling calendars and coffee cups, and dozens of environmental groups offering calendars, T-shirts, and tote bags.

What makes these and similar merchandising activities legally acceptable? For the most part, they're viewed by the IRS as falling into one or more of the following allowable categories:

- activities within an organization's mission
- activities that are not part of an ongoing business, or
- income or activities that are subject to a special IRS exception.

Activities Within Your Nonprofit's Mission

If your sales of goods or services are in some way tied to your organization's mission, you're probably on safe ground, tax-wise. Museum gift shops, for example, stay within their mission by selling items to educate or interest people in the subject on display—such as animal magnets at a wildlife museum or art reproductions at an art museum. Even so, these shops may be required to pay tax on some of the items they sell. For example, the IRS says that an art museum shop that sells souvenirs of the city in which it is located will have to pay tax on those items.

Organizations such as Goodwill further their mission of employing needy people, through selling used goods. Goodwill uses its shops as a training and employment center, as do many other nonprofits that run businesses such as bakeries, bicycle repair shops, and more.

Activities That Are Not Part of an Ongoing Business

A normal, for-profit business needs to keep its doors open on a fairly regular basis, or risk having customers go elsewhere. To maintain a clear separation between these businesses and nonprofits, the IRS allows nonprofits to make sales that occur irregularly or a few times a year. For example, the Girl Scouts sell cookies only once a year (to the frustration of many a sweet-toothed consumer), so their cookie sales are not part of an ongoing business. They could probably sell cookies more often than once a year and still be fine—as long as the sales aren't as frequent as those a commercial business would conduct in order to survive and prosper.

Other examples of irregular nonprofit sales abound—including auctions, bake sales, benefit concerts, car washes, garage sales, calendar sales, and more. Most of these tend to be specially scheduled activities, outside the nonprofit's usual day-to-day work. The one area where you need to be careful, however, is with activities that are sporadic by nature—for example, if you run a catering business that is hired only every few weeks or so, you may look very much like an ordinary catering business—although not a wildly successful one.

Activities That Fall Within IRS Exceptions

You might be encouraged to learn that the IRS has created numerous exceptions and exclusions: Activities or income that fall within these categories are automatically considered nontaxable. Smaller groups that sell the occasional T-shirt or coffee mug (as much to encourage organizational solidarity as to raise money) will be delighted to learn that they needn't report annual earned income amounts less than $1,000. Such small amounts don't even require the nonprofit to file a tax return, even if the business activities were clearly outside or unrelated to the group's mission. The other major exceptions include business activities in which:

- Substantially all of the work of providing the services or creating the products is done by volunteers (for example, if you sell volunteer-created baked goods or crafts, or your volunteers can be hired as translators).
- The product or services are primarily for the convenience of the group's members, students, patients, officers, or employees (for example, an on-site cafeteria or pharmacy).
- The nonprofit accepts money from a company that sponsors its educational, fundraising, or other event and displays the company's name or logo on its premises or publications in return. But it's not okay for the nonprofit to provide the company with advertising or allow it to use the nonprofit's logo in company periodicals. (For example, you can't devote a page of your newsletter to a company ad, or accept payment for having your logo appear in company materials, without paying tax on any income you receive.)
- The nonprofit sells merchandise that was donated to the organization (an important exception that allows for the many thrift shops, donated-goods auctions, and used-car resale businesses run by nonprofits).
- Bingo games are used as fundraisers (as long as bingo is legal in the nonprofit's area, and is not played in a hall that's also used for commercial bingo gaming).
- A nonprofit exchanges or rents its membership list with another nonprofit.
- Entertainment is provided to attract people to a fair or exposition that promotes agriculture or education.

The IRS also excludes from tax any income that comes from:

- dividends, interest, annuities, and other investment income
- royalties earned from allowing use of the nonprofit's trademark, trade name, copyrighted material, or other valuable rights (but not personal appearances or services)
- rents from real property (such as land or buildings; but see IRS Publication 598, *Tax on Unrelated Business Income of Exempt Organizations* for the various exceptions, for example if you're also providing personal services to the renters, or if you've got a mixture of real and personal property, such as equipment)
- income from research grants or contracts, and
- gains and losses from selling property.

> **SEE AN EXPERT**
>
> **Get answers to your questions about unrelated business income.** This section summarizes the IRS's definitions, exclusions, and exceptions dealing with unrelated business income. However, before you make any final business decisions, you'll want to read IRS Publication 598, *Tax on Unrelated Business Income of Exempt Organizations*, available on the IRS website at www.irs.gov. Consult an attorney if anything remains less than completely clear.

If you can think of an activity that would both serve your mission and bring in funds, you're in great shape. For starters, any fees that you charge for special events or client services are no problem—you don't need to worry about the federal tax implications, and you can even charge market rates.

If there aren't any natural ways to raise funds within your mission, then your next step is to consider raising revenues on an occasional basis, or starting up an activity that fits within an IRS exception. Any revenues you earn from any of these ventures will not only be safely within the rules of your tax-exempt status, but will also earn you tax-free revenue.

Activities That Will Be Taxed

What happens if your nonprofit's business activities don't fit within one of permitted categories just discussed and, instead, constitute an "unrelated trade or business"? As long as you're churning 100% of the profits back into your charitable activities, they are still permitted, with one big catch. You'll have to pay corporate income tax—to both the feds and possibly your state government—on any profits ("unrelated business income" or UBI) of more than $1,000 per year. (You pay the tax using IRS Form 990-T; if you earn less than $1,000, there's no need to file the form.) In fact, if it looks like your total tax payment (not income, but the amount you'll owe) will be $500 or more, you'll have to pay quarterly, estimated taxes even before the usual April tax time rolls around.

The IRS definition of income from an unrelated trade or business is remarkably free of tax-code gobbledygook. They call it: ... *income from a trade or business that is regularly carried on by an exempt organization and that is not substantially related to the performance by the organization of its exempt purpose or function, except that the organization uses the profits derived from this activity.*

Of course, it wouldn't be the Internal Revenue Code if there weren't a couple of terms that need defining:

- **"Trade or business"** means selling goods or services in order to produce income. If you think you're in a trade or business, you probably are. For example, if your organization charges nonclients for consultations on organic landscaping, you owe tax on the profits. And the IRS is quick to point out that you can't hide a trade or business by burying it within your exempt activities—for example, a nonprofit hospital pharmacy that sells drugs to its patients (within its charitable purpose) would still have to pay taxes on drugs it sells to the general public. As another example, selling commercial advertising in your organization's newsletter would be considered an unrelated trade or business, even if the rest of the newsletter contains reports on your nonprofit's programs.

- **"Regularly carried on"** is another term that has been the subject of much learned discussion by nonprofit tax experts and the IRS. Whether your business is "regularly carried on" (or, hopefully, is only occasional and, therefore, exempt from tax) depends on whether it's run with the same frequency and continuity as a typical profit-making business. Like any business, however, your own commercial viability may depend on running a continuous operation. So, for example, if you're planning to run a bakeshop, there's no point in closing it on odd days and times in an effort to make it "irregular"—you're better off just paying the taxes. And note that you can't necessarily get around the requirements by choosing a business with "irregular" operations, such as a catering company. If your company caters functions with the same frequency as a commercial catering company, your income will be taxable.

- **"Substantially related"** business activities—those that contribute importantly to your nonprofit purpose—are entirely tax exempt. If you're thinking that any fundraising helps you accomplish your charitable purposes, I'm sorry to report that the IRS is one step ahead of you—and specifically rules out this line of reasoning. The IRS appears to grant tax exemption when the products or services being sold are a spinoff of the nonprofit's existing activities or a direct result of its charitable activities. For example, if your organic agricultural research nonprofit sells milk produced by your herd of experimental dairy cows, the profits are not taxable—but once you start turning that milk into ice cream and the like, it stops being an activity that contributes to your charitable purposes, and you would have to pay tax on any profits.

Here are some of the IRS's examples of activities that are taxable because they constitute trades or businesses that are not substantially related to charitable purposes:

- selling a nonprofit membership list to a for-profit business
- using a school facility to run a summertime tennis club open to the general public
- selling handicrafts made by local members of the public (even if they're sold alongside handicrafts produced by the nonprofit's clients)
- renting studio apartments with dining room services to artists even though the organization's main purpose is to sponsor art events
- offering pet boarding and grooming to the public (even if it's by an organization dedicated to preventing cruelty to animals)
- offering travel tours that don't include an educational component related to the group's purpose, or
- charging for the use of an organization's name on product endorsements.

Activities That Risk a Nonprofit's 501(c)(3) Status

Paying tax on your unrelated business activities is not as good as paying no tax at all, but it's greatly preferable to engaging in activities that call into question your nonprofit's 501(c)(3) tax status. Unfortunately, you can face this unhappy situation if doing business becomes the focal point of your nonprofit's activities. This is doubtless one reason your local YMCA works so hard to raise money for its charitable programs, despite all the profits it is likely to make from fitness centers.

Unfortunately, there's neither a bright line nor a numeric amount (such as a percentage of total income or a flat dollar figure) at which the IRS automatically finds that your profit-making business is too large in comparison to your tax-exempt activities. However, if your programs are shrinking but your business is growing, it's time to take a closer look. And even if both your business and nonprofit activities are growing, if you're lucky enough to enjoy substantial business profits, it may be time to spend some of that money on a nonprofit lawyer who can evaluate the situation for you.

> **TIP**
> **Consider creating a separate tax-paying organization.** If your business activities threaten to overwhelm your nonprofit purpose, you might want to make the business a separate, for-profit venture. For example, if your education-centered nonprofit publishes calendars and books that become hugely popular and profitable, it might make sense to spin those activities off into their own publishing company. This way, the business could channel its profits in your direction, without threatening your 501(c)(3) status. You'll need a lawyer's help for this.

Learn From Other Nonprofits' Experiences

To help you get a sense of the range of business ventures that might work for your nonprofit, this section takes a closer look at how other nonprofits have fared. Although only a minority of nonprofits engage in any significant business activities, the creativity and range among those that do is inspiring. Nevertheless, a number of hard lessons have been learned along the way— which gives you an opportunity to avoid relearning them.

As a broad generalization, nonprofit businesses fall into two categories:

- enterprises centered on client training and employment, and
- sales of goods and services produced by nonclients or outside sources, sometimes but not always with a thematic connection to a nonprofit's mission and work.

Although hybrids of the two models certainly exist, each category is covered separately below, so as best to highlight its advantages and challenges.

Client-Based Businesses

The ultimate in mission-based enterprises is to involve your clients in some part of the business. Sometimes called "social-purpose enterprise," this strategy has been utilized by numerous nonprofits to teach business, vocational, or life skills to low-income, disadvantaged, homeless, recovering, or disabled clients. Instead of training the clients and then sending them elsewhere to get "real" experience, such organizations bring the world of business in-house.

The clients use their newly acquired commercial skills to do everything from selling Christmas trees and moving furniture to woodworking, mechanics, cooking, landscaping, and computing. Typically, they either create things for sale or operate businesses serving the general public. As a result, consumers can now purchase everything from coffins to salad dressing to Web design services for good causes.

Ideally, social-purpose businesses will earn enough to be able to pay the client-employees salaries or stipends, thus reinforcing the larger point that work is rewarding. In rare cases, it might even bring in profits to the organization.

CAUTION

Operating a client-based business is probably not the most efficient way to raise funds. While businesses that use clients as workers may provide the clients with excellent training and life skills opportunities, such businesses' chances of doing much better than breaking even are slim. They're a fine idea if your main goal is to create a setting where clients can gain real business experience, but a poor choice if you need to raise extra funds to cover other programs.

The biggest advantage to running a client-based business occurs when clients are already at the core of your mission and will benefit from your business activities. If the client-based business raises funds you would have otherwise had to get from foundations, individual donors, or other fundraising efforts, you're already far ahead of where you would have been—and probably running a more exciting and educational program to boot. And if your customers are satisfied with what you sell them, and if you make sure they understand the role your nonprofit played in bringing this interaction about, you may turn your customers into donors.

However, if starting this type of business will represent a significant expansion or alteration of your existing programs, you'll also need to take a close look at the disadvantages—and they can be many. Organizations with experience in running client-based businesses—even successful ones—have identified the following unique challenges:

- low worker efficiency and high turnover, as compared to for-profit businesses
- difficulty in finding professional-level managers to oversee operations
- conflicts between mission-related goals and business goals, and
- heightened risk that business failure will harm the lives of client workers.

Worker efficiency and turnover issues. Let's start with the most hopeful scenario: Your new client-based business has been well planned and managed and breaks even almost from the start. Best of all, your clients are learning a new skill—perhaps baking or bicycle repair. Customers appreciate the quality of what they're receiving and are returning for more and sending their friends. Your client workers enthusiastically complete their training in a matter of months and find better-paying jobs in the private sector. But unfortunately, you now have a new problem—you've just lost valuable, trained workers, while you must continue pleasing your growing customer base.

Even with good planning, this problem doesn't always have an easy solution. Assuming that part of your goal is to help your clients develop job skills, you certainly don't want to discourage them from moving on, both to better themselves and to make room for new clients. But the inevitable result is that unless you can carefully phase your "graduations" so as to always have a decent number of experienced workers, you'll always be trying to run a business with new or only minimally trained workers.

Of course, quick success probably won't be your biggest problem. If you honestly consider who your clients are, you may also have to face the very real reasons that they're not already in the workforce. Sometimes a second chance is all someone needs, but often it's not that easy. As worthy of help and respect as they are, your clients may lack not only tangible work skills, but other personal qualities customers have come to expect.

Basic things like showing up regularly or on time and interacting appropriately with others can sometimes be significant problems, depending on a client's personal background and ongoing medical, family, or other needs. For clients with cognitive difficulties, completing tasks will obviously take longer—which can become frustrating to the clients if they're put under pressure. And clients with criminal backgrounds may even fall into old habits around your inventory or cash register.

To some extent, you can factor these issues into your business planning by choosing a type of business that is easy to run, doubling up on personnel on any given shift, and providing extra supervision and separate counseling, for example. But no matter which way you slice it, your business efficiency will be reduced.

Finding qualified managers. If extra supervision is required, you may need some luck to find it. Your existing staffers may be highly skilled in client training and support, but not necessarily in the business aspects of supervising a staff, much less in other business management techniques. You may well have to hire additional staff—but finding a person who has the full plate of business and client interaction skills may not be easy, especially at a salary you can afford.

Once again, high turnover isn't going to help a fledgling business. There is some hope on the horizon, though: As more and more business schools establish nonprofit management programs, the field is receiving growing attention and interest, so the pool of applicants may expand. And the down economy has left many skilled people hungry for work. When you do find a skilled person, he or she will probably have knowledge and talents to lend to other aspects of running your nonprofit.

Conflicts between serving clients and serving customers. If your client-based business doesn't turn a decent profit—and it probably won't in the first few years—conflicts may arise between your organization's goals and needs and the business's requirements. For example, what if you're attempting to pay your clients a salary—but having trouble paying them the minimum amount that will allow them to stick with the program? If neither your business profits nor your agency's budget can accommodate such expenditures, you've got a conflict. Or what if one of your client workers is going through a personal crisis, and others feel that the first priority should be to listen to and support him or her—even if it means setting the work aside? A steely-eyed businessperson might take a more draconian approach to these issues than you can—or should. But you may find yourself choosing whether the organization as a whole or the business suffers—with the added frustration that the business may have been budgeted to be self-supporting.

Impact of failure on client workers. In the worst case, your business may head toward failure. While this is a reality that every business faces—and it does not mean the end of the world—failure of a nonprofit-run business may nevertheless spell unusual rupture and economic difficulty for its client workers. If your business provides the sole source of support for clients who are already on the economic margins, layoffs may, in an instant, push them back toward homelessness, substance abuse, personal crises, or precisely the traps that the program was meant to help them out of. Even if the business merely reduces hours, such cuts can dampen your client workers' morale—and lower their paychecks—at a time when they're vulnerable. You might need to plan ahead for the extra client support that such a scenario would require. You might also find yourself scrambling to find other funding to plug the holes in the failing business.

RESOURCE

Want to learn more about client-run enterprises? See the publications of the Roberts Enterprise Development Fund (REDF), at www.redf.org.

Other Sales of Goods and Services

If you don't have clients to involve in your business, or you've concluded that business activities wouldn't be a good use of your clients' time, that shouldn't stop you from creating a small business that sells goods or services created by your own staff or by others.

Nonprofits operate small businesses at nearly every scale imaginable, from selling the occasional mug, to retail shops and website sales. Some of these business types are covered in more detail below—but first, here are some of the general advantages and disadvantages of running this type of business.

On the plus side, this kind of project can energize people who are tired of feeling like they're begging for money. Your business venture may be just the place to direct the skills or energies of particular board members—like the entrepreneurs or those who drag their feet when asked to do other types of fundraising. If you're really lucky, you may be able to tap into the artistic, culinary, or other skills of existing staff members or volunteers. Also, selling goods and services gives you an opportunity to reach out to people beyond your usual donor base. Everything that you sell with a tag or label on it should loudly proclaim what your organization is about and how the buyer is helping an important cause. The interested buyers may eventually turn into donors as well.

On the minus side, you're launching into an area that is probably outside the expertise of most of your staff. And, while the energy of staff and board members may be high at the beginning, their enthusiasm may flag when it comes time for the real work—or they receive the first customer complaint (complaints being inevitable), or don't see profits coming in at the rate you'd anticipated.

As with client-based operations, another inevitable disadvantage comes up when conflicts arise with your mission-based activities. In fact, these conflicts can look even starker when you're selling something that has very little immediate benefit for your mission, because it doesn't employ or train a client. For example, what if the business needs a cash investment in order to get past a difficult period or produce some inventory, but cash is tight, funding has been cut for one of your other programs, and you're already deeply in debt? Or, what if you're counting on a staffer to write a book for sale, but a pressing environmental or social concern makes it urgent for everyone to spend their time mobilizing your membership instead? If everything is happening under the same roof—or with the same people—tugs-of-war are inevitable.

Fortunately, there is a wide variety of business types and models for you to consider. At the most minimal end of the scale, many nonprofits offer souvenir-like products (e.g., T-shirts or mugs) showing their logos or something thematically related to the work that they do, such as wild animals for an environmental group. (There are scads of companies that will quickly print your organization's logo, a photo, or another design on just about anything you want.) Many nonprofits make such items available as small thank-you gifts for donations, but in part because the unit costs for these items are far cheaper when they are purchased in large numbers, nonprofits often end up with a garage full of items they need to sell separately. Most fundraising staffers will tell you that these small-scale sales are not a good way to raise money, but they keep the sales going for other reasons, such as getting the organization's name into the public eye and increasing membership. Nevertheless, with the right kind of sales strategy and perhaps volunteer commitment, you can turn anything into a moneymaker if you sell it for significantly more than you paid for it.

Another common nonprofit enterprise is small-scale publishing of books, reports, or classroom materials produced by the groups' own staff or supporters. The tricky parts are not so much the writing and publishing—although, done well, these are harder than most people credit—but the marketing. A huge amount of material makes it into print these days but very little of it finds a sufficient audience to be profitable. In a world where information is increasingly delivered electronically, publishing companies are failing right and left. Nevertheless, if your experts really do have valuable information on an issue that people want to know more about, you may be able to realize some profits from publishing it. The Immigrant Legal Resource Center (ILRC) in San Francisco, California, is a good example of making this niche marketing work. The ILRC's mission includes making legal and social services available to immigrants, a mission which it serves primarily by providing support—including on-call advice attorneys, regular email and printed updates, and legal seminars—to legal staff and other nonprofits serving immigrants. Because of its in-house expertise and connections to the broader immigration community, the ILRC is uniquely positioned to create manuals encapsulating its expertise, for use by immigration attorneys and advocates.

Yet another significant niche is selling products that you've sought out or commissioned in order to serve the particular interests of your clients or the larger community that cares about the issue you serve. For example, SightConnection, in Seattle, Washington (www.sightconnection.com), sells products that help the blind and partially sighted. It offers everything from magnifiers to full-spectrum lamps to talking clocks. SightConnection's revenues support its programs to help vision-impaired people maintain their independence and well being.

SightConnection Store

Reprinted with permission

And let's not forget the variety of cards and posters sold by museums and arts and environmental groups—the Sierra Club calendar is a famous, example. However, you should also take a lesson from the Sierra Club's closure of its retail stores. They found it more cost-efficient to sell online or through bookstores. You're not likely to achieve large sales unless you're either a national group with a large audience or have a killer marketing plan.

Marketing is the area where most nonprofit businesses fall down. I learned that lesson the hard way myself, while I was a legal staffer at an immigration nonprofit. I got involved in a project to create greeting cards that featured photos from the four continents, with a regional recipe on the back. I and other staffers had a wonderful time collecting the photos, trying out the recipes, and admiring the cards once we'd spent a few thousand dollars having them professionally printed. The trouble was, we didn't have a solid marketing plan in place, and at a certain point, we could no longer spare time from our client service work to pound the pavement in search of buyers or distributors. I still think the cards look beautiful—and I get to see them often, when my mother-in-law, who kindly bought several packs, uses them to write to me!

Rosie's Place Holiday Card Sales

Rosie's Place is a Boston, Massachusetts, sanctuary for poor and homeless women, offering emergency and long-term assistance with the help of private (nongovernment) funding and numerous committed volunteers. (See www. rosiesplace.org.) Since 2001, the organization has annually offered an attractive selection of nondenominational holiday cards, containing local artists' images of winter, particularly in Boston. The cards have had impressive fundraising years and slow years, as Director of Development Leemarie Mosca describes:

"From the beginning, we were able to keep production costs down in various ways. The artists—who are well-known in our area—allowed us to use images of their works at no cost, and a local printer, with whom we've built an ongoing

Sample Holiday Card

Reprinted with permission

relationship, gave us a discount. Before long, we were earning around $15,000 on the card sales. As the project evolved, we began offering organizations and companies the opportunity to buy customized cards (with their name and message inside) in bulk. That took our sales up to a record $90,000 in 2007. But our proceeds plummeted in 2008, and stayed low for the next few years.

The recession caused companies to slash their marketing budgets at the very same time that people began shifting to use of personal photo cards and e-cards.

"So, we reevaluated. We realized that these cards were more than a fundraiser for Rosie's Place—they are an important marketing and PR tool. Whenever someone sends out one of our cards (which has our mission statement on the back), they're demonstrating support for, and spreading the word about the services that Rosie's Place provides to women.

Rosie's Place Holiday Card Sales, cont'd.

"We called up the companies that had bought from us before, and said, 'We understand you aren't able to buy at the same volume; would you consider buying less as a way to share our mission with people in your network?' Then we asked our constituents (via our website and e-newsletters, print ads donated by local newspapers, bloggers, Facebook, Twitter, and the website CardsThatGive.org), to buy cards and send them to their network as a way of supporting our mission. To further attract buyers, we've made sure to offer a variety of images, so that they can send our cards out year after year without repeating the same one. And, on our order form, we added an opportunity for people to send in additional donations, which resulted in many people who were spending, say, $17, rounding up to $20.

"These efforts have brought our revenue back up to $60,000 (representing an approximately 60/40 split between companies and individuals). Not only is that good news by itself, but we feel the cards give us a springboard to promote other types of giving and engagement. Building relationships with bloggers, for instance, means they'll write about Rosie's Place's other initiatives. And people who come to our website to buy cards then notice that we also sell handcrafted jewelry (and vice versa). In redirecting our focus, we've rebuilt our card program's fundraising potential."

Develop Your Own Great—And Low-Risk—Business Idea

If, after hearing about other nonprofit experiences with developing products or services for sale, you're still enthused about this approach to fundraising, you'll need to decide what to offer. Look for a business idea that will yield a solid return with a minimal risk of failure. If that sounds painfully obvious, reflect on the fact that many fledging for-profit entrepreneurs follow the opposite strategy—they bet their money (and often everything they can borrow) on the Next Big Thing, with the hope of making millions. It's best to leave them to their fantasies.

To minimize risk, you'll need to think about what goods or services your nonprofit is best able to provide, and what the public wants. So that you won't be doing all the thinking alone, I also provide a plan for brainstorming as a group.

> **CAUTION**
>
> **Risk is inevitable.** If a risk-free business niche existed, someone else would have long since filled it. However, the existence of risk shouldn't be a new pill for your nonprofit to swallow: If you're careful, starting a relatively low-risk business should be little different than the risks you take with other fundraising efforts, such as sending out a direct mail package or holding a special event.

What Goods or Services You Can Offer

Looking for a side business for your nonprofit is a little like looking for a night job for yourself. For example, if I wanted to pick up some extra money, the last thing I should do is apply to be a car mechanic or a pet groomer, having spent my life at various research and writing jobs. Conceiving of an added career for your nonprofit should operate on the same principle—don't stray too far from what you or your inner circle knows best.

In fact, your best starting point for a business or sales idea is the very asset list you drafted to create your fundraising plan in Chapter 3. (If you skipped that chapter, go back and look it over now.) Many of the items on your asset list will be relevant to planning a business as well. Good examples are all around you—every hospital that opens its cafeteria to the public, every museum that sells reproductions of its artworks, and every public radio station that sells tapes and CDs of its programs makes use of assets it already has or owns as part of its mission.

Similarly, some organizations identify a good or service already being offered to their clients—such as a seminar on recovering from addiction or learning how to budget—and make it available to the general public for a price. You can get even more creative, as the Red Cross did in designing First Aid Emergency Preparedness Kits for sale (see www.redcross.org). Similarly, various environmental organizations offer test kits for radon, arsenic, and other home and garden toxins.

What Customers Want or Need

There's no point in having a great product or service unless someone will buy it. Customers can be fickle, but you can stay in the safety zone by focusing on goods or services that you know are already needed or wanted. (Especially if your organization is dedicated to protecting the environment, it should avoid selling unneeded junk that will further deplete world resources and quickly end up in a landfill.)

Taking the for-profit business world as a model for the moment, you might notice that some of the most successful, as well as socially responsible businesses, are not begun with the primary motive of making money. Instead, they were born when someone noticed a gap in existing products or services—sometimes out of personal dismay that they couldn't find what they needed—and took steps to fill that gap. For example, Anita Roddick, founder of the Body Shop, says she got her idea of producing natural cosmetics that didn't demean women with false promises of eternal youth from her own irritation that she couldn't find such products. (See her book, *Business as Unusual* (Thorsons), for more information on how her U.K.-based company created a business revolution by treating its employees well, seeking out small, nonexploitative suppliers, and investing its profits in human rights and other campaigns.)

Another example is the founder of Patagonia, Yvon Chouinard, a blacksmith and mountain climber who was disturbed that the very steel pitons he was creating were contributing to damage to the wilderness. He started by creating alternate, aluminum gear, then branched into clothing and other supplies, and Patagonia was born. And finally, let's not forget Nolo, the publisher of this book, begun by legal-aid lawyers who saw that sky-high legal fees meant ordinary people were going without basic legal services and protections, when getting a divorce or writing a will. They published a pamphlet explaining how to do your own divorce, and the rest is Nolo history. (See "About Nolo," at www.nolo.com.)

If you aren't poised to fill a gap like this, your next best bet is to identify goods or services that people already need or are buying, and that they'd be willing to buy from a different source. Food is the classic example here: We all need food—or can at least justify buying it—every day. This is yet another reason that those Girl Scout cookies have been around for so many years. (In fact, anything containing chocolate seems to rank high on the list of what people regard as "necessary.") The salad dressings, popcorn, and spaghetti sauces sold by Newman's Own (which donates all profits to charity) are the stuff of fundraising legend, having earned over $370 million for good causes since the company began in the early 1980s.

Though choosing to sell food means that you'll always be competing with other providers, you have a big potential edge: As Paul Newman once said, "If you can make people aware that things are going to charity, and if there are two competing products on the shelf, maybe people will grab the one where some good will actually come of it" ("Newman's Own: Two Friends and a Canoe Paddle," by Jon Gertner, *The New York Times*, November 16, 2003).

Food is not your only possibility, of course. People also need clothing, though perhaps not a T-shirt or baseball cap from every nonprofit they support. Fleece jackets and other athletic wear seem to be the nonprofits' current clothing sales items of choice. Be cautious, however, in considering the potential profit margins—you'll essentially be reselling something that someone else has put all the labor and materials into, which means that they'll have to charge you a reasonable amount unless they're exploiting someone. If the only thing that makes the clothes that you're selling unique is a logo from your nonprofit, you'd better have a large and enthusiastic membership. You might have better luck, if one of your volunteers is willing, for example, to produce hand-dyed scarves for sale.

People also need shelter. You may not be able to sell them a home, but my college alumni association came up with an interesting idea, by setting up a bed-and-breakfast network. Traveling alumni were linked up with other alums willing to open up their homes, and the B&B fee went straight to the college.

People may not "need" recreation, but they are willing to pay for it. This accounts for the many tours run by nonprofits, in particular colleges, environmental groups, or groups with an international focus. You don't have to plan an overnight, or an international tour—a simple day trip, on a bus, boat, or on foot, can be a great way to start. One advantage you have as a nonprofit is that more and more travelers are actually searching for something more meaningful than a margarita-on-the-beach outing. If you can offer a combination of scenery and education, you may attract people who are genuinely interested in your nonprofit's work and will pay to get involved in it.

> ⊘ **CAUTION**
> **The IRS closely scrutinizes travel tours.** In the IRS's view, tours by nonprofits compete closely with those offered by for-profit businesses and may be required to pay tax accordingly. Still, if you introduce a unique educational component, you should be able to operate tax free. Consult a lawyer for information and advice specific to your tour idea.

People also need information. Because many nonprofits occupy forgotten niches of our society, they have developed expertise in areas that no one else gives much thought to. You might use your in-house expertise to offer classes or create books, classroom materials, or other printed materials for sale. Just be sure you truly do occupy a specialized niche or have information that would be in wide demand—as mentioned earlier, the world is becoming saturated with free information, so it isn't always feasible to make money from selling it.

The lesson here is that the most solid business ideas begin close to home. But you'll still need a little brainstorming and inspiration to come up with an idea custom-fitted to your own organization, as discussed next.

Engage a Brainstorming Group

Like your fundraising plan, thinking up a business is not something you should do on your own. If you're seriously considering a business or sales venture, pull together a small working group (under ten people) of staff and board members to generate ideas. You might also ask people from outside the "usual suspects" list to join the group—perhaps donors or vendors with experience in the type of business you're contemplating, or in sales or marketing. (This type of short-term commitment is ideal for many volunteers.) Ask the group to come together for a brainstorming meeting.

In preparation for the meeting, write down, on a chart or blackboard, the assets you identified on your fundraising list and any additional assets specific to generating business. On a separate chart or half of the blackboard, write down the community needs that your organization recognizes based on its unique expertise and community position. These might be things like "weekend activities for kids," "nutrition counseling," or "morning coffee."

Start by asking your group to help add to both sides of the chart, by suggesting ideas that will utilize or rely on your organization's assets. Also see whether your list of known community needs points to any assets that you forgot your organization had. Tell people to feel free to suggest ideas that will require some outside expertise or help—that may be inevitable. Also be clear that at this point, you're not talking about any particular size or scale of business—everything from an annual sandwich sale to a nationwide Web design service is a potential candidate for consideration.

Be open to, and write down, all the ideas that come up. By starting with the assets list, however, you've made the message clear—any idea worth its salt is going to have to have some grounding in what your organization is already doing (or is capable of doing) without too far a stretch.

After you've brainstormed, take a break (or even close the meeting for that day). Then come back later and evaluate your ideas. Ask your group to help you draw arrows between the assets and community needs, to see whether there are any obvious linkages. Those with linkages should be the first up for consideration. Assets without arrows to known needs should be reassessed, to determine whether they can be linked to a need you hadn't thought of. Listed needs with no assets in place to meet them should be tossed. Take notes on each idea's advantages and disadvantages. See how many of the items below you can answer "yes" to—the winning ideas should have the most "yes" answers. (Your group may not know the answers to all of these questions, but should do the best it collectively can.)

- ☐ Does your organization have special assets, expertise, or potential partners that can be used in this business?
- ☐ Can the up-front costs be kept to a minimum?
- ☐ Can the business be started relatively quickly—preferably in less than six months?
- ☐ Is the business likely to generate enough profit to support other program activities, or, alternately, is your organization content to start a social purpose enterprise that will be self-supporting while it achieves an important mission-related purpose?
- ☐ Is there one person within your organization who can enthusiastically dedicate most of his or her time, thought, and

energy to this project (a factor widely cited as vital to a nonprofit business venture's success)?

☐ Will you be able to deliver a product of high enough quality to compete in the marketplace?

☐ Does the business steer clear of high-risk, potentially high-liability activities, such as working with hazardous materials or caring for children?

☐ Will your intended customers really be able to find your product and be willing to pay for it? (For example, starting a fancy sit-down restaurant in a fast-food neighborhood is almost certainly a bad idea.)

☐ Can your existing staff spare enough time to help launch and run the business? How else could they be deployed to raise money if you didn't start a business?

☐ Will the activities involved in starting and running the business be meaningful—or, hopefully, even enjoyable—for the participants and affected staff and board members?

☐ Can the business be started on a small scale, so you won't be forced into higher overhead costs or production runs than you can necessarily handle?

☐ Is the business likely to stand the test of time, rather than fade due to changes in fads or technology?

☐ Can your organization survive if the business doesn't live up to expectations?

☐ When all is said and done, could you make more money with a simple auction or raffle? Though this sounds facetious, the expenses and effort of running a small business often cancel out many of its profits, while mobilizing your volunteers and collecting donated goods will often reliably produce a one-time major cash influx.

At the end of this meeting, an idea or two may emerge as promising. Remember, this isn't a final decision. You'll need to do some more research on costs and demand and talk to others. You'll also want to reconsider the financial questions on this list with your core group of leaders and accountants. (And don't forget, there's no shame in deciding that your organization isn't in a position to launch any sort of business at all.)

Measure Your Ideas Against Reality

Once you've got some agreement on likely business prospects from the key members within your organization, it's time to do some real-world research. Do not skip this step! Running any kind of business involves risk—an estimated three out of four will close in the first five years. Let's look at some realistic ways of measuring your chances of success in the world of small business generally, including customer research, price research, and competition research.

Customer Research

By now, you should have identified a product or service that you reasonably believe your customers could benefit from. But the big question remains: Will they buy it? For example, many of us need funeral plots, but how many of us plan to shop for one in the near future? And if your business sells something new or innovative, its existence may be so far from any customers' imaginations that they don't think to look for it. Fortunately, multitudes of business and marketing experts who've gone before you have turned customer research into a science. Use as many of the below methods as it takes to get you a set of consistent, logical answers.

Talk to owners of similar businesses. Look for businesses that do what you'll do, in a similar locale. To avoid future competitive problems, focus on those outside your own neighborhood or city. If you can find a business being run by a nonprofit, all the better. Be open about who you are and what your goals include, and ask them to spend a few minutes telling you about what's worked, what lessons they've learned, who their best customers are, what kind of marketing has been most successful, and how long it took their business to get on its feet. You'll be surprised at how eager some businesspeople are to talk, once they realize you're serious and that you respect their need to protect their own interests. Even local business owners may reveal more than you'd expect if you stop by, as a customer, and simply ask, "How's business?"

Observe customers of similar businesses. Let's say you'll be opening a bagel bakery. If you stop by a bagel bakery in a nearby city and munch slowly on your cream cheese and lox for an hour or two, you should be able to pick up scads of relevant information: the going prices, number of customers, number of employees, favorite flavors, number of people who buy sandwiches versus a dozen to take home, discounts the bakery offers in order to boost sales, sources of customer complaints, and amount of leftover inventory at the end of the day. (Remember that if you visit during lunch hour or a busy time, it doesn't represent the entire business day.) An even more effective approach is for someone in your organization to volunteer in the business for a week or two. Yes, it's time consuming, but there is no better way to learn a lot quickly.

Talk to, or survey, your most likely customers. It may be that your customers are people already known to you—for example, patients at your clinic, patrons of your museum, or participants in your classes. You can either talk to them informally or ask them to fill out a survey containing simple questions like, "Would you be interested if we made (a café, gift shop, etc.) available?" "Would $_____ be a reasonable price to pay?" "How often would you be likely to purchase this?" "Is there a related product or service that you wish we'd offer instead?" Also talk, or send surveys to, any sympathetic friends, family, or supporters of your organization.

If your customers are not likely to be people with whom you're already in contact, you'll need to start by defining who you think your customers are most likely to be, such as "middle-income teens involved in sports and living in the nearby suburbs" or "wealthy urban vegetarians with pets." Likely characteristics around which to define your customers include (depending on your business type) age, gender, income level, profession, family size or composition, ethnic background, geographic location, education level, media preferences, buying habits, and hobbies or activities.

Once you've created your customer profile, you can—probably by going through friends and friends of friends—pull together a group of people who fit that profile and are willing to serve as a focus group. Ask them to test your product (if you have it available already) or to offer their opinions as prospective customers. If possible, try to offer choices—would they rather you located your service here or there, do they prefer doughnuts or pancakes, what kind of people do they think would buy your product, and the like. Although commercial operations pay people to serve on focus groups, you have every right to ask for volunteers—but should treat them well and probably serve snacks!

Research demographic data. Using your developing sense of who your customers are most likely to be, research how many of them are around. If your likely customers are clients or visitors to your nonprofit's office, counting them up should be easy. If, however, you're seeking a new customer base, you'll probably need to rely on sources such as the U.S. census (www.census.gov). Your local reference librarian can be a great source of help with such research.

Price Research

If you'll be selling goods or services, a basic question you'll need to answer is whether you can sell enough of them, at a hefty enough markup, to make a profit. Once you add the costs of purchasing or producing the goods or services, plus an adequate profit margin, you may be shocked at how much you have to charge. Although this may result in your developing a new sympathy for small businesses trying to compete in a Walmart world, it may also cause you to conclude that, like so many of them, you simply can't charge a competitive price. No surprise there—the low prices consumers expect to pay for many items are based on low-wage overseas workers, highly automated supply chains, and high-volume discounts at the wholesale level, none of which are available to you.

But one thing you can and should do, if you plan to sell goods and services beyond a small circle of maniacal supporters, is be sure the price you plan to charge is within the realm of reasonableness. Fortunately, it's easy to compare prices on the Internet, or by calling the merchants you find in your local yellow pages.

Even if you find that your survival depends on charging slightly above-market rates, don't despair. For starters, remember that you have no obligation to sell things on the cheap (despite common myths about nonprofit law). And, if enough of your customers will buy from you rather than the bargain warehouse down the block, you may still do well. But, all of your advertising and other materials should clearly explain that by buying your product or service, the customer is supporting a good cause. See "Stand By Your Price," below, for an example of how one nonprofit learned this lesson.

Stand by Your Price

The DAMAYAN Migrant Workers Association came up with a fundraising idea that its volunteers and new members were excited about: to set out a table at the Asia Pacific American Festival in Union Square Park, New York City, and sell homecooked Filipino treats. (DAMAYAN is a nonprofit membership organization that organizes Filipino domestic workers in the New York area to fight for their rights and welfare; www.damayanmigrants.org.) Here's how Amanda Vender, then board member, describes the event:

"It was a beautiful, sunny day. We unfurled our newly painted green banner, propped up the photo display of recent events, and put out stacks of brochures. Most of the table was filled with trays of cassava cake, biko rice cakes, and empanadas—$2 each. Festivalgoers flocked to our table.

"When the time came to pack up, the organizers found the food trays empty and the brochure stack mostly full. And when all of the cooks were reimbursed for the ingredients, we found that we had only broken even. What happened?

"It turned out that a few festivalgoers were more resourceful than we were. They negotiated down the price of our sweets and empanadas, saying that they were cheaper at other tables. And as the day went on, our volunteer salespeople rushed to get rid of the perishable goods. Two dollars apiece became $1.50, then $1.00, then 50 cents, then three for a dollar, and finally four for a dollar!

"We had obviously forgotten an important element: to sell our organization, not just the empanadas. With the help of a fundraising consultant, we learned that we should have been telling customers: 'Your donation of two dollars helps to support our organization. We organize Filipino domestic workers—some of the most isolated and exploited workers in the city—to know their rights and to fight for better conditions.'

"Before our next fundraising event, we resolved that everyone involved would practice and roleplay our fundraising pitch, and will hand out a DAMAYAN flyer to every customer."

Competition Research

Even if you think you know who your likely competition is, double-check this with some research. The purpose is to discover how many other similar businesses there are in the area you plan to serve. (If you'll be selling online, then that area is nationwide and potentially worldwide.)

> (!) **CAUTION**
>
> **Don't ignore businesses that have recently closed their doors.** It does you no good to be the only business of your type if your predecessors tested the waters and drowned. See if you can contact the proprietors to find out what went wrong—people love to share a tale of woe.

What is a "similar" business? For the most accurate research, you'll want to look not only for businesses that provide the exact same thing, but for those that satisfy the same market segment. For example, if you plan to open a bagel bakery, and there's no bagel bakery nearby, that's good so far—unless there happens to be a bread store on the same block. Both of you may be satisfying the market segment of "fresh-baked goods and sandwich providers," which may be more than the local demand can support.

Again, you don't need an M.B.A. to research the competition. Your telephone book, the Internet, and your local Chamber of Commerce should all provide ample amounts of information. On Excite.com's business yellow pages, for example, you can enter a type of business and a city and get a complete listing of names and addresses. If your business will have a storefront and will rely on walk-in traffic, you should also drive around the area to get a sense of where else your potential customers might go.

Create a list of all your competitors, containing their names and addresses, a brief summary of what they offer, and, where possible, price information. If you'll be relying mostly on local customers, plot out your competition's locations with pins or dots on a map. Then try to learn more about your competitors, to see how much of a threat they really pose. Perhaps their businesses are doing well, and they in fact have more business than they can handle. On the other hand, if they're hurting for customers in an oversaturated market, you'd do well to back off. Also evaluate the quality of their goods or services—if yours is higher, you may be able to woo away customers.

Final Planning and Test Runs

If your research has shown that your business is likely to succeed, it's not yet time to open your doors or launch into production. You need to map out your exact plans and expectations, as discussed below. You may also want to ease into a mini or test version of your planned business, as described under Minimize Risk by Starting Small, below. And you may need to be ready with some initial cash, as discussed under Finding Start-Up Money, below.

Create a Meaningful Business Plan

Up to this point, you've been conceptualizing your business and researching its prospects for success. Now it's time to sit down and plot out its future, for approximately the next three years. (Don't bother projecting farther—too much guesswork is involved.) This may or may not involve preparing a written business plan. Although some MBAs and consultants will warn you that few businesses can succeed without a written plan, including an extensive narrative, charts, budgets, and projections, the truth is that for many small nonprofit enterprises, such plans consume more energy than they're worth. Worse yet, they may produce an artificially rosy picture of the future, leading to a false sense of security. ("How can we fail, when we've got two inches of paper saying all will be well?")

What your organization needs to arrive at through planning is a deep understanding of what your business is about. In other words, you must think through every element of starting and running your business. Even if you don't plan to write it up in a fancy document, you should be able to summarize it in a succinct report. To do this, you and the other wise heads in your organization should consider the following:

- What will the business sell or do, and for what types of customers?
- Who will your most likely customers be, and what's your basis for believing they'll be interested in buying?
- Who will be responsible for what tasks, using how much of their time?
- How closely connected will the people who do the work be to your nonprofit "mother ship"?

- How much initial investment will be required to start the business?
- How much will it cost to run the business and produce the goods or services on an ongoing basis?
- What's your break-even point—how much will you need to bring in to cover your running costs and pay back the initial investment?
- At what price will you need to sell your product in order to not only cover your costs but to make a profit?
- How will you deal with any significant foreseeable legal, insurance, or tax concerns?
- How will you market (tell the world about) your goods or services?
- What's your profit timeline—how many months will you go without a profit, when should you expect to see profits, and at what levels?
- After your start-up investment is spent, will your incoming cash flow be enough to cover your costs month by month, or are you likely to require loans or other cash infusions?

Take the time to write up a brief planning document covering these issues. Include the specific research sources or bases upon which you projected any financial figures, market demand levels, or other external facts and figures that may affect the business's success.

Next, bring your marketing and accounting experts into the process. Ask them to help you create forecast budgets for three scenarios:

- **Best case:** if everything goes right, you keep your costs down, and your customers respond as well as can reasonably expected
- **Break-even scenario**: often best calculated backwards, to see how much you'd need to purchase or produce and sell just to cover your costs. (For more information on how to calculate this, see the article entitled "Will My Business Make Money?" free on Nolo's website at www.nolo.com.)
- **Worst case:** what will happen in the case of such foreseeable problems as product cost increases, failure to obtain donated equipment or labor, and, most important, a disappointing customer response.

If the best-case scenario doesn't look too exciting, your business idea may not be worth the effort. Same story if the worst-case scenario would result in losses that would cripple your organization. The break-even scenario should help you determine whether the business is realistic—and hopefully lead you to further planning of how to push it to true profitability.

> ! CAUTION
> **Never hand the entire business planning process over to a consultant.** It's your business and only you can determine whether it will be viable. Business consultants can help you make this decision, but don't turn the whole job over to them: Chances are that all you'll get in return is a long and expensive document that you don't really understand.

You can, of course, develop a much more detailed business plan. In fact, if you plan a large business that will require either major support from donors or foundations or commercial (most likely bank) loans, you'll surely have to do so. Such a business plan should include narratives and formal financial reports, including a break-even analysis, a profit-and-loss forecast, a cash-flow projection, and a start-up cost estimate. See the resource box below for good information on how to draft such a plan. Also contact local business schools; many of them sponsor classroom projects in which students evaluate potential new businesses. You can bring a great deal of free, personalized, and expert attention to your business planning process this way.

> RESOURCE
> **Need help drafting a business plan?** For a quick introduction to what belongs in a formal business plan, see the free article "The Essentials of a Business Plan," at www.nolo.com. For in-depth information on drafting a business plan, *How to Write a Business Plan*, by Mike McKeever (Nolo) offers easily digested, plain-English guidance on general business plans.

Minimize Risk by Starting Small

If your nonprofit is as cash strapped as most, it literally can't afford a business failure. Before attempting a high dive into full-scale production,

It's worth dipping your toes into—and testing—the business waters first. Three good ways to do this include:

- starting with borrowed or temporary resources
- running a test version of the business, and
- lining up customers before you create the product.

As a nonprofit, you have a huge advantage when it comes to minimizing your risk: You're accustomed to getting by with less and being creative about filling your daily needs. For example, the file folders that a corporate office might recycle after one use probably have, in your office, been relabeled so often that you could perform an archaeological dig on the layers. Don't drop these thrifty habits once you enter the business world. A surprising number of new businesses spend far too much, far too soon, precisely because their owners get caught up in creating the appearance of successful businesses—pricey addresses, cherrywood desks, glossy catalogs, and extensive product or service lines. In short, they quickly spend themselves out of business.

If you can't use existing resources, think about how you can avoid expensive investments. A surprising amount of equipment can be borrowed or leased short-term, rather than purchased outright. You may even be able to line up donated facilities, at least for the short term—for example, a restaurant's kitchen on a day when it's closed for business, a church's basement for initial product assembly, or an undeveloped lot for purposes of starting a garden. Look into these possibilities well before you've committed to a business venture.

If you'll need to purchase some products or inventory, see whether the most expensive items can be donated. Talk to local businesses, especially those that you or your clients already patronize. As discussed in Chapter 2, many businesses see charitable donations of goods or services as a normal part of their annual financial cycles—though you may need to catch them early in their fiscal years, before they've made all of their planned donations.

There are limits, of course, to this "just getting by" philosophy. The two most important are that you shouldn't compromise the quality of your goods and services, and the process of soliciting donations shouldn't take more time than it's worth. For example, customers might not mind a hand-printed label on your jar of homemade applesauce, but the applesauce itself should be of top quality. Fortunately, another advantage that you have as a nonprofit is that no one expects you to look like the corporation next door. In fact, because supporting a nonprofit may be part of your customers' incentive in giving you their business, they may actually be put off by an up-market address or the latest, shiniest equipment.

It's usually best to start small, which can include beginning with mini, test versions of your business. If, for example, you're thinking of opening a crafts business, why not try setting up booths at a few fairs first? Or better yet, avoid the costs of retail altogether and sell by mail order or online. This will not only keep your costs down (opening storefronts is notoriously expensive) but will also tell you a lot about whether your staff and/or clients can handle the production and service end of the business. You'll also be learning what your customers like and respond to—or don't. You may even decide that a small-scale operation is all you want to pursue for the moment.

Another excellent strategy when you're starting out is to avoid committing resources to anything until you're sure you've got customers lined up—preferably paying in advance. In some cases, this will be easy—for example, customers who sign up for a class, workshop, or tour usually understand, or can be warned, that the event is subject to cancellation for low attendance. (Just make sure you're ready to return their deposits or payments immediately!) See "Women's Studio Workshop Summer Arts Institute," below, for an example of a successful use of this "keep it small and get advance commitments" strategy. Or, if you take orders for goods, you can tell customers how long they'll have to wait before delivery and use that time to create the goods. (This is another advantage to not opening a store, where you'd have to have a full supply of the goods on hand.) In other cases—particularly for large or expensive orders—you may need to negotiate with the customer and sign a contract, asking them to pay in full in advance but to wait several weeks for delivery.

The one catch to this strategy is that small steps into business won't gain you large returns in the long run. At some point, you'll need to either invest or risk some real money in order to make money.

Women's Studio Workshop Summer Arts Institute

For most of the year, the Women's Studio Workshop (WSW, at www. wsworkshop.org) in Rosendale, New York, focuses on providing arts residencies to people making careers out of art. During the summer, however, they use their 6,500 square feet of professional studios (for printmaking, papermaking, photography, book arts, and ceramics) to offer classes in traditional and experimental studio techniques. Practicing artists and the arts-interested public from across the country participate in classes, private instruction, and intensive workshops, which run from two to five days and cost around $750; there is also a scholarship program.

The institute's classes are a good example of building a small business using existing resources. According to Anita Wetzel, development director and cofounder, "Part of the reason this works for us is that we already have the facilities. We are known in the field and have established connections to artists who teach. Also, we keep our plans small scale, while being flexible enough to expand on short notice. A full class is about six to eight people, allowing participants a lot of hands-on time in the studios and one-on-one interaction with the instructors. We make sure that, at a minimum, we have enough people to pay for the teacher's salary and transportation to get her here. Then, if more than the maximum number of students sign up, we do our best to create an additional class section."

Finding Start-Up Money

If you need more start-up cash than you can scare up from existing sources, you'll have to look to major donors, grantmaking foundations or corporations, or bank lenders. Because none of these sources can ordinarily give you overnight returns, be prepared for at least six months' effort in lining up commitments. For some nonprofits, it has taken one to two years.

Starting up a business provides an interesting focus for a major donors campaign. Your pitch to them is that their gifts will go farther than ever, as they'll help to launch a profit-making enterprise. As you'll remember from Chapter 6, launching a campaign requires your leadership and board members to devote a period of several weeks to meeting with various donor prospects and asking for their financial support. You'll want to show the prospects your plans and forecasts, and demonstrate that your organization is ready to launch into this new venture. With the right presentation, this can give you a chance to approach existing donors in a new way, with a new message, to reinvigorate their support. If your efforts don't lead to sufficient amounts in outright gifts, also consider asking major donors to support you with low-interest loans.

Some foundations will make grants to assist you in starting a small business. As with the major donors, you're in the happy position of offering them something new to support—and as you've probably learned, foundations are much more receptive to new projects than to ongoing support of the "same old thing." At the same time, your track record of good communication with funders and measurable outcomes on past grants will be an important way of demonstrating your chances of business success.

Be aware of—and receptive to—a preference by some foundations to give you technical assistance, such as educational or consulting opportunities in business planning and setup, rather than an outright cash grant. Some foundations are also developing funding alternatives that are something short of cash grants, such as revolving lines of credit or loans that are forgiven when certain benchmarks are reached. See Chapter 10 for more on researching and approaching foundations for support.

As a last resort (given the risks that come with carrying a debt burden), you could also approach banks for small business loans. Bank loans are certainly one of the primary methods used by for-profit entrepreneurs. You're at a bit of a disadvantage here, however, if this is your first business effort. The bank will want to see not only a formal business plan, but also evidence that you're capable of getting a small business off the ground and repaying the loan. This is a good time to enlist the help of any board members and other volunteers who will be participating in this effort, and emphasize their experience, business knowledge, and ongoing roles.

Licensing, Sponsorships, and Other Relationships With Existing Businesses

Rather than developing and implementing your own business idea, you may be able to generate revenue in cooperation with, or through sponsorship by, an existing business. For example, universities can make significant sums by licensing their names and logos for clothing and all sorts of other products. In return for its sponsorship or other payments, a business would normally expect one of the following from your organization:

- **use of your organization's name or logo,** by which the business could give its products a stamp of socially conscious approval. For example, tea and coffee companies sometimes advertise their commitment to fair trade.

- **use of your organization's name or logo on a product again, but with a different fee arrangement,** where a certain percentage of the profits goes to support your organization. This is known as "cause-related marketing." It's similar to the licensing arrangement, but takes it one step farther, not only because of the percentage payment, but because you might also be asked to encourage your organization's supporters to buy the product. (Note: Because of the quid pro quo arrangement, the business cannot deduct from its taxes the amounts it gives your nonprofit.)

- **your display of the business's logo**—for example, in your publications, on your website, on team shirts, or on banners—in return for the business's sponsoring an event or activity. (Also see Chapter 8, on special events, and Chapter 13, on media, for more on the most likely uses of corporate sponsorships.)

- **your assistance with a joint business venture,** in which both you and the business provide a portion of the expertise or services, and share in the profits.

As a practical matter, larger, more established nonprofits— with recognizable names and logos—are the ones in the best position to enter into licensing, marketing, or sponsorship arrangements with major companies. You may need to set your sights on businesses that match the size and reach of your organization. For example, a local sports bar might sponsor your little league team, or a local print or photo shop might be happy to say in its catalog, "We're the choice of environmentally conscious organizations such as [*your organization*]," in return for either a fee or a discount on their services.

The arrangement that will require the most creativity is that of a joint venture, in which both you and the business take some role in business activities. However, having already considered your assets, needs, and business concepts, you may have already identified an area in which an existing business could take part. For example, a local grocery store might partner with you in a catering venture. Or, you might consider short-term ventures. Your bonsai club might arrange to give classes at a local nursery—the nursery would do the advertising through its mailing list, and you would both reap the profits. Or, if you are a cancer-care organization, you might arrange for a local hat store to come to your nonprofit and offer advice and discounts on attractive headwear for people undergoing chemotherapy—and give you a share of any profits from sales.

Approaching a business or corporation has some important things in common with approaching an individual—there are no preset rules, and you'll need to do your research first. By learning about the business's values, how it's doing financially, and who the right person to approach is, you'll vastly improve your chances of success. Be prepared to be quite open with the business about what it will gain—perhaps an increase in its numbers of customers, access to a new customer base, or a boost to its public reputation.

Before embarking on any plan, make sure your arrangement is written up as an agreement signed by a representative of both parties. This doesn't have to be in legalese—the important thing is to use words and phrases that both sides understand and feel comfortable with. If the business provides a document, perhaps drafted by its legal staff, go over it carefully. There's no shame in asking, "What does this mean, and why does it need to be here?"

One of the most effective ways to interest a business in partnering with you is to find points of commonality between your two messages or how you want the public to view you. For example, the American Diabetes Association receives sponsorship from the makers of Splenda, an artificial sweetener. (The match is obvious—diabetics need to avoid sugar.) In fact, part of the sponsorship arrangement allows Splenda to contribute recipes to the ADA's website (http://diabetes.org), many of which use you-know-what sweetener.

Other matches are sometimes based on a company's need to overcome a negative aspect of its reputation—for example, some car manufacturers sponsor Mothers Against Drunk Driving (MADD, at www.madd.org).

With all of these business arrangements, there are ethical issues that your organization will need to discuss and consider before the deal is signed. You're not tainted by mere association with businesses—after all, many of them are no more or less moral than your average nonprofit. However, your reputation may start to suffer if you've got corporate logos plastered all over your website and publications. And, of course, if it's a company that creates harmful products, you'll need to think hard before helping it try to save its reputation. (The Susan P. Komen Foundation, for example, created a PR nightmare by partnering with KFC to provide "Pink Buckets for the Cure.") There's something to be said for letting it atone for its errors through your organization, but make sure your organization gains more than it loses by the association.

The Next Steps

Hopefully, this chapter has guided you toward the front door of your new business, but you'll have to walk through it on your own. A book of this size couldn't possibly advise you on all the aspects of running your small business—obtaining permits, choosing a business name, avoiding trademark disputes, leasing space, managing employees, dealing with customers, paying business taxes, marketing and advertising, riding out hard times, and more.

For a compact guide to all these issues and more, see *Legal Guide for Starting & Running a Small Business,* by Fred S. Steingold (Nolo). It's perfectly appropriate for you to be reading books that aren't geared only for nonprofits at this point—you'll need to play by the same rules as other businesses do, with only a few exceptions. Still, I recommend developing relationships with other nonprofits pursuing business activities, and with organizations that support them, to keep up with new knowledge and developments in this quickly changing area of endeavor.

Seeking Grants From Foundations, Corporations, and Government

The world of grant funding is surrounded by a somewhat unwarranted mystique. Novice fundraisers tend to imagine that if they can only come up with the right combination of words, money will rain down upon their organization. Actually, the truth is more complicated. On the one hand, it's not terribly hard to write a grant proposal—no magic set of talents, other than solid research, writing, and organizational skills, are required. On the other hand, experienced insiders realize that there's a lot more to getting a grant than writing a compelling proposal. As this chapter explains, you'll need to:

- understand who gives out grants in your field
- narrow the list by researching your grant prospects
- understand the entire proposal process, from initial inquiry forward, including how to write a targeted grant proposal
- follow up with the funder, and
- apply for grant renewals.

Understand the Funders

There are two primary sources of grants to nonprofit organizations: foundations (private and public) and the government (local, state, and federal). Each source has unique purposes and requirements for granting funds. For example, a large, corporate-run foundation may seek to have its name associated with a certain positive image; a private family foundation may be primarily motivated to carry out the very personal interests of the family that founded it; and a government grantor may be fulfilling legislative requirements.

To improve your chances of winning support, you'll need to know a lot about any funder you approach—particularly when it comes to private foundations, whose organizational personalities can be, and often are, as distinct and quirky as those of any individual donor.

Characteristics of Private and Public Foundations

Most nonprofits find that public and private foundations are their best bets for obtaining grants. A foundation is essentially another form of charity—

in fact, its tax status, like yours, is covered by Section 501(c)(3) of the Internal Revenue Code. Over 75,000 grantmaking foundations are active in the United States today. Collectively, they've granted between about $30 billion and $45 billion in funds annually for most of the last ten years.

One of the best things about foundations is that they don't just give out money because they want to; many of them give it out because they have to! Depending on their particular tax status, "private" foundations must spend at least 5% of their investment assets on philanthropy every year; this includes money spent on reasonable administrative expenses, such as salaries, facilities, and travel.

Tax laws also affect the foundation's essential character and way of working with you. Private foundations are usually in the hands of a single source of money, such as a wealthy family or a corporation. (The Bill & Melinda Gates Foundation is a well-known example.) Many private foundations are funded by wealthy philanthropists, seeking to change the world to fit their visions. Some of these organizations are quite small or narrowly focused. For example, the Rauch Family Foundation supports programs and activities that enhance the daily lives of its fellow citizens of Rock Island, Illinois—specifically because during the Great Depression, according to its website, "the Rauch brothers remembered how the community, especially the American Federation of Labor Construction Workers, came to the aid of the Rauch family whose husband and father was a paraplegic" and "constructed a storefront—and the means for the family's livelihood—onto the front of their Rock Island Home."

Some family-based foundations are so private that you might think that they want you to just go away and leave them alone. In fact, a few do want just that—as evidenced by the fact that they don't even publish websites. Others are long-established, high-profile players in the foundation world. Whatever their size or provenance, most family foundations tend to focus on one major substantive interest area and two or three other minor ones. This makes it hard for most groups to get in the door, but relatively easy to stay inside once you cross the threshold.

Corporate-sponsored foundations also normally fall into the private foundation category. Although they account for a small percentage of the foundation money granted every year, that's because most corporate giving isn't channeled through foundations alone, but instead is given out directly by the parent corporations. (See "Nonfoundation Corporate Giving," below.)

Any consumer would probably recognize the names of corporate foundations—the Levi Strauss Foundation, the Ford Foundation, and the Merck Company Foundation, to name a few. Some of these make grants that explicitly tie to each of their company's product or philosophy. For example, the Aetna Foundation lists its first giving priority as health—a fitting choice given that its creator company, Aetna Inc., is one of America's largest sellers of health insurance. Other corporate foundations simply try to promote the interests of the communities in which their customers live.

Nonfoundation Corporate Giving

Corporations don't grant money through foundations alone—in fact, many of them find it easier or more advantageous to give by other means. And, of course, not all companies that make charitable gifts are organized as corporations—sole proprietorships, partnerships, and limited liability companies (LLCs) can also be generous with their profits.

If yours is a small, local nonprofit, the majority of business giving available to you will be through nonfoundation avenues, such as employee volunteer or matching gift programs, in-kind donations of services, goods, or facilities, event sponsorship, cause-related marketing (where a business's advertising mentions your nonprofit and cause), or cash gifts.

Because most businesses prefer to keep their giving local (sometimes even at the neighborhood level), and because companies can set their own rules for their gift programs, you should research the companies operating in your area to see what they have to offer.

Nonfoundation Corporate Giving (cont'd)

Here are some tips for tailoring your approach to a business that doesn't operate a foundation:

- **View this as another relationship to be built.** Look for existing contacts between your staff and volunteers and the company's employees. For example, if several people from a local company have adopted animals from your shelter, that's a good entry to ask the business for support.

- **Ask yourself what's in it for the company.** Unlike at corporate foundations, your contact person at a local business will quite possibly be in the marketing department. This means you must focus squarely on how you can improve or advertise the company's image or enhance quality of life for its customers or employees. For example, if you want businesses to contribute a gift of attractive products for your silent auction, be ready to tell them how you'll publicize their donations.

- **Think creatively.** Few rules for business giving are written in stone. Thus, you might approach a small food producer that has never given anything to charity before by proposing an exciting way to partner—for example, featuring its rice-based desserts at an event directed at people with gluten intolerance.

- **Be prepared to sign a contract.** Particularly with event sponsorship, you'll need to sign an agreement with the company, specifying such things as where you'll mention its name and feature its logo.

- **Don't approach a company in financial trouble.** Do your homework before getting in touch—read the business pages and do some online research. You want to catch them when they're feeling generous.

For more information on where to find corporate support, see:

- *National Directory of Corporate Giving* (Foundation Center). Gives descriptions and guidelines for over 2,500 corporations that make gifts directly or through a foundation.

- **www.hoovers.com.** Use this website to check on the health of the nation's top companies, or to look up major companies by industry category or location.

324 | EFFECTIVE FUNDRAISING FOR NONPROFITS

Public foundations, which usually have to forage for their own funding sources in order to turn around and make grants, are slightly different animals than the private ones—hungrier ones, to be precise. Unlike private foundations, which are usually funded by one or a few families or corporations, public foundations must beat the bushes for funds, typically trying to aggregate lots of small donations. The United Way or the Red Cross are examples of public foundations, as are local community foundations. Many public foundations also pursue those not-quite-super-rich philanthropists who would like to give away a little of their largesse, but don't have enough to form their own foundations. In this regard, community foundations position themselves as liaisons between such philanthropists and nonprofits, helping the philanthropists learn more about community needs, and efficiently taking care of the administrative aspects of giving.

For your organization, this means that working with public foundations will help you get around the narrow grant guidelines that otherwise plague the foundation world. Public foundations need you to feed them exciting new ideas that they can use to stimulate their donors' interests. In fact, some grant decisions won't be made by the foundation itself, but will be based purely on the donors' choices. This can add up to some serious money in the case of donor-advised funds, in which major donors pool resources and make their own decisions about who to fund and for what purposes.

Of course, you're at a particular advantage if your nonprofit works in "fun" or "popular" fields like education, health, or the environment. Even if you don't, however, it's well worth courting your local community foundations' favor, because those that lack immediate grant opportunities may be intrigued enough to link you up with an interested donor later.

People Who Staff Private and Public Foundations

After learning how foundations work, your next task is to understand who works for them. Obviously, you won't expect to find the person after whom the foundation was named sitting behind a desk (although this sometimes happens). The main people you'll interact with are a foundation's "program officers." They typically are responsible for reading and evaluating proposals and presenting the ones they like to their boards of directors—who usually make the final call (although program officers may have discretion to approve small grants on their own).

Many program officers cut their teeth in nonprofit jobs, including fundraising, so you can expect them to be fairly savvy about who you are and what you can reasonably expect to achieve. Above all, most are extremely interested in seeing that their money is invested well. So, it will always be important to present your organization as solid, well organized, and able to produce results.

Government Grantmakers

Government grants are made by local, state, and federal agencies. Statistics are hard to come by, but it's a good guess that nonprofits nationwide get about 12% of their revenues from the government. However, the distribution is uneven, with some nonprofits in certain fields, such as health services or education, relying almost completely on government funds, while others receive none at all. If you are one of the lucky ones that gets funded, the amount granted is likely to be quite substantial—the feds, in particular, rarely mess around with pocket-change grants. Although the purposes of government grants have traditionally been fairly narrow, they are now turning toward outsourcing and privatization, which means that grants will increasingly be available for a broader range of purposes. But before you leap clapping from your chair, you should know that the government tends to be very risk averse, so new organizations and untested projects will have a tougher time getting funded.

Government grants can also be affected by the political goals of the current administration or party in power. For example, during the George W. Bush administration, family planning projects whose primary focus was anything but abstinence became difficult to fund through federal sources.

> TIP
>
> **The more reproducible your project, the more likely it is to be funded.** The federal government loves to see evidence that your program will serve as a pilot and model for others to follow. After all, in a huge country, there is little to be gained from pouring huge funds into creating one local success story. But if you can show that your effort—whether it be curbing gun violence, teen smoking, or accidents on the farm—can be rapidly rolled out in other communities across the nation, you are much more likely to receive a big check.

A big downside to any government grant is the overwhelming amount of red tape involved. The application alone can be more than some nonprofits can handle. Although you'll likely need to submit it digitally, the hard copy version of your federal grant application would likely stack up to two inches or more once you've completed all the forms, narrative, statistical information, lists of collaborators and advisory committees, and so on. Worse yet, federal grant opportunities are often announced a mere six weeks before applications are due. State and local grant applications are less onerous when it comes to paperwork, but often include other requirements, such as mandatory attendance at dull meetings with large groups of other applicants or grantees.

People Who Staff Government Grantmaking Offices

The administrators with whom you'll interact on a government grant may be far away geographically and may not seem attuned to the nonprofit world. Their background is likely to be more state university than Ivy League. They may have worked their way into their current job from another branch of government—and, as a gross generalization, tend to be highly attuned to rules, requirements, and obedience to orders from higher up. So don't expect your prospective grant administrator to overlook deficiencies in your application based on its wonderfully creative concept.

None of this is meant to say, however, that you shouldn't try to establish human contact with government grant administrators—their very remoteness means that you can set yourself apart from the pack by picking up the phone and trying to get to know them, as well as keeping in regular contact after you receive your grant.

Research Grant Prospects

Researching your most promising funders, and the grants that they offer, is a critical part of the grantseeking process—and sadly, one that too many people zoom through. While different funders report very different success/rejection ratios, all agree that they receive scads of applications proposing programs that are 180 degrees away from their stated purposes or guidelines—in other words, that are completely unfundable.

The common wisdom is that a mere one of each ten submitted grant proposals gets funded, with a significant portion of rejections attributable to the applicants' failure to understand the guidelines. Knowing this, you'll understand why, before you can even begin entering an online application for a grant at some foundations, they make you take an eligibility quiz. You'll need to affirm that you're with a registered nonprofit, that it's located in the United States, that you're not asking for money for something outside the foundation's guidelines (such as religion or scholarships), and so forth.

> CAUTION
> **Don't get too excited if a funder sends you a notification that it's accepting grant applications.** Especially once your nonprofit is established, funders may mail you grant proposal requests out of the blue, as a courtesy. However, this doesn't mean that your application is any more likely to be accepted. Unless your application is both competitive and relevant to the funder's mission, you'll just be joining the ranks of all the other nonprofits who submit grant applications cold.

To get your application to the top of a grantmaker's pile, take the time to do some basic research. Your object is to make sure your proposal is a likely match for the funder's stated—and in some cases, unstated—interests and priorities. Begin your research with some library or online work, but also be ready to act like an investigative reporter, determined to sniff out the real-deal grant opportunities. Your research progression should typically go something like this:

1. Decide what you're looking for.
2. Research public information.
3. Make personal contacts with funders.
4. Create files to track funders.

Choose a Goal for Each Research Project

Seeking grant money is probably the area where the "plan first, act second" approach gets violated the most. If you get a request for proposals (RFP) from your local city government inviting you to apply for funding, you shouldn't start by writing a proposal, but by first figuring out whether your group is any more likely to be funded than the multitude of other groups in town who received the same solicitation. (If a can't-pass-it-up RFP comes along, you can, of course, alter your fundraising plan—but be realistic about the costs that come with every grant you pursue.)

Sticking to Your Mission

During her time as development and communications coordinator with the World Institute on Disability (WID), Marisa Lianggamphai became all too familiar with the temptation to apply for grants that don't quite fit. "WID focuses primarily on issues affecting adults with disabilities, at the policy level. Although several of its programs have components that serve youth with disabilities, they are not the main focus of the organization. Unfortunately, there are a lot more funding opportunities for youth with disabilities than for adults with disabilities. I often thought it would be great if WID could change its programs to go where the funding is, but that really isn't WID's purpose. Every possible funding opportunity must be run through the question of 'Is this within our mission?' Otherwise, an organization's strength and purpose gets watered down."

Once you're clear on your funding goals, break them into categories and fill out Worksheet 8 below (available online, see Appendix B for the link) for each grant-seeking effort.

Most of the chart's criteria should be fairly self-explanatory. Your **clients or issue** depends on how you've defined your fundraising goal. Your answer could be as broad as the entire populace served by your agency, such as the homeless, the blind, or wild birds, or as narrow as the purchase of a new drinking fountain for your dance studio. The **greater goal** would be all or part of your agency's mission, such as "reducing maternal mortality" or "ending youth violence." This goal is important because it should dovetail neatly with goals set out by a funder.

Set yourself a **minimum grant amount**, or at least have an idea of how many grant proposals you're able to write in order to reach your funding goal. You don't want to stretch too far and end up preparing 15 small grant proposals to raise $30,000, when two larger ones would have done the same job. **Geographic area** is a common limitation placed by funders, so you'll need to know exactly what area your agency plans to cover, bearing in mind any future plans for expansion. The funding source will no doubt define other **restrictions** on what you can do with the money, so be clear about which ones your organization can't accept. Prohibitions on legislative advocacy or on working with certain populations are common ones. For example, in the immigrant services field, certain governmental funding sources will not give support to agencies whose clients include undocumented ("illegal") immigrants, which makes it virtually impossible for agencies serving immigrants to accept this money.

Some organizations also struggle with whether it's moral to accept money from a **funding source** like a drug or tobacco company. You certainly don't want to help one of the sources of society's troubles clean up its reputation at the expense of your own. But it doesn't mean you're crass or ruthless if you don't set such limitations—plenty of nonprofits figure that it's time these corporations gave a little back, and that it's nearly impossible to find money that wasn't raised through someone's exploitation in the not-too-distant past.

TIP

Don't hide what you're doing. Occasionally, you may be able to get around funders' limitations by casting what you're doing in a different light. For example, if you work with a mountain biking association that seeks to have more trails opened to bikes, and you apply to a funding source that funds education, not advocacy, you may nevertheless be able to develop a fundable program to educate the public and governmental decision makers as to why biking doesn't necessarily harm trails. However, if you have to resort to hiding part of your activities or mission to get a grant, it will backfire. Even if you get the grant, the grantmaking community is a tight one—and if your transgression is discovered, word will spread quickly, hampering your ability to get any future grants.

With your Grant Priorities Summary Chart in hand, it's time to start researching individual foundations and other grantmakers. Although you could just use the chart as a general checklist to identify good matches, it's better to go one step further and assemble detailed information on the most

Fundraising Worksheet 8: Grant Priorities Summary Chart

Clients or issue to be served: _____

_____

_____

_____

_____

_____

Greater goal being pursued: _____

_____

_____

_____

_____

_____

_____

Minimum useful grant amount: $_____

Geographic area served or covered: _____

_____

_____

_____

Any unacceptable restrictions: _____

_____

_____

_____

_____

Any unacceptable sources of funds: _____

_____

_____

_____

_____

promising-looking funders. To do this, use the following Grant Prospect Summary worksheet (available online; see Appendix B for the link); you can, of course, add to and customize the worksheet to fit your organization's needs and interests. The information on this worksheet will help you decide whether the possible grant is a good fit for your organization and what your next steps should be.

Most of the information on this worksheet is self-explanatory. Taking a look at the funder's application deadlines and schedule for answers will also help you decide whether the grant prospect fits into your annual fundraising plan. You're likely to wait three or four months for an answer to your proposal, but some funders can take up to a year—which is a problem if you were counting on this grant to fill a particular, more immediate need. Also, not all funders set specific application deadlines—some accept applications on a rolling basis. However, they're likely to make decisions at one of their board meetings. Therefore, if you can find out when their upcoming board meetings are, you can put yourself in the best position by submitting your proposal two to three months in advance of that date.

The entry regarding similar grants given to other organizations is there as a reality check. No matter what the grantor says it wants to fund, the grants it has actually made tell the real story, helping you interpret what it means by generalized phrases like "vocational training" or "leadership development." For example, a foundation that says it funds environmental projects may really be interested only in water issues or forests. Part of your job is to find out the funder's unspoken, internal guidelines.

Public Information About Grants and Funders

Researching grant opportunities isn't difficult. A number of nonprofit-support organizations and public libraries are dedicated to assisting nonprofits, and the Internet can bring a wealth of helpful information right to your desk.

The Foundation Center (www.fdncenter.org) is an excellent organization with lots of helpful funder information. It has main branches in Atlanta, Cleveland, New York, San Francisco, and Washington, DC, and affiliate relationships with hundreds of "cooperating collections," so chances are good that information is available near you. Many of these centers offer

Fundraising Worksheet 9: Grant Prospect Summary

Basic Information

Foundation/funder's name and address: _____

_____

Foundation's stated mission and purpose: _____

_____

Contact person: _____

Contact person's telephone, email: _____

Names and titles of other staff members: _____

_____

_____

Names of board members and trustees: _____

_____

_____

_____

Total grants made annually: $_____

Eligibility Information

Grant subject matter: _____

_____

Grant eligibility requirements: _____

Geographical limitations: _____

_____

Other limitations: _____

_____

Maximum grant amount: $_____

Funding duration : _____

"Good Fit" Indicators

Other organizations that have received grants for similar work (name the organization(s), list how much received and for what work): _____

_____

_____

_____

Typical grant amount: $_____

Limitations on overhead/administrative costs: _____%

Prospects for grant renewal: _____

Special considerations: _____

Application Process

First steps: ☐ query letter   ☐ full proposal

Printed application form or guidelines: ☐ available   ☐ obtained

Next application deadline(s) (if any): _____

Board meeting dates: _____

_____

Likely to hear answer by: _____

Research Trail

Have checked:

☐ Website

☐ Directories (name them):

☐ Form 990

☐ Annual report

personal or group orientation sessions to help you best use their research materials. If you have ready access to such a resource, you can skim the rest of this section, which covers:

- online resources, and
- printed directories.

Online Resources

Here's some of the best of what's on the Internet, for free or by subscription:

- **The Chronicle of Philanthropy,** at www.philanthropy.com. A limited number of articles are posted for free, but you must subscribe to the print or online version to see the remaining articles and access its grants database.
- **The Foundation Center,** at www.fdncenter.org. This stellar website pulls together much of what you'll need—substantive advice, research studies, a "Foundation Finder" that lets you look up basic information on foundations whose names you already know (including their IRS Forms 990 or 990PF), a "Philanthropy News Digest" that publishes daily requests for proposals (RFPs) and archives news articles on foundations back to 1995, and links to myriad other helpful sites.
- **Foundation Directory Online.** Updated weekly, this subscription-based service offered by the Foundation Center comes in various plans, with the most basic simply providing profiles of the top 10,000 U.S. foundations, and the most expensive offering information on over 100,000 foundations, corporate donors, and grantmaking public charities, plus program details and application guidelines. Prices in early 2013 ranged from $195 to $1,295 per year.
- **FirstGov,** at www.usa.gov/Business/Nonprofit.shtml#fundraising. This U.S. government website has helpful information for nonprofits, from available federal grants (including grants by federal agencies, such as the Environmental Protection Agency) to U.S. Postal Service regulations.
- **Guidestar,** at www.guidestar.org. This offers information on all kinds of nonprofits, foundations included. You'll need to register and pay for the advanced search capabilities, allowing you access to Form 990s, 990-PFs, and publications.

- **The Grantsmanship Center,** at www.tgci.com. By clicking "Funding Sources," you can find links to today's *Federal Register* grant announcements and to foundation websites, accessible state by state.
- *The Philanthropy Journal* at www.philanthropyjournal.org contains news about foundations, and recent tips about fundraising trends and other nonprofit issues.
- **The *Federal Register*'s Notices of Funding Availability** (federal grants only). The *Federal Register*, which is printed daily and is available at many main larger public libraries, is available online at www.gpoaccess.gov/fr/index.html. Unfortunately, reading it every day is hardly practical—you're more likely to find out about good opportunities through other sources, such as a nonprofit-related newsletters, magazines, or listservs.
- **The *Catalog of Federal Domestic Assistance*** (federal grants only) is also available online at www.cfda.gov.

Printed Resources

Printed resources aren't yet obsolete (I hope)—and may be a great choice if your only time to research is while sitting on the bus going home. See, for example:

- **The *National Directory of Corporate Giving*** (the Foundation Center), a guide to grants and direct giving by nearly 4,000 corporations and corporate foundations. The cost in 2013 was $195.
- *LGBTQ Grantmaking by U.S. Foundations* is a free report by Funders for LGBTQ Issues on which foundations have supported gay, lesbian and related issues, www.lgbtfunders.org.

Subscribing to newsletters or magazines that keep abreast of the funding world is also a great way to learn about grants, changes in the grantmaking world, and broader issues, such as nonprofit management or other types of effective fundraising. These publications are a rich source of ideas:

- *The Chronicle of Philanthropy.* Contains news on the foundation and nonprofit world; available via http://philanthropy.com
- *Grassroots Fundraising Journal,* at www.grassrootsfundraising.org
- *The Nonprofit Quarterly,* at www.nonprofitquarterly.org
- *The NonProfit Times,* at www.thenonprofittimes.com, and
- *Nonprofit World,* at www.snpo.org.

Information From Funders

Although general information from printed directories or independent websites can be helpful, they're only the start of your research (and the information you find there may be out of date). Your next step is either to call the foundation or agency to request a copy of its annual reports and grant guidelines or (more likely with all but the smallest foundations) to go online to view and download them.

The annual reports are useful not only to get a sense of the foundation's personality, but also to find out what programs the foundation is proud to have funded and who has received grants in the past. Many reports present useful lists of every group funded, including the amount of the grant and a brief description of its purpose.

The funder's grant guidelines will provide more detail than secondary sources about the foundation or government agency's eligibility requirements, funding priorities, types of projects funded (for example, new or pilot projects, research or direct services only), submission requirements, and timelines for decisions.

> **TIP**
> **Revisit the funder's website regularly.** Requirements and opportunities may change overnight. The funder's website will be your most up-to-date source of information—short of personal conversations with the grantmakers (covered next).

After you've researched funders through the various sources described above, you should have some good information on your most likely grant prospects. For the hottest prospects, create separate files containing your summary worksheets, notes, and any application materials or other information and instructions.

Make Personal Contact With Funders

By now you should have a short list of the hottest prospects—and you are probably champing at the bit to start working on your proposals. That will get you points for enthusiasm, but not for common sense. As perfect a match as your organization and the funder seem to be on paper, any experienced fundraiser will tell you that there is always more to the story. Your next step is to attempt to make telephone or personal contact with a decision maker within the foundation or other funder's office.

Now is where the real detective work begins. That "Contact person's telephone, email" entry on your summary worksheet is probably still blank. And for good reason: Grants officers could spend all of their days and nights talking to people seeking funds—most of them for proposals that will never get off the ground. While there are exceptions, many foundations are about as accessible as a 14th-century fortified castle.

It may take perseverance and even a little luck to get the needed phone number. First, get a list of the foundation's grant officers and board members, and circulate it among your staff and board. If your people know anyone on the list, that can be your critical link. As you gain experience in the development world, every conference, meeting, or special event will be an opportunity for you to meet people who work for foundations or colleagues who can tell you the right person to call or email. And never think of this as just a preliminary step to your "real" work—making contacts and establishing relationships is your real work. There's no need to be surprised, or worried, if you spend large amounts of time on it.

> **EXAMPLE:** Iris, a development director, is looking for funding for a needle exchange program—never an easy sell. She spends part of one morning reading her email listservs and the *Chronicle of Philanthropy.* Though much of the information doesn't help her, she does notice that Dave, a program officer at an area foundation that has previously funded her organization, has moved to a large foundation—and because it works in health areas, the new foundation is on Iris's prospect list. Unfortunately, Dave is now in charge of grants for children's issues. Iris starts by calling someone she knows at Dave's old job to get his new number. She gives him a call, schmoozes a little, and then pops the key question: "Who's the best one to talk to about our needle exchange program?" Dave suggests Iris talk to Radhika, and gives Iris her direct line number. Bingo. And because Dave thinks Iris and her organization do good work, he volunteers to pave the way with Radhika. A couple of days later, Iris has a cordial conversation with Radhika, learns how to structure the grant to meet several explicit and not-so-explicit foundation guidelines, and eventually receives funding.

Sometimes the first person you get on the phone may be an administrative support person or a receptionist. Don't treat this person as a low-level gate-keeper (though gatekeeping might indeed be part of his or her role). Your goal is to develop a long-term relationship with this and every other person in the foundation. Support staffers can be invaluable contacts later—for example, if you have a last-minute question, or need to know whether your proposal arrived by the deadline. In addition, if you needlessly alienate these frontline folks, your organization may develop a reputation for rudeness—one you never find out about, but that may come back to haunt you.

As shown in the example above, knowing a friend or colleague of a foundation staff person can often be your password to a constructive conversation. This isn't simple nepotism (although sometimes it can also be that), but a reflection of the fact that all funders operate, at least in part, on trust. They don't want to spend their time—or, further down the line, a chunk of their foundation's money—without knowing that it's going to a legitimate, responsible organization. If the grants officer trusts someone who thinks your organization deserves attention, you have a solid reference—someone who says "this group is okay, there's no need for us to look for a quick excuse to hang up." (Of course, this will be harder to achieve when your organization is young.)

> ### TIP
> **What if foundation guidelines prohibit phone calls?** In most cases, this rule really means that the foundation doesn't want unsolicited phone calls from strangers. If you've already done your detective work, preferably have been referred by a trusted intermediary, and have some real questions to ask, by all means give it a try—or at least send an email. If the person hangs up on you, it won't set your group back (as long as you take the rejection graciously). In the case of some large or institutional foundations, however, they may really mean "No phone calls." Jennifer Castner, director of The Altai Project, says, "As head of a small nonprofit, I try to think of this as a way they put grantseekers on an equal footing with one another. I may have no more access to such foundations than the head of a charity that's a household word!"

Look Solid, But Needy

In any interaction with funders, consider what kind of impression you want to make. First and foremost, you want them to realize that you're a solid operation—not one that will take their money and patch up a few holes in your circus tent before folding it up and leaving town. On the other hand, you want them to know that you genuinely need the grant.

The first requirement is the harder to prove, because it depends partly on intangibles and things beyond your control, like your organization's reputation both on the street and behind the closed doors of the funding community. However, some things that will help bolster your professional and dependable appearance include:

- well-designed stationery (but don't use fancy paper)
- communications materials (such as an annual report and a brochure)
- audited financial statements
- newspaper articles quoting or describing your organization
- a relatively up-to-date, engaging website (see Chapter 12), and
- letters of recommendation from those who have funded you in the past.

In your narrative, refer to evidence of your organization's good reputation, steady income, and staying power, such as "Our core funders, who include [*name*] and [*name*] have been supporting us for [*number*] years."

Demonstrating that you need the money is the easier part. After all, what nonprofit couldn't use three or four times the amount it has? To distinguish your group, focus not on your abject need, but on how the foundation's funding will help your group meet a documented community need. If possible, also try to show how the grant will fill a particular project gap—something along the lines of "We have everything in place to make this a go except $_____." The bottom line is, you want to appear to be the most effective program to accomplish a goal that the funder strongly supports.

If one of your staff or board members knows someone at a funder's office, he or she may be the best person to make the initial call. Your ED is the next best bet. The development director is a reasonable choice too, but some grantmaking officers will take the ED more seriously.

The initial conversation should be brief and to the point: "Hello, my name is [*your name*]. Your colleague [*name*] suggested that I call you. I'm the [*your position*] with [*name of your organization*], and I'd like to talk with you a bit about our [*name of your program*]." Your opener shouldn't last longer than a minute. If the officer seems harassed or perhaps even hostile, ask if there is a better time for you to call. Assuming your initial verbal sally is well received, give a very brief overview of your program's purpose and goal—making sure to convey your enthusiasm about it. Then ask your specific questions. This should break the ice with all but the stuffiest grants officers.

If you can get the grants officer chatting, you have done your job. Remember, you're not applying for a grant on the spot. You'll rarely get an outright "no" to funding over the phone, unless your program doesn't fall within the foundation's guidelines, in which case now is the best time to find out. One of the good things about starting with a telephone call is that the person you're talking to probably doesn't have enough information to justify telling you that funding is impossible. By the same token, because a written proposal (or even a query letter, discussed under The Proposal Process, From Query Letter Onward, below) is very easy to reject, calling first is a great way to introduce your request—and help ensure that it will receive some consideration once you submit it more formally.

If the conversation goes well, you and the officer might agree to meet, or you might be asked to submit a query letter. Meetings are usually held at the foundation offices, though in rarer cases the officer might start with a site visit. If you've got an exciting chance for the officer to come view what your organization is doing—such as Save The Bay's canoe outings, discussed in Chapter 6—this may even be a good time to extend the invitation (depending on the tenor of your conversation, of course). If you are invited to the foundation's offices, it's best to take two people along—a funding person, such as the ED, development director, or a board member, and a program person, who can describe how the funding will be used.

This isn't much different from meeting with an individual supporter, as discussed in Chapter 6. You'll want to bring along written materials, such as your organization's brochure, annual report, project description, and budget.

At any meeting, whether at lunch, your program site, or the funder's office, you'll want to spend a fair amount of time listening. Try to find out what the grants officer's interests are, where he or she sees the greatest community needs, what types of program successes the officer gets particularly excited about, and the like.

Also, remember that the officer probably doesn't have the last word on funding your organization (unless he or she is a senior officer and your grant application is small). If you submit a proposal and the officer likes it, he or she will probably have to present it to the foundation board or at least to director for approval. This isn't entirely a bad thing; once a foundation staff person agrees to support your proposal, he or she will usually coach you on how to present it to the board.

At the end of your meeting with foundation staff, you may be invited to submit a proposal. By now, you understand that this is not your first step, as many novice fundraisers believe, but a milestone well on your way to your goal. Even if you're told, "This isn't quite right for us," ask whether you can get in touch in a year or so to see whether your program needs have become a better match for their funding opportunities.

Keep Files to Track Funders

Your research process should be ongoing. Starting with the information you gather to submit your first proposals, you'll want to build a system that not only tracks the foundations that fund you, but also profiles those most likely to do so in the future.

Any time you read something of interest in the *Chronicle of Philanthropy* or your email listservs—such as a new grants officer, a new program focus, or a particular grant made to another organization—make a copy or printout for the appropriate file. Similarly, if you attend a social event and meet someone from a foundation on your A-list or someone who has relevant information about it, promptly enter all relevant facts in your database.

Over time, this attention to detail will help you develop an insider's view of your funding prospects and put you in a better position to plan and execute a targeted fundraising strategy.

As part of this process of keeping current, do your best to maintain cordial relationships with grants officers—even those who haven't yet funded you! Jim Lynch of TechSoup Global tells the following story: "I had developed a phone contact with an officer at the Crocker Foundation. Every year, I called to ask what they had going, and every year, the officer told me that it wasn't a good fit. Finally, one year I called, and something did fit— and we got the grant! I think the officer was partly relieved to be able to give me some good news for once. All this had happened without the two of us having met. But when we finally did meet, we fell on each other like long-lost friends."

The Proposal Process, From Query Letter Onward

Lest you get overwhelmed by all the details of the grant application process, this section leads you through it step by step. Depending on the foundation's guidelines and preferences, your path to funding will probably include some combination of the following:

- a query letter
- a written grant proposal
- a site visit
- a presentation or meeting with the funder, and
- grant approval.

Query Letters

A query letter is often the first written communication between you and the funder (particularly if you're dealing with a foundation rather than the government). Other names for a query letter are "letter of interest" or "letter of inquiry"). The letter's purpose is to give the recipient foundation a quick sense of who you are and what you're seeking, and to find out whether you should take the next step in the proposal process. A sample query from a fictional organization is provided below.

Many foundations require you to submit a query (often online) as the first step in the funding process. In some instances, as discussed earlier in this chapter, the grants officer may have asked you to submit a query. And, of course, there may be times when you have tried but failed to make personal contact and decide to send a query as your next-best alternative.

Find out whether the foundation publishes guidelines for the query letter (on its website or in its printed guidelines) or has already created an online submission format. If not, don't worry: Query letters are short (one to three pages) and follow a fairly standard format. But even within the expected or required format, you can and should write a letter that inspires the foundation and grants officer to ask for more information. Don't however, hold back good material to include as a "surprise" in the full grant proposal. Unless you highlight your best points in your query, you probably won't be invited to submit a full proposal.

The key elements of a query are:

- **Your purpose.** In the opening paragraph, give your organization's name and an overview of the reason for your letter: namely, to seek a particular amount of funding for a purpose or project that you briefly describe. Don't be coy—they are funders, and they expect people to ask for money. And don't beat around the bush when explaining why your proposal fits within the funder's mission and guidelines—explain directly how your project will help the funder further its own goals. You will also briefly want to establish that your organization will be able to accomplish the proposed project. To do this, it's helpful to mention the names and qualifications of key project staff. If someone in the foundation knows your organization and thinks well of it, this is also worth mentioning.

- **Who you are.** In the next paragraph, briefly describe your organization's mission, history, and current programs. Your focus should be on establishing your organization's credentials, in particular its ability to identify and meet community needs. If prominent board members have helped drive your efforts, mention their names.

- **Who or what needs your help.** Here you get to the heart of the matter: the community need that your organization seeks to address. Find the most powerful way to establish that a need exists, whether by statistical data, vivid examples, or both. Be precise about

Sample Query Letter

Oakland African-American History Project
123 1st Street, Oakland, California

March 18, 20xx

The California Historical Foundation
321 6th St.
San Francisco, California 95123

Dear Ms. Officer:

I'm writing to you at the suggestion of your colleague Bob Everbuddy, who is familiar with our work at the Oakland African-American History Project. Our organization has, since 1995, taken the lead in collecting and cataloging the personal histories and documents of Oakland's African-American community. We are particularly interested in African-American migration to California during the late 1800s, when many came to work for the railroads. Our organization is currently seeking $65,000 to support a new project—interviewing the children of this migratory generation to preserve their oral histories, before their generation also passes into history. Given your foundation's special interest in collecting histories of California's diverse communities, we ask you to consider a full proposal for support of this project.

Our organization's mission is to preserve Oakland's African-American history, for the education of future generations as well as the inspiration of its existing African-American community. The enthusiasm and commitment of our board members, including such community luminaries as [names], helps drive all our efforts.

We pay special attention to getting young people involved in our projects. In fact, a component of this new project will be to work with schools, churches, and youth groups to locate and train high-school-age volunteers to help out. With the historical information we collect, our staff and volunteers regularly prepare photo brochures and catalogs and maintain an educational website. However, we do not keep the collected materials at our offices, but rather place them with Oakland's public libraries and museums to ensure that they are preserved and made widely accessible to the public.

Without oral history projects such as the one we propose, personal perspectives on historical events are often lost forever. In fact, as earlier mentioned, we must act quickly to preserve the memories of the remaining members of this aging population. Our research specialist, Stella Amanuensis, Ph.D., has collected the names of over 30 potential interviewees, and believes there are at least as many

Sample Query Letter (cont'd)

more out there. However, the average age of these interviewees is 78 years, and some have significant health problems. In addition, the project will serve a secondary community need—to excite African-American high-school-student volunteers about their community's history, and train them in historical research methods. Studies have shown that Oakland's high school students perform poorly in history as compared to other courses and seldom study history in college.

Our plan is to have our staff and volunteers visit each interviewee at least three times, spending 90 minutes per visit. They will ask the interviewees questions about their early home life, stories their parents told them about where the family came from and why they left, family traditions and recreation, basic household economic issues, such as what they ate, when and how they bought or made clothes, how many people shared living space, and more. We'll also focus on the steps migrants took to forge new community ties within the Oakland area and how these ties have developed or changed over the years.

By the end of the project, we intend to have trained at least ten volunteers, met with at least 35 interviewees, recorded the interviews digitally, and transcribed the interviews into hardcopy for public reading. We also plan to publish a paperback book containing photos and excerpts from the various interviews.

The $65,000 we intend to request from The California Historical Foundation will cover staff salaries, recording equipment, and promotion and incidental expenses associated with finding and visiting interviewees. In addition, we have a commitment of $5,000 from a board member to allow our ten most committed volunteers to attend a special oral history training seminar at a local college. A local printer has also agreed to produce the final publication at no cost.

The beauty of our proposed project is that it has both present and future benefits. In the short term, it will teach the student volunteers important research skills, help them understand and take pride in their place in history, and bring them in touch with an older generation. In the long term, it will gather important information about a critical time in African-American history and make it available for this and future generations. Thank you for your interest in our project. We look forward to hearing from you.

Very truly yours,

Carter Pastime

Carter Pastime
Executive Director

the who, what, and where of those you'll be serving, always looking
for ways to tie your project to the foundation's purposes and the
people it hopes to serve.

- **How you'll help.** Present a detailed and convincing account of what
  you'll be doing and how it will meet the stated community need.
  Explain how you'll measure the project's success. If you haven't
  already done so, this is a good place to include names and titles of
  the main project staff, who will bring your project to fruition.
- **Other supporters.** If you've gotten commitments from other
  grantors or donors, mention them here. You might also mention
  who else you'll be approaching for support.
- **A wrap-up.** Briefly recapitulate the goal of the project. If possible,
  mention a few new facts, such as planned future steps or mutual
  contacts, and thank the potential funder for considering your request.

The letter should preferably be signed by your organization's executive
director or board chairperson. Don't include attachments unless the
foundation's guidelines request them.

Grant Proposals

The next step in the process—or, in rare cases, the first step—is to submit a
full grant proposal. A proposal usually contains a written narrative explaining
who your organization is, the project for which it seeks funds, and the reasons
why the project is important and will succeed. This narrative will be backed
up by a budget, proof of your 501(c)(3) status, and other relevant attachments.

By this time, you should have checked the funder's guidelines. These will
specify the format, length, content, and documentation required.

Carefully read the guidelines, noting the most important information.
Any little item you forget decreases your chances of getting funded.

Unless the foundation in which you're interested wants (old-fashioned)
paper proposal submissions, you may not be able to see the full application
form yet. Most foundations (especially the larger ones) now require that
proposals be submitted online. But they haven't yet achieved consistency
in their respective submission systems. As Susan Messina, Director of
Grants and Special Projects at the National Hospice Foundation (NHF,
at www.nationalhospicefoundation.org) has found, "The systems vary

wildly and widely in user friendliness. Many of them don't even let you see the application until you've logged in to their site. And then, not all of them allow you to save as you go. You will need to figure out the system's requirements, and possibly get everything ready in advance, so that you can upload your proposal and hit 'send' in one visit."

> **TIP**
> **Does that maximum character count include spaces?** For online, "fill-in-the-box" proposal submissions, you'll obviously want to prepare the text separately, ahead of time. But don't make the mistake that some proposal writers have, and count only the number of word characters, not realizing that the system may count spaces as characters, too. (Some funders will make this clear in advance, while others won't; and some systems don't count spaces anyway.) Be ready for anything! And whatever you do, don't use the old typewriter convention of putting two spaces between sentences—one is fine and normal.

Use the information that follows to help:
- Use the right tone and style.
- Respond to all requests for information.
- Polish your final draft and compose a cover letter.

Writing Style

Clear, communicative writing is important in almost every fundraising endeavor, but it's especially crucial when drafting grant proposals. Here are some tips to keep in mind:

- **Know what you want to say before you begin.** A surprising number of organizations whip out grant proposals without any sense of the program or project they're proposing. But, as Susan Messina puts it, drawing on her consulting experiences, "People forget that it's a two-step process; first you plan, then you write. Often, I've been handed a proposal project where I had to go back to the organization and work with them on the details of program planning."

- **Remember that there's a human being at the other end.** In your effort to respond to the foundation's guidelines and to set a professional tone, it's easy to write a proposal that reads like a master's thesis and is just as turgid. Remember that your audience is a real person who will surely appreciate it if you convey the passion and conviction you feel about your organization's work. This person wants, above all, to be inspired and moved—something that's easiest to accomplish if you are able to write directly and clearly (but still within the guidelines).

- **Convey authority.** In addition to writing convincing and moving prose, you must also demonstrate that your organization can handle a seemingly overwhelming task. Try drawing the reader deep into the world your organization understands best. For example, if your work consists of assisting people in administrative hearings to claim disability benefits, make sure that the reader understands the expertise you've developed in analyzing doctors' reports, interpreting Social Security regulations, and coaching the applicants in preparation for their hearings. Also show your organization's business acumen—even using some business vocabulary may help show that your organization has a well-thought-out plan for success, understands how it stacks up against the competition, and is prepared to make good and efficient use of the funder's investment.

- **Use their jargon.** Every funder has its favorite words—ones like "authentic," "outcomes," or "personal empowerment"—chosen because the meanings resonate for it. No need to confuse the issue by substituting your own words. It's a good idea to identify the funder's key words and echo them back within your proposal—just don't overdo it, and always use the words in their proper context.

These tips may at times seem contradictory. But the beauty of writing is that you can, with a little practice, weave many strands of thought together into a cohesive and convincing whole. In the words of Marisa Lianggamphai, formerly of WID, "The more personal, yet professionally conversational I can make the proposal, the more likely I am to reach someone."

TIP

Find a good editor. There's not a writer in the world whose words can't use improving or who will catch every last typo, ambiguity, or other glitch. Leave time for a talented writer within your organization, or even a freelancer, to review and edit your draft proposal.

Responding to the Standard Application Questions

A grant proposal may remind you of a college application, with questions that require you to write mini essays. Fortunately, as you gain experience, you'll see that most funders ask for similar information, which allows you to reuse good material you've written in the past. In fact, some funders use a so-called "common grant application," the format of which may have been developed on a statewide or local basis.

Funders usually ask for:

- a title page and table of contents
- an executive summary
- a background statement and/or list of your organization's qualifications
- a statement of community need
- a description of your project's grand goals or purposes
- a description of the project's more immediate objectives
- an action plan or project description
- a timeline
- an explanation of the methods by which you'll evaluate the project's success
- a budget (sometimes with line item explanations)
- an explanation of where future funding will come from, and
- various attachments containing the facts necessary to convincingly back up your assertions.

> ⓘ **CAUTION**
>
> **Don't get bogged down on the introductory sections.** According to Susan Messina, "The Number One mistake I've seen my nonprofit clients make is spending way too much time writing the perfect statement of who they are and what they've done. These issues are important, but what you really need is a program plan that makes sense, an evaluation plan that's rigorous, and a budget that's detailed and complete. These can be much harder than describing how fabulous you are as an organization."

Title Page and Table of Contents

The title page normally lists basic information like your organization's contact information and the project title. Give your project a name that's short and catchy, but still descriptive. The table of contents simply lists the various headings and page numbers.

Executive Summary

The executive summary should outline all the key segments of your proposal, from background about your organization and a clear statement of the good work you hope to do, to your proposed solution. The summary shouldn't be more than two paragraphs long. You may even be able to use language from your query letter.

Background and Qualifications

Here's where you show that your organization is the best one for the job. Your mission, history, major programs, reputation, receipt of awards, and particular strengths may all be worthy of mention. If your organization has been around for a long time, emphasize its experience and ability to weather the tests of time. If your group is relatively new, emphasize how innovative, exciting, and responsive to current needs it is. Also name the key players in your organization and describe their qualifications, interests, and experience. For example, if your new ED just came on board after running a similar and noteworthy program in another part of the country, be sure to mention it. Even your physical facilities may be worth a mention—a state-of-the-art research boat, learning lab, or health clinic, for example.

This can also be a good place to mention where you fit in with the "competition"—that is, with other organizations doing similar work.

Understanding the competition has become an increasingly important concept in funding circles, so don't be squeamish about addressing it head-on. Funders will be most interested if you don't present your competition as groups to be elbowed out, but as worthy organizations working in slightly different niches.

> ⓘ **CAUTION**
>
> **Never badmouth another nonprofit.** Even if some of your competitors don't produce high-quality results, you have little to gain by pointing this out—except perhaps a reputation as a backstabber. If a competitor really is doing poor work, funders will figure it out fast enough on their own. This means it makes sense for your group to quietly position itself as a reliable alternative that can pick up the slack, if necessary.

Statement of Community Need

The section on community need provides an excellent opportunity to establish your organization's professionalism. Though the community need may seem very real and obvious to you, it's probably much less so to a busy foundation officer inundated by other "crucially needed" funding proposals. In short, you'll want to describe exactly what the need is—and what the consequences are of not acting promptly to meet it.

One way to do this is to run all your statements through the "so what?" test. For example, "There are no suicide prevention hotlines in our city" may seem like an important need to you—but a "so what?" skeptic might ask whether such hotlines actually make a difference or whether callers can simply use national hotlines instead. So, to really rivet the funding officer's attention, take your explanation one step deeper, and express the need like this: "Citizens of River City who might call the suicide hotline we hope to establish have absolutely no other access to this highly effective method of suicide prevention. As a result, many deaths will occur that our program could help avoid."

Statistics, results of reliable studies, other information from neutral sources, and your own organization's surveys should all be assembled and presented concisely and coherently to support your assertion of need.

Depending on the funder's guidelines, you may want to add charts or graphs within the text or as attachments at the end.

Especially if yours is a local or regional organization, finding recent and appropriate statistics can be a challenge. But with a little imagination, you can usually patch together credible numbers. For example, if you're working to straighten out drug-involved youth, it may be impossible to say how many kids abuse drugs in your area. But you can find out the number of teenagers in your area and the percentage who didn't complete high school, which is a significant indicator of drug-related problems. To this, you might add the percentage of kids in the country as a whole (and possibly in your state) who regularly use drugs and perhaps a quote from a local high school principal pointing out that local teenage drug use is a serious problem.

If no numerical or statistical information is available, you'll have to fill this section in with more anecdotal material—but make a note to ask your program leadership to put more effort into finding ways to quantify the need for your services for future proposals.

RESOURCE

The U.S. Census is still one of the best sources of statistical information. Check it out at www.census.gov.

Project Goals or Purposes

The purpose or goal of your project should be presented broadly and optimistically. To do so, answer this question—if all goes well, what will our organization have achieved? For example, "reduce teen drug addiction" is a goal or purpose; "provide counseling" is not. Don't get too lofty, however. While working to save Riverfront County's historical buildings is a measurable and realizable goal, "saving the world" is neither. Also make sure your goals are consistent with your mission statement.

Objectives

In your "objective" statement, you tell the funder exactly what you plan to use its grant money to accomplish. Objectives should be tangible and should include numerical targets and other signs of success. An example might be "provide job training and counseling that helps 40 develop-mentally disabled youth develop and market their skills."

In picking hard numbers, it's well to follow the old adage "underpromise and overperform." Otherwise, you may find that your organization can't achieve the goal you set, no matter how hard and effectively it works. For example, if you were to say, "provide job training and counseling that results in 40 developmentally disabled youth's finding jobs," you may have given your program staff an impossible task, especially if the job market turns sour. Ask your program staff to carefully review the objectives section of your proposal to make sure you have chosen realistic milestones that will also satisfy the funder.

Another reason to beware of choosing overly optimistic numerical goals is that they can actually result in your organization's taking on only the "easy" cases, because the tougher ones are less likely to show measurable results. I know this trap all too well, from my experience working at a nonprofit that helped immigrants. Our clients included people who'd fled persecution in many of the world's most violent regions. To stay alive, they needed to obtain political asylum in the United States. We could never predict how many cases would be granted—that depended on multiple factors, such as how talkative and convincing an often traumatized client was, whether a doctor could confirm the client's experience of torture and other mistreatment, and the attitudes and prejudices of the immigration officer who decided the case. Yet, until we got wise to dealing with objectives, our promises to some funders included "political asylum gained for ten clients," and the like. If we had succeeded in only seven cases as we neared the end of the funding year, the pressure was on to find at least three more likely winners.

Some funders will accept outcome measurements based simply on your organization's carrying out the steps in its action plan—for example, giving five workshops or meeting with 50 clients. Others will insist that your outcomes relate to your overall goals, such as protecting a natural resource, establishing a cultural center, or opening a recreational facility for elderly veterans. Even in these latter cases, however, a little creativity may yield a way to style your outcomes conservatively. In the job training for developmentally challenged youth example, you might promise to serve 40 youth, but predict job placement for only 20 of them. Incidentally, we eventually followed a similar approach with our immigrant services project, by explaining to one funder that our goal was to take on a certain number of the most challenging cases requiring such a high level and investment of legal expertise that the clients probably would likely be rejected elsewhere. By first establishing the difficulty of our task, we were then able to show that the number of people served and the number of cases won were impressive.

> **TIP**
>
> **If possible, promise more results than the funder's money will cover.** Many projects have multiple funders, or include money or in-kind contributions from individuals. If you're in this situation, never hesitate to set projected outcome at the total project level, not just for the donor's portion. Funders will be pleased to see that you plan to enhance the bang for their buck.

Action Plan or Methods

The action plan (also called the "methods" section) is the most fun part of the proposal. Here, you get to bring your organization's work to life. To do this, explain what particular activities your organization has chosen, and why and when it plans to meet its goals and objectives. And don't forget to mention behind-the-scenes aspects of the work, like staff training or client selection.

The "what" and "when" of your work are the easiest, because these will summarize your daily activities, such as establishing curricula, planning field trips, mounting events, and explaining how staff will interact with clients or the public. If you aren't asked to include a project timeline elsewhere, you'll also want to fit that in here.

For the "why" of your activity, avoid repeating the old "need plus your project equals success" equation. Instead, explain why your chosen approach was elected over other possibilities. For example, if you've found that your antibullying project works best if you arrange group sessions with the children away from the school campus, explain this. This helps show your organization's expertise and thoughtful approach. Also, be sure to give the project staff credit for any challenges they've learned to overcome—past failures can be advertised as important learning experiences! Make your plan sound effective without making it sound easy.

Timeline

You'll no doubt be asked for a project timeline, whether in a separate section or as part of the action plan. This is fairly self-explanatory. Don't feel that you have to wrap the project up by the end of the funding cycle, but be prepared to say what you will have achieved by that time and what milestones you expect to reach along the way.

Outcome Evaluation Methods

Providing a solid explanation of how you'll evaluate the results of your project affords you another chance to set your organization apart from the rest. Foundations are used to a certain "flake factor" in this area—a mushiness about accounting for results. They also know that many nonprofits regard data collection as a bothersome task that's imposed upon them by foundations. This means that if you can propose a serious and effective system of project evaluation and outcome reporting, you are likely to really impress your readers.

Unfortunately, it's not easy to achieve tight, accurate evaluation and reporting. Nonprofits tackle some of the toughest, most intractable problems in society. They're not like businesses that can tell their shareholders, "We sold 400,000 wombits, hired 200 new workers, and increased profits by 200%!" So how do you shine in this tough endeavor? If you've been realistic in establishing objectives, your task of evaluating the project as a success will be easier—but may at the same time be labor intensive, because you'll likely have to do more than just present raw numbers of people fed, books read, or acres of land preserved.

Creating methods for evaluating your projects will require input and cooperation from program staff. It's not something that you, as the proposal writer, can simply dream up. But working together, and depending to some extent on what your organization does, you usually will want to choose from a couple of broad evaluation methods.

One is to keep the focus on what you did, reporting on numbers of people served or tasks accomplished. If you adopt this approach, you shouldn't have too much trouble developing a systematic and reliable method of data gathering. Even if you don't have sophisticated technological capabilities, you can still point to a well-organized office system and set of written records, typically including forms completed by clients, schedules of meetings, your employee supervision system, minutes of board meetings, and the like.

Your other main evaluation alternative is to focus more subjectively, by trying to answer the question, "How did we do?" This could involve as simple a method as passing out evaluation forms to your clients, trainees, or participants in activities.

Such an approach might be particularly appropriate in a setting where you aren't working with people over the long term, or toward a major life turnaround. If, for example, you go to high schools and show an antismoking videotape, the funder may be less interested in how many kids sat (or slept) in a darkened classroom than in how they reacted to your message. Of course, you can, and often should, mix and match numerical and judgmental evaluation methods, as appropriate. For example, the funder would certainly be interested in knowing that you showed the videotape in more than one classroom, to more than one student.

Budget and Budget Narrative

The person reading your proposal is likely to turn to the budget section first. Never mind all your fancy explanations: It's the raw numbers that many of them feel tell the real story. Though you'll probably be asking for a nice round number, you'll have to show more precisely how you arrived at this figure and how this money will be spent.

Often the funder will provide a budget format. Usually, the breakdown will include salaries, office and other project supplies, and a miniscule amount for administrative overhead (usually no more than 15%). Your project budget should reflect not only new expenses, but also existing costs for staff (at full time or a percentage of their time), supervision, office space, and so on. If the funder to whom you're applying isn't going to be the project's only source of funds, list other prospective or actual grantors, as well as in-kind donations, such as volunteer time. Funders are always delighted to see that their financial input will be leveraged in these ways, especially if your individual donors will cover administrative expenses so that all foundation money can go directly to programs.

TIP

Think big. I asked the former head of one of America's most prestigious foundations what he considered to be a grant applicant's biggest mistake. "Asking for too little," he immediately responded. "Once you sell a foundation on the worthiness of your proposal and your ability to carry it out, it's only logical that most will want it to be bigger, not smaller."

I'm assuming that you are not your office's chief budgeteer, and that someone in the accounting department will actually run the numbers, after consultation with you and with program staff. Just be sure to give this person plenty of advance warning! And remember to consult with both your program staff and your accountant to arrive at a consensus about how much money is realistically required and what the numbers mean.

Many funders will ask not only for columns of numbers, but for a narrative explanation as well. Having consulted with program staff, you should be ready to do this in a way that brings your numbers to life for the potential funder. Along the way, be sure to explain any expenses that might seem unusual, and highlight any ways that you've managed to keep costs down. Keep it short: You don't need to rehash issues like the overall need for the project.

RESOURCE

Want additional help with your budget? Check out the Foundation Center's tutorial on developing a project budget for grant proposal purposes, at foundationcenter.org (click "Get Started," then "Proposal Writing" under "Learn About," then "Proposal Budgeting Basics").

Future Funding Sources

More and more funders want to make sure that they're not just going to create a bubble project—one that will burst as soon as its funding stops, without having achieved anything. And, given that renewals are anything but guaranteed (especially because of the current penchant among foundations for funding new, innovative, start-up or pilot projects), this should be a real concern for your organization as well. (The exception, of course, would be if you truly are proposing a project with a limited time span, such as restoring a community fountain.) Hopefully your leadership has thought ahead about the sustainability of the project you're proposing and how it fits into your overall strategic plan.

Of course, you can hardly guarantee where this year's funding will come from, much less next year's. Your best bet when writing the proposal is to describe your carefully constructed development plan (see Chapter 3). You might also mention the development office's record of success—for example, that you've increased individual contributions in the past year or years and can project continued success in this area. If you can name particular funders that you believe are likely to fund the proposed project in the future, great—but don't just toss names around. More likely, you'll simply want to describe the types of funding, whether from foundations, individuals, or others, that you'll be trying to obtain.

Supporting Documents

Most funders will require supporting documents to accompany your grant proposal—at a minimum, a copy of the IRS letter proving your 501(c)(3) status. (For online submissions, be ready to make a lot of PDFs.) Don't wait until the last minute to look at the funder's requirements. For example, you may be surprised to find a requirement that you assemble names of influential people willing to serve on a project advisory committee, which can take weeks or months to accomplish. And, if you're applying to the federal government, the attachments will dwarf the narrative part of the grant proposal and require input from program staff and others.

You may also be permitted to attach documents of your own choosing. Your brochure and latest annual report may be relevant and helpful. Strong and convincing letters of support from funders, city officials, or other influential people can be particularly helpful. Such letters should describe your track record on past projects and express the letter writer's great confidence in your ability to carry out future projects. Depending on your field of work, you could also get letters of support from other figures of authority, such as someone in the administration of a hospital or school with which you're affiliated. Such letters won't arrive on your doorstep spontaneously—you'll have to ask for them. This is an accepted and traditional practice, however, so your friends and funders should not be surprised to hear from you. In fact, many of them will be pleased that you are applying for additional money to expand your programs.

Final Preparation and Cover Letter

The last few steps in preparing your grant proposal are too easily forgotten. First, run your final draft past the executive director and anyone else who needs to approve it (you certainly don't want to have to amend it after it's submitted). You'll also want to prepare a short, optimistic cover letter addressed to the appropriate program officer or other contact person, and typically signed by your ED. Refer to any past grants or positive history with the funder. Make sure that the letter indicates who in your organization the funder should contact for questions, follow-up, and its response. Provide that person's direct-line phone number and email address.

Though I could tell you to plan ahead so you won't be working on the proposal until the last possible minute, that's the sort of advice that rarely changes anyone's behavior (including my own). If you are able to get things in before the deadline, however, you've got an advantage—foundations think of the deadline as the "last possible day," not as a simple due date, and are delighted to have an opportunity to read a submission that comes in before the flood.

> **CAUTION**
> **Snail mail can be tough on lateniks.** If your proposal cannot be submitted online, find out the addresses and hours of all U.S. post offices, Federal Express locations, or other delivery offices well in advance. There's nothing worse than finally packaging up your proposal on the eve of the deadline, realizing you've missed the closing time at the nearest post office, and making frantic calls as evening turns into night.

Site Visits

A site visit is just what it sounds like—one or more people from the prospective funder's office schedule a visit to your program site to see for themselves what's going on. Usually this happens after your proposal has been received by the funder and gone through one or more layers of review. If your prospective funder requires or is willing to make a site visit, let out a cheer! This is one of those "picture is worth a thousand words" opportunities—and it indicates that your proposal is under serious consideration.

Grant Din, of the Angel Island Immigration Station Foundation, can testify to the great opportunity a site visit gives your organization: "Back when I worked as a grants officer at a foundation that had very limited funds, I well remember how heart-wrenching it was to say no to a good project after a site visit. Perhaps we weren't cutthroat enough, but we sometimes ended up giving out many small grants just to avoid rejecting a group outright. Do everything you can think of to get funders to visit!"

The site visit will be scheduled in advance. So don't worry that a black limo will pull up full of people wearing white gloves—you'll have time to plan. If possible, try to schedule the visit for a time when your organization is at its most active, seeing clients or engaging in field work. You want to give the visitor a hands-on experience, to the extent possible. Your chances of success go up if they can meet your clients, handle an art project, savor a tomato in your community garden, or do anything else that involves something other than talking to the ED and meeting board members. Remember, you've already engaged their minds with the grant proposal— now is the time to more fully engage their hearts. If the most interesting work of your organization isn't at its central office, then take the visitors where the action is (unless it's a wilderness trek, a toxic dump site, or some other dangerous or messy spot).

Advise all program staff and any relevant clients of who's coming, and ask staff to tidy up their workspaces. Also ask staff members or clients to be ready to talk to the visitors about their activities and, if appropriate, to do a "show and tell" presentation—with the emphasis on "show."

But keep things low-key. The visitors want to see your site as it really functions, not turned into a theater. Foundation officers say that one of the biggest mistakes nonprofits make during site visits is putting on a big to-do rather than engaging in business as usual. Ron Rowell, a program officer with the Common Counsel Foundation, once told me, "Having worked in the nonprofit sector myself, I understand the urge to stage things for the funders' benefit. But now that I'm in the foundation world, the most important thing to me at a site visit is honesty. If all I hear is that everything is just peachy, one success after another, I start to worry about what's really going on."

On the other hand, foundation officers tend to like it when the organization doesn't spend all its time passively waiting to be judged, but actively asks the foundation officers what they're interested in, how their proposal can be improved, and the like. (In fact, if the site visit is conducted before your written proposal goes in, this is an ideal chance to pick up some tips on how to present the relevant information most effectively.)

When the visitors arrive, the executive director should take the lead in showing them around. Make sure you've got enough clean mugs ready to offer coffee or tea. Depending on how long they'll be staying, snacks or a light lunch might also be appropriate. Most site visits last from two to three hours.

> **TIP**
>
> **Out-of-town site visitors need more attention.** Though they'll probably book airplane and hotel reservations on their own, you'll want to be ready with recommendations, plus tips on good restaurants and entertainment. There is usually no need to be a tour guide, but be ready to suggest or join in on dinner plans, if appropriate. Also, give them any needed tips on transportation or getting to your facility.

Meetings With the Funder

Some funders will ask members of your organization to come to their offices for a formal presentation or question-and-answer session. Again, this is a good sign and a grand opportunity to put a human face on your work. Make sure to find out exactly who will be at the meeting—it may or may not be your main contact person. The United Way, for example, brings in "allocation volunteers" who help decide what gets funded. Though the volunteers are briefed beforehand, they'll require a lot more background and introductory information than a foundation staff person with whom you've been in contact for years.

Be careful in choosing who will represent your group at this meeting—the proposal will be judged, in part, by the personality of the person or persons attending. A foundation officer once told me that he was quicker to grant money to an average project with good leadership than to a great-sounding project with leaders who didn't inspire confidence.

Though your executive director should definitely attend the meeting, there will probably be room for some additional people. Ironically enough, the development person who wrote the proposal may not be the best one to go along, because foundations often regard development staff as hired-gun salespeople. A program person is usually the best choice—someone who is actually doing the work and can articulate, passionately and in colorful detail, what it involves.

If your program person isn't used to such activities, sit down with him or her beforehand. Work together on organizing a short presentation, if one is required or expected. Often the program person takes the lead here, relating events from his or her own working experience: how a client was helped, how an arts project was received by the public, how a research project was undertaken, and so forth.

The Funding Decision

After more time than you'd probably like—usually from three months to a year after you submitted your proposal—you'll receive an answer. If months have passed and you haven't heard anything, it's okay to call your contact person to check in.

If the funding decision is negative, the ED may want to call and politely ask why. Not all foundations will be candid about why you were turned down, but if they are, it's important to listen carefully to the answers and not argue. Remember, a "no" doesn't mean you'll never be funded by a funder. It may be that your proposal didn't quite fit the mix of grants the foundation was trying to achieve or that it misinterpreted some element of your proposal for some reason that would never occur to you. Either way, be alert for information that will help you approach the funder next time.

If the decision is positive, congratulations! This is one of those moments that makes the stress and long nights of fundraising worthwhile. Be loud about your joy. Board members and staff can always use some good news and will be especially gratified if they had any hand in preparing the proposal or in supplying the information that went into it. If it's a truly substantial grant or will fund something that's story worthy, mention it on your website, Facebook page, and Twitter feed and consider trying to get some local media coverage (see Chapter 13). The funder may be willing to help in this effort.

And don't forget to thank the funder! Many development pros make it a habit to send out a thank-you letter before even cashing the check. In addition, having your ED or board chair call the funder to say "thanks" offers a good opportunity to get feedback that may help you craft your follow-up reports. In particular, try to solicit information about which part of your proposal was most persuasive and what could have been done to make it even better. Don't skip this important step! There's no better time to get constructive feedback about how to improve your proposal writing than when everyone is in a good mood.

> **TIP**
>
> **If your overall funding falls short, try to renegotiate the terms of the grants.** Nonprofits will often approach more than one foundation simultaneously, asking each to pitch in enough to reach the total needed for the project. However, if some foundations say "yes" and others "no" to your grant request, what do you do? It's rare that a nonprofit would have to decline the grant money in such circumstances. Your first choice is to ask the foundation or foundations who approved your request to grant a bit more to cover the shortfall. If that doesn't work, ask them to accept a scaled-down version of the project, or reduced outcomes.

Follow Up With the Funder

As you surely know, your grant work doesn't end when you deposit the check. All funders follow up to find out how their money has been spent and what results it has achieved. As soon as you've got the grant paperwork in hand, make sure that the people in your organization understand their role in this process. Program people will typically need to track their activities and outcomes for progress reports. Your accounting department may need to track expenses, particularly if the funder operates on a reimbursement basis. Someone will have to set aside time on the calendar for drafting a progress report. Though these reports won't be as time-consuming as the initial grant proposal, they often ask for similar information.

If progress reports are to be drafted by a program person, make sure that a development staff person or the ED gives it a thorough review before it goes out. The object is to scrutinize the report to make sure that promises made in the grant proposal are being kept, or at least that there's an explanation for any changes to the action plan. It's also important that your organization speak with a consistent voice.

This required follow-up should not be pushed to the back burner. Maintaining strong and cordial relationships with funders is crucially important. Not only are you more likely to get a grant renewal if your reports are well organized and timely, but demonstrating your ability to perform may also result in a number of other benefits. For example, the foundation may feature your organization on its website or in its annual report. In addition, a foundation that sponsors donor-advised funds may recommend your organization to individual donors looking for a group that fits their philanthropical inclinations. And, last but not least, because funders talk to each other, your reputation can be burnished or tarnished on the basis of your follow-through.

Beyond just complying with the funder's reporting requirements, think of ways you can use your reports to increase its interest and involvement. Start by treating the contact person at the foundation as you would an important individual donor—who appreciates receiving the occasional update, positive news clipping about your work, or even an invitation to participate. For example, the Zen Hospice Project has invited foundation representatives to its monthly donor lunches, informal events at which volunteer caregivers share their experiences before they tour the residential house. Also see "Women's Studio Workshop Uses Regular Letters to Reach Funders," below.

Women's Studio Workshop Uses Regular Letters to Reach Funders

The Women's Studio Workshop (WSW) is an artist's residency and educational program located in idyllic Rosendale, New York (in the Mid-Hudson River Valley). While WSW already provides visiting women artists with studio and living space in which to explore their voices and visions, its ambitions go beyond this—they'd like to routinely pay women a reasonable wage to come to WSW and do art. To this end, foundation funding has been an important resource. In particular, the Andy Warhol Foundation for the Visual Arts has offered WSW significant support.

As Anita Wetzel, development director, describes the course of WSW's relationship with the Warhol Foundation, "WSW had received a good-sized grant from Warhol in 1992. In 1998, a two-year award from the foundation helped us make a big leap forward, increasing the number of funded opportunities we could offer artists. In 2002, WSW received another two-year grant to fund artists working at WSW.

"Part of the reason we got the 2002 grant may have been that I'd been sending the Warhol Foundation and our other major funders regular letters—about once every three months—telling them what had been happening. For example, my letters might talk about an international artist spending time with us, or describe a session of the Arts-In-Education program, where kids from Kingston City Schools come and develop their art skills. In fact, the program officer remarked on the letters when she came to visit.

"It's funny, because no one ever told me to start writing these letters. Like many people, I happened into fundraising because I wanted to make our project happen. But I had come to realize that you need to reach out to anyone giving you a significant amount of money. And, I enjoy writing the letters—it's a chance to tell people what we think is interesting and important, instead of always just answering the questions on their required reports. Also, by writing regularly, I can highlight colorful information before we've moved on to the next project and forgotten the details."

> **TIP**
> **While things are going well, ask for a letter of recommendation from your funder.** It can be very useful when you apply for other funding. The best time to ask for this is after you have submitted several progress reports detailing how you are successfully spending the funder's money.

Grant Renewals

Putting "renewals" in the title of this section is a bit misleading, because only a minority of foundation grants come with any expectation of renewal (or in nonprofit lingo, "re-upping" the grant). Many funders specifically prefer that after your one-, two-, or even five-year grant period is completed, you go elsewhere for subsequent funding. Though you may be lucky enough to locate a funder who makes a tradition of long-term support, such funders are getting rare. Nevertheless, having invested time and effort in educating the funder about your work, it's worth inquiring whether a new grant is a possibility.

Even though re-upping may be difficult to accomplish with a particular funder, it may nevertheless be easier than finding a new funding source. By now, you have the advantage of personal contact with someone in the funder's office. For a one-year grant, the time to bring this up is no longer than nine months into your grant, when things are hopefully going well but you're not yet desperate about how you'll continue. Have a frank talk with your contact person. Ask for his or her views on whether the foundation might be interested in funding continuation of your program or another part of your activities.

The funder may require that your next proposal contain something new and different. (Be ready with some ideas before holding any conversations.) Finding or creating something new to propose can be tricky, especially if you provide ongoing services that don't culminate in anything. This is one of those times when you need to be especially wary of letting the funding stream determine the program—altering or expanding your services just to get a grant can lead to trouble down the line. But realize that not everything about your proposed activities needs to be new. The funder may be happy to support a new phase of your program, an increased focus on the needs of certain members of your clientele, a collaborative effort encompassing existing services, or a heightened need for your services due to new legislation or social or environmental pressures.

If the funder truly can't support your organization any longer, ask for recommendations to other funders. Don't forget to take down the names and telephone numbers of the contact people!

Creating Printed Communications Materials

Every organization needs certain printed materials on hand—such as a well-written, professional-looking brochure—to educate the public about its mission and activities. Newsletters and annual reports are also great for this purpose. And because these materials are not designed primarily as fundraising tools, they can have great credibility with your current and potential supporters. Once you have an attractive, up-to-date publication, you can send it to existing supporters, use it to inspire new ones, hand it to people you meet at conferences, meetings, or fundraising events, and, of course, post it online. Like a businessperson handing out his or her card, these publications are an instant way of showing that your organization is ready to be taken seriously.

Although producing a high-quality brochure should be well within the reach of virtually every nonprofit, creating newsletters and annual reports can be far more time-consuming and costly. The audience for these publications often expects something with higher production values than the everyday letter—although most donors aren't looking for something as slick and costly as your average corporate report. So if you're on a bare-bones budget, you'll do just fine producing these items using decent page layout software (such as *InDesign*), supplemented by a copy machine and stapler. But if you have the financial resources, a modest investment in professional design and print services can be well worth the expense.

How a Newsletter Paid for Itself

Kate McNulty, then with Sacred Heart Cathedral Preparatory School, described this "happy ending" to the school's production of its newsletter. "We'd been putting out a newsletter to our donors reporting on how our capital campaign to fund the new Student Life Center was going. The newsletter itself cost a couple of thousand dollars to produce, and contained investor profiles, a construction report with photographs, and a fundraising update. After we sent the last newsletter out, one of our major supporters took an interest in one of the naming opportunities we listed. He pledged $15,000, and in recognition the school put his name on one of its Campus Ministry Offices. He had been cultivated and asked earlier in the campaign for a gift, but it was the newsletter that clearly tipped the scales—and thereby paid for itself."

This chapter covers:
- brochures
- newsletters, and
- annual reports.

RESOURCE

For more detailed information: See *Every Nonprofit's Guide to Publishing: Creating Newsletters, Magazines & Websites People Will Read*, by Cheryl Woodard & Lucia Hwang (Nolo).

Brochures

As emphasized above, every organization should have an up-to-date brochure on hand. You simply don't want to be in the room when a prominent visitor or potential supporter asks for more information about your organization and you're caught empty-handed.

Your brochure should explain what your organization is and what it does. It should include information on:
- why your organization was founded and continues to exist (your basic mission, but spelled out in compelling language)
- what activities your organization currently carries out to address your mission
- your organization's hopes and plans for the near future
- how your organization is funded, and
- how readers can become involved or make contributions.

The simplest brochure is an 8½" by 11" piece of paper folded into thirds, which gives you six panels to fill with text and graphics. It's even smarter to use an 8½" by 14" sheet of legal-sized paper folded into fourths, which creates eight panels. Either size allows you to turn the right-most panel into a tear-off reply or donation card. But with the larger version, a professional can do something even snazzier—attach a tear-off reply envelope.

Because you want your brochure to have a reasonably long shelf life, you should include only general information about your group. Avoid adding dates or detailed descriptions of time-specific projects that will soon be in your rear-view mirror. Instead, focus on continuing programs and long-term results. Keep the text short and snappy—bold headings and bullet points will make your points far better than long-winded explanations. Photos are also an excellent way of giving readers an instant understanding and appreciation of your work.

The brochure is also a good place to provide key information for people who might need to contact or make use of your organization—perhaps your address and phone number, website address, hours of operation, a map to your facilities, fees for services or admission, and the like.

> **TIP**
>
> **Hiring a freelance designer can be a bargain.** Like a well-designed tool, vehicle, or building, a visually pleasing brochure will be far more attractive and effective than a slapdash one that's thrown together without much thought or skill. In just a few hours, a freelance design professional can turn an amateurish effort into something you can be proud of.

Below are some sample pages from an elegant and effective brochure from the Haas-Lilienthal House in San Francisco. You'll see the front page, which shows an attractive photo and the necessary contact information, as well as the tear-off membership/donation page. Note that this page points out both the importance of donations and the various benefits to which membership entitles the donor.

Newsletters

Many nonprofits send out regular newsletters as a way to communicate with their dues-paying members and, in some cases, potential members. (And many others have given up, convinced that no one reads the newsletters—which may be true, given how many nonprofit newsletters are utterly boring—unlike what yours will be, of course.) Although newsletters take a fair amount of money and effort to produce, a well-crafted one can provide a series of ongoing tugs designed to pull donors toward deeper engagement with your organization.

Many organizations send their newsletter by both print and email and ask willing supporters to accept only emailed copies. But the world

Haas-Lilienthal House Brochure

The Haas-Lilienthal House

Photo © Douglas Keister

A property of
San Francisco Architectural Heritage
City Landmark No. 69
National Register of
Historic Places

2007 Franklin Street
San Francisco, CA 94109

House Information Phone: 415.441.3004
SF Heritage Phone: 415.441.3000
House Rental Phone: 415.441.3011
Fax: 415.441.3015
Email: info@sfheritage.org
Web Site: www.sfheritage.org

MEMBERSHIP REPLY CARD

Become a Member – San Francisco Architectural Heritage depends on membership dues and contributions to support its education and conservation activities. Membership and donations are tax deductible.

Benefits include:
- Our bi-monthly newsletter, *Heritage News*
- Free admission for you and your guests to the Haas-Lilienthal House, and on regularly scheduled walking tours
- Free admission to the Holiday Open House
- A 20% discount on educational events and book store items
- Advance invitation to special events

JOIN TODAY!

Yes! I'd like to join!
Please sign me up at the following level:

❑	$45	Senior/Student
❑	$60	Individual
❑	$75	Family
❑	$125	Supporting Member
❑	$250	Contributing Member
❑	$500	Sustaining Member

Name _____

Address _____

City/State/Zip _____

Phone/Fax/Email _____

We accept checks, VISA, MasterCard and American Express. If paying by credit card:

Account Number _____ Expiration Date

Signature _____

Tax exempt status: Heritage is exempt from Federal income tax under Section 501 (a)(3) of the Internal Revenue Code and has been classified by the IRS as a public foundation. Heritage is exempt from California State franchise or income tax under Section 2370 (d) Revenue and Taxation Code.

Please return to: San Francisco Heritage, Attn: Membership, 2007 Franklin Street, San Francisco, CA 94109

Designed by: PTI, Printers for Nonprofits
Reprinted with permission

doesn't yet seem to be fully ready for email-only newsletters. As JoLynn Taylor, Membership and Publications Manager at WildCare in San Rafael, California (www.wildcarebayarea.org), explains, "Many of our members don't want all the email! Besides, more than half of the people who receive our printed newsletter haven't yet shared their email addresses with us. And another advantage to the printed newsletter is that we can drop off free copies at various places around the county, which serves not only fundraising but educational purposes."

Your printed newsletter can take many forms, but probably the most common consists of four or eight double-sided 8½" x 11" pages, sent out four times per year, containing photos and one to four substantive stories about your organization and its work. (The newsletters that contain only one main story typically contain various other brief blurbs or, if using an email-only format, teaser summaries and links to online articles.) Wealthier organizations might produce a magazine, complete with a glossy cover.

TIP

Your social media efforts need not undercut your newsletter. Many nonprofits happily report that the ability to broadcast time-sensitive material via social networks serves as a handy pressure release valve. It means they no longer need to either sit on hot news until the newsletter goes out or try to hurry up the publication date before the news gets stale. Of course, you should still try to put newsy material into the newsletter, but you can go deeper, such as with opinion pieces or discussions of the impact of your group's work. Your social media postings are actually a great way to test what topics are of interest to your readership and might deserve a full newsletter article.

While one person in your organization—or, if you can afford it, a cost-efficient freelancer—should edit your newsletter, the articles can be written by anyone. In fact, writing newsletter articles makes a fun—and educational—project for board members and other volunteers with the necessary skills.

Take a look at other organizations' newsletters to see what types of format and content appeal to you. Shown below is an example from WildCare, a California organization that provides care for ill, orphaned, or injured wild animals (www.wildcarebayarea.org).

Sample WildCare Newsletter

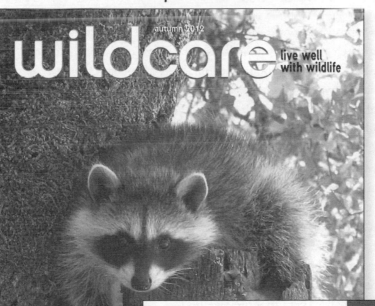

autumn 2012

wildcare

live well
with wildlife

| in this issue |

🐾 project in patholog

🦴 adventures with w

🐾 canine detective st

patient gallery

River Otter (#0681) was rescued in Larkspur on May 27. Residents had observed an otter family playing in Corte Madera Creek but piercing distress calls alerted Jane Sherman. Using their kayak Jane pulled the drowning pup, too young to swim, from the water and called the Marin Humane Society. The baby arrived at WildCare hypothermic and exhausted. Two siblings were later found drowned; their mother was never found.

Supportive care, including heat, oxygen, fluids, antibiotics and formula fed from a bottle revived her, and by Monday she was alert and very feisty. River Otters need specialized facilities and other otters to thrive, and Lake Tahoe Wildlife Care responded to our email for help.

Patient #0681 was transferred there on May 30, but following California Fish and Game regulations, she will be released in Marin County. You can view a video of her at WildCare at www.wildcarebayarea.org.

Gopher Snake (#0853) was one of three tangled in garden netting and brought in from Novato by the Marin Humane Society on June 14. Two were dead and had begun to decompose, but miraculously, #0853 was still alive.

The netting was painstakingly removed, and it was clear they had all sought the mice nesting in the netting.

Patient #0853's scales were badly damaged, and he had minor lacerations all over his body. The snake was put in a pool of warm water to hydrate, and he began to gulp down the water.

Snakes are not the only animals that become tangled in garden netting. This non biodegradable plastic has snared birds, raccoons, opossums, skunks, lizards and other animals.

He went to foster care with Nat Smith on June 18 where he will stay until late summer, after his skin has healed and he sheds the damaged layer.

Long-tailed Weasel (#0712) was found sitting on Kathleen Sartori's porch in Tomales on May 30. He was in good condition, with beautiful teeth that indicate he is relatively young. That he was "approachable" could indicate that he was in the early stages of distemper, a viral disease of carnivores that causes neural damage. Tameness was another possibility. Keeping any wild animal in California is not legal, but weasels are small relatives of ferrets, popular as pets in other states. Baby animals seem like good pets until sexual maturity occurs. Then the no-longer-sweet babies are often abandoned.

Patient #0712 had a great appetite and showed no sign of distemper. He was transferred to quiet outdoor off-site caging where he will be released slowly, with supplemental food.

Western Gray Squirrel (#0234) was brought to WildCare from Novato by Sonia Fuetsch on March 29. She had been found under a palm tree with a severe laceration deep into the muscles across her back, from hip to hip. Unwilling to use her rear legs, her tail was completely flaccid. This is a concern, because squirrels use their tails for balance and temperature regulation in both winter and summer.

Radiographs showed no fractures, but a subtle spinal injury might not show up on our equipment, and we called Dr. Lynne Lankes of the Central Marin Cat and Exotic Hospital. Dr. Lankes prescribed a wound treatment for the next week as the baby regained strength, then performed surgery to close the wound on April 6. Over the next weeks several more visits and treatments were needed, amounting to more than $1,000 in veterinary services which Central Marin Cat and Exotic Clinic generously donated to WildCare.

Miraculously, this little squirrel made a complete recovery with full function of her tail, and on June 2 was released with a nest box in a tree.

#0681

#0053

#0712

#0234

The stories in your newsletter don't have to sound like they were written by hard-nosed reporters—but your pieces need to be interesting, timely, and appropriate. For example, your taxpayers' rights organization might appropriately run a story about waste in the mayor's office, but not a board member's long poem about freedom. Take a look at Chapter 13 for information on what the professional media considers a worthwhile, attention-grabbing story. It also helps to keep your newsletter's mission in mind. Go light on the chatty updates about what's happening within your organization, in favor of educating readers about the cause you work on. Everyone loves stories about people and animals.

Also be sure to include stories that follow up on any plans, projects, or emergencies that you've already described in mailed appeals. For example, if your donors were sent an emergency appeal for funds to deal with the aftermath of a flood, and your subsequent newsletter doesn't mention what happened next, your donors will lose interest in your stories at best, or at worst, may become suspicious that you exaggerated or even fabricated the emergency to convince them to write big checks.

From a direct fundraising standpoint, your newsletter is also a good place to advise readers of any upcoming special events and other opportunities to get involved. If warranted, you can also include a tear-out or cut-out slip of paper to facilitate donations and enclose a reply envelope.

Annual Reports

You don't have to produce an annual report, but it can be very effective for purposes of fundraising, educating others about who you are, and helping satisfy various nonprofit watchdog organizations that your group is on the up-and-up. (See "BBB Wise Giving Alliance Recommendations Regarding Annual Reports," below.) Unlike a newsletter, which often contains articles that zoom in on particular things your organization has done, your annual report should provide a wider-angle picture of your organization and what it stands for. The report should be published soon after the close of your fiscal year.

Somewhat like a corporation's annual report, yours should concentrate on a one-year period—usually your fiscal year—and include detailed financial accounting, often straight from your auditors. Also like a corporate report, your annual report will play a role in marketing your organization.

The trend is, however, clearly moving away from the lengthy bound volumes that were once the gold standard for annual reports. For one thing, your audience's attention span has shortened. For another, producing a multipage, glossy report can cost many thousands of dollars, while online-only versions are increasingly gaining acceptance. If a printed version still seems best for your audience, consider making it short and sweet, focusing on key numbers and impact. Some organizations have reduced their print report to a postcard. WildCare presents it as a section of one of its quarterly newsletters, and VolunteerMatch got its 2011 report down to a single online infographic!

BBB Wise Giving Alliance Recommendations Regarding Annual Reports

The BBB Wise Giving Alliance, a nonprofit affiliated with the Council of Better Business Bureaus, has established itself as an industry standard setter when it comes to nonprofit fundraising practices, disclosure, and more. Although the Wise Giving Alliance Standards are voluntary, their widespread use as a tool by which to judge your work makes them worth heeding. The group includes the following recommendation among its standards for charitable accountability:

"[The organization shall] [h]ave an annual report available to all, on request, that includes:

- the organization's mission statement
- a summary of the past year's program service accomplishments
- a roster of the officers and members of the board of directors
- financial information that includes (i) total income in the past fiscal year, (ii) expenses in the same program, fundraising and administrative categories as in the financial statements, and (iii) ending net assets."

For the complete list of standards, see www.bbb.org/us/Charity-Evaluation.

The elements to include in a classic annual report are:

- **An attractive cover.** Make sure your organization's name, as well as the year the report covers, are clearly displayed. Include a visual image that both conveys your organization's personality and identity and makes people want to open the report.

- **Your mission or "about" statement.** This should appear on the inside of the front cover or in some other highly visible spot.

- **Message from the top executive.** A short "letter" from the executive director or chairman of the board (or both) is traditionally included near the beginning of the report. This is the executive's chance to express his or her vision about the core message the report conveys and to remind the donor-reader about his or her key role in bringing it about. See, for example, the introductory letter by Kate Kendell, executive director of the National Center for Lesbian Rights (NCLR) in its 2011 annual report below (www.nclrights, a national legal organization that works to advance the civil and human rights of lesbian, gay, bisexual, and transgender (LGBT) people and their families).

- **Short descriptions of the year's major projects or endeavors.** You don't have to cover everything. Highlight important or successful work that supports the overall message of that year's report. If you began an exciting new initiative, be sure to cover it, even if it's still in the start-up phase.

- **Work that remains to be done.** No need to imply that you wrapped up all of your projects by year's end—in fact, such a message works against your ultimate fundraising interests. Your report should highlight ongoing challenges and projects.

- **Photos or illustrations.** Pages of pure text aren't likely to catch anyone's eye, especially if they're reading off of a computer or smartphone screen. Including photos of your organization's work (with good explanatory captions) as well as drawings, graphs, or charts conveying relevant information will help reel in the readers. See, for example, NCLR's interesting pie chart showing its "work at a glance," below.

- **Where the money came from.** Give credit to the various foundations, donors, and others who supported your organization over the past year. You might include narrative descriptions, charts (for example,

Sample Letter From the Executive Director

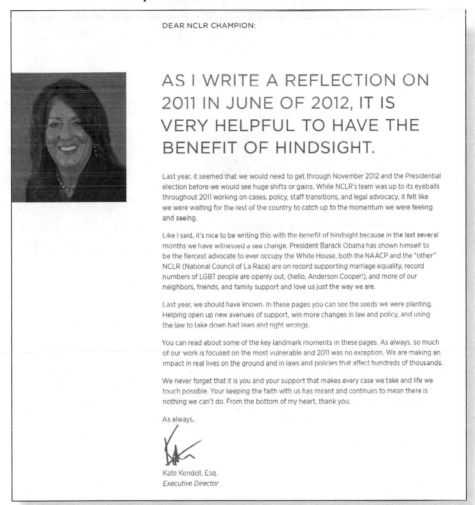

DEAR NCLR CHAMPION:

AS I WRITE A REFLECTION ON 2011 IN JUNE OF 2012, IT IS VERY HELPFUL TO HAVE THE BENEFIT OF HINDSIGHT.

Last year, it seemed that we would need to get through November 2012 and the Presidential election before we would see huge shifts or gains. While NCLR's team was up to its eyeballs throughout 2011 working on cases, policy, staff transitions, and legal advocacy, it felt like we were waiting for the rest of the country to catch up to the momentum we were feeling and seeing.

Like I said, it's nice to be writing this with the benefit of hindsight because in the last several months we have witnessed a sea change. President Barack Obama has shown himself to be the fiercest advocate to ever occupy the White House, both the NAACP and the "other" NCLR (National Council of La Raza) are on record supporting marriage equality, record numbers of LGBT people are openly out, (hello, Anderson Cooper!), and more of our neighbors, friends, and family support and love us just the way we are.

Last year, we should have known. In these pages you can see the seeds we were planting. Helping open up new avenues of support, win more changes in law and policy, and using the law to take down bad laws and right wrongs.

You can read about some of the key landmark moments in these pages. As always, so much of our work is focused on the most vulnerable and 2011 was no exception. We are making an impact in real lives on the ground and in laws and policies that affect hundreds of thousands.

We never forget that it is you and your support that makes every case we take and life we touch possible. Your keeping the faith with us has meant and continues to mean there is nothing we can't do. From the bottom of my heart, thank you.

As always,

Kate Kendell, Esq.
Executive Director

Reprinted with permission

a pie chart showing the amounts that came from foundations, donors, and other types of sources), and an explanation of any changes in your pattern of support from past years. And whatever you do, don't fail to include a list of individual donors, usually ranked in categories of gift levels. (That's all some people look at; and their names had better be spelled right, too!) If you've received

Sample Chart From NCLR Annual Report

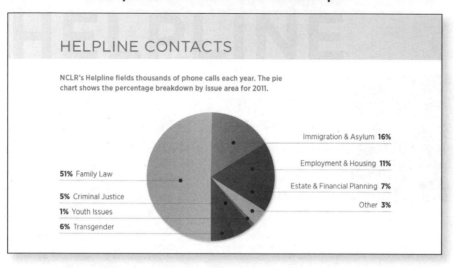

Reprinted with permission

anonymous gifts, mention them; this not only demonstrates your full range of support, but it also shows that, on request, you will you respect your donors' privacy.

- **Where the money went.** Include audited financial information and an explanation of what the numbers mean for the budgetarily challenged. Readers will be particularly interested in stories of money well spent.

- **Introduction to your staff and board members.** If your organization is large, you may want to include only your key staff. In general, however, readers love to see the faces of those involved with the work, even interns or part-timers. So include lots of photos of staff if your people will agree to them.

- **A reply device.** An envelope and fill-out form for donations is not required with your annual report, but it's never a bad idea to add one.

Tips for Keeping Down Design and Printing Costs

Designers and printers who work with nonprofits should be familiar with producing the frugal but competent look you're after. But, if you're working with one who's less sensitive to nonprofit sensibilities, be sure to educate him or her. The last thing you want is a highly produced, glossy report that conveys that you are flush with cash. Even worse, you don't want to spend precious dollars on a report that looks unprofessional, fails to convey the spirit or accomplishments of your organization, or otherwise falls short of the mark.

Here's how to make the most of your relationships with publishing professionals:

- **Before choosing a designer or printer, ask for references, and find someone you can trust.** Ask other nonprofits for recommendations—in every urban area there are designers and printers who specialize in working with nonprofits.
- **Especially on your first job, work closely with your designer and/or printer.** Be ready to visit his or her office, look over samples, express your opinion on paper and color, and more. You may be able to nip expensive propositions in the bud, and find out about lower-cost options.
- **Don't take offers of free services at face value.** For example, a free layout may not be such a great deal if you are overcharged for paper, ink, and printing.
- **Plan your year's printing needs in advance, to maximize what can be printed in one lot**—for example, don't have new envelopes printed for every mail appeal.
- **Find out the costs of mailing—and weigh a prototype of your package—before producing it.**
- **Don't print anything until you have a plan in place for distributing or marketing it**—otherwise you could end up with a pile of expensive material in your closet.
- **Always bid out your good-sized printing jobs, such as your annual report, and get estimates from at least three printers.** Nothing will cost you more in the long run than making a "best friend" out of the printer.
- **Avoid full color unless money is no object; even then, consider whether your donors will see it as too costly.** A single shade of ink plus black on a well-chosen color of paper can look great and allow for legible, attractive photographs. Ask your designer or printer for suggestions.

Designing Your Website to Draw in Donors

E very nonprofit that can scrape together the necessary funds and talent should set up a website. Because people now use the Web as a telephone book, research tool, contact method, and much more, your absence in cyberspace makes about as much sense as deciding not to have a telephone. Given this reality—and that most nonprofits have long since gotten at least a bare-bones website up and running—I don't cover the mechanics of establishing a website (see the resources listed below if you need such help). Instead, this chapter will help you make sure that your website works to effectively achieve your fundraising goals.

The checklist below gives you eight simple ways to assess your website's ability to help you raise money. Each of these topics is discussed at greater length in the sections that follow. If you are still in the organizational start-up phase, it will obviously be most efficient to address these various issues during the design of your website. But these strategies can help you even if your website is already up and running—particularly if it's running in the wrong direction.

> ## CAUTION
>
> **Few websites attract random donors.** In the early days of the Web, nonprofits hoped that generous people would surf the Net, looking for worthy organizations. But this rarely (if ever) happens, so you should assume that most of your website's visitors have some previous connection to your organization. They may have heard of it through a news story, a member friend, a Facebook link, or the interesting written materials you've produced. Your website should be ready for anyone, whether the viewer still needs a basic introduction to your organization or is looking for detailed information.

After you've created a website that meets as many of these criteria as financially feasible it should become one of your principal communication devices. Post the address prominently on business cards, stationery, brochures, T-shirts, and every printed document you put out. Encourage newsletter readers to check your website for further information or updates on issues they're reading about. And include links to your website within emails sent to supporters, allowing them to click for further information or to donate online.

Fundraising Worksheet 10:
Check Your Website's Fundraising Effectiveness

☐ **Basic identifying information:** Does your website clearly state what your organization does, where it's located, and every possible way to get in touch with development and other staff?

☐ **Your organization's personality:** Does your website convey your organization's personality in a manner that's consistent with your fundraising and other marketing materials?

☐ **Freshness:** Does your website appear current and up to date?

☐ **Content:** Does your website present interesting content about your organization's cause?

☐ **Donation information:** Does your website lead viewers easily to information on how to donate or get involved?

☐ **Information on where the money goes:** Does your website tell donors how their money will be spent?

☐ **Funder and donor information:** Does your website find space to publicly thank funders and donors?

☐ **Tracking users:** Does your website allow you to track where viewers go within the site and how successfully you're leading them to donation or involvement options?

☐ **Optimization for searchability:** Will a Google or another search for your organization's name, or for whatever subject your group provides authoritative information on, actually bring people to your site?

> **RESOURCE**
>
> **Need more information on building a website?** Check out these resources:
> - TechSoup, at www.techsoup.org. Under "Solutions," choose "Web, Multimedia, and Design."
> - Network for Good (www1.networkforgood.org). This nonprofit is focused on online fundraising and offers handbooks, training, and services nationwide, and links to Web-building resources.

Include Basic Identifying Information

In the course of writing this book, I looked at countless nonprofit websites. Although the overall quality goes up every year, I still couldn't believe how many were truly awful in the sense that they lacked (or hid) even the most basic information about an organization. In some instances, I couldn't even tell what city or state the nonprofit was located in, much less find its actual address.

My personal pet peeve is when I click the "Contact Us" button and receive only an email popup, without a phone number or any hint of where the organization is located outside of cyberspace. Do these groups really expect visitors to undertake extensive research just to figure out where to send their checks?

Your nonprofit's full name, address, telephone number, and email address should be prominently displayed on your website's home page, and on the bottom of every page. If yours is a national nonprofit, or affiliated with one, there should be easy-to-find information on the nature of the affiliation and links to any national, subsidiary, or sister offices.

A one- or two-sentence statement of what you do should also appear somewhere on the home page. You can use your mission statement, as long as it's clear, concise, and readable; if your mission statement is lengthy, create a more succinct version for your site. For example, the home page of Common Good Radio (www.commongoodradio.org) prominently says, "sharing hope with children through music, word, prayer and scripture." That of Carbonica (www.carbonica.org) states simply, "Carbonica is a leading carbon offset provider for businesses."

How far you go to explain who's who in your organization is partly a matter of your workers' privacy preferences. However, you'll really help supporters feel personally connected to your organization if you provide links to its staff, with bios, photos, telephone numbers, and email addresses. This personal approach encourages people to get in touch with you. It has the added bonus that, due to human curiosity, many viewers will read your staff members' biographies, which may enhance their confidence in your organization as well as their sense that you're all like-minded people.

To get Web visitors to the right page, many groups post an "About Us" or "Who We Are" link on the home page. The next page may include a detailed description of (or links to) the group's mission and activities, contact information, and job openings—as well as a link saying "Meet Our Board and Staff," "The [*group name*] Team," or something similar. Other groups put both "About Us" and "Contact Us" tabs on the home page, but make sure that each leads readily to information contained in the other.

Convey Your Organization's Personality

Remember, your organization is trying to build a personal relationship with donors—and that's going to be a tall order if donors perceive that your organization has a multiple personality disorder. Hopefully, you already have an idea of what image your organization is trying to present, whether it's traditional, scientific, homey, offbeat, ethnic, left, right, center, or whatever. Take a look at the fundraising materials you've been producing— your letters to donors, grant proposals, newsletters, annual reports, and so on. Ask yourself what personality is emerging. Then look at your website and make sure it's got the same one.

You can present your organization's personality through the use of colors, graphics, words, photographs, and more. It's a broader issue than I can cover in this book—the important point here is to look for consistency. If your website seems to be reflecting a personality you don't recognize (perhaps that of your Web developer!), it may be a simple matter of borrowing images or text from your other materials to get it back in line.

For an example of a consistent presentation, compare the website and annual report produced by Share Our Strength, whose "No Kid Hungry" campaign connects kids in need with nutritious food, teaches families how to cook healthy, affordable meals, and engages the public to make ending childhood hunger a national priority. As you can see, photos of the children take center stage in Share Our Strength's website and materials. The organization's beautifully designed apple core logo is always prominently displayed. And, if we could only bring you color illustrations, you'd see that bright orange is used as a unifying color between the website and many of Share Our Strength's other printed materials.

Share Our Strength Home Page

Reprinted with permission

Share Our Strength Annual Report Excerpt

Reprinted with permission

According to Jason Wilson, Associate Director of Digital Communications at Share Our Strength, "One of the most important things we did during our recent website redesign was to make a commitment to our brand as a starting point. The heart of our brand is simple: Solving childhood hunger in America. All of our follow-up conversations about what to present on the website and in other communications materials, and how to best present it, flow from there."

Another way to create consistency is to treat Web visitors in a manner true to your organization's mission and ideals. An organization that works with the elderly, for example, shouldn't use a tiny text font. An organization working with the disabled should ensure that its website is accessible to its clientele, as discussed below.

Making Your Website Accessible to Visitors With Disabilities

If your nonprofit happens to work with disabled persons as a clientele, website accessibility should obviously be a top priority. But other organizations would be smart to take accessibility into account as well. Don't forget that 10% to 20% of Americans have some form of disability. One of your supporters might be a bestselling author who's legally blind or a venture capitalist with carpal tunnel syndrome.

Making your website accessible to users with disabilities doesn't have to require a lot of extra programming or cost a lot of money. Often, it's a simple matter of choosing to do things one way rather than another. In fact, the complex, expensive websites with lots of graphics and video are sometimes the hardest ones for persons with disabilities—and for plenty of people without disabilities, as well—to navigate. In the words of Anthony Tusler, owner of About Disability and former coordinator of the Technology Policy Division of the World Institute on Disability, "An easily navigated, well-designed website is better for everyone."

Because the requirements for website accessibility are highly technical however, I'm not going to attempt to review them in detail here. After emphasizing to your Web designer this priority for your organization, encourage him or her to visit the website of the Worldwide Web Consortium (W3C), at www.w3.org, and to click "Accessibility" in the left column.

> **TIP**
>
> Once you've got an accessible website, you can advertise that fact by **displaying a WAI conformance logo** (see www.w3.org/WAI/WCAG2-Conformance. html for details). The logo looks like this:
>
> **W3C WAI-AA WCAG 2.0**

Keep It Fresh

Yes, it's important to have a website—but your Web presence can actually work against you if your organization bites off more than it can chew. I've seen many a website where the nonprofit clearly went through a major push to get material online—articles, descriptions of their projects, upcoming events, volunteer opportunities, and the like—and then left them up unchanged for months, while the projects were completed and the events became history. A potential donor who sees all this stale material is likely to think that the organization is stagnating as well.

The ideal, of course, is to keep your material up to date and to replace old items with new ones as soon as possible. With enough interesting and timely content, your website can become a draw for people who are tracking or researching the issue you cover, as discussed further on in this chapter. Becoming a regular news source (even if you're only compiling links to relevant news stories from other sources), or providing a favorite blog, is one of the few ways you might be able to turn anonymous Web visitors into eventual donors.

If you can't reach the ideal of regular updating, however, your next best bet is to simply avoid putting time-sensitive information in prominent places on your website. Your organization probably has plenty of stories and information to share that aren't likely to become dated, such as its history, its sociological or scientific approach, success stories of particular campaigns or clients, and more. Look at your other communications materials, such as your annual report, for materials that you can borrow or adapt.

If even that seems like too much to tackle, you might reasonably create a website that presents nothing more than your organization's "name, rank, and serial number"—that is, an explanation of its identity, location, mission, and activities. This sort of website isn't going to wow anyone, but at least it won't turn them off.

TIP

Use clever wording to avoid sounding dated. Sometimes, a simple solution like using the word "recently" instead of "last July" or "July 24th" can save a Web article from imminent staleness. Also avoid telling phrases like "with the holidays coming up" or "as the birds begin their autumn migration."

Know Your Organization's Limits When Planning Your Website

Leanne Grossman, then-director of communications at the Global Fund for Women (www.globalfundforwomen.org), was integrally involved in its website redesign—no small task for a site that includes 500 pages, with multilingual portions for French, Spanish, Russian, Arabic, and Portuguese speakers. According to Leanne, "The biggest caution I would give people concerns putting up content that will need updating. Any time you have to change content, it can be expensive and time-consuming. I spent about 10% of my time keeping up our current Web content—and we did a yearly review and overhaul—but I still felt like we could do more.

"One solution is to have some portions of your website that can stand on their own, without facts, figures, the 'new this,' or the 'new that.' It also helps to be clear when defining your website's parameters. We had some donors ask us to locate and post articles with content pertinent to our mission, but as an alternative, we provided links to relevant articles on other websites."

Provide Interesting Content

The best websites contain substantive information, preferably information that the reader might not get elsewhere. This information usually falls into one of two broad categories. First, readers might be interested in your nonprofit's current activities—such as news about ongoing projects; follow-up stories on issues they've heard about before, such as whether a rescued animal survived or a park has been saved from development; or details and signup information for upcoming events and classes. (Remember that you can easily post copies of your press releases online.)

Advantages of Providing Content Within a Blog

Pat Joseph, former editor and blogger at the Sierra Club (www.sierraclub.org), notes that blogs are "the best way to keep fresh content up on your site. It means there's always something new, no matter when you stop by."

Blogs are also inherently casual, and even personal. No one expects a blog to present your organization's fully researched, last word on a topic. Topics might include everything from updates from your various departments (fundraising, client services, and ED) to postings of videos showing your work to comments on relevant news events. (In fact, it's best to strategize possible topics in advance, to spur ideas later.) Short entries of about 300 to 600 words are just fine. Even a few sentences announcing an event or a quick update will fit in, no problem. If a post looks out of date within a week, that's okay. Even the occasional typo can be forgiven (but try to avoid them).

Of course, if your nonprofit is already having trouble keeping its website up to date, blogging may not be for you. For example, Pat Joseph says maintaining the Sierra Club's "Compass" blog was the biggest part of his job. "But," he explains, "I posted at least once a day, and usually three or four times a day." (Once a week is widely considered the minimum.)

Still, from a technical standpoint, blogging is much easier than actually updating your website. Many nonprofit bloggers sign on with Web-based blog supporters, such as Blogger, TypePad, or WordPress. Doing this makes it so easy that, once you've set up the blog, you can basically type in your content, upload a photo or video, and press "submit." (Your blog will appear on the provider's website, not yours, but you can link back and forth fairly seamlessly.) Don't forget to add an RSS feed, so that loyal readers can subscribe.

As with everything new, there are aspects of blogging that will take getting used to. One is the reader comment feature, assuming you choose to include it. Yes, anyone can potentially post anything on your blog, for the world to see—and you'll get tons of spam. Pat Joseph explains, "You can set the program up so that you have a chance to approve comments before the public sees them, but that discourages people from commenting (they lose the satisfaction of seeing their posting right away), and it makes the blog seem less real. I set mine up so that I could delete comments after the fact. Fortunately, I received very few hostile comments."

Another concern is the stream-of-consciousness element. Whoever writes your blog should be excited about the topic, and even opinionated—but should also be careful to avoid late-night rants that might, for example, offend a funder or sound overly political, thus possibly jeopardizing your nonprofit status.

The second category is information that doesn't derive directly from your nonprofit, but that you've either written or collected for your readers, such as articles about relevant national or local news issues, updates on the state of the environmental, legal, health, or social issues with which your nonprofit is concerned, and the like. This may seem a bit far from the fundraising theme, but studies have shown that readers place substantive content number one in importance when evaluating a nonprofit's website.

Some websites take their news provider role one step farther and offer readers regular email newsletters or news alerts. It's a great way of collecting email addresses of potential future supporters—whom you can cultivate with other electronic communications. At WildCare, for example (an urban wildlife rehabilitation center in San Rafael, California; www. wildcarebayarea.org), Web visitors are offered a chance to sign up for informative, free newsletters and weekly updates. These contain stories about rescued animals, tips on interacting with wildlife (such as "Please don't feed the ducks!"), photos (including photo contests), and more. According to JoLynn Taylor, Membership and Publications Manager, "This seems to be where fundraising for us is really growing." And, there's no harm in including a line or two within every emailed newsletter mentioning donation and volunteer opportunities and providing links to your website for further information.

Of course, all of the content described above can do double or triple duty if your organization has a Facebook fan page, a Twitter feed, and so forth. Be sure to set up cross-links between these.

Encourage Donations

Everything on your website should be easy to find—and, from a fundraising perspective, finding information about donating or otherwise getting involved should be especially easy. Visitors may have landed on your website by chance after searching for content on the Web, or they may already have some history with your organization. Perhaps, they are catching up on an issue they care about or checking out a special event. A small but important minority might be one mental step away from donating, given the right opportunity.

At the same time, you don't want to rush people to the payment page, especially without offering them some background information about why, how, and how much to give. Give careful thought to your organization's home page, introductory donation or support page, the nondonation pages of your website, and the mechanism for online donations, all of which will help boost the ease with which viewers can fund your group—and the likelihood that they will do so.

Donation Information on the Home Page

If you look at other nonprofits' websites, you'll see that a fairly standard set of home page tabs and links is coming into use. Most nonprofits place a set of tabs across or alongside their home page, with links to such topics as "About Us," "Contact Us," "Media Center," "Upcoming Events," "Publications," and—the important one for this discussion—"Get Involved." Other examples I've seen for that critical "Get Involved" tab include "Get Active," "Become a Member," "How You Can Help," "Join Today," or "Support [*name of organization*]." How to choose tabs that both represent your organization's identity and will best guide your likely visitors— without confusing those of them who've become accustomed to standard navigation methods—can require some balancing. At Share Our Strength, Jason Wilson says, "We were able to distill our main navigation tabs down to a simple four: The Problem, The Solution, Take Action, and Give. This setup both matched our analysis of why people visit our site, and created a useful structure for going forward. Now, when preparing new content, we always think, 'What section will that fit into?' All roads ultimately lead to the Take Action section—we want to get people engaged."

In addition, many display a separate button saying "Donate Now!" or something similar, important for viewers who are ready to make a donation that instant. If you look at Share Our Strength's home page, for instance (shown above), you'll see a Donate button (bright orange) just above the main four navigation tabs. "From everything I've read and seen," says Jason Wilson, "that top right corner is a great spot for the Donate button."

Not everyone uses a separate "donate" button. Some simply title one of their tabs "Donate"—which fulfills the requirement of an easy link, but may turn away people who were hoping for other ways to get involved with your organization. If you go this route, be sure to have a separate "Volunteer" tab.

Introductory Support Page

Unless your viewers have decisively clicked a "Donate Now" button or link, it's best not to confront them too quickly with a credit card or other payment form. In many of the best websites, if you click on a link called "How You Can Help," "Get Involved," "Ways to Give," or something similar, you're led to an introductory page explaining how different dollar amounts and types of gifts will help the cause, as well as other relevant links, such as "Make a Memorial Gift," "Leave a Legacy," "Events," "Donate While You Shop," and "Volunteer/Intern." Orient donors to their options—and to any premiums or benefits they'll get in return for their support—before proceeding to the bottom line.

There are alternate ways to design this introductory page, depending on your organization's strengths and range of giving options. Many organizations start the page with a brief introduction, then subdivide the remainder into summaries of various memberships or other options, each of which contains a link to further information.

Just don't make things too complicated—at the top of any range of options should be a basic procedure to give a modest amount of money, without frills or fanfare.

Links to Donation Page From Other Pages

Websurfers may take a crazy ride through your website, clicking on items at whim and often forgetting how they got to their current landing spot. Where does that leave them if their intent was to make a donation?

Reprinted with permission

No matter where someone is on your website, the pages should either repeat the home page tabs (though they can be relocated), contain a "Donate" button, or provide another link to opportunities to get involved.

At Share Our Strength, Jason Wilson notes, "We definitely try to offer an easy way to give on every page of our website. When you scroll down a page (the likely path, since our content is presented vertically), the header follows you, including the Donate button and Give tab. Importantly, this function works well on tablets, too."

If you can invest a little more time, review the text of the nonfundraising sections of your website and add sentences where relevant. For example, in a description of a particular program, you could add a linked sentence saying "To find out how you can support [*name your client base or issue*], click here." This type of customized linking—assuming it's tastefully done—can be very effective in drawing people to your donation page.

Option for Online Donations

Any user who is Web-savvy enough to check you out online is likely to prefer giving online as well. Online credit card donation services are available through application service providers (ASPs), such as Acceptiva, BlueFire Donations, and contribute.com. Ideally, you'll find (or already have) an ASP that offers a package deal, including such other services as website maintenance, donor tracking, email messaging, event registration, and more.

Among the advantages of going through an ASP is that donors will not only see the online giving option on your organization's website, but their credit card statements will show your group's name. Another, typically simpler and less expensive option is to use a third-party processor, such as PayPal or Network for Good. In these cases, however, donors will likely see only the third party's name on their credit card statements, and your nonprofit may wait a little longer for the funds.

TIP

If you truly can't afford an online donation system, tell website visitors how to donate. Whatever you do, don't skirt the issue! You can, for example, offer a downloadable page that contains all the information on your regular reply card, along with information on where to fax or mail the completed form. In fact, such information is useful for any website visitors who would prefer to fill out a form and send money via the U.S. mail.

CAUTION

Online donors expect an immediate thank you. Without the lag time provided by the U.S. mail, electronic donors expect to hear from you right away. Most ASPs will instantly email a message of thanks, but make sure that this is part of their packages of services. You should then follow up with a mailed thank-you letter, which looks more formal, can be customized to express a more personal message, and guarantees that the donor will have something in print for tax record keeping.

Provide Information on Where the Money Goes

Where and how supporters' gifts will be spent is a topic worthy of a separate page on your website—and it's a page that should be easy to find. Remember, supporters want to know that their money is funding worthwhile projects and programs. Studies have found that users rank information about how donations are spent high in importance when visiting a charity's website. You might title your link, for example, "How Each Dollar Is Spent," "Financial Highlights," or even "Click here to learn more about our budget and funding."

At the website charitywater.og, for instance, clicking "About Us" quickly leads you to a page called "The 100% Model," an excerpt of which is shown below. This gives readers a graphically presented, easily understood promise that 100% of their donations go directly to funding water projects (while the charity finds other ways to cover its operating expenses).

charity: water webpage

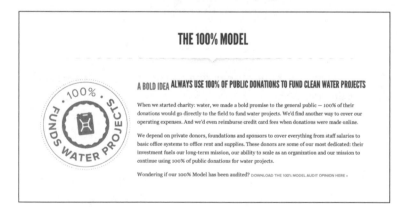

If you've received positive press coverage or a high rating from one of the various watchdog organizations, such as the BBB Wise Giving Alliance or Charity Navigator, include links to those (and take advantage of such a watchdog's offer to use its logo on your site). This portion of your website should also include links to your annual report (if available online) and Form 990.

Mention Funders and Donors

If you've been scrambling to find ways to publicly thank your foundation funders and major private donors, a website can really take the pressure off. Many organizations add a simple link to "Our Funders," whether on their home page or a page deeper within the site. Your annual report may contain this information, and it may be posted online. However, this shouldn't stop you from separately repeating some of the most relevant information—not everyone knows to look in your annual report.

Mentioning your funders and donors online serves purposes beyond recognition. It's also a way to build trust in your organization. You want Web viewers to think, "If the ABC Foundation and So-and-So support this group, it must be okay."

Some nonprofits go further than merely listing their funders and donors, and post profiles of individual donors, complete with photos and personal accounts of why they give. (You would, of course, have to get permission from the donor first.) Again, this is a way to inspire potential supporters to realize that others "just like them" have been moved to give, and to rally them to join the club.

Track Users

Up to now, I've been talking about the parts of your website that users see. But let's shift gears and consider what's behind the scenes. It doesn't take particularly advanced technology for your Web designer to add a feature allowing you to keep "site traffic statistics." This information tells you not only how many people are visiting your site, but also where your site visitors came from (what website) and where they go within your site—what links are enticing them to click, what pages they're leaving unviewed, what they're downloading, which pages they most commonly exit from, and the like.

If your site was set up without such a feature, you can install Web-tracking software or use an online service, such as eXTReMe Tracking (extremetracking.com). (Some of the online services are free, but be aware that they may irritate your viewers with pop-up ads.)

Once you make a habit of collecting and interpreting your traffic statistics, they can be invaluable for measuring and enhancing your website's fundraising effectiveness. The numbers will look particularly meaningful as you monitor them over time, leading you to evaluate, for example, the comparative success of an email campaign, the drawing power of a video posted on Facebook, or who your best referral sources are. "Conversion" statistics are particularly important, showing what pages caused people to click through and actually make donations, sign up to volunteer, or fulfill some other goal.

> **TIP**
>
> **Get to know your referral sources.** If another organization or website is referring a lot of visitors your way, perhaps with a link to an article on your site or an outright recommendation of support, it may be worth contacting them to talk about ways to deepen the relationship.

You might also learn where not to waste your energies. If, for example, you're putting a lot of time into writing updates on your organization's latest project or research, but no one is reading them—or, worse yet, users are exiting your site from that page—your time might be better spent on a more productive task. (On the other hand, maybe your updates just need better drafting or promotion.)

Help Online Searchers Find Your Site (Basic SEO)

Is your nonprofit's team of Web planners and online content generators familiar with the concept of search engine optimization (SEO)? It's important: And, despite the technical name, it's easier to deal with than you might think.

Here's why you should care: Imagine that you're the only nonprofit in the known universe dedicated to conservation of banana slugs—but that, when someone plugs "banana slug conservation" into Google or some other search engine—or even the exact name of your organization—the first page of results that pops up lists a bunch of other environmental organizations, plus some ads for slug poison. Or, imagine that you've posted a number of articles about banana slug science on your website, but even typing their exact titles into Google doesn't bring them up until page three of the results.

You've got an SEO problem. Search engine optimization is the process by which website owners attempt to analyze (or in some cases, guess at) and respond to whatever systems the people behind the scenes at Google and other search engines devise to instantly determine what people really want when they type in a set of search words, and which Web pages are most likely to deliver it to them. In effect, these search engines award "points" to websites that meet certain criteria, and demote the ones that don't.

Think about when you do a Google or similar search. You will instantly be given several pages of results. All of those pages may contain the exact words that you typed in. So what determines the order in which you see those results? It's a complex algorithm, and each search engine has a different one—guarded as carefully as any secret recipe.

In large corporations, entire SEO teams spend their days tracking the latest changes to the various search engine algorithms and making sure that their companys' names and products rank as high as possible in search results. As a nonprofit, you won't have that luxury. So let's keep it simple, with these top tips to help your nonprofit rise to the top of the search results list:

- **Consider what keywords are important for your nonprofit to use.** Independent searches are now a primary way that people find their way to websites, whether or not they know the URLs. You want to make sure that you know what keywords your potential website visitors are most likely to enter into search engines—or are already using, which you can find out using the sort of analytic software discussed in the previous section. Then, feature those words often and in prominent places on your website, so that search engines will pick up on them. For example, even if you would normally refer to banana slugs by their Latin name, *Ariolomax*, make sure to use the name "banana slug" as well, for searchability.

- **Put keywords high up in the article.** Look at my very first sentence in this section, above. It mentions "nonprofit" and "SEO." That would work well if people were searching for this as an online article. If I'd just launched in with "Imagine that you're a banana slug organization," then guess what type of visitors I'd more likely get? Every banana slug aficionado might find his or her way to my article, while the people wanting to know about SEO for nonprofits would be led elsewhere. Think about what words are important to people looking for the type of information your nonprofit offers, and (without overdoing it), plant them early and often in your Web pages.

- **Post lots of fresh content.** A stale, unchanging site gets fewer points in SEO-land. Adding a blog within your site will help with this, as will posting your recent press releases and other publications.

- **Encourage inbound links.** As a nonprofit, you have inherent credibility—make use of it! The more other sites link to yours (for example, by listing your site in their "Resources" section), the better your site will rank. This is especially true if the referring sites are authoritative ones, such as major newspapers or government. (When one site links to another, search engines like Google look upon it as a "vote" in favor of that site.) Some site owners will find their way to your website simply by virtue of your being a nonprofit and providing good content, including in social media. If you have contacts at affiliate organizations, it's also worth bringing their attention to your content and asking them to link to it.

- **Make sure your content is getting attention on social media.** Search engines are increasingly bringing readers to relevant content that their friends on Facebook, Twitter, Google+, and other social media sites have linked to or liked. In other words, the search engines see "likes" (and the like) as a mark of quality, raising the rankings of the content accordingly. To take advantage of this, make sure your organization has a social media presence and that you're posting your new and best content to it.

- **If you are already analyzing traffic to your site, look for patterns of visitor entries, exits, and more.** In the previous section, I discussed tracking your site's users. The more you learn about who is visiting your site and what they're doing there (such as how long they're spending on various pages and which pages are causing them to lose interest and go elsewhere), the more significant patterns will emerge. You may, for instance, find that gardeners are the biggest readers of your banana slug content—in which case you could either make sure to further address their interests or work harder to attract a wider audience. (Or both.)

How a Search Engine "Sees" Your Page

When you look at your nonprofit's Web page, you see a title, maybe some pictures, and the content itself. Google, Bing, Yahoo, and all the other search engines see a bit more, and use that additional information (called "signals" by those in the biz) to help analyze the page and improve their respective search results. Almost every modern blog- and Web-publishing software will allow you to customize most if not all of these signals. Following are some of the important ones that you should consider (or make sure your tech geek is taking the time to consider) when publishing any new Web page.

Title Tag/Page Title. This is probably the most important SEO signal you can control for a given Web page, even though it's not visible by your reader on the page itself. It's included in the source code as an HTML tag that looks like this:

<title>This Is My Page Title</title>

This text gets displayed within the results after someone performs an online search. Not only does this tag have to describe the contents of your page to a search engine in a very small space, the keywords that were used to perform the search will be bolded in the search results. You want to make sure they are near the front of your page title so they don't get cut off—there's only so much real estate on a search engine's result page.

For example, if you post an article titled, "What We've Done This Month to Help Save the Banana Slug From Extinction," your page title should read something like: "Saving the Banana Slug From Extinction: What We've Done This Month."

The idea is that the words unique to this page and its content are up front, and the common words used all the time take a back seat. This helps ensure that those all-important keywords are big and bold on your potential visitors' search results.

Subtitles. Similiar to the page title, search engines add emphasis to terms included in subtitles. Using the article title above, you might have a subtitle telling readers you "Rescued a Family of Banana Slugs in Santa Cruz." The terms in a subtitle are wrapped in HTML code that makes it larger, bolder, and or colorful, to make it stand out from the rest of the text. A search engine may pick up on that extra emphasis and determine that those words should be weighted more heavily, as an indicator of the terms for which this page should be served as a search result.

How a Search Engine "Sees" Your Page, cont'd.

Links and Anchor Text. You see links all over the Web. They are means by which one page refers users to another. For search engines, they provide different, critical signals. When one page links to another, the "linking page" is "voting" or "vouching" for the "linked-to" page, telling search engines that the linked-to pages are valuable or authoritative. As a matter of fact, this concept of using links as votes to determine which pages are best served up by a search engine is what originally separated Google from other search engines and made it the behemoth it is today.

There are two parts to every link (commonly called a hyperlink); the destination URL and the anchor text. Let's say you give readers a link to a Wikipedia article on banana slugs. While they will see the term "banana slugs" colored and underlined, Google sees this: <a href="http://en.wikipedia.org/wiki/Banana_slug">Banana slugs</a>

The destination URL is http://en.wikipedia.org/wiki/Banana_slug. The anchor text is "banana slugs." These are two distinct signals telling a search engine that, 1) your page vouches for the Wikipedia page located at http://en.wikipedia.org/wiki/Banana_slug, and 2) that page is "about" banana slugs.

Be sure to vote for your website's own related pages when appropriate for the person reading it (but without going overboard).

For example, our hypothetical article above might include a sentence saying, "Our most recent trip to Santa Cruz was part of our ongoing effort to protect banana slugs from gophers." If you have another article specifically about gophers' impact on banana slugs, you'd want to hyperlink the term, "protect banana slugs from gophers," pointing it to your gopher article. Alternatively, you could specifically call your readers' attention to that article by including something like, "To learn more about these impacts, see our article, 'Gophers and Banana Slugs.'"

RELATED TOPIC

Your website's not your only place in cyberspace. In the next chapter, I'll discuss other ways that a nonprofit can establish an online presence, namely through social networking.

Outreach Via Traditional and Social Media

Fundraising gets a whole lot easier when people have heard of your organization. Better yet, they should have positive impressions of its work, and a sense of how they can get involved. That's why this chapter is devoted to getting or creating coverage in traditional or social media.

Such activities may or may not be the job of the fundraising staff in your organization. Many nonprofits are hiring communications staff, realizing both the importance and the time-consuming nature of getting their message out and engaging in dialogue with supporters. But no matter whose job this is, you'll all need to keep talking to one another, sharing stories and ideas.

To that end, this chapter will discuss:

- knowing when and how to place stories with traditional media outlets, such as newspapers, television, and radio, and
- creating your own news and communications using social media and networking.

Don't skip the first section, even if you think the traditional media is dead and you plan to rely more heavily on social media. It contains important lessons on what topics will catch readers' or listeners' attention.

Placing Stories With Traditional Media

Many organizations put no energy into media outreach, which gives you a potential edge. Of course, you'll want to be sensible and appropriate about your media efforts; the last thing you want is negative public attention.

Don't wait for the phone to ring. Far more media coverage than you'd imagine is generated by businesses, politicians, authors, and yes, even nonprofits that have learned to place their stories. To help you develop a smart and effective media strategy, and learn to make your own news, this section will address how to:

- identify and develop stories that will attract journalists' attention
- get to know your local media
- pitch or place stories, and
- protect your organization's reputation and interests in media interactions.

> **TIP**
>
> **Track the buzz on your organization.** You may be getting media coverage you don't know about, including mentions in blogs. A handy way to find out is using Google alerts, which will send you regular emails covering a broad variety of online sources. Go to www.google.com/alerts.

What Makes a Good Story

Engaging the media will require a shift in how you think about portraying your organization. A pitch that you might make to a donor—for example, "For 20 years, our organization has been offering tutoring to homeless children," is likely to fall flat with reporters. They want a story that's newsy, contains drama, is different, or, most often, is closely connected to a current issue or event.

Many organizations simply don't understand that the word "new" and "news" are virtually identical. They call reporters and say, "I'm so-and-so; my organization is doing great work; how about a story?" Needless to say, this kind of approach won't lead to any headlines or airtime. Most journalists are looking for a "hook" or an unusual angle with which to entice the audience into reading or viewing the particular story right then and there. By becoming aware of the different types of stories that the media produces—from hard news to gossip about personalities to community interest features—you can style your publicity pitches accordingly.

Come Up With a Hook

When I say that journalists look for stories that have a hook, I'm not just describing some subtle or subliminal process—most journalists will immediately ask, "What's the hook?" as they evaluate a potential story. It follows that you have to know the answer to this yourself before you pitch a story.

Here's how Nick Parker, former communications director at the California School Age Consortium put it: "When I worked in the film industry, we had to condense ideas for a movie into one sentence, like, 'The earth's computers have been taken over by aliens, and humans have 24 hours to get them back before our planet is blown up.' Getting a nonprofit-generated story into the media is not much different: You've got to be able to quickly sum up the central conflict in a way that grabs their attention."

A true hook, for a news story or any other kind, involves a shift in how the audience views the world. Common hooks involve conflict, shock, laughter, something new and different in your community, identification of a trend, a marking of time, such as with an anniversary or holiday, or a "first," such as the first person to be cured of a disease, or the first sighting of a supposedly extinct bird.

Something that just happened in your organization, such as receiving a small grant, may be big news to you. But it's not necessarily interesting enough to hook anyone else's attention. If it was a huge grant, however, with which you will build a new community center, that may warrant at least local coverage. Kids and animals also seem to be perennially interesting to the public.

The media often develops its own, internal trends regarding what's supposedly exciting. They all read, watch, and listen to each other, and borrow madly—a phenomenon that's only gotten worse as social media has provided a platform for stories to go viral. Fads and cycles develop, some of which you may be able to take advantage of. For example, the 2013 media frenzy around the so-called "poop cruise" (stranded for days in the Gulf of Mexico with no running water, little food, and ultimately disgusting conditions) presented an opportunity for savvy nonprofits to get out their messages concerning marine environmental issues, the real global health issues caused by poor sanitation, and of course, journalistic priorities.

No matter the current media mood, certain stories are always difficult to pitch and gain coverage for. One is the depiction of the endless train of human suffering: endemic hunger, disease, and injustice all over the world, Compassion fatigue is common, and many people take long breaks from reading the newspaper or watching television. The ever-ratings-conscious media know 0 it, and try to leaven the doom-and-gloom coverage with hopeful material. Your local newspaper is thus more likely to cover a story about how a local nonprofit helped homeless girls get dressed up for the prom than to do a feature on the root causes of homelessness.

Take a step back and recognize what aspects of your group's work are new, different, or shed some light on current news or thought. And think about how to present your facts or findings in a light that will make others appreciate their significance. If, for example, you're dealing with dry facts and numbers, try to put them in terms that people can understand. The Straphangers Campaign does this well, with its annual "Pokey Award" (a golden snail on a pedestal) given to NYC's slowest bus. The New York City–based group advocates for improved public transportation on behalf of subway and bus riders. That could elicit yawns from readers. But in describing the two buses that tied for the "winning" spot in 2012, the group cleverly noted that the two would "lose a race to any amusement park bumper car." (See www.straphangers.org for more information and links to its press releases.)

How the Traditional Media Categorizes Stories

Though virtually every potential story needs a hook, you also need to recognize the different categories of stories that the media feature. For your purposes, the three most important include:

- breaking news
- feature stories, and
- arts or other events.

Breaking news is just what it sounds like—something that's in the headlines. Journalists who work in this area tend to be news junkies who think everything else is mere fluff. A nonprofit can make its own breaking news. For example, your group's successful boycott of a corporation's products resulting in its decision to stop using an endangered type of Southeast Asian hardwood is certainly newsworthy. A demonstration or protest is always news; although whether it's big or interesting enough to cover might be questionable. Some cities see protests so regularly that the media loses interest. And if the media perceives an event as solely staged to make news, many reporters will ignore it. Releasing a study or report can be news, especially if your conclusions shock or break new ground. Thus, if your study found that organically grown vegetables were actually bad for you, media outlets would likely line up to cover it.

Alternately, you can tie your work or insights to a story that's already in the news. For example, if one of your elderly nursing home clients attempts suicide, that's probably not news by itself. But if you can legitimately present it as part of a pattern of suicides caused by gaps in public health care benefits and patients' fears of being kicked out of nursing homes, you've got yourself a news story.

Feature stories are a different animal and are usually handled by a different set of journalists. Though feature stories may tie into news of the moment, they usually offer more background and reflection on their subject, and go on at greater length. (Think about the human interest stories that fill the middle sections of your local newspaper, or hour-long radio interview shows.)

Nearly every type of media devotes separate attention to **arts, literary, and social events**. These might include everything from the opening of your nonprofit's fall music or theatre season to a small lecture, dinner, or garden tour—though you'll find that some media outlets report only on events of a certain size or perceived quality, or want to know whether any "big names" will be in attendance. (If anyone famous does attend your event, be sure to get photos for after-the-fact coverage.)

If you ask for coverage of an arts or theatre event, you may have to open yourself up to the world of critics, with their ability to make or break a show's success—but even criticism is a form of publicity. You'll find more about how to invite the press to attend your events later in this chapter.

Who to Approach With Your Story

Let's assume now that you've got a story with a great hook that's just dying to be told. Now you need to decide whom to contact. Because most media operations work against deadlines and on low budgets, there's a very real risk that if you simply prepare a press release and mail or email it out, your effort will land in a dead file, unread. To boost your chances of success, you need to understand how the media is organized to accept stories.

Print Media Contact Persons

At a newspaper, your contact point is probably either a reporter, for straight news stories, or a columnist, for feature stories. Check the "bylines" on stories that look similar to ones that you'd like to place. The writer may be on staff, a freelancer, or may be from another paper, such as *The Los Angeles*

Times, through syndication. (Or you may see no name at all, because the article came from a wire service such as the Associated Press (AP) or Reuters.)

On big-city newspapers, reporters and columnists are assigned a particular topic area or "beat," such as arts, education, environment, food, religion, or city/community issues. If you follow the stories on issues similar to those that your nonprofit would like to weigh in on, you'll see the same names popping up regularly.

> **TIP**
>
> **Your nonprofit can be covered in the business section.** Business reporters are often hungry to cover something more interesting than the bottom line. For example, an organization that rehabilitates drug addicts by offering training in how to cook for—and run—a restaurant, is likely to attract the attention of the newspaper's business journalists. And, your nonprofit is itself a sort of business, so your own creative strategies for success may inspire media interest.

If a story you're presenting will be of interest to a national audience—for example, your tips to parents on choosing a good summer camp (as opposed to ratings of local summer camps)—you might try to get it covered by newspapers nationwide. One way to do that is to send it to major wire services, most of which have regional bureaus.

As a non-news alternative, you might offer the newspaper an editorial or op-ed piece, in which case, you would separately contact the editorial page staff. Also look for newspapers that have regular opinion columnists (although many editorials are provided by national news syndicates). They're always looking for something new to opine about—with a quick phone call, followed up by your expert factual materials, you may provide that very something.

Magazines tend to rely on submissions, often approved in advance, from freelance writers. Many freelancers regularly work for the same publications, however, so if you see a name appearing often, that person is probably your best contact.

Radio Contact Persons

At a radio station, your contact point depends on the type of show. For news shows, reporters or news directors are your best bet. (Listen carefully, though—many stations license news programs from larger outlets, such as National Public Radio (NPR) or the BBC, which means they're less open to locally generated news.) Keep your ears open for the local shows, especially those with a one-hour format.

For public affairs or talk shows, the host is rarely the best one to contact—especially for more popular shows, it's the producer's job to select and schedule guests. Often the producer's name is mentioned briefly at the end of each show or you can identify him or her by checking the station's website. If you can find a producer interested in your line of stories, you're in good shape, because he or she might keep your group's experts' names on file for future shows.

If a leader or an expert from your organization will be visiting another city, think about contacting radio journalists there, as well. Although telephone technology allows you to be interviewed from anywhere in the world, the sound quality and general ambience aren't as good as if you are there in person.

Television Contact Persons

At a television station, whom to contact depends on the type of show and the size of the station. In general, you'll have the best luck with local stations. If you're seeking rapid attention to breaking news, such as the birth of an endangered bird in captivity, track down contact information for the "assignment desk"—that's where producers tell their crews, "Go to this location, now." For news events with a little more lead time, you'd normally contact the planning desk or assignment editor. Some television programs have less news-oriented formats—for example, focusing on consumer affairs, local events, or travel. If you're interested in placing a story with one of these, get in touch with a producer of that show.

A number of local television stations also offer community event alerts, usually flashed on the screen now and then. Call the station or check its website for submission guidelines and eligibility rules.

Educate Know-Nothing Hosts

In both radio and television, many show hosts—often called "talent" by real journalists—aren't personally familiar with the stories they cover. In other words, though they may look good, sound good, and project an aura of celebrity, they won't even have read your press packet. For example, a friend of mine had long respected a San Francisco television talk show host—but when he finally appeared on her show, he was dismayed to hear her ask, with just a few minutes to air time, "So, what are we talking about today?"

Fortunately, unprepared hosts are a problem only if you aren't ready for them. Don't bug the producers for advance contact with the host or withhold your best information for when you get to talk to him or her. Instead, fully cooperate with the producers, to get them excited about the topic, and to help them develop materials and questions that will prepare the host to sound like an informed expert.

It pays to create a short list of potential questions, together with your name, organization, and information on how people can reach your organization. In appreciation of your efforts to make the host sound like an expert, many hosts will not only follow your suggestions, they'll also toss in several plugs for your activities.

Get to Know the Media Serving Your Area

Journalists are not all as remote as they might appear. Although a few broadcasters think they're movie stars, most of them, particularly at the local level, have chosen their life's work because they are genuinely interested in people and information. Add to that the fact that all news people are always on the lookout for a good story, and it's easy to see that they need you as much as you need them.

But, as with any relationship, you've got to hold up your end. Even if you never talk to these journalists personally, doing your part to understand what they cover—so that you can, someday, knowledgeably say to one of them, "I've got a story that's perfect for you"—can make all the difference. It's a matter of matching journalist's names (many of which may already be in your media file) to personalities, interest areas, and even job descriptions.

Simply observe what types of stories the media serving your area cover, and who's writing or producing the pieces. Don't forget special interest and ethnic papers, free weeklies or monthlies, neighborhood papers, community association newsletters, and magazines and newsletters produced by other nonprofits or public-oriented groups. Take notes or develop a file or document showing how their interests might dovetail with your group's. Also notice what they don't cover, and don't expect to change that.

Make Your In-House Experts Available

After you've figured out which media venues might be interested in covering your nonprofit's work, you should let them know about your group, and about any experts you have available to help them. The most prized possession of most journalists and media producers is their "experts" list.

Your goal is to get your name, or the names of your organization's staff and board, on those lists. Then, when a news story hits—say, the federal government's plan to spend more money on highways—there's a good chance that the ED of your rapid-transit-oriented organization will be called and have a chance to point out that the money could be far better spent on light rail alternatives.

TIP

Make your experts available on short notice. When news breaks, journalists often need to reach experts in minutes or, at most, an hour or two. If you can provide the experts' cell phone and home phone numbers, you are far more likely to see their names—and the name of your organization—in the news.

Pitch and Place Stories

Once you know which media cover particular types of stories, and you've perhaps made some initial contacts with journalists and producers, you can begin trying to place stories. The best ways for nonprofits to approach or attract the media include:

- press releases
- publicity and press invitations for special events
- media stunts, and
- letters to the editor and op-ed pieces.

You'll notice that press conferences don't appear on this list. Unless you're the U.S. president or a well-known spokesperson for a very large organization, your press conferences are unlikely to attract a crowd—if anyone at all.

> **TIP**
> **Alert your supporters and colleagues to your organization's media appearances.** If someone from your organization will be appearing on television or radio, it's a perfect time to email your members and post heads-ups on social media. For radio call-in shows, ask them to phone in with questions—to tip the balance against less sympathetic callers!

Press Releases

Anyone can write and send a press release. You don't have to have any special credentials or invitations. You simply write up the story you want to convey, preferably in one or two pages, and send it out while it's still fresh and interesting. If you've got some spare minutes, you'll also want to tweak your basic wording to fit the interests of your different news targets.

Craft your release to grab the reader's attention within a few seconds. All journalists receive more press releases than they can read or cover, and they leave many unopened.

> **TIP**
> **Your press releases can do double duty.** Publish them on your website, within the "Press" or "About Us" section. You'll give Web viewers a sense that your organization is a happening place. The press release's long-term availability there will also help educate the broader public and any journalists later doing research about your organization's work or the underlying issue.

Formatting and Drafting Your Press Release

For the appropriate format for a printed press release, see the template below (also available online; see Appendix B for the link) and the sample following that, an actual press release from the Save the Redwoods League (www.savetheredwoods.org) announcing an art contest for kids. Notice how the release presents key facts, the organization's mission, and a quotable quote, all within a page.

View From the Radio Newsroom

Harry Lin, former news anchor at KQED, an NPR affiliate station in San Francisco, tells the following about the many press releases he received from nonprofit organizations: "Since we covered local news on a daily basis, we received press releases from nonprofits all the time. Much of my daily routine, in fact, was sifting through releases … deciding which ones to toss, which ones to file as 'just background info,' which ones to give reporters to follow up on, and which ones got tacked to our communal bulletin board so that we could all laugh at them. All of which is to say that news organizations are swamped every day with releases, so to cut through the clutter and stand out is not easy. However: No matter how flashy or elaborate one's release, you can bet that someone else sent in something even flashier. So, the trick to getting noticed isn't to send in the wackiest, weirdest, loudest, most unorthodox release.

"For example, I can still remember the freshly baked icing-covered chocolate cake that was messengered to our newsroom one morning accompanied by a press release about … well, I can't remember what the press release was about, but we ate the cake in two seconds flat, and no, we didn't attend the event the release was touting.

"The most important factor is actually the most basic: The headline must be relevant, intriguing, timely, and newsworthy. News organizations aren't interested in anything that smells old, already-happened, or historical."

Press Release Template

[Your organization's name; preferably with logo]

FOR IMMEDIATE RELEASE

Contact: *[Name of one or preferably two persons they can call]*

[Date]

[Phone number of contacts]

[Email address of contacts]

[Centered title of press release, in larger font]

[Your state, in capital letters, such as "OKLAHOMA"]

[Text of press release, in short paragraphs, ending with a brief description of your organization and where to obtain more information, such as on your website.]

###

[traditional signal of end of text]

Save the Redwoods League Press Release

PRESS RELEASE

Contact: Jennifer Benito, Outreach Director, (415) 820-5814 or jbenito@SaveTheRedwoods.org

Save the Redwoods League Launches National Art Contest to Encourage Kids to Protect Redwoods

SAN FRANCISCO (September 7, 2012) – Save the Redwoods League, the only nonprofit organization dedicated to protecting redwood forests throughout their natural range, **today announced its third annual redwoods art contest for kids**. The League's **Find Me in the Redwoods art contest** is a simple way to encourage America's students to have fun, connect with nature and help protect one of our country's most iconic natural wonders.

Beginning September 10, K–12 students across the nation are invited to create a work of art that features them **playing, learning or exploring** redwoods. Their art will help Save the Redwoods League raise awareness of redwood forests. Students can draw, paint or sketch their way toward a chance to win fabulous redwoods prizes while learning about the tallest and some of the oldest and largest living things on Earth.

"Save the Redwoods League's **Find Me in the Redwoods** art contest uniquely combines art, science and civic participation, while encouraging students to protect redwood forestlands," said Jennifer Benito, outreach director for Save the Redwoods League, "This contest is a wonderful way to encourage children to have fun, be creative, connect with nature and help protect a natural wonder."

Contestants compete in the following three grade categories: K–3, 4–8 and 9–12. **Winners will be announced on November 15** via email and on the League's website. Winning entries will also be showcased in League publications. **All artwork will be mailed to Ken Salazar, Secretary of the U.S. Department of Interior.** Salazar is in charge of protecting America's great outdoors. **Teachers also win.** Educators associated with the first-place winners will win fabulous redwood prizes. The hope is to inspire teachers to educate students about the wonders of the redwood forests.

All entries must be mailed or hand-delivered to Save the Redwoods League, 114 Sansome Street, 12th floor, San Francisco, California, 94104, Attn: Redwoods Art Contest by **October 19, 2012, 5 p.m. US Pacific Time.** No late submissions will be accepted. No fee is required to enter the contest. Spanish and English entry forms will be available online on Monday, September 10.

Prizes generously donated by Balloons Above the Valley; Cavallo Point, The Lodge at the Golden Gate; FolkManis Puppets; Mount Hermon Redwood Canopy Tours; Redwoods & Rivers Rafting; REI; Sequoia Park Zoo; and Skunk Train. Media sponsored by the Bay Area News Group

About Save the Redwoods League
Walk through a redwood forest—home of the tallest, largest, and some of the oldest living beings on Earth—and you can't help but feel an overwhelming sense of awe and peace among these magnificent giants. Since 1918, Save the Redwoods League has led the effort to protect the coast redwoods and giant sequoias for all to experience and enjoy. To date the League has completed the purchase of more than 190,000 acres of redwood forest and associated land. For more information, please visit SaveTheRedwoods.org, or to receive monthly email updates, sign up at SaveTheRedwoods.org/signup.

###

114 Sansome Street, Suite 1200, San Francisco, California 94104-3823
Telephone (415) 362-2352 | Facsimile (415) 362-7017 | website SaveTheRedwoods.org

WALK AMONG GIANTSSM

As mentioned in "View From the Radio Newsroom," you should spend some time on the title of the release. This doesn't mean being so clever that you obfuscate the meaning—but it also doesn't mean a tired-sounding scholarly title. For example, let's say you work for an environmental organization that's reporting on new findings about ocean temperatures and otters. As possible headlines, "Hotter Otters Make Shark Fodder" would be silly and incomprehensible. At the other extreme, "Recently Published Studies Show that 0.75% Increases in Ocean Temperatures Negatively Impact Otter Populations and Increase Vulnerability to Predation" would make readers eyes glaze over. A nice middle ground might be "Otters in Hot Water as Ocean Temperatures Rise"—it gets the main point across with a pun that isn't too annoying, and could itself be used as a newspaper headline.

Journalists love to lift words straight from press releases, to help them meet their ever-looming deadlines. To make their jobs easier and increase your chances of publication, write the body of your release in the same style you see in newspaper articles. It's best to start with a colorful story or set of facts, move to the background information, and wrap it up quickly with a snappy closing line. Don't forget to include the "five W's" early on—what, when, where, who, and why. Don't use long sentences or ponderous words—the person reading your release is going to be skimming it amid the noise and bustle of a newsroom, not reading it word for word. Most news sources figure that their audience members haven't finished high school, so eloquent literary language is not what they're looking for.

TIP

Line up colorful interviews in advance. Because reporters know that people like to read about people, most feature stories rely on anecdotes about—and quotes from—real folks. Thus, if your press release is about a summer program that teaches wilderness skills to inner-city kids, you'll want to include some names, photos, and contact information about your star pupils. And don't forget to prep them so they say something appropriate should a reporter call.

Be sure to include accurate and complete contact information on the release. One of a reporter's pet peeves is getting a release that lists "Contact Person X," then calling the number and getting no answer, or being led into voicemail purgatory. At that point, the reporter is likely to kiss the story goodbye.

Sending Out Your Press Release

Once you've prepared a catchy press release, don't just send it out scattershot. The evening news doesn't want to hear about your upcoming garage sale fundraiser, unless it's of a truly staggering size. Your community newspaper, however, might be willing to give it a mention. You'll preserve your credibility with the press by demonstrating that you send only stories that fit their areas of interest. (You'd be amazed at how many people don't follow this rule, so journalists tend to get swamped and stop reading the releases of the serial senders.)

When to Send

Different outlets have different schedules, and it can be just as bad to send something too early as too late. If you're targeting daily news outlets, they work a day or three ahead, tops. If you send a release about something you want covered two or three weeks from now, you'll be long forgotten once that time rolls around.

On the other hand, feature stories and talk-radio interviews often need a week or two of advance notice. Monthly magazines often need a lead time of three months, and they sometimes want high-quality photos to go with your story, so plan and send accordingly. As you establish contact with members of the media, ask about their schedules.

Sending not only a press release but a whole "press packet" can convince the journalist to pursue the story. You might add:

- photos (high resolution and available for reprinting)
- a pamphlet about your organization
- the text of an interview with or a speech by one of your leaders or experts, and
- copies of previous articles about your organization.

If you have hard-to-send materials, such as podcasts or videos, add a tip sheet explaining where to find these online.

Check Out Media Watch Groups

A handful of nonprofits and other organizations keep an eye on what news the media covers and how often, with an implicit critique of the lack of coverage of the very issues in which your nonprofit may be interested. While these groups probably can't help you directly, you may learn more about the media from them, and they sometimes offer training or tips on getting underreported issues into the public eye. For example, check out:

- **www.alternet.org.** AlterNet is an online source of alternative, public interest, and opinion stories to help feed the media.
- **www.media-alliance.org.** Media Alliance, based in San Francisco, is a resource center for media workers and nonprofits. It offers training in media skills and advocacy techniques.
- **fair.org.** Fairness & Accuracy in Reporting, or FAIR, is a media watchdog group that works with activists and journalists to critique existing news coverage and help get underreported stories into the news.

There are several ways to send your press release. The traditional printed, mailed copy is still used by some, and still effective. Email is good for getting the word out quickly, but it is also easy for journalists to delete or ignore. You may want to combine snail mail with email. One journalist told me that he always opened press release packages sent via by Federal Express or another courier first, even though he knew that the extra expense didn't necessarily translate into a better story.

Because you never know what's getting read and what's getting tossed, it's a good idea to follow up on your press release with a phone call, particularly to journalists whom you know should be interested in the story. Ask whether they saw your release, take a few seconds to pitch the story and make it sound exciting, and be ready to send another copy right away.

> ### 💡 TIP
>
> **Or, just pick up the phone.** There are times when a full press release isn't appropriate. For example, maybe you've got a simple tidbit of colorful information or gossip—such as a tip regarding a natural event or a local politician—to pass on to an interested journalist. Or perhaps you're watching an event that merits immediate media attention—a beached whale, or a face-off between demonstrators at your family planning clinic, for example. Don't waste time writing a press release—just call, or send an urgent email.

Publicity and Press Invitations for Special Events

An event that your organization sponsors or participates in is, by its very nature, "news." Whether it's interesting news is another matter—a theater piece will probably attract wider attention than your annual spring car wash. If you think your event is sufficiently colorful, will attract enough people, or fits an existing media outlet's area of interest, then by all means send out press releases and get in touch with your favorite media professionals to get the word out.

At the very least, many media outlets collect information on events for their entertainment or community calendars. Find out who carries these calendars, their criteria for submission, and—perhaps most important—how far in advance you need to advise them of the event. Don't forget events calendars on cable access channels.

The best way to get journalists to pay attention to your event is to invite some of them to attend—for free, of course. If your group or event is large enough, you might even set up a separate press night, prescreening, or the like (they'll love it if you include free food). Don't just send press members a stack of tickets, or you won't know how many to expect. Instead, contact selected journalists (by press release, phone call, or email) and ask them to call you for free tickets or a press pass. Remember to offer two tickets to each journalist, so that he or she can bring a companion—few people like to attend an event alone.

Will a journalist who attends your event necessarily do a story about it? No. Many consider freebie invites to be a perk of their no-doubt low-paying job. But even if no story is forthcoming, this is a valuable way to build relationships.

Hosting Members of the Press at Events

When inviting members of the press to theater, musical, or other major events, it's customary to ask them to pick up their ticket at "will call" or, if enough journalists will be attending, at a special "press table," usually in the lobby. When they arrive, you can give them not only a ticket and program, but also a "press packet"—a folder with additional background information, and copies of any other media coverage. Having a press table also gives you an opportunity to make personal contact and gently nudge the journalists about when and whether they're planning to feature your event or the artists or other participants—with the emphasis on gently. Mostly, you should just be welcoming. If it's a sit-down event, and seats aren't otherwise assigned, be sure to reserve seats for the journalists. They don't have to be in the very front row, but seat them close enough to appreciate what's going on.

TIP

Hosting a benefit concert or another musical event? Invite radio DJs. Local stations may be interested in playing music by the group you're featuring, along with mentioning the upcoming event on the air. If you offer the DJ free tickets and CDs for audience giveaways, your odds of coverage go up even higher.

Staging a Media Stunt or Direct Action

If your organization has an activist bent, you may want to attract the media with a march, hanging a controversial banner, or delivering something humorous or damning to a government or corporate office. Fortunately, you don't need to court arrest to score lots of ink—something as innocent as staging a one-day count of migrating birds in the park can garner media attention.

Doing something that's visually interesting—for example, with costumes, signs, puppets, or props—will help you attract television coverage. This strategy is particularly useful for organizations that don't have visually interesting clients or activities, but have a message that needs to be heard. However, because many of the standard stunt techniques have already been tried, you will need to think up something clever and creative.

One California group came up with a headline grabbing—and conveniently low-budget—stunt by cleaning up a clothing-optional beach while wearing nothing at all. At the other end of the fabric spectrum you'll find the Raging Grannies, a group of women who dress up in aprons, shawls, and old-fashioned hats and sing humorous—and sometimes shocking—songs to promote global peace, justice, and economic and social equality. They've attracted major media attention, from *The Washington Post, The New York Times*, and C-SPAN.

Promoting a media stunt is just like any other event. You typically issue a press release and make follow-up phone calls or emails. The catch is that if you're planning to surprise anyone, giving advance notice may not be safe. In such a situation, it's best to tell only your most trusted journalist contacts, and place last-minute phone calls to others. Alternately, you can simply arrange for your own footage and photographs of the event, with written materials, recorded interviews, and contact information for follow-up interviews, and offer it to the media immediately afterward.

RESOURCE

Want to know more? For more information on staging nonviolent direct actions, see the manuals and other information on the website of the Ruckus Society, at www.ruckus.org (click "Ruckus Action Toolbox"). For free, practical guides to planning media events and interacting with the media, check out Jason Salzman's website at www.effectcommunications.com.

Ask Your Funders About Joint Media Efforts

Not all foundations have a media strategy, but some understand that helping garner media attention for their grantees helps everyone in the long run. It boosts the reputation of and possibly donations to the funder and grantees alike, and lifts a burden from the shoulders of nonprofits that are already plenty busy delivering services.

One of the leaders in this effort is The California Wellness Foundation, which published a 2003 report titled "Reflections on Communications Strategies th at Accent Grantees." The foundation asserts: "We strongly believe we owe it to our grantees and the people they serve to use our non-grantmaking resources to tell their stories. So our entire communications program is focused on our grantees and their work." (The report is available at www.calwellness.org.)

Letters to the Editor and Op-Ed Pieces

Letters to newspaper and magazine editors and op-ed (opinion-editorial) pieces are great ways to demonstrate your organization's expertise and to affect public opinion (or perhaps correct the public record) on issues of importance. And, the piece will be all in your own words (probably minus a few after it goes past an editor), unmediated by the bias or boredom of a reporter.

Letters to the editor are shots in the dark—you'll have to prepare and send them with little or no guarantee that they'll get printed. Experienced nonprofits count themselves lucky to place one to three per year.

However, the fact that your letter will represent your organization, which presumably has some expertise on the topic, increases your chances of publication. Another way to improve your odds is to carefully follow the publication's guidelines regarding letters, particularly word count. The upward limit is often 200 words. You can often further increase your odds by sending a letter when your topic is in the news. In that case, you may want to style your letter as a response to or commentary regarding an article in the publication. Email your letter within 24 hours of the story you're responding to.

The gamble of sending in a letter to the editor can pay off nicely—such letters are one of the most widely read parts of the newspaper or magazine.

Op-ed pieces are different from letters to the editor—they run to around 700 words and are usually given a special spot on a newspaper's editorial page, essentially as a guest editorial. For this reason, it's best to contact the editor of the relevant page in advance. Your chances of acceptance are best if you're willing to take a reasonably controversial (but not totally wacky) stand on an issue—including one that the newspaper doesn't agree with, but doesn't mind printing to stir up a bit of excitement.

For example, an editor might print an article by the ED of an education-oriented nonprofit opposing affirmative action, but would be unlikely to print one advocating segregated education. Again, you'll need to jump on any hot issues quickly. If timing permits, the newspaper may arrange to place your op-ed piece next to one written by a person representing the other side.

As with press releases, your letters and op-eds can, whether published or not, be posted to your group's website and on social media.

Protecting Your Nonprofit in Media Interactions

Here are the primary sources of difficulty you might encounter in working with the media:

- **You may spend a lot of time for little reward.** For example, never agree to write large portions of text for a print journalist without a mention of your organization's name. Also, be wary of freelance journalists who are shopping an article to publications without a firm commitment. Either way, you can spend many hours with no payoff.

- **The article or piece may be careless, wrong, or unflattering.** Print journalists are famous for talking to you by phone, scribbling down some notes, then putting quotation marks around something that you don't remember saying. In any personal interviews, try to speak slowly and carefully, avoid sarcasm or parodies that could be quoted out of context, and never, ever, say anything "off the record" if you don't want to see it in print.

- **You won't be sent a copy of the article or show.** People commonly ask journalists for copies or tapes of the final piece, but unless you're famous or the journalist owes you a favor, you'll likely find that both the journalist and the media outlet are too busy to provide it. Try to find out when the piece will be run, and then follow the news yourself, making your own copy or tape. Some larger television and radio stations allow you to buy copies of shows.

- **You may be surprised at whose side the journalist was really on.** Especially if your organization does controversial work, you can be sure that some of the reporters who call will be taking the other side. And if they do, they may try to bait you with innocent-sounding questions like, "Wouldn't you like to tell your side of the story," or "I'm very interested in why you believe such and such."

With good planning and care about who you agree to speak with, you should be able to develop relationships with a select list of media professionals who are accessible, interested in your work, and can be counted on not to misuse your time and trust.

> **TIP**
>
> **Track and save any favorable articles.** Good media coverage is worth its weight in gold for establishing your credibility with funders and prospective donors. You can send these pieces out with mailings, reprint them in your newsletters (after getting permission of course, to avoid copyright violations), mention and link to them on your website, and attach copies to grant proposals.

Making Your Own News: Social Media

The statistics about how many people participate in social media get more zeroes tacked onto them every time you look. As of early 2013, Facebook had an audience of 600 million, Twitter 500 million, Google+ 343 million, Pinterest 25 million, and so on. And, a growing number of people of all ages donate to charity online.

Unfortunately, the link between nonprofits using social media and their attracting online (or any other) donations is anything but a direct one. As Susan Messina, Director of Grants and Special Projects at the National Hospice Foundation (NHF, at www.nationalhospicefoundation.org) says of her work in establishing a social network presence for NHF, "We figured, starting out, that social networks had created a space that nonprofits like ours simply had to be in—even though we yet didn't yet, and perhaps still don't know what would emerge as a result. It's now looking like social networks are unlikely to be primary fundraising vehicles. Still, they allow nonprofits to reach a certain demographic, which makes them an essential part of any communications strategy and therefore solicitation strategy." NHF is active on Facebook and Twitter, putting it in league with the over 90% of top U.S. charities that have joined at least one social network.

It's the indirect route between social media and fundraising that's becoming most important. Nonprofits that successfully participate in social media can raise their profiles and public awareness. That leads to interest and engagement (such as volunteer participation) and perhaps to one-time donations from people spurred on by a friend, all of which may eventually lead to some long-term support from donors who wouldn't have found or maintained interest in the group otherwise.

If your executive, development, and communications staff haven't already done so, I recommend that they get familiar with the social network scene by joining a few of the most popular sites. Then, use the tips below to establish or enhance your nonprofit's social network presence and develop compelling content.

TIP

Say goodbye to your inner control freak. As Jennifer Gennari, consultant and former Communications Director at Greenbelt Alliance explains, "The casual nature of Facebook and Twitter is a shift for communications and development professionals, who are used to very carefully monitoring every word and every image when talking about our work. In my case, I started out thinking, 'How much oversight will I need to have about what gets posted?' And then I realized I should stop worrying. The social network scene is by definition casual, and within 24 hours, most everyone has moved on to the next hot tweet."

Be Selective in Joining Up

Which sites should your nonprofit join? As of this book's publication, Facebook and Twitter were the apparent category killers for most nonprofits, with some move into Pinterest, as well. By the time you're reading this, that could have changed; and your nonprofit's choice of sites should depend on current trends and the demographics of whomever you're hoping to reach.

If your organization ends up with several online presences, there are features that will allow automatic postings of content from one source, such as your website or blog, to other sites such as Twitter or Facebook. But if this is your only source of social media content, it may backfire, as people get no sense that there's a human being behind the postings or tweets. Twitter users, for example, report irritation when they see truncated tweets that take people to another page, or utterly unenticing entries like, "We posted a new photo to Facebook" (with a link).

Create a Strategy: Who Will Post, About What, and How Often?

In people's personal social networking lives, they post whenever the mood strikes—meaning that some people update readers on every morsel of food they take in, while others emerge only occasionally to announce a new job or a divorce. A nonprofit, however, needs to be more systematic in its postings.

Some ideas that have emerged for tackling this include:

- **Assign only one or two people to post content.** That avoids overlaps or long hiatuses between postings. Ideally, that person will be an experienced member of your organization, not an intern chosen because, "She's young; she gets how to use this stuff."
- **Decide what voice and tone your nonprofit wants to convey.** Not stiff and boring, obviously. But look at other organizations' posts to see what you admire and what sounds strident, inappropriate, or immature. Use these insights to create some guidance for your in-house social networkers.

- **Create an annual content calendar.** This should show all the important events happening both within your nonprofit (such as appeal mailings and special events) and outside (such as holidays or commemorative days, which often provide tie-ins for thematic postings). Plan ahead for posts to issue (or hold back on) at specific times.

- **Arrange for other staff to report in regularly on specific topics.** Your networkers might want to hear, for example, about volunteer activities, progress on advocacy, rescue, or other work, funding, and so forth. This practice will provide a regular feed of potentially interesting information. (Also see Chapter 2 for advice on fostering communication and storytelling within the organization.) Some nonprofits foster even more personal insights into the lives of their staff, for example posting fun photos about how they decorate their workspace, or photos of their pets.

- **Encourage picture taking by staff and volunteers (if appropriate).** For example, the Berkeley East Bay Humane Society sent a message to all its volunteers in 2013 saying, "I imagine many of you have camera phones and are taking cute pictures and videos of the animals when you're here, and so we'd like to request that you send some of them (whatever you're comfortable having posted online) on to . . . our marketing manager, to be used on social media. Everything from dog play groups, to cat cuddling, to snuggling with recovering surgery patients, to you all being your awesome selves…."

- **Plan to post regularly.** At least once a week is optimal and will keep your existence in readers' minds. Some nonprofits, however, aim for once or twice a month.

As your audience responds, you'll start to get a sense of what works and what doesn't, and can refine your strategy accordingly.

To maximize your nonprofit's presence online, you can encourage (but shouldn't require) people within your nonprofit who have joined a networking site—staff, board members, and volunteers—to mix cause-related messages (whether information, announcements about events, or actual appeals) with their personal ones. If they're willing, people's own birthdays can become a time to ask for donations. Staff members doing this should, however, recognize the risks of mixing the personal with the professional. Some people deal with this by creating more than one profile per site for themselves.

> ⓘ **CAUTION**
>
> **For staff, create guidelines (but not outright mandates) on the amount of time that's appropriate to spend on social networking sites while at work.** Add other appropriate cautions, like "Be aware of the damage you could do to our nonprofit's reputation by complaining about your boss or long work hours on the same site where you ask people to attend a fundraising event."

Create Meaningful Communication With Members

Social media offers a great way for your nonprofit to establish regular communication with existing members without always asking for money. Your posts remind people that you're hard at work on your mission every day and that they, too, can get further educated and involved.

An important (and easy to overlook) aspect of this newly close communication is that it will be two-way. Your audience will want to "like," comment on, argue over, and share your content.

It's worth fostering this type of dialogue and trying to create content that your core audience will want to share more widely. In fact, one of the most likely ways to pick up new followers is by posting a photo, video, or story about your work that is so compelling that people will feel like, "My friends have to see this."

Susan Messina of the National Hospice Foundation notes, "We often get the greatest Facebook response to questions of all types, whether open-ended, true/false, or a quiz. For example, I've asked, 'If you've been with someone when they died, what would you say to others who haven't yet had that experience?' It was an intense question, but it brought in amazing answers, such as, 'I wouldn't miss it. . . . There is a quiet and a peace that fills the room' and 'I was there when my dad died, and I know the last thing he heard was my voice.' In fact, we got multichannel use from this question because I wrote it up, with a sampling of the answers, for our next newsletter."

You can also have fun with promoting dialogue. The Cornell Lab of Ornithology, for example, asks readers to identify what bird is shown in a photo and sponsors contests to vote for a favorite bird species. Other groups invite readers to take a test on a topic, enter a contest (caption a photo or devise the group's next slogan), or otherwise compete to receive a freebie, like a T-shirt with the group's logo.

And let's not forget posting petitions to sign, or offering letters to Congresspeople or other leaders that members can quickly send in their own name. This practice has become a regular way for nonprofits to advise members about urgent issues—and expand their own mailing lists.

Two-way communication does not, however, end the day you publish the post. Someone needs to go back to the site regularly to see what responses have come in, and then respond to them. Sometimes all you need to do by way of response is to say thank you to someone who openly admires your work. Other times you'll face more difficult conversations. Treatment organizations, for example, sometimes become aware of a person in need of services via a social network comment. They may then post a response inviting the person to contact them.

You may also receive comments from critics or people who've come a bit unhinged. The same rules here apply as in personal communications—take a deep breath, remember that whatever you write will live on the Web for years, and don't press "send" when mad. Fortunately, many nonprofits report that they find they don't need to do a thing about "haters"—their supporters step in to defend them.

Post Lots of Visuals

People love, love, love, pictures. Whether it's photos or videos, this is what now gets noticed, liked, and shared the most on social networking sites.

For example, when asked what content works best on the Facebook page of The Altai Project (which protects nature in a mountainous region of Siberia, dealing with issues ranging from poaching to oil pipeline construction to preserving indigenous peoples' way of life), Director Jennifer Castner says, "Frankly, it's pictures of cute fuzzy animals. Any time I can post a photo or video of an Altai snow leopard, it will get more 'likes' than anything else. Fortunately, I regularly receive photos and video from

The Altai Project's collaborators. I'll also share photos from outside sources if there's a direct connection to our work."

Your group is probably not creating as many visual records of its work as it could. If you're savvy enough to hire professionals to take photos of your special events, that's a great start; but now's the time to also get your staff and volunteers to record their everyday work—keeping a sharp eye out for any cute, fuzzy animals!

To increase quality, consider creating volunteer positions or internships specifically around photo taking or video production, filling new marketing and communications positions with people who have skills in these areas, or applying for a small grant to foster your group's photo and video skills and production.

> **CAUTION**
>
> **Avoid copyright violations.** Contrary to popular belief, photos and other content found online are not free for the taking. You can link to other people's work, and share photos circulating on Facebook and the like, but uploading a photo for your nonprofit's use is a no-no unless you've either gotten permission or ascertained that it's already in the public domain. For more information, see the free articles on the "Patent, Copyright & Trademark" section of nolo.com.

Turn First-Time Social-Networking Donors Into Repeat Donors

Now let's imagine that you've been fortunate enough to bring in some donations from new members via your social networks. How will you bring them back for a second gift?

The forces lined up against you are a bit daunting. The first gift may have been in response to a request from a friend, perhaps in honor of a birthday, wedding, or funeral. But once that moment has passed, the donors were most likely left without any direct sense of connection with your nonprofit. What's more, they may have since been bombarded with donation requests by other friends.

However, you can take steps to enhance their feeling of connection. Possibilities include:

- **Encourage a recurring gift right from the start.** There's no better way to guarantee repeat donations than to arrange for them from the outset—an option that appeals to some donors who don't have much cash on hand. Make sure your online donation processing provider can offer this function, and highlight it as an option in your first and every communication with donors.
- **Track who's following you.** On Facebook, for example, your organization can get detailed demographics on who its "friends" are—their ages, genders, where they live, and more. Use this information to tailor your future postings.
- **Thank donors who arrived via social networks not only online, but off.** If you've heard the maxim that donors should be thanked via the same method through which the donation was made, that's still true. But there's no harm in going beyond this. If you've obtained the person's home or email address, send an occasional newsletter or other communication. This helps emphasize that your group has a very real existence outside the cyber-world.
- **Thank donors profusely and often.** That's true for all donors, but those who arrive via social networks sometimes feel like their gifts are treated casually, with a terse, impersonal thank you and nothing more.

Giving Via Mobile Text Message: Can It Work for Your Nonprofit?

Given the speed of technological change, it's surprising that the effectiveness of mobile text giving seems not to have risen much since the last edition of this book two years ago. It continues to be a tool best suited to large organizations raising funds for disaster relief. I first became aware of the power of mobile text giving while having dinner with friends, one of whom began excitedly describing her experience of having donated $10 to a Haiti relief charity. Her words, more or less, were: "It was so easy! I didn't have to call a number or fill out a form—all those steps that might normally make me feel like I'd taken on a chore and might want to give up in the middle. Within seconds, I'd made the donation, and felt good about it." She, and then I, were among the 77% of Americans who got the word that texting money for Haiti relief was an option.

Here's what mobile phone donors literally experience: They're told (via various advertising and marketing means, online and off) that, by simply typing a word and a numeric code into their mobile phones, they can make a donation of a particular amount—usually $1, $5, or $10 (the max). For the American Red Cross's Haiti efforts, for example, donors were advised to text the word, "HAITI" and send it to 90999.

Donors then get a message asking them to confirm their wish to donate, to which they hopefully respond by typing the word "yes," at which point they get another automated confirmation message. When their mobile phone bills come, they see the extra charge representing their donations.

My friend isn't the only one who has found it easy and satisfying to give via text message. The numbers are, in some cases, eye-popping—especially given that the mobile donation systems limit people to $10 per text message (apparently to protect people from having their kids start happily pressing buttons on their phone). They also impose per-cause or per-month limits, typically around $30. It's a volume business, which sometimes works: More than $30 million was raised for Haitian earthquake relief via text message donations.

Of course, such big numbers are partly explained by the fact that fundraising for emergency relief efforts tends to dwarf (or even take away from) fundraising for ongoing needs. Meanwhile, *Consumer Reports* noted that the American Red Cross's intake was more than three times the amount of money that all U.S. charities had raised via text in the previous two years combined.

So, will mobile text giving become a realistic fundraising method for smallish nonprofits any time soon? The numbers look iffy. First off, you need to pay a third-party processor. Among the widely acknowledged go-to places for setting up such arrangements is the MGive Foundation (www. mgive.com). When this book went to print, it charged a one-time setup fee of $150, plus $349 a month (at its lowest program level) for ongoing services with a one-year minimum contract, plus a per-transaction fee of 35 cents and 3.5% of the donation. This obviously works best for large nonprofits with a big public presence.

The fees would be worth the price even for a smaller nonprofit if, of course, the dollars coming in swamped the up-front investment; but none seem to have pulled that off yet. Perhaps text message campaigns will continue to emerge as a possibility—or perhaps they will actually become less relevant as other mobile payment options come into play, such as use of a PayPal account or small card-swiping devices.

Worksheets

Worksheet Title	Chapter in Book
Sample Cost Analysis	Chapter 3
Fundraising Assets	Chapter 3
Fundraising Strategy Chart	Chapter 3
Mailing Evaluation	Chapter 4
Meeting Checklist	Chapter 6
Projected Special Event Expenses	Chapter 8
Projected Special Event Income	Chapter 8
Grant Priorities Summary Chart	Chapter 10
Grant Prospect Summary	Chapter 10
Check Your Website's Fundraising Effectiveness	Chapter 12
Press Release Template	Chapter 13

Fundraising Worksheet 1: Sample Cost Analysis

Item	Cost per Year	Notes
Salaries and benefits	$_____	_____
		_____
Fees to independent contractors and consultants	$_____	_____
		_____
Travel (trainings, donor visits)	$_____	_____
		_____
Office supplies	$_____	_____
		_____
Graphic design/printing	$_____	_____
		_____
Dues and publications	$_____	_____
		_____
Staff trainings and networking events	$_____	_____
		_____
Web, database, and other technical support	$_____	_____
		_____
Telephone	$_____	_____
		_____
Postage	$_____	_____
		_____
Food (such as coffee or meals with donors)	$_____	_____
		_____
Special event costs	$_____	_____
		_____
Other special program costs	$_____	_____
		_____
Total	$_____	

Fundraising Worksheet 2: Fundraising Assets

Asset Type	Asset Description	Possible Fundraising Use
Organization's mission		
Organization's programs		
Organization's reputation or history with certain foundations or individuals		
Organization's access to certain members of community		
Organization's physical facilities or resources		
Physical facilities or resources owned or accessible by board, staff, or volunteers		
Executive director		
Development director		
Development assistant		
Other development staff		
Board members		
Board fundraising committee		
Particularly active individual volunteers		
Volunteer program generally		
Other friends of your organization		

Fundraising Worksheet 3: Fundraising Strategy Chart

Activity or Funding Source	Amount It Should Raise	New or Unusual Expenses	Total Amount (Column 2 minus Column 3)
_____	$ _____	$ _____	$ _____
_____	$ _____	$ _____	$ _____
_____	$ _____	$ _____	$ _____
_____	$ _____	$ _____	$ _____
_____	$ _____	$ _____	$ _____
_____	$ _____	$ _____	$ _____
	$ _____	$ _____	$ _____
		Grand Total:	$ _____

Fundraising Worksheet 4: Mailing Evaluation

For mailing sent [_____], consisting of:

_____

_____

_____

_____

Describe appeal and any special enclosures:

_____

_____

_____

A. Number of letters sent out   _____

B. Total expenses of mailing $ _____

C. Number of new supporters   _____

D. Total amount of donations $ _____

E. Usual donation amount $ _____

F. Percentage of response (C divided by A)   _____ %

G. Net profit (D minus B) $ _____

H. Cost of acquiring each new supporter (B divided by C) $ _____

Comments:

_____

_____

_____

_____

_____

_____

_____

Fundraising Worksheet 5: Meeting Checklist

Here's a summary of things to consider bringing to your donor meeting:

- [ ] Brochure

- [ ] Annual report

- [ ] Historical information

- [ ] Mission description

- [ ] Case statement

- [ ] Budget

- [ ] Plans for the future

- [ ] Publicity materials

- [ ] Copies of any recent newspaper articles

- [ ] Premiums and recognition opportunities

- [ ] Pledge card

- [ ] Return envelope or instructions for giving online

- [ ] Receipt book

Fundraising Worksheet 6: Projected Special Event Expenses

Expense Category	Projected Cost	Description of Reasoning or Assumptions, Particularly for Discount or Donated Items
Physical Space		
Room, building, outdoor space	$_____	_____
Chairs, tables, performance platform	$_____	_____
Site manager and other staff fees	$_____	_____
Heating or air conditioning	$_____	_____
Sound system, projector, screen, other equipment	$_____	_____
Municipal permits (traffic, etc.)	$_____	_____
Subtotal:	$_____	_____
Decorations		
Banners	$_____	_____
Lighting	$_____	_____
Flowers	$_____	_____
Candles	$_____	_____
Balloons	$_____	_____
Party favors, gifts, award plaques, and certificates	$_____	_____
Other	$_____	_____
Subtotal:	$_____	_____
Food and Drink		
Snacks or appetizers (for participants and volunteers)	$_____	_____
Main meal	$_____	_____
Extra catering or corkage fees	$_____	_____
Alcohol, other drinks, ice	$_____	_____
Plates, cups, napkins, cutlery	$_____	_____
Waiters and bar staff	$_____	_____
Subtotal:	$_____	_____

Fundraising Worksheet 6: Projected Special Event Expenses

Expense Category	Projected Cost	Description of Reasoning or Assumptions, Particularly for Discount or Donated Items
Performers/Speakers		
Performers' or auctioneer's fee or honorarium	$_____	_____
Transportation and parking (airfare, shuttle, rental car, cabs, or limousine)	$_____	_____
Hotel	$_____	_____
Meals	$_____	_____
Telephone and other extras	$_____	_____
Subtotal:	$_____	
Publicity		
Graphic designer and/or artist	$_____	_____
Printing (invitations, posters, programs, ad books, auction catalogs)	$_____	_____
Stationery, envelopes	$_____	_____
Postage (invitations, press releases, thank yous)	$_____	_____
Professional mailing services	$_____	_____
Event photographer	$_____	_____
Subtotal:	$_____	
Miscellaneous		
Taxes on goods sold	$_____	_____
Photocopying	$_____	_____
Supplies for volunteer meetings and information packets	$_____	_____
Reimbursement of volunteers' expenses (i.e., gasoline, telephone)	$_____	_____
Name badges	$_____	_____
Insurance	$_____	_____
Unexpected or emergency expenses	$_____	_____
Subtotal:	$_____	
Total:	$_____	

Fundraising Worksheet 7: Projected Special Event Income

Income Category	Projected Amount	Description of Reasoning or Assumptions
Tickets	$_____	_____ of guests at $_____ per ticket
Ad books or ad space in program	$_____	_____ of advertisers at $_____ per _____
Exhibitors' or vendors' rental fees	$_____	_____ of exhibitors/vendors at $_____ per booth
Corporate sponsorships	$_____	_____
Sales of food or goods	$_____	_____
Silent auction or raffle proceeds	$_____	_____
Total:	$_____	

Fundraising Worksheet 8: Grant Priorities Summary Chart

Clients or issue to be served: _____

_____

_____

_____

_____

Greater goal being pursued: _____

_____

_____

_____

_____

Minimum useful grant amount: $_____

Geographic area served or covered: _____

_____

_____

_____

Any unacceptable restrictions: _____

_____

_____

_____

Any unacceptable sources of funds: _____

_____

_____

_____

Fundraising Worksheet 9: Grant Prospect Summary

Basic Information

Foundation/funder's name and address: _____

_____

Foundation's stated mission and purpose: _____

_____

Contact person: _____

Contact person's telephone, email: _____

Names and titles of other staff members: _____

_____

_____

Names of board members and trustees: _____

_____

_____

_____

Total grants made annually: $_____

Eligibility Information

Grant subject matter: _____

_____

Grant eligibility requirements: _____

Geographical limitations: _____

_____

Other limitations: _____

_____

Maximum grant amount: $_____

Funding duration : _____

"Good Fit" Indicators

Other organizations that have received grants for similar work (name the organization(s), list how much received and for what work): _____

_____

_____

_____

Typical grant amount: $_____

Limitations on overhead/administrative costs: _____%

Prospects for grant renewal: _____

Special considerations: _____

Application Process

First steps: ☐ query letter   ☐ full proposal

Printed application form or guidelines: ☐ available   ☐ obtained

Next application deadline(s) (if any): _____

Board meeting dates: _____

_____

Likely to hear answer by: _____

Research Trail

Have checked:

☐ Website

☐ Directories (name them):

☐ Form 990

☐ Annual report

Fundraising Worksheet 10:
Check Your Website's Fundraising Effectiveness

☐ **Basic contact information:** Does your website clearly state what your organization does, where it's located, and every possible way to get in touch with development and other staff?

☐ **Your organization's personality:** Does your website convey your organization's personality in a manner that's consistent with your fundraising and other marketing materials?

☐ **Freshness:** Does your website appear current and up to date?

☐ **Content:** Does your website present interesting content about your organization's cause?

☐ **Donation information:** Does your website lead viewers easily to information on how to donate or get involved?

☐ **Information on where the money goes:** Does your website tell donors how their money will be spent?

☐ **Funder and donor information:** Does your website find space to publicly thank funders and donors?

☐ **Tracking users:** Does your website allow you to track where viewers go within the site and how successfully you're leading them to donation or involvement options?

Press Release Template

[*Your organization's name; preferably with logo*]

FOR IMMEDIATE RELEASE

Contact: [*Name of one or preferably two persons they can call*]

[*Date*]

[*Phone number of contacts*]

[*Email address of contacts*]

[*Centered title of press release, in larger font*]

[*Your state, in capital letters, such as "OKLAHOMA"*]

[*Text of press release, in short paragraphs, ending with a brief description of your organization and where to obtain more information, such as on your website.*]

###

[*traditional signal of end of text*]

Using the Interactive Worksheets

The forms provided in this book can also be accessed as interactive files, available online at:

www.nolo.com/back-of-book/EFFN.html

To use the files, your computer must have specific software programs installed. The types of files provided by this book, as well as the software programs you'll need to access them, include:

- **RTF.** You can open, edit, print, and save these form files with most word processing programs such as Microsoft *Word*, Windows *WordPad*, and recent versions of *WordPerfect*. Underlines indicate where to enter information. After filling in the needed text, delete the underline. In most word processing programs you can do this by highlighting the underlined portion and typing CTRL+U.

- **PDF.** You can view these files with Adobe *Reader*, free software from www.adobe.com. PDFs are designed to be printed out and completed by hand.

TIP
Note to Macintosh Users. These forms were designed for use with Windows. They should also work on Macintosh computers; however Nolo cannot provide technical support for non-Windows users.

Every word processing program uses different commands to open, format, save, and print documents, so refer to your software's help documents for help using your program. Nolo cannot provide technical support for questions about how to use your computer or your software.

CAUTION
In accordance with U.S. copyright laws, the forms provided by this book are for your personal use only.

Files Provided on Nolo's Website

Form Title	File Name
Sample Cost Analysis	SampleCost.rtf
Fundraising Assets	FundAssets.rtf
Fundraising Strategy Chart	FundStrat.rtf
Mailing Evaluation	MailEvaluation.rtf
Meeting Checklist	MtgChecklist.rtf
Projected Special Event Expenses	SpEventExp.rtf
Projected Special Event Income	SpEventIncome.rtf
Grant Priorities Summary Chart	GrantPrior.rtf
Grant Prospect Summary	ProspectsSum.rtf
Check Your Website's Fundraising Effectiveness	WebsiteFund.rtf
Press Release Template	PressRelease.rtf

Index

sending out, 420–422
template for, 417
titles for, 419
See also Media outreach
Printed communications materials
brochures, 371–372, 373
cost control, 381
design consistency with web-based
communications, 387–390
hiring freelance designers/editors,
372, 374
including website links on, 384
layout considerations, 371–372
overview, 370–371
press packet, 421
See also Annual reports; Marketing;
Newsletters
Printing costs, 381
Print media contacts, 410–411
Private foundations, 320–322
Product endorsements, 286
Professionalism, 80, 83–84, 339
Professional services donations, 58, 237
Program staff, 18–23, 289–291
Project Open Hand, 110, 119–120,
126–129, 138–141
Promotional items, 94–95
Property donations, 92–93, 212–213,
223–224
Property rentals/sales, tax treatment
of, 284, 286
Public foundations, 320–322,
324–325

Q

Query letters, 340, 342–346
Quid pro quo contributions, 93, 134,
315

R

Radio coverage
announcing upcoming spots to
supporters/colleagues, 415
contacting radio stations, 412
educating show hosts, 413
insider tips for, 413, 415, 419
obtaining copies of your interview,
427
publicizing musical events, 423
ticket giveaways during interviews,
423
timing of press releases and, 420
See also Media outreach
Radio nonprofits, 59, 94–95,
241–242, 297
Raffles, 58, 62, 93, 106, 234, 238–239
Raging Grannies, 424
Ratios for spending, 78–80, 83
Receipts for donations, 94, 135, 247
Receiving donations. *See* Accepting
donations
Receptionists, 18, 35
Recognition of donors
beyond a thank-you note, 276
legacy donors, 203–204, 218–222
plaques, tiles, bricks and other
printed mentions, 176, 179, 185,
202, 221
respecting donors' wishes, 192, 203
Recreational tours, as business activity,
299–300
Recycling, use of recycled products,
121
Regular donors, 151, 152, 216–218
"Regularly carried on" business,
285–286
Renewal letters, 94–95, 138–141, 172

and direct mail campaigns,
122–123
as face of the organization, 28
fundraising strategy reviewed by,
70–72
manual for, 26
motivation of, 21, 25
online resources for finding, 24, 27
as potential supporters, 97–98
promoting special events, 266
recruiting and motivating, 22–25, 27
showing appreciation for, 28
social media networking by, 431,
433
soliciting/collecting in-kind
donations, 58
for special events, 233, 234, 238,
246–247, 250
and start-up of your nonprofit, 54
tax deductions for unreimbursed
expenses, 94
thank-you phone calls by, 155–156,
168
training and expectations, 25–26,
168
volunteer coordinator, 25
volunteer matching organizations,
22, 24, 26–27
working with the public, 27
See also Fundraising tools; Staff

W

WAI website conformance, 391
Walkathons, 243–244
Wealthy, soliciting the, 196–198
Website content and design
blogs, 391, 393, 402, 407, 429

checklist for website's fundraising
effectiveness, 385
conveying your organization's
personality, 387–390
for crowdfunding campaigns,
104–105
encouraging donations, 394–395
featuring funder/donor information,
398–399
funders' websites, 336, 364
help online searchers find your site,
400–404
as "home base," 35, 42, 148
the home page, 386, 395
including basic identifying
information, 384, 386–387
introductory support page, 396
keeping it fresh, 391–392, 402
links to donation page from other
pages, 396–397
marketing your, 148, 384
option for online donations, 397
overview, 386
planning and design, 387–390, 392
posting letters to editor/op-ed
pieces, 426
posting press releases, 392, 415, 416
product sales online, 294
providing information on where the
money goes, 398
providing interesting content,
392–394, 402, 427
random donations and, 384
sharing financial information with
supporters, 81–82, 83, 398
updating information, 391–392,
393, 402

⚖ NOLO *Online Legal Forms*

Nolo offers a large library of legal solutions and forms, created by Nolo's in-house legal staff. These reliable documents can be prepared in minutes.

Create a Document

- **Incorporation.** Incorporate your business in any state.
- **LLC Formations.** Gain asset protection and pass-through tax status in any state.
- **Wills.** Nolo has helped people make over 2 million wills. Is it time to make or revise yours?
- **Living Trust (avoid probate).** Plan now to save your family the cost, delays, and hassle of probate.
- **Trademark.** Protect the name of your business or product.
- **Provisional Patent.** Preserve your rights under patent law and claim "patent pending" status.

Download a Legal Form

Nolo.com has hundreds of top quality legal forms available for download—bills of sale, promissory notes, nondisclosure agreements, LLC operating agreements, corporate minutes, commercial lease and sublease, motor vehicle bill of sale, consignment agreements and many more.

Review Your Documents

Many lawyers in Nolo's consumer-friendly lawyer directory will review Nolo documents for a very reasonable fee. Check their detailed profiles at **Nolo.com/lawyers.**

⚖ NOLO — *Save 15%* *off your next order*

Register your Nolo purchase, and we'll send you a
coupon for 15% off your next Nolo.com order!

Nolo.com/customer-support/productregistration

On Nolo.com you'll also find:

Books & Software

Nolo publishes hundreds of great books and software programs for consumers and
business owners. Order a copy, or download an ebook version instantly, at Nolo.com.

Online Legal Documents

You can quickly and easily make a will or living trust, form an LLC or corporation, apply
for a trademark or provisional patent, or make hundreds of other forms—online.

Free Legal Information

Thousands of articles answer common questions about everyday legal issues
including wills, bankruptcy, small business formation, divorce, patents,
employment, and much more.

Plain-English Legal Dictionary

Stumped by jargon? Look it up in America's most up-to-date source for
definitions of legal terms, free at nolo.com.

Lawyer Directory

Nolo's consumer-friendly lawyer directory provides in-depth profiles of lawyers all
over America. You'll find all the information you need to choose the right lawyer.

EFFN4